UNCERTAIN CAUSATION IN MEDICAL LIABILITY

'Proving' the cause of the plaintiff's injury in personal injury litigation often entails significant challenges, particularly when science cannot identify the cause of a biological phenomenon or when the nature of this cause is debatable. This problem is frequently encountered in medical malpractice cases, where the limitations of scientific knowledge are still extensive. Yet judges must decide cases, however uncertain the evidence with regard to proof of causation. Reluctant to leave patients without compensation, courts have in some cases challenged their traditional approach to causation through recourse to such techniques as reliance on factual presumptions and inferences, the concept of loss of chance, and reversal of the burden of proof. This book analyses and criticises the use of these various techniques by the courts of England, Australia, Canada, France, and the civilian Canadian province of Québec in confronting evidentiary causal difficulties caused by the uncertainties of medical science.

Winner of the Prix Minerve 2004

Uncertain Causation in Medical Liability

Lara Khoury

•HART•
PUBLISHING

OXFORD AND PORTLAND, OREGON
2006

Published in the USA by
Hart Publishing
c/o International Specialized Book Services
920 NE 58th Avenue, Suite 300
Portland, OR 97213-3786
USA
Tel: +1-503-287-3093 or toll-free: (1) 800-944-6190
Fax: +1-503-280-8832
E-mail: orders@isbs.com
Website: www.isbs.com
Published in Canada by Éditions Yvon Blais (Thomson)

Hart Publishing, 16c Worcester Place, Oxford, OX1 2JW
Telephone: +44 (0) 1865 517530 or Fax: +44 (0) 1865 510710
E-mail: mail@hartpub.co.uk
Website: http//:www.hartpub.co.uk

British Library Cataloguing in Publication Data
Data Available
ISBN-13: 978-1-84113-517-5 (hardback)
ISBN-10: 1-84113-517-8 (hardback)

Typeset by Compuscript Ltd, Shannon
Printed and bound in Great Britain by
TJ International Ltd, Padstow, Cornwall

ACKNOWLEDGEMENTS

In the middle of the 1990s, Professor Robert P Kouri, of the Faculty of Law of the University of Sherbrooke, offered me advice that would prove decisive for my research aspirations when he pointed out the value of pursuing doctoral work on the issue of causal uncertainty. He had great vision since this was to become one of the most dynamic and interesting areas of civil liability litigation throughout the following decade.

This book is based on the text of my doctoral thesis completed at the University of Oxford between 1998 and 2002. Throughout my doctoral work, as well as in the process of this manuscript's preparation, I was lucky to receive the support of many people. First and foremost, my gratitude goes to my supervisor, Professor Bernard A Rudden, for his helpful and inspiring comments, for his admirable human qualities and for providing me with constant and unfailing trust and encouragement. I am also greatly indebted to the late Professor Peter BH Birks, who joined as second supervisor upon Professor Rudden's retirement, for his helpful comments and advice, and his kind and generous support in the pursuit of my academic projects. He has been a wonderful, inspiring and touching inspiration to his students. Professor John Cartwright and Dr Duncan Fairgrieve have also been instrumental in the preparation of this book, through the helpful advice they offered as examiners of my D Phil thesis.

My gratitude also goes to my administrative assistant, Ms Hélène Lajeunesse, for her devoted and indispensable assistance in the preparation of the thesis. It must also be expressed to my colleagues of the Faculty of Law of McGill University, in particular those who have kindly offered thoughts on various aspects of my work, Professors Lionel Smith, Shauna Van Praagh, Geneviève Saumier, Stephen Smith, Jaye Ellis, Richard Janda, Nicholas Kasirer, and Marie-Claude Prémont. My gratitude also goes to Professor Paul-André Crépeau, whose work as the precursor of modern Quebec medical liability, as well as his kind and joyful support, were a source of inspiration. I would also like to thank: Dr Jean-Pierre Tétreault and Dr Raymond Duperval of the Faculty of Medicine of the University of Sherbrooke, as well as Me Stéphane Reynolds, for their precious comments on excerpts of the thesis; Assistant-Principal Louis Marquis, Assistant-Deans Suzanne Philips-Nootens and Geneviève Cartier , and Professor Nathalie Vézina, of the Faculty of Law of the University of Sherbrooke, for their assistance in my search for funding; Catherine Simard and Élise Labrecque for their research assistance; as well as Sylvain Robert for his technical and personal support.

I am also grateful to the scholarship and fellowship awarding bodies which have generously funded this work: the *Fonds Formation Chercheurs & Aide Recherche (F.C.A.R.)*; the I.O.D.E.; the *Social Science and Humanities Research Council of Canada*; the *Boulton Research Fellowship* (Faculty of Law, McGill University); the *Max-Planck-Institut für ausländisches und internationales Privatrecht* Research Fellowships; the *Plummer Award* and *Waterson Scholarship* (St-Anne's College); and the *Overseas Research Students Scholarship* (Oxford University). I would also like to thank *Les Éditions Yvon Blais* for awarding this text the Prix Minerve 2004, and to Hart Publishing for their excellent work in preparing the manuscript of this book.

Enfin, mes sincères remerciements à ma famille sans qui rien de tout ceci ne serait possible.

I wish to dedicate this work to my family, as well as to the memory of Peter BH Birks.

Lara Khoury, Montréal, March 14, 2006

CONTENTS

TABLE OF CASES

United Kingdom

AUSTRALIA

CANADA

FRANCE

Cour de cassation

Court of Appeal

Tribunal de Grande Instance

Conseil d'État

Cour administrative d'appel

Tribunal administratif

Tribunal des conflits

Québec

Others

ADDENDUM

As the book was going to press, the House of Lords issued its reasons in the case of *Barker v Corus (UK) plc.*[1] It was therefore not possible to deal with the impact of this important case in any detail. Though the Law Lords make it clear that *Barker* is not intended to change the law in respect of the treatment of causation in medical liability instances, it will nonetheless impact on the law in a number of ways which ideally should have been commented on here. These impacts concern more precisely the future application of the decision in *Fairchild v Glenhaven Funeral Services,*[2] as well as the interpretation of this decision, which are both commented on in this book. Prominently, the majority decision in *Barker* stands for the fact that the defendant's material increase of risk in *Fairchild* did not demonstrate the causal connection, but rather *liability* (Lord Rodger dissenting). Moreover, *Barker* goes further in an important way by deciding that, for fairness reasons, once liability is found based on increase of risk in the *Fairchild* situations, the injury must be redefined as the risk increase (Lord Rodger and Baroness Hale dissenting). Damages are accordingly apportioned proportionally to the degree of risk contributed to by each specific defendant, but only if the risk eventuates (Lord Rodger dissenting), a reasoning that bears close resemblance to that of the French Cour de cassation in its loss of chance case law. The majority judgments in *Barker* are careful, however, to limit the application of this ratio to very restricted situations exemplified by the facts of *McGhee v National Coal Board,*[3] *Fairchild* and *Barker.*

[1] [2006] UKHL 20.
[2] [2002] 3 All ER 305 (HL).
[3] [1973] 1 WLR 1 (HL).

Introduction

Section 1

A Society of Risks and Uncertainty

Recent decades have seen tremendous improvements to our way of life and our prosperity, as well as our power to heal. Progress has come at a cost, however, that of incurring new and sometimes unknown risks which may exact a toll years and even decades after their incorporation into everyday life. We are currently discovering more and more adverse impacts of developments we initially thought harmless. That we live in an age of risks is now a truism. Though some comfort may be derived from the fact that knowledge and risk control increase with advances in science and technology, many of the consequences of innovative activities are still unknown at the time when exposure to risk occurs. Modern life thus presents us with a contradiction: it grants us greater control over our destiny while increasing the hazards to which we are subjected and the uncertainty of their consequences.

We have long known that '[t]he growing industrial power magnified the potential for large-scale accidents and massive exposure to toxic, environmental and other hazards.'[1] This fact has changed the face of modern civil liability.[2] However, in recent decades, the relevance of this observation has extended beyond the realm of industry to a vast sector of our society's activities, including continuing developments in pharmacology, genetics, medicine, technology, and so on. All these fields have given rise to radical changes in the accustomed distribution of risk in our society. At the same time, public awareness and consequent fears about these risks have also grown. It suffices to open the daily papers from time to time to realise the breadth of this awareness and the place the question of modern risks occupies in people's everyday concerns. Indeed, questions of risk, damage, and causation, as well as debates on the uncertainty of causal links between everyday agents and human health, have become part of everyday life. Classic examples are

[1] A Porat and A Stein, *Tort Liability under Uncertainty* (Oxford, OUP, 2001) 3.

[2] For convenience, *civil liability* will refer to contractual and extra-contractual *responsabilité civile* in civil law, as well as to the tort of negligence in common law.

numerous and include the DES and thalidomide litigation around the world; claims by Vietnam veterans for injury caused by *Agent Orange* used during the war to destroy dense flora; claims following the worldwide contaminated blood scandal, from which victims continue to emerge, infected by either HIV or the hepatitis C virus; and the scandal arising in the mid-1980s from the development of Creutzfeldt-Jakob disease (CJD) by recipients of cadaveric human growth hormone.

Numerous further examples could be culled from the current events of the past years. Common concerns relate mainly to human consumption of products suspected or confirmed to entail risks to human health, for example, genetically modified organisms, mobile phones (feared to cause brain and ear cancer), and cigarettes, known to cause cancer and cardiac disease amongst other conditions. Injury caused by pharmaceutical products also occupies an important place in people's concerns; for example, in recent years, claims have been launched against Johnson & Johnson on the basis that Propulsid, a drug that controls gastric reflux, caused cardiac arrhythmia leading to the death of 38 persons. Lyodura, a brand of cadaveric dura mater grafts, has also prompted several claims against its German manufacturer because of its suspected link to CJD. In August 2005, Merck & Co Inc was ordered by a Texas jury to pay more than US$253 million to the family of a man who died after taking the painkiller Vioxx. Damage allegedly caused by vaccination has also played a part in society's worries, as, for instance, in the case of the suspected link between neurological diseases in young infants and DPTP vaccine, which has been the subject of claims in England and Canada.[3]

Damages caused by working conditions are not a new issue, but they continue to be a feature of modern life despite the existence in several countries of legislation aimed to protect workers' health. Such damages continue to prompt litigation, as their development can be insidious, their manifestations often arising several years after exposure.[4] For instance, claims by miners for British Coal, for damage caused to them by coal dust, were settled in the amount of £3 billion on 26 March 1999, after 10 years of negotiations during which British Coal had contested the causal link between the miners' work and their conditions of chronic bronchitis and emphysema, from which hundreds had died.[5] On 17 May 2002, British workers who had contracted mesothelioma, a type of lung cancer, follow-

[3] *Loveday v Renton* [1990] 1 Med LR 117 (QBD) (Stuart-Smith LJ) and *Rothwell* v *Raes* (1988) 54 DLR (4th) 193 (OntHCJ); (1990) 76 DLR (4th) 280 (OntCA). Some compensation schemes have been implemented to compensate victims of vaccine damage, eg, England: the 'interim' scheme of The Vaccine Damage Payments Act 1979 (UK); Québec: Public Health Act RSQ c S-2.2 §71.

[4] In Canada, workers are compensated through the Worker's Compensation Scheme and no tort claim is possible; in Québec, they also benefit from a compensation fund, which does not preclude civil claims, however, as in England; in Australia, no-fault workers' compensation is also dealt with by each state's legislation; finally, in France, workers' compensation is part of the general organisation of the social security system.

[5] Following *Griffiths v British Coal Corporation* [1998] EWJ No 4656 (QB, 23 January 1998).

ing exposure to asbestosis, also succeeded in their claims against their various employers, but only by taking their cases all the way to the English House of Lords.[6]

Finally, pollutants and their links to human disease also constitute a growing concern. Salient examples are claims by residents of Walkerton, Ontario, following contamination of their water supply with *E coli* in 2000, settled in the amount of C$50 million; and claims against the French state in 2001 by 51 French citizens suffering from thyroid cancer, who alleged that their condition was caused by the Chernobyl nuclear accident of April 1986. One could go on and on. That concerns such as these should be so prominent in the lay literature demonstrates the extent of public interest and disquiet about the effects on health of industry, new technologies and products, and modern developments in science and pharmacology.

The time is long past when questions of liability involved an identified agent causing risk, in whose ambit damage obviously fell. Today, causal connections between disease, death, and modern forms of risk have become more complicated, in particular because their relationship is easier to suspect than to prove and scientific controversies about them are not uncommon. And indeed, the main hurdle in determining the relationship between modern developments and danger to human health is also one of the most difficult aspects of modern civil liability: scientifically uncertain causal connections.

Despite continued impressive advances, scientific knowledge is still offset by uncertainties. These uncertainties can have a tremendous impact on the law. Law and science are in ongoing relationship and have a mutual influence which increases as technological, industrial, and medical developments take place. On one hand, law constantly affects science by imposing boundaries within which it must contain its activities and its development. On the other hand, science leaves its impress on many judicial and administrative decisions. This is true in several legal spheres, including criminal law and environmental, pharmaceutical, and medical liability, as well as cases involving industrial diseases. These legal areas all have one thing in common: they involve scientific questions which are often difficult to understand and resolve.

Problems of proof of causation that are the result of scientific uncertainty are consequently not uncommon in cases involving mass pollution, industrial disease, and medical malpractice. In mass pollution instances, while it may be possible to establish a statistical link between the emission of a pollutant and a specific damage, establishing the causal link in the case of an identified plaintiff or claimant[6a] may present serious hurdles. Other potential complicating factors

[6] *Fairchild v Glenhaven Funeral Services* [2002] 3 All ER 305 (HL): The House of Lords granted damages in three test claims. It is now expected that settlements shall be reached in more than 500 claims.

[6a] Althougth the word 'claimant' is in use in England, this text employs the term 'plaintiff', as do Canadian, Québec and Australian courts.

include the fact that a large segment of the population was subjected to the source of the damage, that the disease in question could be due to other causes, that epidemiological studies are impossible to conduct, and that the aetiology[7] of the disease is not known, making it impossible to say whether it was contracted gradually or by a triggering mechanism. Cases of industrial man-made diseases caused by agents such as dust, asbestosis, and chemical products are also a problematic area. These ailments typically develop following more or less prolonged exposure to an occupational risk which can make their relation to the work setting less than self-evident. Some conditions are in fact not immediately evident and produce undesirable effects years or even generations later. Moreover, these effects may be subtle and difficult to assess. Finally, ageing, environmental pollution, smoking habits, and individual predisposition may play a role in illnesses' development. Indeed, most industrial diseases are multi-factorial. It may be impossible to apportion the respective contributions of the different causes in order to assess whether working conditions played a sufficient role in the disease's onset.

One of the main benefits of modern life is derived from developments in medical science; but this field also still involves areas of great uncertainty. These uncertainties are reflected in instances of medical liability heard by the courts, where they may present tremendous hurdles as the parties and the court attempt to shed light on the relevant events and undertake scientific inquiries into still uncertain areas of medicine in order to do so.

Section 2

Uncertainty in Medical Malpractice

The field of medicine is in constant evolution and important scientific developments have taken place in recent decades. As a result of this progress, medicine today entails new dangers, as well as risks that are not always totally understood and that can engender damage whose origin may be difficult to establish. The words of Lord Denning, written in 1954 in *Roe v Minister of Health*, remain relevant today:

> Medical science has conferred great benefits on mankind, but these benefits are attended by considerable risks. ... We cannot take the benefits without taking the risks. Every advance in technique is also attended by risks. Doctors, like the rest of us, have to learn by experience; and experience often teaches in a hard way.[8]

[7] Aetiology refers to the study of the causes of ailments: M Garnier, et al, *Dictionnaire des termes de medicine*, 24th edn, (Paris, Maloine, 1995).

[8] *Roe v Minister of Health* [1954] 2 QB 66, 83. See also: PA Crépeau, *La responsabilité civile du médecin et de l'établissement hospitalier* (Montréal, Wilson & Lafleur, 1956) 30–32.

When a person sues the alleged negligent author of his physical injury, the link between the defendant's fault and the damage suffered must be demonstrated. Already recognised as a problematic requirement, the proof of the cause of the damage suffered by the patient involves serious challenges when science is not able to identify the origin of a biological phenomenon or when it is controversial. This situation is far from exceptional in the sphere of medical liability, where the tribunal of fact[9] is constantly confronted with causal problems which prevent one from determining the exact causes of the injury or the role played by the defendant in its realisation. These difficulties derive from the circumstances that scientific inquiry may be needed into areas of medicine in which the causal mechanisms are not yet completely understood; that the aetiology of some sicknesses, such as cancer, is still poorly understood; that one phenomenon may have several scientific explanations without the experts being able to identify which played a role in a specific case; that some conditions emerge years and even generations later or have subtle effects that are hard to assess; and, finally, that the human body's reactions are often unpredictable and difficult to explain with current medical knowledge. These uncertainties create two problematic situations: either it is impossible to know whether the doctor's fault[10] contributed at all to producing the damage; or, while it is known that it did, it is impossible to measure the exact extent of its contribution. The impact of these uncertainties may be exacerbated by the judge's and patient's lack of scientific background, as well as by deficiencies in the medical records available in evidence. Yet despite the uncertain causal evidence, the judge must take a decision.

Under the traditional rules of evidence, a plaintiff having to deal with uncertain or contradictory scientific evidence of causation may in consequence be doomed to failure. This result has been a source of concern for the courts of common law and civil law. They have been faced with a difficult dilemma in refusing to disrupt the traditional rules concerning the standard and burden of proof of causation, yet being unwilling to let an innocent victim of a proven wrong go uncompensated. A complicating concern is the equally important desire not to prejudice equity for the defendant by holding him liable for the whole of the plaintiff's loss in cases where it is impossible to identify his exact contribution. It is in the light of these conflicting interests that the courts have had to answer the difficult question of *who should bear the consequences of the scientific evidential gaps*.

[9] The words 'tribunal' and 'court' used in this text include judges and jury where appropriate. Civil cases are occasionally tried by jury in England and in some Canadian jurisdictions (Ontario and British Columbia). In Australia, civil trials by jury are still available, but their importance is declining. Due to time and space constraints, the interesting question of the impact of the presence of a jury on the evaluation of the quantum, as well as on approaches to scientific evidence in cases involving scientific uncertainty, will not be studied.

[10] The terms 'fault' and 'negligence' are generally used to refer both to the civilian concept of fault, and to the common law concept of breach of the duty of care.

The tension between the desire of the courts to compensate the patient and their respect for the traditional rules of evidence has led them to design conceptual and evidential techniques that are subject to criticism and arguably incapable of yielding the desired results. The courts have challenged the traditional approach that leaves the patient uncompensated by relaxing the burden or standard of proof of causation, resorting, in order to do so, to such approaches as factual presumptions and inferences, the concept of loss of chance, and the reversal of the burden of proof. This text analyses and critiques the different techniques used by the civil courts[11] to grant compensation to the plaintiff despite the uncertainty affecting the causal link in medical malpractice cases. This is mainly a case law study which concentrates on the practical problems encountered in the proof of causation and its judicial evaluation, namely the procedural question of evidence of causation. It therefore adopts an empirical and pragmatic approach, attempting to demystify the case law on the subject of scientific uncertainties in medical malpractice, without seeking to address and solve philosophical or theoretical issues related to causation. It also attempts to advocate for an appropriate approach towards the evidentiary difficulties caused by the uncertainties of science in medical liability.

Section 3

Jurisdictions, Fields of Law, and Methodology

This book mainly adopts a comparative model focusing on two legal traditions, common law and civil law. Four main jurisdictions have been chosen as the object of inquiry, those of English and Canadian common law, French civil law, and civil law prevailing in the Canadian Province of Québec.[12] Without undertaking an exhaustive review of the law of this jurisdiction, the text will also make brief incursions into the main Australian developments which have specifically dealt with uncertain causation in medical malpractice cases. The choice of these jurisdictions is not random. English law has greatly influenced the Canadian and Australian common law in this field, even though Canadian and Australian courts have taken a more expansive turn in the last decade. Common law developments have, in turn, influenced the Québec courts, which, in some cases, even rely on famous common law decisions to solve causal uncertainties. Finally, while Québec developments in

[11] Due to time and space constraints, this book does not examine exhaustively decisions by French administrative courts, aside from a brief review of their treatment of loss of chance, ch 4, text to fns 137 to 148. Administrative courts have jurisdiction over issues of public hospitals' liability in France.

[12] This text refers to the separate legal jurisdiction of the Province of Québec simply as Québec. Canada refers to the Canadian common law Provinces.

the field of civil liability are often true to their roots in French law, there are clear contradictions between the Québec and French positions in the domain of causal uncertainty. Close examination of French jurisprudence in this field in conjunction with its North American cousin is thus of inherent interest.

Québec law constitutes an interesting point of junction of the main jurisdictions studied in this text. The Province of Québec is one of two jurisdictions of North America where the French legal tradition has survived, despite the fact that it is a member of a federated nation ruled by the common law tradition.[13] But though this heritage has subsisted in the area of private law, public law in the Province of Québec is governed by common law.[14] The mixed nature of the Québec legal system and the sometimes difficult relationship between its French roots and the direct influence of the common law tradition makes it a fascinating jurisdiction to study.[15] Moreover, with regard to evidence of causation, Québec is situated at the crossroads[16] of common law and civil law, both systems perceptibly influencing its case law and legislation. This is due particularly to the fact that Québec rules of civil liability are of French origin while its rules of evidence are mixed, of common law and French descent.[17] An examination of Québec law on the subject of scientific causal uncertainties is thus of great interest, especially when paralleled with English and Canadian common law and French civil law, the three legal systems which have had the most impact on its historical development.[18]

[13] The other is the American state of Louisiana.

[14] This is the result of historical factors flowing from the conquest of Nouvelle France by Great Britain in the XVIIIth century. On these historical developments: FP Walton & M Tancelin, (trs), *Le domaine et l'interprétation du Code civil du Bas-Canada* (Toronto, Butterworths, 1980) 35. While predominantly of French origin, Québec private law is also composed of federal statutes and some rules of common law origin.

[15] In 1866, the distinctiveness of Québec private law was confirmed by the drafting of the Civil Code of Lower-Canada ('CcL-C') which aimed to protect the French legal tradition from foreign influence: Office de révision du Code civil, PA Crépeau (Chair), Rapport sur le Code civil du Québec, vol I (Québec, Éditeur officiel, 1978) XXVI–XXVII cited in M Guy, 'Le Code civil du Québec: Un peu d'histoire, beaucoup d'espoir' (1993) 23 *Revue de droit de l'Université de Sherbrooke* 453, 461. This code was extremely close to the French Napoleonic Code of 1804, and many of its articles employed almost identical style and terminology: JL Baudouin, 'The Impact of the Common Law on the Civilian Systems of Louisiana and Quebec' in J Dainow, (ed), *The Role of Judicial Decisions and Doctrine in Civil Law and in Mixed Jurisdictions* (Baton Rouge, LA, Louisiana State University Press, 1974) 4. The CcL-C was reformed in 1991 by the adoption of the Québec Civil Code ('CcQ') which came into force on 1 January 1994.

[16] 'Point de rencontre'. The expression is that of Crépeau (1956) (n 8 above) 40.

[17] Louis Baudouin emphasised, as early as 1953, that Québec is a 'living model of comparative law, since there comparative law is a living reality, not a mere intellectual conception.'[Translation by author]: L Baudouin, *Le droit civil de la province de Québec; Modèle vivant de droit comparé* (Montréal, Wilson & Lafleur, 1953) 40.

[18] Constraints of time and space have compelled exclusion of American case law and doctrine from this study, despite the fact that American writing on the question of scientific uncertainties and causation is both prolific and inspiring.

For historical reasons, the common law of torts has resulted in a fragmented system including different torts, all more or less independent of one another, and, traditionally, in a broad refusal to recognise a general principle of liability in the civil law style.[19] At the other extreme, the main feature of the French and Québec system is the generality of its principles and its focus on subjective rights.[20] At first sight, it may appear pointless to undertake a comparative analysis of legal traditions which address liability on such apparently different bases. Nevertheless, such an exercise can be useful, not only in providing a better understanding of one's own legal system, but also as a 'theatre of observation' permitting one to find one's 'own paths through "the forest"'[21] through examination of how other legal systems at a comparable stage of social and economic development have dealt with similar problems.

In the context of our study, the interest of the comparative venture goes beyond this, however. The problems encountered in both traditions with regard to the assessment of factual causation are extremely similar, and scientific uncertainty affects its determination in the same manner. These hurdles are in fact neither typical of common law, nor of civil law.[22] They have produced the same dilemmas in both traditions and the same desire to assist victims, although expressed with varying explicitness. In all the jurisdictions, courts have relied on similar kinds of evidential means or conceptual constructions to provide such assistance. And in all, confusion is observable in the tools used to achieve this generous approach. Comparison is rendered a helpful and extremely stimulating exercise by the fact that, despite all these resemblances, the jurisdictions studied have ultimately taken disparate avenues.

The similarities amongst the systems have prompted the adoption of two methods of analysis: comparative and integrated. For the most part, this text adopts the comparative model.[23] However, whenever possible, specific questions are addressed on the basis of an integrated approach. The latter seeks to address questions not through insistence on a strict comparison of the differences and resemblances amongst the systems, but rather by focussing on the underlying concepts

[19] Although reliance on *Donoghue v Stevenson* [1932] AC 562 (HL), as well as—in Canada—on the test of *Anns v Merton London Borough Council* [1978] AC 728 (HL), for the evaluation of the existence of a duty of care comes close to establishing a general principle of liability in the tort of negligence.

[20] For an interesting historical and comparative overview: G Viney and B Markesinis, *La réparation du dommage corporel: Essai de comparaison des droits anglais et français* (Paris, Economica, 1985) 3–11.

[21] MA Glendon, MW Gordon and C Osakwe, *Comparative Legal Traditions*, 2nd edn, (St Paul, West, 1994) 10.

[22] See generally: J Gordley, 'Comparative Legal Research: Its Function in the Development of Harmonized Law' (1995) 43 *American Journal of Comparative Law* 555, 561–62.

[23] Debates of course exist as to what constitute a 'comparative model' or what 'comparative methodology' is: A Watson in Glendon, et al (n 21 above) 2–8; CC Emanuelli, 'Le droit comparé selon une perspective canadienne' (1980) 40 *Revue du Barreau* 75, 77 and ff.

and ideas engaged with by the jurisdictions studied. In other words, it concentrates on the inherent nature and value of the ideas rather than on whether the ideas are in harmony with the systems they originate from. The rationale for this choice is that some of the concepts studied herein are not necessarily specific to one system but instead are shared amongst them, although there are sometimes noticeable differences in the reasoning with which they are presented or the importance they are assigned.[24] Through the comparative-integrated analysis, this text seeks to brush a critical portrait of the different solutions existing at a conceptual level without being constrained by jurisdictional boundaries.[25] In order to do so, however, it pays a close look at the solutions experimented with by each jurisdiction, while being alert to particularities of each tradition that may explain differences in the solutions resorted to.[26] It is hoped this comparative-integrated approach contributes to providing a dynamic look at the legal developments of the jurisdictions studied.[27]

Section 4

Structure

This book is divided into five chapters. First a general overview of the applicable rules of law in this field is presented (chapter 1); then comes an account of judicial developments in the four jurisdictions (chapters 2 to 5). Within each of these chapters, analytical and critical study aims to yield approaches to a solution.

Chapter 1 seeks to prepare the ground by undertaking a brief review of the rules regarding causation and evidence law in common and civil law, as well as describing the types of problems of proof encountered in the area of medical malpractice and how they may affect attempts to demonstrate causation. The main aim of this first chapter is to define the problems confronting the courts, which,

[24] The text is careful to emphasise any differences that might exist in each system's treatment of the relevant concepts or ideas, however.

[25] Using comparative law as an '*école de vérité*' which may supply solutions: Zitelmann, cited in K Zweigert and H Kötz, T Weir, (tr), *Introduction to Comparative Law*, 3rd edn, (Oxford, Clarendon Press, 1998) 15. See also: R David and C Jauffret-Spinosi, *Les grands systèmes de droit contemporains*, 10th edn, (Paris, Dalloz, 1992) 4; Emmanuelli (n 23 above) 80.

[26] We are however conscious of the limitations of such an approach and the necessity for a solid integrated-comparative approach also to situate the legal rules studied in their economic and cultural context, a task that unfortunately goes beyond the scope of this text: A Watson in Glendon, et al (n 21 above) 11.

[27] The sources enumerated in the footnotes are divided by jurisdiction only when the amount of references justifies it. The research is up to date as of 31 May 2005.

it is believed, cannot be addressed without a good understanding of how scientific uncertainties interact with the different causal processes in medical malpractice cases.

Chapters 2 to 5 are devoted to an analysis of the various solutions courts of common law and civil law have devised to relax the traditional rules of evidence and thereby assist patients who see their claims jeopardised by the impossibility of providing traditional evidence of causation because of medical uncertainties. They first deal with ways in which the law of the jurisdictions under review have expressed the need for judicial flexibility in assessing factual causation (chapter 2). They then examine the three main techniques which have interested the courts, namely reversal of the burden of proof (chapter 3), the proportional assessment of damages through the technique of loss of chance (chapter 4), and reliance on inferential reasoning (chapter 5).[28] With regard to the last, chapter 5 also looks at the courts' tendency to devise justifications on which they ground their decision to infer causation despite the limited evidence available using concepts such as creation or increase of the risk of harm, creation of a danger, absence of other explanations, the defendant's particular knowledge of the causative facts, and negligent impairment of the plaintiff's means of proof. The main aim of these three chapters is not only to present the different existing judicial solutions, but also to shed light on the way they are applied by the courts. Moreover, by treating all the different avenues available and experimented with by the courts in the same text, this book aims to avoid giving a fragmented view of this subject.[29]

While chapters 3 to 5 proceed to, first, merely present and analyse the results yielded by empirical study, they thereafter, in their respective critical analysis section, include a thorough critique of the findings. These critiques seek to determine whether the current solutions succeed in addressing the problem of uncertain causation in medical malpractice. Our working hypothesis is that none of these solutions is really workable and none allows for adequately balancing the desire to assist the victim with an assurance of fairness to the defendant. The critical analysis goes further, however, and attempts to identify the most suitable option to follow *within* the existing avenues available to the courts in the law of civil liability and evidence in view of all of the competing sets of interests concerned. A comprehensive and critical portrait of the interactions amongst the different solutions is also attempted in order to lead to a general assessment of the adequacy of the various judicial efforts to address causal uncertainties.

[28] The term inferential reasoning is used to refer to both the drawing of inferences and factual presumptions in common law, and to the drawing of factual presumptions in civil law. The term presumptive reasoning is used as a synonym.

[29] This approach is adopted in the hope of avoiding the trend emphasised by Gerecke. In 1990, he observed that, on this subject, commentators have chosen to tackle only one or two patterns at the same time, the result of which has been 'a patchwork of theories and proposals': D Gerecke, 'Risk Exposure as Injury: Alleviating the Injustice of Tort Causation Rules' (1990) 35 *McGill Law Journal* 797, 801.

This text has not been written in the frame of reference of recent work proposing such alternative ways of dealing with causation as mathematical approaches to probability or the creation of new torts. We advance the view that a more proper and realistic answer to causal uncertainties lies in the adoption of a flexible approach to the evidence but one that eschews arbitrariness and subjectivity in the decision-making process. Ultimately, this book seeks to defend the position that existing legal rules provide tools for the courts of the four main jurisdictions under study to address the uncertainty problems encountered in medical liability in a way that will ensure proper compensation for the plaintiff on the one hand, while preserving respect for the fundamental principles of the law, promoting their effectiveness, and ensuring fairness to the defendant on the other.

1

Problems in the Proof of Causation

S'il est un domaine juridique dans lequel il est périlleux de s'aventurer, c'est bien celui de la causalité
P Esmein

Section 1

Proof of Causation

Causation is a fundamental concept in the common law of *negligence* and the civil law of *responsabilité civile*. In both systems, a plaintiff to an action in damages for physical injury must prove that the tortious act of the defendant has caused the damage for which he claims compensation. Causation is probably one of the most problematic elements of modern tort law and *responsabilité civile*. Prosser describes it as a 'tangle and a jungle, a palace of mirrors and a maze';[1] Starck is of the opinion that '*la causalité, c'est la quadrature du cercle*';[2] Giesen argues that: '[e]stablishing the causal connection between medical negligence and the injury complained of is probably the most difficult task in medical malpractice litigation (as indeed in many negligence actions).'[3]

[1] WL Prosser, 'Proximate Cause in California' (1950) 38 *California Law Review* 369 (on proximate cause) approved in H Mazeaud, L Mazeaud and J Mazeaud, *Traité théorique et pratique de la responsabilité civile délictuelle et contractuelle* t II, 6th edn, (Paris, Montchrestien, 1965) para 1439, fn 1 bis.

[2] B Starck, *Droit civil: Les obligations* (Paris, Librairies Techniques, 1972) para 264.

[3] D Giesen, *International Medical Malpractice Law: A Comparative Law Study of Civil Liability Arising from Medical Care* (Boston, Martinus Nijhoff, 1988) 163. See also: Canada: *Bigcharles v Dawson Creek and District Health Care Society* [2001] 91 BCLR (3rd) 82 (BCCA) para 5; *Dixon Estate v Holland* [1997] 1 WWR 130 (BCSC) 134; MA Ross, 'Rules of the Road to Judgment in Medical Malpractice Cases: Standard of Care and Causation' (1998) 20 *Advocates' Quarterly* 274, 281; Australia: A Beever, 'Cause-in-Fact: Two Steps Out of the Mire' (2001) 51 *University of Toronto Law Journal* 327, 327, who however argues that it is less convoluted than one would imagine; *Chappel v Hart* (1998) 195 CLR 232 (AustHC) paras 87 and 93 (Kirby J); France: J Flour and JL Aubert, *Droit civil: Les Obligations 2) Le Fait juridique* (Paris, Armand Colin, 1997) para 162; B Starck, H Roland and L Boyer, *Obligations 1): La responsabilité délictuelle*, 5th edn, (Paris, Litec, 1996) para 1066; Demogue, cited in Mazeaud (n 1 above) para 1673; G Ripert, note under Cass civ, 27 December 1944, D 1945.237; G Boyer-Chammard

Legal theorists and philosophers have spilt much ink in recent centuries in an attempt to frame underlying theoretical principles to provide the courts with a coherent way of assessing causation.[4] Despite these efforts, the practical difficulties raised by the analysis of causation are often not properly met by the theoretical solutions.[5]

Not only have the theoretical efforts not resolved the problems of application of the causation requirement; they have also played a minor role in their solution by the judiciary.[6] Judges have resisted being 'trapped into endless philosophical discourse on the concept of causation.'[7] The intellectual process of common law and civil law judges has not been systematically based on any theoretical ground, logical explanation, or search for a scientifically exact solution. Judicial assessment of causation is generally fact-based, pragmatic, and empirical, and depends on judges' sovereign and subjective appreciation, as well as the application of their

and P Monzein, *La responsabilité médicale* (Paris, PUF, 1974) 98; G Ripert and J Boulanger, *Traité de droit civil* t II (Paris, LGDJ, 1957) para 904; Durry, note under Cass civ 1st, 18 March 1969, JCP 1970. G. II. 16422; Dorsner-Dolivet, note under Cass civ 1st, 17 November 1982, D 1984.Jur.305 (case also found at Bull civ 1982.I.n333, D 1983.380, JCP 1983.G.IV.41, JCP 1983.G.II.20056 (note Saluden); Québec: *Boucher v Rousseau* [1984] CA 85, 92; A Bernardot and RP Kouri, *La responsabilité civile Médicale* (Sherbrooke, RDUS, 1980) 72. Against: J Gaudron in *Naxakis v Western General Hospital* (1998) 197 CLR 269 (AustHC) 278–79, para 31: Difficulties associated with proof of causation are exaggerated, even in medical negligence cases.

4 England: HLA Hart and T Honoré, *Causation in the Law*, 2nd edn, (Oxford, Clarendon Press, 1985) 431 and ff; T Honoré, 'Causation and Remoteness of Damage' in A Tunc, (ed), *Encyclopaedia of Comparative Law*, vol XI (The Hague, Tübingen, 1971) 23–66; RF Heuston and RA Buckley, *Salmond and Heuston on the Law of Torts*, 21st edn, (London, Sweet & Maxwell, 1996) 511–16; France: P Conte and P Maistre du Chambon, *La responsabilité civile délictuelle*, 2nd edn, (Grenoble, Presses Universitaires de Grenoble, 2000) 133–37; Starck, *et al* (n 3 above) paras 1077–88; G Viney and P Jourdain, J Ghestin, (dir), *Traité de droit civil: Les conditions de la responsabilité*, 2nd edn, (Paris, LGDJ, 1998) paras 333–31 to 347; Flour and Aubert (n 3 above) paras 155–62; P le Tourneau and L Cadiet, *Droit de la responsabilité civile* (Paris, Dalloz, 1998) paras 821–25; Ripert and Boulanger (n 3 above) paras 1004–7; G Marty, 'La relation de cause à effet comme condition de la responsabilité' (1939) *Revue trimestrielle de droit civil* 685, 690–709; Tunc, note under Paris 18 April 1955, DS 1956.354; Québec: JL Baudouin and P Deslauriers, *La responsabilité civile*, 6th edn, (Cowansville, Yvon Blais, 2003) paras 570–97; M Tancelin, *Des obligations: L'acte illégitime et les modes d'exécution* (Montréal, Wilson & Lafleur, 1993) 132–35.

5 WVH Rogers, *Winfield and Jolowicz on Torts*, 16th edn, (London, Sweet & Maxwell, 2002) 224; Flour and Aubert (n 3 above) paras 161 and 182; Conte, *et al* (n 4 above) p 133: '*La causalité du juriste ne peut pas être celle du physicien ou du philosophe*'; *March v E & MH Stramare Pty Ltd* (1991) 171 CLR 506 (AustHC) 509 (Mason CJ) and 522 (Deane J); *Chappel v Hart* (n 3 above) paras 23 (McHugh J) 62 (Gummow J); *Rosenberg v Percival* (2001) 205 CLR 434 (AustHC) para 85 (Gummow J). See also: R Fumerton and K Fress, 'Causation and the Law: Preemption, Lawful Sufficiency, and Causal Sufficiency' (2001) *Law and Contemporary Problems* 83, 102.

6 Ripert (n 3 above). See also: Starck, *et al* (n 3 above) p 1060; Flour and Aubert (n 3 above) para 161; P Lesage-Jarjoura and S Philips-Nootens, *Éléments de responsabilité médicale: Le droit dans le quotidien de la médecine* (Cowansville, Yvon Blais, 2001) para 95; Viney and Jourdain (n 4 above) para 333 and *Dodds v Schierz* [1986] RJQ 2623 (CA) 2627 (Monet J).

7 AM Linden, *Canadian Tort Law*, 7th edn, (Markham, Butterworths, 2001) 109. See also: M McInnes, 'Causation in Tort Law: Back to Basics at the Supreme Court of Canada' (1997) *Alberta Law Review* 1013, 1013.

common sense.[8] In common law, the central role played by common sense is often restated in connection to causation by referring to the famous words of Lord Salmon in *Alphacell Ltd v Woodward* (1972):

> The nature of causation has been discussed by many eminent philosophers and also by a number of learned judges in the past. I consider, however, that what or who has caused a certain event to occur is essentially a practical question of fact which can be best answered by ordinary common sense rather than by abstract metaphysical theory.[9]

In civil law, commentators also recognise that causation cannot be explained logically[10] and depends on the judge's 'feeling.'[11]

While proving causation is often straightforward, it can become overwhelmingly difficult when evidence is lacking or is uncertain as to the chain of events leading to the damage, as well as when there exist multiple possible explanations of the injury. This practical difficulty, far from being an academic hypothesis, regularly challenges the parties, as well as the judges who have to assess the causal requirement.[12] Viney and Jourdain have indeed argued that even though theoretical efforts to define causation have been vain, it is imperative that the doctrine be

[8] C von Bar, *The Common European Law of Torts*, vol 2 (Oxford, OUP, 2000) para 412; England: *Roe v Minister of Health* [1954] 2 QB 66, 85 (Lord Denning); *Alphacell Ltd v Woodward* [1972] AC 824 (HL) 834 (Lord Wilberforce), 847 (Lord Salmon); *McGhee v National Coal Board* [1973] 1 WLR 1 (HL) 4–5 (Lord Reid); Hart and Honoré (n 4 above) p 1; Rogers, (n 4 above) pp 212–13; Australia: *March v Stramare* (n 5 above) pp 513 (Mason CJ), 522 (Deane J); *Chappel v Hart* (n 3 above) paras 6 (Gaudron J), 23 (McHugh J), 93 (Kirby J), 111 (Hayne J); *Rosenberg v Perciva* (n 5 above) para 85 (Gummow J). But see the scepticism expressed by McHugh J in *March v Stramare* (n 5 above) pp 532–33. Outside of medical liability: *Bennett v Minister of Community Welfare* (1992) 176 CLR 408 (AustHC) 413 (Mason CJ, Dean J and Toohey J), 419 (Gaudron J), 428 (McHugh J). Canada: *Athey v Leonati* [1996] 140 DLR (4th) 235; [1996] 3 SCR 458, 467; *Ostby v Bondar* (1998) 218 AR 132 (AltaQB) 146; *Meyers (Next Friend of) v Stanley* (2003) AJ No 685, ABQB 468 (AltaQB, 27 May 2003) para 54; *Bear (Litigation Guardians of) v Lambos* (2005) CarswellSask 232 (SaskQB, 28 March 2005) para 49; *Adair Estate v Hamilton Health Sciences Corp* (2005) WL 1244381, CarswellOnt 2180 (OntSCtJ, 25 April 2005) para 111; Linden (n 7 above) p 109; M McInnes, 'A Decade in the Supreme Court of Canada' (2000) 62 *Saskatchewan Law Review* 445, 445; McInnes (n 7 above) p 1014; France: Demogue cited in Mazeaud (n 1 above) para 1673; Starck, *et al* (n 3 above) paras 1070 and 1074; Flour and Aubert (n 3 above) para 165; le Tourneau and Cadiet (n 4 above) para 825; P Leroy, 'Le juge judiciaire et le lien de causalité médical' (1994) 90 *Petites Affiches* 19; Québec: J Pineau and M Ouellette, *Théorie de la responsabilité civile*, 2nd edn, (Montréal, Thémis, 1980) 174–75; Bernardot and Kouri (n 3 above) p 80. Against: *Boucher v Rousseau* (n 3 above) p 92 (Monet J diss); Flour and Aubert (n 3 above) paras 154 and 165.

[9] (N 8 above) p 847. Approved in Canada in *Snell v Farrell* [1990] 72 DLR (4th) 222; [1990] 2 SCR 311, 328.

[10] Starck, *et al* (n 3 above) para 1074.

[11] P Esmein, 'Le nez de cléopâtre ou les affres de la causalité' (1964) 33 *Dalloz* 205. See also: Flour and Aubert (n 3 above) paras 162 and 165 and Starck, *et al* (n 3 above) para 1070.

[12] MA Jones, *Medical Negligence*, 3rd edn, (London, Sweet & Maxwell, 2003) paras 5–3; Starck, *et al* (n 3 above) para 1060; Pineau and Ouellette (n 8 above) p 174; and *Dodds v Schierz* (n 6 above) p 2627 (Monet J).

subjected to an analytical effort on this problem with which the courts are constantly confronted and on which the faith of victims often depends:

> *On se résignerait volontiers à ce constat d'échec si la définition de la causalité apparaissait comme un problème purement théorique imaginé, plus ou moins artificiellement, pour exercer la subtilité des juristes. Mais il suffit d'ouvrir un recueil de jurisprudence pour constater que les tribunaux sont quotidiennement confrontés à cette question et qu'ils ne peuvent, pour leur part, éluder sa solution dont dépend d'ailleurs très souvent le sort des victimes. Dès lors, la doctrine manquerait, selon nous, gravement à sa mission si elle renonçait à tout effort d'analyse et à toute tentative d'orientation du droit positif en ce domaine.*[13]

Before we address the particular problems of proof arising in the area of medical negligence, a brief review of the general principles of causation developed in common law and civil law is necessary.

A. Common Law

1. Factual and Legal Causation

In Canada and Australia, even though the doctor–patient and hospital–patient relationships are normally considered contractual,[14] doctors' and hospital's liability is generally dealt with under the tort of negligence, of which causation is an essential part. The same applies in England, although private health care is also governed by contract.[15] To be successful, a plaintiff to a claim for negligence has to show that he suffered harm as a consequence of the defendant's breach of a duty of care owed to him. No conclusion can be reached as to a doctor's liability based on the mere fact that an accident happened or that the result was not in accordance with the patient's expectations.

Courts and legal writers distinguish between two stages in the assessment of the existence of a causal link: *causation in fact*[16] and *causation in law*.[17] The cause in

[13] (N 4 above) para 335.

[14] As well as of a fiduciary nature. The same applies in Australia, even when the treatment is billed to Medicare or other insurance: M Wallace, *Health Care and the Law,* 3rd edn, (Pyrmont, NSW, Lawbook, 2001) para 10.1.

[15] A Grubb and J Laing, *Principles of Medical Law,* 2nd edn, (Oxford, OUP, 2004) para 8.42. In England, the relationship between the National Health Service patient and his doctor or hospital is not considered contractual: Grubb and Laing, above, para 5.06.

[16] Also causation in fact, cause in fact, or but-for cause.

[17] Also direct, proximate, or foreseeable (or, conversely, remote). Stapleton interestingly suggests abandoning the 'legal cause' terminology, in favour of the expression 'scope of liability for consequences': J Stapleton, 'Cause-in-Fact and the Scope of Liability for Consequences' (2003) 119 *LQR* 388, 389 and ff, a suggestion adopted by the 2002 Australian legislative reform: Civil Liability Act 2002 (NSW) §5D and E; Civil Liability Act 2003 (Qld) §11–12; Civil Liability Act 1936 (SA) §34–35; Civil

fact process inquires whether the defendant *in fact* caused the damage. This step involves a mainly factual inquiry resolved by the production of evidence and the drawing of inferences from that evidence.[18] At this stage, the question is whether the defendant's act or omission should be excluded from the events which contributed to the occurrence of the plaintiff's loss.[19] The goal of the exercise, however, is not to compile an exhaustive list of causes; nor is it concerned with determining whether the defendant's act was the sole or main cause of the plaintiff's damage, since it needs only to be *a* cause.[20] The factual inquiry aims to identify the causally relevant factors,[21] but acts only as a preliminary filter and is not determinative of liability. A subsequent choice must be made amongst all the identified causes in order to select those to which the court will attribute legal responsibility. This is where *causation in law* enters in. This second step aims to determine whether the defendant's act or omission was a sufficiently legally effective cause amongst the complex of other causes.[22] It asks whether the defendant *ought* to be held liable for the loss suffered by the plaintiff.[23] This question is considered to be more one of value, fairness and legal policy,[24] than one concerned with the factual existence or absence of a causal link.

Inherent in this divide is the belief that the ascertainment of facts should be distinguished from the elucidation of values.[25] This ground for distinguishing between cause in fact and cause in law has been criticised as misleading, as it gives the impression that policy factors are assessed only at the second stage of the inquiry and that the first stage is only a technical and evidentiary one.[26] The present study

Liability Act 2002 (Tas) §13–14; Civil Liability Act 2002 (WA) §5C and D; Civil Law (Wrongs) Act 2002 (ACT) §45–46; Wrongs Act 1958 (Vic) §51–52. On the distinction between cause-in-law and cause-in-fact, England: S Deakin, A Johnston and BS Markesinis, *Tort Law,* 4th edn, (Oxford, Clarendon Press, 2003) 185–86; Honoré (n 4 above) p 9; Rogers (n 4 above) pp 209–12; EJ Weinrib, 'A Step Forward in Factual Causation' (1975) 38 *MLR* 518, 518; Australia: *March v Stramare* (n 5 above) pp 530–31 (McHugh J); Canada: EI Picard and GB Robertson, *Legal Liability of Doctors and Hospitals in Canada,* 3rd edn, (Toronto, Carswell, 1996) 218; Ross (n 3 above) p 281; R Roth, 'Causation and the Burden of Proof: An Age Old Dilemma and a New Age Approach' (1992) 14 *Advocates' Quarterly* 70, 71. But see: Honoré (n 4 above) p 67.

18 Weinrib (n 17 above) p 518.

19 Rogers (n 4 above) pp 208–9.

20 England: *Cork v Kirby MacLean Ltd* [1952] 2 All ER 402 (CA) 406–7 (Lord Denning); Rogers (n 4 above) pp 210–11; Honoré (n 4 above) pp 8–9; Jones (n 12 above) paras 5–4; Canada: *Athey v Leonati* (n 8 above) pp 467–68; GHL Fridman, *The Law of Torts in Canada,* vol 1 (Toronto, Carswell, 1989) 322–23.

21 JG Fleming, *The Law of Torts,* 9th edn, (London, Sweet & Maxwell, 1998) 193.

22 Rogers (n 4 above) pp 210–11.

23 P Cane, *Atiyah's Accidents, Compensation and the Law,* 6th edn, (London, Butterworths, 1999) 99.

24 Rogers (n 4 above) pp 210–11; Weinrib (n 17 above) p 518; Roth (n 17 above) p 71; *Cork v Kirby MacLean Ltd* (n 20 above) p 407 (Lord Denning) citing *Jones v Livox Quarries* [1952] 2 QB 608.

25 Weinrib (n 17 above) p 529; *March v Stramare* (n 5 above) p 534 (McHugh J).

26 *March v Stramare* (n 5 above) pp 515–16 (Mason CJ) and *Naxakis v Western General Hospital* (n 3 above) p 314; Deakin, *et al* (n 17 above) p 186. Against: WS Malone, 'Ruminations on Cause-in-Fact' (1956) 9 *Stanford Law Review* 60, 61.

in fact confirms that the divide is not so clear cut and that policy considerations and values form an intrinsic part of the assessment of factual causation.

2. Factual Causation

Factual causative inquiry is most frequently carried out with the assistance of the *but-for test*, which has met with near universal acceptance as a tool for achieving the determination.[27] This test constitutes direct application of the *causa sine qua non* theory.[28] According to this theory, every condition in the absence of which the harm would not have occurred in the way it did occur is a cause of it.[29] Conversely, the condition which made no difference to the course of events is excluded from the realm of causes. Adherents of this theory believe that the selection of one condition over another at the factual level would be irrational and unscientific. All the conditions are consequently considered equally necessary to produce the harm.[30]

The practical application of the test is usually straightforward.[31] It has even been described as unimportant in practice, because its satisfaction is usually obvious.[32] It involves asking whether the harm suffered by the plaintiff would have occurred but for the defendant's action or omission?[33] If the answer to this question is

[27] Fleming (n 21 above) p 194. See also, England: Honoré (n 4 above) p 67; G Williams, 'Causation in the Law' (1961) *CLJ* 62, 63; Rogers (n 4 above) pp 213–14; Canada: *Athey v Leonati* (n 8 above) p 466; *Walker Estate v York Finch General Hospital* [2001] 198 DLR (4th) 193; [2001] 1 SCR 647, para 87; and Giesen (n 3 above) p 177.

[28] Commonly referred to as the *equivalence theory* or the *condition theory*: Honoré (n 4 above) p 33. This theory has fallen out of favour in civil law and common law except as a test of cause in fact: pp 31 and 36.

[29] *Ibid*, p 33.

[30] *Ibid*, p 34.

[31] Eg, England: *Corn v Weir's Glass (Hanley) Ltd* [1960] 1 WLR 577 (CA) 583 (Willmer LJ), 584–85 (Devlin LJ); *Barnett v Chelsea Hospital* [1969] 1 QB 428, 438; *Robinson v Post-Office* [1974] 1 WLR 1176 (CA); *Titchener v British Railways Board* [1983] 1 WLR 1427 (HL) 1434; *Stockdale v Nicholls* [1993] 4 Med LR 198 (QB) 199; Canada: *Hock (Next Friend of) v Hospital for Sick Children* (1998) 106 OAC 321 (CA) 355; *Jaskiewicz v Humber River Regional Hospital* [2001] 4 CCLT (3rd) 98 (OntSC) 111. In England, if the inquiry reveals that had the defendant acted lawfully, his subsequent treatment or intervention, or absence thereof, would have resulted in the same damage to the plaintiff, one has to ask whether this would have been contrary to accepted medical practice (*the Bolam test*): *Joyce v Merton Sutton and Wandsworth Health Authority* [1996] PIQR 121 (CA) 141, 151–53; *Bolitho v City and Hackney Health Authority* [1998] AC 232 (HL) 239–43; *Wisniewski v Central Manchester Health Authority* [1998] PIQR 324 (CA) P329 and ff; Jones (n 12 above) pp 5–10. See also: Hart and Honoré (n 4 above) p 415: The correct test in England is what the defendant would probably have done and not what the reasonable defendant would have done.

[32] Rogers (n 4 above) p 212.

[33] Or, as put by Weinrib (n 17 above) p 522, 'what would have happened if what had happened had not happened.' See also: MA Jones, *Textbook on Torts,* 8th edn, (London, Blackstone, 2002) 228–29 and Fleming (n 21 above) p 195.

negative, the plaintiff meets his threshold.[34] Conversely, if the loss would have occurred in any event, or if the loss had already occurred before the defendant's negligent intervention, the plaintiff fails on this issue.[35] This ease of application is demonstrated by the famous English decision in *Barnett v Chelsea Hospital* (1969).[36] Barnett and two other men had started vomiting shortly after drinking tea. They were seen by a nurse, but the doctor, when phoned at home, negligently refused to see them. Barnett died a few hours later of arsenic poisoning. The medical evidence showed, however, that he would have died of poisoning even if he had been admitted to the hospital and treated with all care. Indeed, the drip antidote had to be administered immediately to save him; even without negligence, this would not have occurred.[37]

As illustrated by *Barnett,* the but-for test necessarily involves questions about what would have happened if the past chain of events had been different. The answer to these questions may depend on the assessment of a hypothetical state of facts, as well as on an inquiry into the hypothetical behaviour of the plaintiff,[38] a third party,[39] or the defendant.[40] Direct evidence about hypothetical situations rarely being available, the matter must be decided on the basis of generalisations about how things and people normally behave or ought to behave in given circumstances.[41] This is often an evident inference, but in some cases, reconstructing historical events in order to prove that things would have been different, absent the alleged negligence, may constitute an insurmountable difficulty.[42]

While in most cases the application of the but-for test adequately meets the needs of the causal inquiry, there are some areas in which the test is unworkable[43]

[34] Eg: *Brown (Next Friend of) v University of Alberta Hospital* [1997] 145 DLR (4th) 63 (AltaQB) 126.

[35] Eg: *Hotson v East Berkshire Area Health Authority* [1987] 1 AC 750, 785, 789–90 (Lord Mackay), 792 (Lord Ackner); *Re R (A Minor) (No 2)* (1996) 33 BMLR 178 (CA) 199.

[36] [1969] 1 QB 428.

[37] *Ibid*, p 438. Using *Hotson*'s terminology, one could say that, on arrival at the hospital, the man was 'doomed'. Outside medical liability: *Robinson v Post-Office* [1974] 1 WLR 1176 (CA) and *Titchener v British Railways Board* [1983] 1 WLR 1427; [1983] 3 All ER 770 (HL).

[38] *Nolan v Dental Manufacturing Co Ltd* [1958] 1 WLR 936 (ManAss); and *McWilliams v Sir William Arrol & Co Ltd* [1962] 1 WLR 295 (HL).

[39] *Allied Maples Group Ltd v Simmons & Simmons (A Firm)* [1995] 1 WLR 1602 (CA); and *Scott v Northern Devon Healthcare Trust* (QB, 31 July 2000) 7–8.

[40] *Bolitho v City and Hackney HA* (n 31 above). It involves particular difficulties in cases of omission, where the defendant is not the immediate cause of the damage but rather fails to act to prevent damage being caused by someone or something else: Cane (n 23 above) p 62. Cane criticises the distinction, however: 63–64.

[41] Honoré (n 4 above) p 76.

[42] Suffice to recall the often-cited example of Pascal's assumption that if the nose of Cleopatra had been shorter, the whole face of the earth would have been changed: G Williams, 'Causation in the Law' (1961) *CLJ* 62, 67; P Esmein, (n 11 above).

[43] *Athey v Leonati* (n 8 above) p 466; *Cottrelle v Gerrard* (2003) OJ No 4194; (2004) CarswellOnt 1623 (CA, 22 April 2004) para 30; *Trajdos (Litigation Guardian of) v Bala* (2003) OJ no 4953 (OntSCtJ, 11 December 2003) para 65. See also: JA Campion and DW Dimmer, *Professional Liability in Canada* (looseleaf) (Toronto, Carswell, 1998) 3–28.

or produces unfair or absurd results. For instance, it may in some cases *prevent the selection of any cause,* with the inevitable result that the plaintiff fails to meet his burden of proof. Such a hurdle is most frequently encountered where a plurality of causal factors are involved in the production of the injury. For instance, it occurs where damage is caused by two (or more) events, which combine to produce the total outcome, in circumstances in which each of them would have been sufficient to individually produce it.[44] In such cases, the strict application of the *causa sine qua non* test leads to the absurd result that neither event would qualify as a cause since the defendant can invoke the existence of alternative explanations for the plaintiff's injury as proof that the damage would have happened without his negligence.[45]

The unfair results the but-for test can lead to in some situations have given rise to affirmations that it is not determinative and can serve only as an inclusion tool.[46] Others have argued that, even though it is considered one of the most helpful devices to resolve the question of factual causation without relying solely on the judiciary's discretion, the but-for test is no more than a tool for the judge:

> The dominance of the 'but-for' test is itself a result of the urge to banish evaluative considerations from the realm of cause in fact. This test is the most mechanical method of handling cause in fact, and therefore it seems to be the most suitable for excluding the considerations of policy which by their nature are too flexible and delicate to be susceptible to an automatic form of treatment. But it is noticeable that even here the purely factual approach breaks down on occasion, and it is necessary, whether explicitly or not, *to supplement the mechanical formula with an infusion of policy.* (emphasis added)[47]

The but-for test of causation has therefore not been applied in a rigid way in the common law. Neither has it been considered the exclusive test in negligence cases[48]

[44] As when two fires are lit by two different tortfeasors, one at each end of a building, which is consequently destroyed: Hart and Honoré (n 4 above) p 206; *March v Stramare* (n 5 above) p 523 (Deane J).

[45] Problems also arise when different causes overtake and defeat one another: Fleming (n 21 above) p 225, referring to JA McLaughlin, 'Proximate Cause' (1925–26) 39 *Harvard Law Review* 149, 155 and, generally: 239–49; Hart and Honoré (n 4 above) p 2; or in cases involving *supervening causes*, ie, successive and causally unrelated injuries, eg: *Carslogie Steamship Co Ltd v Royal Norwegian Government* [1952] AC 292 (HL); *Performance Cars Ltd v Abraham* [1962] 1 QB 33; *Baker v Willoughby* [1970] AC 467 (HL); *Jobling v Associated Dairies Ltd* [1982] AC 794 (HL).

[46] Weinrib (n 17 above) pp 521–23. Some consider it obsolescent, as observed by Von Bar: C Von Bar, *The Common European Law of Torts*, vol 1 (Oxford, Clarendon Press, 1998) para 413.

[47] Weinrib (n 17 above) pp 530 and 522–23. Weinrib adds that problems of application of the but-for test come from a tendency to look upon it as being normative. See also: *Kerry v England (PC)* [1898] AC 742, 746; McLaughlin (n 45 above) pp 153–55.

[48] Canada: *Dybongco-Rimando Estate v Jackiewicz* (2001) CarswellOnt 3219 (OntSC, 28 August 2001) para 35; *McLeod v Ridyard* (2001) CarswellBC 186, BCSC 158 (26 January 2001) para 55 (obiter); *Adair Estate v Hamilton Health Sciences Corp* (n 8 above) para 109; Australia: *March v Stramare* (n 5 above) pp 508 (Mason CJ), 522 (Deane J), 524 (Toohey J) (non-medical); *Chappel v Hart* (n 3 above) paras 24 (McHugh J), 62 (Gummow J), 93 (Kirby J), 117 (Hayne J). Against: *March v Stramare* (n 5 above) p 534 (McHugh J).

and courts have recognised that the but-for test needs to be 'supplemented by considerations of justice and legal policy.'[49] Concerned to resolve the unfairness but-for causation can lead to, courts and scholars have admitted that common sense may in some cases require an alternative test of factual causation.[50]

Alternatives to the but-for test become pressing where uncertainty in the scientific evidence prevents one from identifying which of several possible causes produced the damage. In these cases, the strict application of the *causa sine qua non* test has clearly offended the judges' sense of justice and they have responded by finding alternative ways of assessing the existence of the causal link in order to reach what they thought was the just result. This shows that beyond any rigid theoretical notion of cause lies the judges' sense of fairness, which has found particular expression in the present field of study.

English, Australian,[51] and Canadian[52] courts have indeed proven to be ready to find causation proven in cases where it is not possible, in the light of the facts and the expert evidence, to say that the defendant's act or omission actually caused the damage on the but-for test. This has long been achieved through reliance on the concept of *material contribution to the damage* under the authority of *Bonnington*

[49] Expressed most emphatically in Australia: *March v Stramare* (n 5 above) pp 515–17 (Mason CJ), 522–23 (Deane J) and 524 (Toohey J). Against: McHugh J, pp 532–33. See also: *Chappel v Hart* (n 3 above) paras 62 (Gummow J), 93 (Kirby J), 148 (Hayne J). Outside of medical liability: *Bennett v MCW* (n 8 above) p 413 (Mason CJ, Dean J and Toohey J).

[50] *Fairchild v Glenhaven Funeral Services* [2002] 3 All ER 305 (HL) para 40 (Lord Nicholls): Only in exceptional cases; para 62 (Lord Hoffmann): When the ordinary rule empties the duty of its content. Alternatives include the *material contribution test;* the American *substantial-factor rule*; and the *NESS test* where, to be causally relevant, a factor must be a necessary element of a set of antecedent actual conditions that was sufficient for the occurrence of the plaintiff's injury: A Beever (n 3 above) p 330. See also: Hart and Honoré (n 4 above) pp 111–14; RW Wright, 'Actual Causation vs Probabilistic Linkage: The Bane of Economic Analysis' (1985) 14 *Journal of Legal Studies* 435; Fumerton and Kress (n 5 above); J Stapleton, 'Scientific and Legal Approaches to Causation' in I Freckelton and D Mendelson, (eds), *Causation in Law and Medicine* (Hampshire, Ashgate Dartmouth, 2002) 19; J Stapleton (n 17 above) pp 393–94; Civil Liability Act 2002 (NSW) §5D; *Finch v Rogers* (2004) NSWSC 39 (NSWSC, 13 February 2004) para 148; D Hamer, 'Chance Would Be a Fine Thing: Proof of Causation and Quantum in an Unpredictable World' (1999) 23 *Melbourne University Law Review* 557, 572. A detailed analysis of this test is beyond the ambit of this work; the NESS approach attempts to deal with the classic inadequacy of the but-for test in cases where the outcome is 'over-determined', while the present text is rather concerned with the difficulty that arises where the evidence is inadequate to even apply the but-for test. On the distinction: J Stapleton, 'Lords a'Leaping Evidentiary Gaps' (2002) 10 *Torts Law Journal* 276, 280.

[51] G Edmond and D Mercer, 'Rebels without a Cause? Judges, Medical and Scientific Evidence and the Uses of Causation' in I Freckelton and D Mendelson, (eds), *Causation in Law and Medicine* (Hampshire, Ashgate Dartmouth, 2002) 99; PJM MacFarlane, *Health Law in Australia and New Zealand* (Sydney, Federation Press, 2000) 129; B Bennett, *Law and Medicine* (North Ryde, NSW, LBC Information Services, 1997) 50.

[52] The French and Québec law's approach to cumulative processes has not provoked exceptional developments such as those which have taken place in common law.

Castings v Wardlaw (1956).[53] This case involved a steel dresser whose employment exposed him to silica dust emanating from the pneumatic hammer at which he worked, as well as from swing grinders. The swing grinders were not kept free from obstruction and in this respect the defendant factory owners were in breach of statutory duty. Having contracted pneumoconiosis, the worker sued his employer for damages. Medical evidence demonstrated that pneumoconiosis is caused by a gradual accumulation of minute particles of silica. While both sources of dust contributed to produce the disease, it was impossible to assess the proportion of dust inhaled by the plaintiff which came from the swing grinders (*guilty* dust). While this prevented from concluding that, but-for the guilty dust, the steel dresser would have suffered injury, the court nevertheless granted his claim on the basis that it had materially contributed to it.[54]

The material contribution test thus allows for a departure from the traditional but-for test of causation and flows in fact from the recognition that this test is sometimes unworkable or, more precisely, leads to results considered unfair.[55] The more liberal material contribution test considers it sufficient to show that the defendant's negligence *materially contributed* to producing the damage, even though his act alone was not sufficient to create it. Materiality is a question of degree and is met by any contribution which does not fall within the exception *de minimis non curat lex.*[56] This test has allowed recovery in cases in which it was impossible to even approximately quantify the contribution of the defendant to the plaintiff's injury.[57] Even though the material-contribution-to-the-damage test was developed primarily in industrial disease cases, it has been applied to medical malpractice cases which could not be solved under the but-for test.[58]

[53] *Bonnington Castings Ltd v Wardlaw* [1956] AC 613 (HL). This case is the main authority on this alternative way of assessing causation, even though the concept of material contribution to the damage has been relied on since the middle of the nineteenth century in England and Scotland: *Senior v Ward* (1859) 1 E1 & E1 385, 392; *Wakelin v London and South Western Railway Co* (1886) 12 App Cas 41, 47; *Craig v Glasgow Corporation* [1919] SC 1 (HL) 6.

[54] P 623 (Lord Reid), pp 626–27 (Lord Keith). Such test is only relevant where courts are faced with a multiplicity of causes that operate cumulatively: Below, text to n 254.

[55] *Athey v Leonati* (n 8 above) p 466.

[56] The law does not take notice of small or trifling matters. Lord Reid in *Bonnington Castings v Wardlaw* (n 53 above) p 621. See also: *Meyers v Stanley* (n 8 above) para 56; *Grass v Women's College Hospital* (2003) OJ no 5313 (OntSCtJ, 31 December 2003) para 95.

[57] *Bonnington Castings Ltd v Wardlaw* (n 53 above); and *Nicholson v Atlas Steel Foundry and Engineering Co Ltd* [1957] 1 WLR 613 (HL). In both cases, the Court believed the contribution was not so negligible that the maxim *de minimis* applied. See also: *Smith v Leech Brain* [1962] 2 QB 405, 413 (Lord Parker) 416.

[58] England: *Wilsher v Essex Area Health Authority* [1988] 1 AC 1074 (HL); *Stockdale v Nicholls* (n 31 above). It has also been significant in cases involving psychiatric damage (non medical), eg: *Jones v Wright* [1991] 1 All ER 353 (QB) 382; *Page v Smith (No 2)* [1996] 1 WLR 855 (CA); *Vernon v Bosley (No 1)* [1997] 1 All ER 577 (CA). Generally: AM Dugdale and KM Stanton, *Professional Negligence,* 3rd edn, (London, Butterworths, 1998) 390. Canada: *Parkin v Kobrinsky* [1963] 43 DLR (2nd) 519 (ManCA) 526; *Myers v Peel County Board of Education* [1981] 123 DLR (3rd) 1; [1981] 2 SCR 21, 35;

Some courts grant full recovery on the basis of material contribution without discounting damages to account for the fact that part of the damage was contributed to by other causes.[59] Others hold that if the evidence shows that part of the damage is not due to the defendant's contribution, damages are to be reduced accordingly.[60] Such evidence does not, however, affect the assessment of causation

Couillard and Labutis v Waschulewski's Estate (1988) 87 AR 161 (QB) 166 and 172 (non-medical); *Athey v Leonati* (n 8 above) pp 466 and 477; *Webster v Chapman* [1997] 155 DLR (4th) 82 (ManCA) 92; *Hock v Hospital for Sick Children* (n 31 above) p 345; *Sohal v Brar* (1998) 211 AR 81 (AltaQB) 104–5; *Bigcharles v Dawson Creek* (n 3 above) para 5; *Allen (Next Friend of) v University Hospitals Board* (2002) AJ no 1041, ABCA 195 (AltaCA, 27 August 2002) para 41; *Martin v Inglis* (SaskQB, 17 April 2002) para 18 (obiter); *Keane v Adams* (2002) AJ No 93, ABQB 63 (AltaQB, 23 January 2002) para 80; *Cottrelle v Gerrard* (n 43 above) para 30; *Grass (Litigation Guardian of) v Women's College Hospital* (n 56 above) para 94; *Williamson v Kozak* (2003) AJ no 1467, ABQB 953 (AltaQB, 21 November 2003) para 64; *Duffy v St Joseph's Health Care System* (2003) OJ No 3078 (OntSCtJ, 4 July 2003) para 12; *Lurtz v Duchesne* (2003) OJ no 1540 (OntSCtJ, 16 April 2003) para 347; *Michener v Doris* (2003) BCJ No 2301, BCSC 1541 (BCSC, 8 October 2003) para 175 (obiter); *Doiron v Haché* [2003] NBJ No 23, NBQB 26 (24 January 2003) para 110; *Trajdos v Bala* (n 43 above) paras 65, 143 and 193; *Ibrahim v Hum* (2004) 33 Alta LR (4th) 323; (2005) 6 WWR 564 (AltaQB) para 143; *Fournier v Wiens* (2004) 33 Alta LR (4th) 114 (AltaQB) para 96; *Bystedt (Guardian ad litem) v Hay* (2004) BCJ No 401, BCCA 124 (BCCA, 4 March 2004) para 3; *Smith (Guardian ad litem of) v Grace* (2004) BCJ No 583, BCSC 395 (BCSC, 23 March 2004) para 8; *O'Grady v Stokes* (2005) ABQB 247, Carswell Alta 578 (AltaQB, 26 April 2005) para 122; *Adair Estate v Hamilton Health Sciences Corp* (n 8 above) paras 7 and 109; *Bear v Lambos* (n 8 above) para 49; *Dybongco* (n 48 above) para 35; *McLeod v Ridyard* (n 48 above) para 53 (obiter); *Meyers v Stanley* (n 8 above) paras 56 and 83. See also: *Walker Estate v York Finch* (n 27 above) paras 88 and 97 (Major J): The Supreme Court of Canada considered the but-for test unworkable, opting for the material contribution test, to ultimately find causation proven on the but-for test even though there was no evidence of even a material contribution of the defendant's fault to the third party's decision to donate his contaminated blood. Outside medical liability: *Marcotte v Martin* (2004) NJ no 27, NLSCTD 15 (Nfld & LSC, 30 January 2004) para 116; Australia: *Stacey v Chiddy* (1993) NSW Lexis 7679 (NSWSC, 23 April 1993) 38; *Naxakis v Western General Hospital* (n 3 above) paras 26 (Gaudron J) and 127 (Callinan J); *Tamworth Base Hospital v Durant* 2000 NSW Lexis 225 (NSWSC, 8 August 2000) 86 (Handley J); and, outside medical liability, *March v Stramare* (n 5 above) p 514; *Ren v Mukerjee* (1996) Aust ACTSC Lexis 78 (AustCapTerrHC, 12 December 1996) 36; *Bendix Mintex PTY Ltd v Barnes* (1997) 42 NSWLR 307 (NSWSC) 311; *Wallaby Grip (BAE) PTY Ltd (In Liq) v Macleay Area Health Service* (1998) NSW Lexis 2423 (NSWSC, 18 December 1998) 11. Some cases rely unnecessarily on the material contribution test although causation is proven under the but-for test: *Comeau v Saint John Regional Hospital* [2001] 9 CCLT (3rd) 223; (2001) 634 APR 201; (2001) 244 NBR (2nd) 201 (CA) paras 69, 71, 73; *Phillip v Whitecourt Gen Hosp* (2003) 22 CCLT (3rd) 27 (AltaQB) para 75; *Grass v Women's College Hospital* (n 58 above) para 255; *Crawford (Litigation Guardian of) v Penney* (2003) 14 CCLT (3rd) 60 (OntSCtJ) para 219; *Zaiffdeen v Chau* (2004) AJ No 513, ABQB 331 (AltaQB, 30 April 2004) para 55; and outside of medical negligence: *Brazel v Nicholls* (2003) NSWCA 387 (1 December 2003) para 69.

59 *Nicholson v Atlas Steel Foundry* (n 57 above); *Fairchild v Glenhaven, Bonnington Castings Ltd v Wardlaw* (n 53 above). See also *Athey v Leonati* (n 8 above) p 478: Major J nevertheless observed that if the trial judge had found the existence of a realistic chance that injury would have occurred at some point in the future without the accident, a reduction of the damages would have been considered. For a French example: CAA Paris, ch 3, 8 November 2004, No 01PA03602. Stapleton critiques the lack of apportionment in material contribution cases: J Stapleton (2002) (n 50 above) p 284 and ff and 298 and ff.

60 *Griffiths v British Coal Corporation* [1998] EWJ No 4656 (QB, 23 January 1998) 121–24; *Holtby v Brigham & Cowan (Hull) Ltd* [2000] 3 All ER 421 (CA) 428; *Ibrahim v Hum* (n 58 above) para 146. When assessing damages, account can also be taken of the possibility that the loss, or part of the loss,

and in the absence of demonstration of the exact extent of the defendant's contribution, the claimant is still fully compensated. In *Allen & Ors v British Rail Engineering Ltd* (2001), recognising that even with expert evidence it can be difficult or impossible to determine precisely the extent of the contribution, Schiemann LJ stated the court should do its best to make the apportionment but should not deny plaintiff relief because he cannot accurately establish the proportion of his injury attributable to the defendant.[61]

Despite numerous referrals to the material contribution test, few judges and authors have expanded on what amount of contribution is needed to avoid falling within the *de minimis* rule.[62] Such a wide test is capable of including a large range of situations. Some judges and authors have attempted to be more precise about what contribution may comply with the requirement by stating that it must be more than minimal or trivial or insignificant;[63] or by being satisfied with the fact that the defendant was *part of* the cause of the injury.[64] In *Couillard and Labutis v Waschulewski's Estate* (1988), material contribution was assimilated to the but-for test, however.[65] This last interpretation contradicts the fact that material contribution was devised to meet cases in which the but-for test was unworkable. In *Bonnington* itself, it was impossible to say whether or not but for the guilty dust, the plaintiff would have suffered the damage through inhalation of the innocent dust. Moreover, cases applying the material contribution test have not endorsed this position, nor have they imposed the quantification of the contribution to any specific extent.[66]

Doctrinal scholarship has not provided better guidance, arguing that the *de minimis* principle suggests that to qualify as being causative of the damage, the

would in any event have been suffered in the future independently from the defendant's fault: *Smith v Leech Brain* [1962] 2 QB 405, 413 and 416. Reductions in the amount of recoverable damages which reflect absence of certainty of the causal link, or the victim's predisposition to suffering more serious consequences than normal from the harm, are not admissible, however: *Smith v Leech* Brain, above. See also: Hart and Honoré (n 4 above) pp 205–35; J Stapleton, 'Law, Causation and Common Sense' (1988) 8 *OJLS* 111, 128; A Porat, A Stein and SM Cohen, 'Indeterminate Causation of Damages: An Essay on Holtby, Allen, and Fairchild' (2003) 23 *OJLS* 667.

[61] *Allen v British Rail Engineering Ltd* [2001] ICR 942 (CA) para 20. On this case and *Holtby:* Porat, *et al* (n 60 above) p 673 and ff. See also: *Thompson v Smith Shiprepairers Ltd* [1984] 1 QB 405, 443–44 (Mustill J); and, eg: *Brooks v J & P Coates (UK) Ltd* [1984] 1 All ER 702 (QBD); *Nilon v Bezzina* [1988] 2 Qd R 420; and F Trindade and P Cane, *The Law of Torts in Australia,* 3rd edn, (Victoria, OUP, 1999) 478: The total loss in cases where there is no evidence as to the relative contributions of the sources of the injury can be divided between the tortfeasors on any basis not inconsistent with the evidence.

[62] The test is often mentioned but rarely explained however: G Demeyere, 'The "Material Contribution" Test: An Immaterial Contribution to Tort Law: A Comment on *Briglio v Faulkner*' (2000) 34 *University of British Columbia Law Journal* 317, 318.

[63] *Page v Smith* (n 58 above) p 858 (Bingham MR).

[64] *Athey v Leonati* (n 8 above): The defendant's contribution was assessed at 25% by the trial judge, which appears material enough.

[65] (N 58 above) p 172.

[66] Eg: *Bonnington Castings Ltd v Wardlaw* (n 53 above); *Nicholson v Atlas Steel Foundry* (n 57 above).

guilty dust in *Bonnington* had to amount only to something between 10 per cent and 25 per cent;[67] or, after recognising that the concept is imprecise and vague enough to be manipulated, stressing that the contribution must be substantial and significant, an opinion which, once again, is contradicted by the cases.[68]

It may be legitimately questioned whether the extent of the contribution can be measured at all where the evidence contains serious gaps and is not conclusive as to the exact role the defendant played in the production of the damage. The main cases which have applied the material contribution test have done so in circumstances in which it was impossible to quantify the contribution or in which the assessment of the contribution was not attempted.[69] In fact, they show that very little contribution is needed to meet the *material* requirement. Thus the test seems to be overly favourable to the plaintiff, who recovers his full damages even though he cannot prove the defendant's exact contribution, the existence of which may even be inferred in doubtful cases.[70] This results in the incongruous situation that the plaintiff who is able to show the defendant's exact contribution to his damage is treated more severely than the one who cannot do so, as his damages should normally be reduced accordingly.[71]

Klimchuk and Black argue that the normal but-for test of causation can solve cases such as *Bonnington Castings* which involve a contribution between tortious and non-tortious causes,[72] as well as those where two faults combine in order to produce a damage which could not have been caused by only one of them.[73] In their opinion, the but-for test is unworkable only where there is uncertainty as to the effect of the contributing causes[74] and where there are two factors, both tortious, which could each have individually caused the damage. It is true that in many cases in which the material contribution test is applied, the but-for test is not really unworkable. One must not forget, however, that this concept was not only devised to palliate the fact that the but-for test was unworkable in some

[67] W Scott, 'Causation and Material Contribution' (1999) *Health Care Risk Reports* 12, 13.

[68] PH Osborne, *The Law of Torts*, 2nd edn, (Toronto, Irwin Law, 2003) 54. But see: *Derry v Ministry of Defence* (1999) 49 BMLR 62 (CA) 15 (noted to WL): A 'substantial cause' signifies that the causal link must not be *de minimis* (in the context of the application of §10(1) of the Crown Proceedings Act 1947). This comment shows how easily the explanation becomes circular. For a critique of the test, B Pardy, 'Risk, Cause and Toxic Torts: A Theory for a Standard of Proof' (1989) 10 *Advocates' Quarterly* 277, 286: It changes the issue from whether the defendant in fact caused the injury to whether his conduct warrants the imposition of full liability (legal causation question of remoteness).

[69] *Bonnington Castings Ltd v Wardlaw* (n 53 above); *Nicholson v Atlas Steel Foundry* (n 57 above). See also: Jones (n 53 above) p 231.

[70] *McGhee v National Coal Board* (n 8 above).

[71] J Stapleton (2002) (n 50 above) pp 301–2; J Stapleton (2003) (n 17 above) p 400, however commenting on contribution to risk.

[72] D Klimchuk and V Black, 'A Comment on *Athey* v *Leonati:* Causation, Damages and Thin Skulls' (1997) 31 *University of British Columbia Law Review* 163, 167 and ff.

[73] They classify *Athey v Leonati* (n 8 above) in this category.

[74] Such as in *McGhee* which they treat as a cumulative cause case: (n 72 above) p 168.

instances, but also to respond to the fact that the but-for test, while perfectly applicable to the facts of these cases, led to results the courts considered unfair, which they sought to remedy.[75] Thus the question is not necessarily whether or not the but-for test is workable, but rather whether some specific situations deserve, for policy or other types of reasons, an alternative approach.

B. Civil Law

In French and Québec civil law, a plaintiff to a contractual or extra-contractual claim in damages benefits from a general right of action which comes into play each time three prerequisites are met: the defendant has committed a fault, the plaintiff has suffered harm, and there is a sufficient causal relation between the two. In Québec, the relationship between patient and doctor is normally contractual.[76] The contractual framework also applies in France, but only if medical care is given in a private clinic setting.[77] In both jurisdictions, the physician is in principle held only to an *obligation de moyens* (obligation of means).[78] He is not bound to cure his patient, but only to provide him with attentive and conscientious care in conformity with the current state of science.

While the French and Québec civil codes clearly state the causation condition,[79] they are silent on how it should be assessed. No strict divide between factual and legal causation exists,[80] and the only indication given is that the damage must

[75] See also: Osborne (n 68 above) p 54 (referring to L Klar, *Tort Law,* 2nd edn, (Scarborough, Carswell, 1996) 323).

[76] Unless treatment is given without consent, *eg*, in emergency situations, or by medical staff (nurses, anaesthetists, and radiologists) with whom the patient has not contracted. See also: *Hôpital de l'Enfant-Jésus v Camden Bourgault* [2001] RJQ 832 (CA) which, contrary to the current line of authority, found the relationship between hospitals and patients to be extra-contractual.

[77] The liability of doctors exercising in a public hospital setting, as well as that of the public hospitals themselves, is subject to administrative law: Cass civ, 20 May 1936, DP 1936.I.88, S 1937.I.321 (note Breton), Gaz Pal 1936.2.41 (*Mercier*). Administrative liability is autonomous from civil liability in French law: T Confl, 8 February 1873, Lebon.61 (*Blanco*); J Rivero and J Waline, *Droit administratif,* 19th edn, (Paris, Dalloz, 2002) para 279.

[78] France: Cass civ, 20 May 1936 (n 77 above); Cass civ 1st, 29 October 1968, Bull civ 1968.I.n252; H Lalou, *Traité pratique de la responsabilité civile,* 6th edn, (Paris, Dalloz, 1962) para 426; le Tourneau and Cadiet (n 4 above) paras 2025–31; F Chabas, 'Vers un changement de la nature de l'obligation médicale' [1973] *La Semaine Juridique*; J Penneau, *La responsabilité médicale* (Paris, Sirey, 1977) para 14; Québec: Jarjoura and Nootens (n 6 above) para 55 and references cited at fn 24, Baudouin and Deslauriers (n 4 above) para 1451. See generally: PA Crépeau, *L'intensité de l'obligation juridique ou des obligations de diligence, de résultat et de garantie* (Cowansville, Yvon Blais, 1989).

[79] Contractual liability: CN, Arts 1146–51 and CcQ, Art 1458; Extra-contractual liability: CN, Arts 1382–83 and CcQ, Art 1457. The generality of these provisions is in contrast with the specificity of the provisions of other civil codes, such as §823 of the German *Bürgerliches Gesetzbuch,* which enumerates an exhaustive list of protected rights.

[80] Québec courts sometimes distinguish between material or physical causation (*causa sine qua non*) and legal causation concerned with linking the causal factors to a person's faulty behaviour: Tancelin (n 4 above) p 130; Baudouin and Deslauriers (n 4 above) para 580.

have been the certain, direct,[81] and immediate consequence of the fault.[82] It is however generally agreed the inquiry should seek to identify the *necessary* conditions of the damage, ie, those without which the damage would not have occurred.[83] This determination is in many cases straightforward, but it can become a difficult exercise when several factors are susceptible of having caused the damage.[84] The courts have therefore relied on various theories of causation for guidance.

While there is no judicial consensus in France and Québec as to which theory should be favoured,[85] the theory of *causalité adéquate* (adequate causation) is the one that has received the most support and application from the courts.[86] This theory seeks to eliminate the mere circumstances of the damage and isolate its immediate cause(s), namely those event(s) of a nature to have caused the damage in a normal state of affairs (*dans le cours habituel des choses*). This theory necessarily involves objective probabilities and the notions of logic and normality.[87] The alleged negligence does not need to be the sole cause of the damage to be legally effective, however.[88] Courts also tend to rely on the theory of *prévision*

[81] Directness of damage amounts to causation: Baudouin and Deslauriers (n 4 above) para 297; Tancelin (n 4 above) p 111. The same applies in French administrative law: Rivero and Waline (n 77 above) para 284; D Chabanol, *La pratique du contentieux administratif*, 5th edn, (Paris, Litec, 2003) para 664; M Lombard and G Dumont, *Droit administratif* (Paris, Dalloz, 2003) para 927.

[82] CcQ, Art 1607 and CN, Art 1151 (extended by the doctrine from contract law to *responsabilité civile:* Starck, *et al* (n 3 above) para 1063).

[83] Conte, *et al* (n 4 above) p 132; Viney and Jourdain (n 4 above) paras 352–53; le Tourneau and Cadiet (n 4 above) para 877; Jourdain (n 95 above) p 10; Flour and Aubert (n 3 above) para 163.

[84] A Nadeau & R Nadeau, *Traité pratique de la responsabilité délictuelle* (Montréal, Wilson & Lafleur, 1971) 607–8.

[85] Viney and Jourdain (n 4 above) para 341; Nadeau (n 84 above) p 608; Baudouin and Deslauriers (n 1 above) para 580.

[86] France: Conte, *et al* (n 4 above) p 137; le Tourneau and Cadiet (n 4 above) paras 824–25; Viney and Jourdain (n 4 above) paras 340–41; Flour and Aubert (n 3 above) paras 150 and 157; J Carbonnier, *Droit civil 4) Les obligations,* 22nd edn, (Paris, PUF, 2000) 395; Québec: Baudouin and Deslauriers (n 4 above) para 588; Pineau and Ouellette (n 8 above) pp 177–78; Tancelin (n 4 above) pp 123–24, 133–34. French administrative courts also tend to favour the adequate causation theory: Lombard and Dumont (n 81 above) para 927; M Deguergue, 'Causalité et imputabilité' (Fasc 830) in *Jurisclasseur administratif* (Paris, Éditions techniques, 2000) para 4.

[87] J Favier, *La relation de cause à effet dans la responsabilité quasi délictuelle* (Thèse de doctorat, Université de Paris, 1951) n 74 above; Tancelin (n 4 above) p 134. Baudouin and Deslauriers believe that there are two views of the adequate causation theory, one that focuses on the objective possibility of the realisation of the damage, the other on the criterion of the 'usual experience': (n 4 above) para 573. Chabas, however, describes these two views as part of the same reasoning process: F Chabas, *L'influence de la pluralité des causes sur le droit à la réparation* (Paris, LGDJ, 1967) 102–11, 86–90.

[88] Savatier, note under Cass civ 1st, 27 March and 9 May 1973, JCP 1974.G.II.17643. When damage is the consequence of several causes, all its faulty authors are held liable *in solidum* and damages are apportioned between them at a latter stage: le Tourneau and Cadiet (n 4 above) paras 847–48. If damage is the result of a combination of the defendant's fault and a non-faulty cause, the defendant is held liable only for the damage he has caused: Baudouin and Deslauriers (n 4 above) para 627. See generally, on plurality of causes: Mazeaud (n 1 above) pp 523 and 526; Starck, *et al* (n 3 above) paras 1119,

raisonnable des conséquences (reasonable foreseeability), inquiring whether the kind of damage caused could have been reasonably foreseen by the author of the fault.[89] The *équivalence des conditions* (equivalence theory or *causa sine qua non theory*), which retains as causal all the facts without which the damage would not have occurred, plays a minor role as a preliminary screening device.[90] Even though civil law judges rely sporadically on the theories outlined above, their intellectual process is usually not based on any theoretical ground, logical explanation, or search for a scientifically exact solution. It rather is empirical and depends on their sovereign and subjective evaluation, and the application of their common sense (*bon sens*).[91]

Finally it must be noted briefly that the context in which the causal inquiry takes place in civil law is quite different from the one that prevails in common law. Indeed, *responsabilité civile* in civil law does not benefit from the same limitative device that shapes the scope of defendants' liability in common law, namely the requirement of demonstrating a 'duty of care' owed to the plaintiff by the defendant. Moreover, it does not require, as prominently as its common law counterpart,[92] that the type of injury suffered by the plaintiff was reasonably foreseeable to the defendant at the moment the negligent activity was undertaken; it is normally contented with a demonstration that the loss is the *direct* consequence of the fault, although courts do sometimes rely on foreseeability to limit the results obtained by the directness test.[93] The concept of causation in civil law may, in the

1130–32 and 1140; B Starck, 'La pluralité des causes de dommage et la responsabilité civile: La vie brève d'une fausse equation: Causalité partielle = responsabilité partielle' (1970) I *La semaine juridique* 2339, paras 1 and ff; Viney and Jourdain (n 4 above) para 408.

89 Viney and Jourdain (n 4 above) para 347; Esmein (n 11 above) p 207; *Brisson v Potvin* [1948] BR 38; *Canéric Properties Inc v Allstate Co d'assurances* [1995] RRA 296 (QuéCA); Baudouin and Deslauriers (n 4 above) paras 589–90. Recourse to this theory is marginal, however, and foreseeability is usually required only in contractual liability: CcQ, Art 1613 and CN, Art 1150.

90 Previously, the equivalence theory was preferred, however. France: Flour and Aubert (n 3 above) para 163; Viney and Jourdain (n 4 above) para 53 and cases cited at fn 60; Conte, *et al* (n 4 above) p 137; Carbonnier (n 86 above) p 395; le Tourneau and Cadiet (n 4 above) para 821; Québec: *Beausoleil v La Communauté des Soeurs de la Charité de la Providence* [1965] BR 36, 55; *Dame Cimon v Carbotte* [1971] CS 622, 630; *Lachambre v Perreault* [1990] RRA 397 (CA) 396; *Kirschenbaum Green v Syrchin* [1997] RRA 39 (CA); [1993] RRA 821 (CS). See also: D Jutras, 'Expertise médicale et causalité' in *Congrès du Barreau du Québec* (Montréal, Service de la formation permanente du Barreau du Québec, 1992) 897, 898; Bernardot and Kouri (n 3 above) p 80; Giesen (n 3 above) p 178.

91 Starck, *et al* (n 3 above) paras 1066, 1070 and 1074; Flour and Aubert (n 3 above) paras 154 and 165; Demogue cited in Viney and Jourdain (n 4 above) para 335. In administrative law: Deguergue (n 86 above) para 3.

92 In its cause-in-law inquiry: *Overseas Tankship (UK) Ltd v Mort's Dock Engr Co (The Wagon Mound (No 1)* [1961] AC 388 (HL); *Overseas Tankship (UK) Ltd v Miller Steamship Co (The Wagon Mound (No 2)* [1967] 1 AC 617 (HL); and *Hughes v Lord Advocate* [1963] AC 837 (HL).

93 See (n 89 above). Civil law applies predominantly the adequate causation test in its evaluation of directness, however, a test more restrictive than the *causa sine qua non* test.

absence of these two limitative tools, play a more prominent restrictive role in civil law than in common law, which may in turn explain some of the hesitations that Québec courts have in extending the notion.[94]

As in common law, the civil approach to factual causation leaves untouched the problem that arises when the *causa sine qua non* or the adequate causation theories do not allow for the selection of any cause of the damage or lead to results considered unjust by the tribunal.[95] When this is the case, both the adequate causation theory and the *causa sine qua non* test may lead to the rejection of the plaintiff's case.[96] Consequently, civil law has also been confronted with a conflict between the courts' sense of fairness and the result to which its theoretical approaches to causation lead.

Conclusion to Section 1

While the above gives some indication as to how the causal relationship between an event and its alleged consequences is assessed by the courts, it does not discuss the type of evidence necessary to convince a court of common or civil law that a causal relationship exists. More specifically, in the presence of evidential uncertainty, the questions of who has the responsibility for demonstrating the existence of this relationship, and how convincing the demonstration must be to lead to a positive conclusion, acquire great importance. Moreover, uncertainty makes the possibility of using the existing rules of evidence to assist the parties in dealing with evidential uncertainties through indirect evidence of causation become central.

Section 2

Evidence in the Four Jurisdictions

In ordinary language, proof is a way of establishing truth. Truth can never be absolute, however, and civil evidence cannot be about proving in the absolute the existence or non-existence of a fact or a right. It is concerned, rather, with

[94] Such hesitations are less prevalent in France perhaps because of the fact that the higher standard of proof imposed on plaintiffs also serves as a limitative device, at least in theory, see below text between fn 147 and fn 150. This hypothesis may prove to be wrong given the fact that typical medical negligence cases in common law do not raise difficulties in the demonstration of duty of care and reasonable foreseeability of the type of injury.

[95] P Jourdain, 'Droit à la réparation: Lien de causalité' (Fasc 160) in *Jurisclasseurs* (Paris, Éditions techniques, 1993) 5.

[96] Flour and Aubert (n 3 above) para 163.

convincing the trier of facts (judge or jury member) of the veracity of the facts or rights alleged,[97] ie, with making the balance of his belief shift one way rather than the other. The right alleged must generally *appear* to be true or at least be *probable*.[98] If fact-finding were to require certainty, it would become 'stalled in indecision.'[99]

Evidence plays an essential role in the claim of substantial rights: *idem est non esse aut non probari*.[100] In fact, many cases fail not because the plaintiff does not possess the right claimed, but simply because he is not able to prove such possession.[101] This section therefore looks briefly at the civil rules of evidence that apply to the demonstration of causation, in order subsequently to assess the impact on them of scientific uncertainties.

A. Burden and Standard of Proof of Causation in Civil Cases

The traditional burden and standard of proof of causation in Canada and England, as well as in Australia, are that the plaintiff must prove causation on the balance of probabilities. The same burden and standard apply in Québec, where, for historical reasons, the common law approach has permeated the French law of evidence, with the result that Québec's rules of evidence are truly mixed, originating from both common law and civil law.[102] The burden of showing causation also rests on the French plaintiff's shoulders, but the standard of proof is different in theory and merits separate assessment.

1. Burden of Proof

The expressions *burden of proof* and *onus of proof*[103] are generally used to describe the legal obligation imposed on a party to persuade the tribunal of fact, to the

[97] J Ghestin and G Goubeaux, *Traité de droit civil: Introduction générale*, 3rd edn, (Paris, LGDJ, 1990) 609.

[98] J Carbonnier, *Droit civil: Introduction*, 27th edn, (Paris, PUF, 2002) para 174.

[99] A Porat and A Stein, *Tort Liability under Uncertainty* (Oxford, OUP, 2001) 16–17.

[100] Not being proven is the same as not being.

[101] Ghestin and Goubeaux (n 97 above) para 564.

[102] YM Morissette, 'L'influence du droit français sur le droit de la preuve au Québec' in HP Glenn, (ed), *Droit québécois et droit français: communauté, autonomie, concordance* (Cowansville, Yvon Blais, 1993) 424 and ff; JC Royer, *La preuve civile*, 3rd edn, (Cowansville, Yvon Blais, 2003) paras 43, 48 and 56–65; OS Tyndale, 'The Quebec Law of Evidence Compared with that of France' (1934) 12 *Canadian Bar Review* 641, 641; KM Clermont and E Sherwin, 'A Comparative View of Standards of Proof' (2002) 50 *American Journal of Comparative Law* 243, 270. Moreover, the Québec trial system and rules of procedure are based on English practice: Tyndale, above, p 642.

[103] Or legal burden, persuasive burden, probative burden, ultimate burden. In France: *charge de la preuve*.

required standard of proof and on the whole of the evidence, of the truth of every essential fact at issue.[104] In claims for damages, these include causation. The incidence of the burden of proof is a question of substantive law[105] and the general rule is that the elements forming the basis of a claim must be demonstrated by the party who asserts a proposition.[106] In most cases this places the burden onto the plaintiff's shoulders.[107] A party who fails to discharge the burden resting on him to the requisite standard of proof loses on the issue in question. Respect for this rule is crucial: 'It is an ancient rule founded on considerations of good sense, and it should not be departed from without strong reasons.'[108] This firm principle flows from the fear of legal uncertainty that would arise if the rules governing the legal burden of proof allowed the tribunal to allocate it according to its perception

[104] P Murphy, *Murphy on Evidence*, 8th edn, (London, Blackstone, 2003) 76 and 80; MN Howard, R Bagshaw and SL Phipson, *Phipson on Evidence*, 15th edn, (London, Sweet & Maxwell, 2000) 55.

[105] England: S Uglow, *Evidence: Text and Materials* (London, Sweet & Maxwell, 1997) 65; P Murphy, *Evidence and Advocacy*, 5th edn, (London, Blackstone 1998) 6; Australia: JD Heydon, *Cross on Evidence (Australia)*, 7th edn, (Sydney, Butterworths, 2004) 235; J Gans and A Palmer, *Australian Principles of Evidence*, 2nd edn, (Sydney, Cavendish Publishing, 2004) 29; A Ligertwood, *Australian Evidence*, 2nd edn, (Sydney, Butterworths, 1993) para 6.04, stressing that the allocation of the burden is a matter of policy; Canada: J Sopinka, SN Lederman and AW Bryant, *The Law of Evidence in Canada*, 2nd edn, (Toronto, Butterworths, 1999) 57; France: R Legeais, *Les règles de preuve en droit civil* (Paris, LGDJ, 1955) 170; X Lagarde, *Réflexion critique sur le droit de la preuve*, t239 (Paris, LGDJ, 1994) 220–22.

[106] *Actori incumbit probatio:* CcQ, Art 2803, CN, Art 1315 and NCPC, Art 9. See also: Heydon (n 105 above) p 246; Viney and Jourdain (n 46 above) p 362; Flour and Aubert (n 3 above) p 163; Conte *et al* (n 4 above) p 140; Lalou (n 78 above) p 268.

[107] Generally, and with regards to causation, England: *Donoghue v Stevenson* [1932] AC 562 (HL) 622 (Lord MacMillan); *Bonnington Castings Ltd v Wardlafw* (n 53 above) p 625; *Brown v Rolls Royce* [1960] 1 WLR 210 (HL) 213 (Lord Cohen) and 215–16 (Lord Denning); *Henderson v Henry E Jenkins & Sons* [1970] AC 282 (HL) 301; *McGhee v National Coal Board* (n 8 above) p 11; *Hotson v East Berkshire AHA* (n 35 above) p 782; *Brown v Lewisham and North Southwark Health Authority* [1999] Lloyd's Law Rep Med 110 (CA) 116; Rogers (n 4 above) p 218; Australia: Trindade and Cane (n 61 above) 475; Heydon (n 105 above) p 246; Gans and Palmer (n 105 above) p 29; Ligertwood, (n 105 above) para 6.01; Canada: *Snell v Farrell* (n 9 above) p 321; *McGowan v King* (OntCtJ, 25 April 1991) 5; *Jourdain (Litigation Guardian of) v Hogg* (OntCtJ, 3 November 1993) para 45; *Meyers v Stanley* (n 8 above) para 53; *Grass v Women's College Hospital* (n 58 above) para 94; *Strachan (Guardian ad litem of) v Reynolds* (2004) CarswellBC 1564 (BCSC, 9 July 2004) para 562; *Wilson v Byrne* (2004) WL 1201437, Carswell Ont 2314, OJ No 2360 (OntSCtJ, 4 June 2004) para 81; *Fournier v Wiens* (n 58 above) paras 92–93; *McPherson v Bernstein* (2005) WL 1231377, Carswell Ont 2165 (OntSCtJ, 27 May 2005) para 148; *O'Grady v Stokes* (n 58 above) para 119; *Bear v Lambos* (n 8 above) para 44; Sopinka, *et al* (n 105 above) p 154; Fridman (n 20 above) p 341; France: Lagarde (n 105 above) p 208; Legeais (n 105 above) p 170; R Rodière, *La responsabilité délictuelle dans la jurisprudence* (Paris, Librairies Techniques, 1978) 72; Ripert and Boulanger (n 4 above) para 1003; Jourdain (n 95 above) p 14; Carbonnier (n 86 above) p 390; Lalou (n 78 above) p 205; Viney and Jourdain (n 4 above) para 362 and cases cited at fn 103; Québec: H Kélada, *Notions et techniques de preuve civile* (Montréal, Wilson & Lafleur, 1986) 359–60; Baudouin and Deslauriers (n 4 above) para 598. The same applies in French administrative law: Rivero and Waline (n 77 above) para 226; R Chapus, *Droit du contentieux* administrative, 11th edn, (Paris, Montchrestien, 2004) para 988.

[108] Viscount Maugham in *Joseph Constantine Steamship Line Ld v Imperial Smelting Corporation Ltd* [1942] AC 154 (HL) 174.

of fairness or of expediency in a particular case.[109] The need for predictability in the litigation process demands that the burden of proof be allocated according to rules of law and not to *ad hoc* decisions by the trier of fact.[110]

In both the common law and Québec doctrine and case law, a great deal of confusion flows from the fact that the expression *burden of proof* is also used to refer to the notion called in common law *evidential burden,*[111] which forms part of the normal fact-finding process.[112] The evidential burden refers *inter alia* to the fact that a party who bears it is subject to adverse ruling for failing to meet its threshold test.[113] Usually, the party who bears the legal burden of proof of a particular fact also bears the evidential burden.[114] The burden of proof and the evidential burden do not always coexist, however, and the evidential burden in one case may be distributed between the parties depending on the evidence adduced. In theory, when a *prima facie* case[115] is made in relation to a particular issue, the other party does not have the obligation to adduce evidence in rebuttal. If, however, he does not, an adverse conclusion may be reached against him.[116] One might therefore say that he *acquires* the evidentiary burden; even though at law, he has no burden of proof, it is tactically advisable that he present evidence contradicting the opposing party's evidential demonstration.[117] A *prima facie* case does not, however, automatically result in an adverse ruling since the tribunal is not compelled to make a determination unless a rule of law demands it.[118] Moreover, the court must still admit the evidence of the party bearing the legal burden on the other issues; these, taken together, will determine the case once the whole of the evidence has been adduced.[119]

The risk of confusion between the two notions is real and has led judges and commentators to state that the burden of proof of causation may be *shifted* or

[109] Sopinka, *et al* (n 105 above) p 57.

[110] *Ibid*, pp 57–58.

[111] Or burden of adducing evidence, duty of passing the judge, tactical burden, provisional burden.

[112] Heydon (n 105 above) indeed argues that this concept is the product of trial by jury and of the possibility of withdrawing an issue from that body. Thus, it is not a logical necessity of litigation about questions of fact: 265.

[113] Sopinka, *et al* (n 105 above) p 56.

[114] *Ibid*, pp 61 and 63; Ligertwood (n 105 above) para 6.06.

[115] Here, *prima facie* refers to situations where there is enough evidence to entitle the tribunal of fact to find in the plaintiff's favour if this prima facie evidence is left uncontradicted: Murphy (n 104 above) p 77; DW Elliott, *Elliott and Phipson on the Law of Evidence* (London, Sweet & Maxwell, 1987) 60. For the different meanings of prima facie evidence: Heydon (n 105 above) pp 116–17.

[116] *Brown v Rolls Royce* (n 107 above) pp 215–16; Elliott (n 115 above) p 60.

[117] Generally: IH Dennis, *The Law of* Evidence, 2nd edn, (London, Sweet & Maxwell, 2002) 373–74.

[118] Doctrinal and judicial divergences exist as to the meaning and effect of a prima facie case, however: Sopinka, *et al* (n 105 above) pp 64 and 68–70 emphasise that the Supreme Court of Canada has sometimes treated it as leading, in the absence of evidence to the contrary, to a *compelled* fact determination.

[119] *Ibid*, p 67. The trial judge's determination as to the sufficiency of the evidence to discharge the evidential burden, its incidence and the evidentiary effect of its discharge are questions of law: pp 56 and 59.

reversed by the court during a trial.[120] This obscures the fact that the legal burden does not normally shift unless a rule of law says that it does.[121] Consequently, common law commentators[122] and judges[123] have insisted that a clear distinction be made between legal burden and evidential burden.[124] One should therefore avoid speaking of the reversal of the burden, or of its shifting to the defendant, in referring to the general evidential dynamics between the parties,[125] ie, to signify that the tactical balance passes back and forth from the plaintiff to the defendant during the course of a trial, depending on the evidence adduced:[126]

> These references speak of the shifting of the secondary or evidential burden of proof or the burden of adducing evidence. I find it preferable to explain the process without using the term secondary or evidential burden. It is not strictly accurate to speak of the burden shifting to the defendant when what is meant is that the evidence adduced by the plaintiff may result in an inference being drawn adverse to the defendant. Whether an inference is or is not drawn is a matter of weighing the evidence. The defendant runs the risk of an adverse inference in the absence of evidence to the contrary. This is sometimes referred to as imposing on the defendant a provisional or tactical burden. ... In my opinion, this is not a true burden of proof, and use of an additional label to describe what is an ordinary step in the fact-finding process is unwarranted.[127]
>
> *Cummings v City of Vancouver* [1911] 1 WWR 31 (BCCA), *Hollis v Young* (1909) 1 KB 629 and *Dunlop Holdings Ltd's Application* [1979] RPC 523 (CA).

The question of whether the burden of proof has been discharged normally arises after all the evidence has been adduced.[128] If, after hearing and weighing the

[120] Especially in Québec: Beauregard J in *Houde v Côté* [1987] RJQ 723 (CA) 729–30; Chouinard J in *Gburek v Cohen* [1988] RJQ 2424 (CA) 2439–40; Baudouin and Deslauriers (n 4 above) paras 443 and 600; Kélada (n 107 above) pp 151–52. See also: (n 217 below) on the confusion between the effect of factual presumptions and the reversal of the burden of proof.

[121] Eg, as a result of a legal presumption: Uglow (n 105 above) p 65. But see: *Geffen v Goodman Estate* (1991) 81 DLR (4th) 211; [1991] 2 SCR 353, 397 (Sopinka J). Writers and courts are divided on whether presumptions of law affect only the evidential burden or both the evidential and legal burden.

[122] England: Howard, Bagshaw and Phipson (n 104 above) pp 55 and ff and 64; R Emson, *Evidence*, 2nd edn, (London, MacMillan, 2004) 420; Dennis (n 117 above) p 373 and ff; Elliott (n 115 above) pp 53–65; Uglow (n 105 above) pp 64–65; Australia: Heydon (n 105 above) p 235 and ff; Ligertwood (n 105 above) paras 6.02 and ff; Canada: Sopinka, *et al* (n 105 above) pp 53–63.

[123] Lord Denning in *Brown v Rolls Royce* (n 107 above) pp 215–16; Lord Pearson in *Henderson v Henry E Jenkins & Sons* (n 107 above) p 301.

[124] The distinction was in fact made in *Gouin-Perreault v Villeneuve* [1986] RRA 4 (CA) 9–10. For critiques of the terminology: *Jayasena v R* [1970] AC 618 (HL), 624; Sopinka, *et al* (n 105 above) pp 53–54.

[125] Elliott (n 115 above) p 59; Sopinka J in *Snell v Farrell* (n 9 above) pp 329–30.

[126] Lord Denning in *Brown v Rolls* (n 107 above) p 216: It may even remain suspended between them. See also: *Wakelin v London and South Western Rly* (n 53 above) p 45, Heydon (n 105 above) p 265; Hart and Honoré (n 4 above) pp 421–22; Uglow (n 105 above) p 64.

[127] Sopinka J in *Snell v Farrell* (n 9 above) 329–30. See also: Hart and Honoré (n 4 above) pp 421–22; Heydon (n 105 above) p 267.

[128] Sopinka, *et al* (n 105 above) p 57.

evidence, the tribunal reaches a determinate conclusion, the incidence of the onus of proof does not need to be considered.[129] On the other hand, it determines which party succeeds when the available evidence does not permit a decision in favour of one side or the other. Such situation may be found where the judge's indecision flows from the existence of equally probable explanations of the cause of damage, or from uncertainty or debates preventing the identification of the cause of damage.[130] Decisions taken on the incidence of the burden of proof are relatively rare, however. In cases of uncertainty, identification of the weight the evidence must have to convince the trier of facts of a proposition is in fact even more important than identifying who bears the burden of proof.

2. *Standard of Proof*

The expression *standard of proof* describes the degree to which the proof must be established by the party on which the legal burden of proof rests.[131] In England, Australia, Canada and Québec, the rule is that causation must be proven on the balance of probabilities. French law deserves a separate consideration, since it requires in theory that causation be proven with certainty.

(a) In Common Law and the Province of Québec

In England, Australia, Canada and Québec, the elements of civil liability, including causation, need not to be proven with absolute, mathematical, certainty.[132] The law is satisfied with a demonstration, on the balance of probabilities,[133] of the existence of causation based on the whole of the evidence.[134] This signifies that evidence is sufficient if it renders the existence of a fact more probable than its

[129] *Robins v National Trust Co* [1927] AC 515 (PC) 520; [1927] 2 DLR 97, 101 (obiter). See also: Heydon (n 105 above) p 235; France: Lagarde (n 105 above) p 206.

[130] England: *Wakelin v London and South Western Rly* (n 53 above) p 45; *Brown v Rolls Royce* (n 107 above) pp 215–16; *Rhesa Shipping SA v Edmunds* [1985] 1 WLR 948 (HL) 955–56; Howard, Bagshaw and Phipson (n 104 above) p 56; M Stockdale and C McAlhone, *The Elements of* Evidence, 3rd edn, (Newcastle upon Tyne, Northumbria Law Press, 1997) 13; Murphy (n 104 above) p 75; Australia: P Bayne, *Uniform Evidence Law: Text and Essential Cases* (Leichhardt, NSW, Federation Press, 2003) para 4.310; Canada: *Snell v Farrell* (n 9 above) p 325 (Sopinka J); *Hollis v Dow Corning Corp* (1995) 129 DLR (4th) 609; [1995] 4 SCR 634, 699 (Sopinka J, diss on another question); *M(CP) (Guardian ad litem of) v Quinn* (2004) para 149; Québec: *Gburek v Cohen* (n 120 above) p 2445.

[131] Howard, Bagshaw and Phipson (n 104 above) p 55.

[132] Generally: Dennis (n 117 above) p 370 and ch 2, text to fns 44 ff.

[133] Or preponderance of probabilities.

[134] England: *Bonnington Castings Ltd v Wardlaw* (n 53 above) p 620 (Lord Reid); *Fairfield Shipbuilding and Engineering Co Ltd v Hall* [1964] 1 Lloyd's List Law Rep 73 (HL) 80; *McGhee v National Coal Board* (n 8 above) p 11 (Lord Salmon); *Whitehouse v Jordan* [1980] 1 All ER 650 (CA) 659 (aff'd [1981] 1 WLR 246 (HL)); *Hotson v East Berkshire AHA* (n 35 above) p 784 (Lord Mackay), 793 (Lord Ackner); *The CJD Litigation: Group A and C Plaintiffs* (1998) 54 BMLR 100 (QBD) 102; *Newbury v Bath District Health Authority* (1999) 47 BMLR 138 (HCJ QBD) 12; *Macey v Warwickshire Health Authority* (2004) EWHC 1198 (QB, 26 May 2004) para 73; Rogers (n 4 above) p 218; Jones

non-existence.[135] There is no need for the relationship to be *highly probable, very probable* or *substantially probable.*[136] On the other hand, it is not enough to prove that there is a *possible* causal connection between a fault and an injury.[137] Moreover, it is not sufficient for the party who bears the burden of proof merely to present a version of the events that is more probable than that of his opponent, since, even if such a threshold is met, neither of the two versions may meet the required standard.[138]

The balance of probabilities requirement as applied to the proof of causation is usually understood to mean the plaintiff must show that the probability the defendant has caused the damage is higher than 50 per cent.[139] Yet courts do not undertake accurate probabilistic calculations when evaluating whether this requirement is met; rather, they proceed intuitively on the basis of their general impression of the lay and expert evidence. The validity of mathematical approaches to the evaluation of the standard of proof is in fact viewed by some judges with scepticism:

> The concept of 'probability' in the legal sense is certainly different from the mathematical concept; indeed, it is rare to find a situation in which the two usages co-exist

(n 12 above) pp 3–144; J Stapleton, 'The Gist of Negligence, Part II: The Relationship Between "Damage" and "Causation"' (1988) 104 *LQR* 389, 389; A Boon, 'Causation and the Increase of Risk' (1988) 51 *MLR* 508, 508; A Keane, *The Modern Law of Evidence*, 5th edn, (London, Butterworths, 2000) 67, 83 and 88; Canada: *Levesque v Comeau* (1970) 16 DLR (3rd) 425; [1970] SCR 1010, 1012; *McGowan v King* (n 107 above); *Jourdain v Hogg* (n 107 above) para 45; *Athey v Leonati* (n 8 above) p 467; *Briffett v Gander and District Hospital Board* (1996) 137 Nfld & PEIR 271 (CA) 288 and 301; *Trajdos v Bala* (n 43 above) paras 65 and 192; *Bauer v Seager* (2000) 147 Man R (2nd) 1 (ManQB) 31; *Lurtz v Duchesne* (n 58 above) para 345; *Strachan v Reynolds* (n 107 above) para 562; *Fournier v Wiens* (n 58 above) paras 92–93; *McPherson v Bernstein* (n 107 above) para 148; *O'Grady v Stokes* (n 58 above) para 119; *Miller v Budzinski* (2005) BCD Civ J 516; (2004) BCD Civ J Lexis 1530 (BCSC, 24 December 2004) para 466; Fridman (n 20 above) p 322; Linden (n 7 above) p 110; Campion and Dimmer (n 43 above) pp 3–28; JG Fleming, 'Probabilistic Causation in Tort Law' (1989) 68 *Canadian Bar Review* 661, 661; Québec: *Laferrière v Lawson* (1991) 78 DLR (4th) 609; [1991] 1 SCR 541, 609; *Gralewicz v Thirlwell* (2004) WL 1434625, Carswell Que 1711 (QuéSC, 22 June 2004) para 112. The same standard applies in Australia: §140(1) of the Uniform Evidence Acts (referring to the Evidence Act 1995 (Cth) [Available at www.austlii.edu.au/au/legis/cth/consol_act/ea199580 (23 August 2005)] and the mirror legislation of New South Wales, Tasmania and Norfolk Island); Gans and Palmer (n 105 above) p 32; *Rufo v Hosking* (2004) NSWCA 391 (1 November 2004) para 4; Ligertwood (n 105 above) para 2.37; Bayne (n 130 above) para 4.400, referring to *Newis v Lark* (1571) 2 Plowden 403; J Gunson (2001) 58; Trindade and Cane (n 61 above) p 474.

[135] Compare Art 2804 CcQ with Lord Denning's definition in *Miller v Minister of Pensions* [1947] 2 All ER 372 (KB) 374. See also: Murphy (n 104 above) p 108; Markesinis and Deakin (n 17 above) p 189 and Honoré (n 4 above) pp 149–50, citing *Briginshaw v Briginshaw* (1938) 60 CLR 336 (AustHC); Trindade and Cane (n 61 above) p 479.

[136] *The CJD Litigation* (n 134 above) p 103.

[137] *Kovats v Ogilvie* (1970) 17 DLR (3rd) 343 (BCCA) 346.

[138] *Rhesa Shipping SA v Edmunds (The Popi M)* (n 130 above) pp 955–56 (Lord Brandon); Emson (n 122 above) p 454; Uglow (n 105 above) p 87.

[139] Against: Fleming (n 134 above) p 662: Sample testing suggests that the balance of probabilities is generally understood by judge and jury to require a 75% probability.

> although, when they do, the mathematical probability has to be taken into the assessment of probability in the legal sense and given its appropriate weight.[140]

With regard to causation, the balance of probabilities is often termed an *all-or-nothing* rule. This expression reflects the fact that once causation is shown to exist on the balance of probabilities, full compensation is granted. No discount is applied to account for the fact that there is greater or lesser probability that the harm would not have occurred in the absence of any wrong on the defendant's part.[141] Conversely, if the balance of probabilities requirement is not met, the claim fails altogether, even though there is a possibility that the plaintiff's loss was caused by the defendant.[142]

It has been suggested that a higher standard of proof is in practice required in cases involving professional negligence. The argument is that, though professionals are entitled to no rule requiring a higher standard of proof, the burden is in effect greater when one is investigating the complicated and sophisticated actions of a lawyer, doctor, accountant, builder, or motor engineer.[143] This view is confirmed by the courts' recognition of, and their attempts to counteract, the fact that in many cases involving medical uncertainty, the plaintiff's burden of proof of causation is impossible to meet or more burdensome than the theory requires.

The balance of probabilities criterion is satisfied by the common sense examination of the whole of the lay and expert evidence.[144] Its assessment lies within the judge's discretion; some have even gone as far as stressing that the standards of decision in adjudicative decisions evaluating evidence are not enforceable but only lay down guidelines for the exercise of the fact-finder's discretion.[145] In addition, some believe that decisions with regard to the standard of proof and the sufficiency of the evidence required to meet it may be determined by policy concerns. For instance, Sopinka, *et al*, have contended that if the threshold evidential test is either too rigorous or too permissive, the substantive law may be altered to address new policy considerations,[146] a view borne out by this empirical study.

[140] *Re JS (a minor)* [1980] 3 WLR 984 (CA). See also: Gans and Palmer (n 105 above) p 32; Ligertwood (n 105 above) para 1.25.

[141] *Hotson v East Berkshire AHA* (n 35 above) p 793 (Lord Ackner); Rogers (n 4 above) p 218.

[142] *Wilsher v Essex Area Health Authority* (n 58 above).

[143] *Whitehouse v Jordan* (n 134 above) p 659 (Lord Denning); *Dwyer v Rodrick,* The Times, 12 November 1983 (CA); Jones (n 12 above) p 3–144.

[144] *Rhesa Shipping SA v Edmunds (The Popi M)* (n 130 above) p 956 (Lord Brandon) and (n 134 above).

[145] T Anderson and W Twining, *Analysis of Evidence: How to Do Things with Facts* (London, Weidenfeld & Nicolson, 1991) 344–45 and 365.

[146] Sopinka, *et al* (n 105 above) p 137.

(b) In France

In France, the standard of proof of causation is in theory very different, since it requires showing the certainty of the causal relationship between the fault and the damage,[147] thus leaving no place for doubt.[148] The standard is high, demanding the *intime conviction* ('inner, deep-seated, personal conviction'[149]) of the judge.[150] This more demanding standard has an obvious effect on the French judicial responses to causal uncertainty, as evidential uncertainty is easier to accept under the balance of probabilities requirement.[151] The *intime conviction* required of French judges may in fact prompt them to draft substantive rules that directly impact the outcome of litigation, rather than achieve such results through the application of flexible rules of evidence:

> A high civil standard, combined with a burden of proof that requires plaintiffs to prove elements of their claims, quite obviously makes it difficult for plaintiffs to succeed. The same high standard, coupled with rules and presumptions that sometimes shift the burden of proof, permits the law to choose between favoring defendants and favoring plaintiffs.[152]

This apparently strict requirement is not, however, applied in its absolute sense. Doctrinal writings acknowledge that life is not always made of mathematical certainties[153] and the conditions in which the judicial debate is conducted and the need to find a solution increase the difficulties of the search for truth and often reduce the assessment of the evidence to probabilities and likelihood.[154] Acknowledging this reality, French judges are in some cases happy to relax this standard of proof and consider the certainty of causation proven based on the

[147] Viney and Jourdain (n 4 above) para 362 and cases cited at fn 106, Mazeaud (n 1 above) para 1677; Lalou (n 78 above) p 195; Starck, *et al* (n 3 above) p 449; Jourdain (n 95 above) pp 7–8, 10, and 14; Conte, *et al* (n 4 above) p 140; Carbonnier (n 86 above) p 391; le Tourneau (n 4 above) para 828; Azard, note under Grenoble 16 May 1962, D 1963.jur.137; YM Serinet and P Mislawski, note under Cass civ 1st, 23 September 2003, D 2004.898, 899 (case also found at Pet Aff 2004.n12.p14 (note Gossement), Pet Aff 2004.n81.p9 (note Mémeteau), JCP 2003.Entreprise et Affaires.II.1749 (note Faict et Mistretta), JCP 2003.G.II.10179 (note Jonquet, Maillols, Mainguy, Terrier), D 2004.1344 (note Mazeaud)). For an historical explanation of this difference between civil and common law: Clermont and Sherwin (n 102 above) p 258 and ff.

[148] Jourdain (n 95 above) p 14; X Lagarde, 'Finalités et principes du droit de la preuve' [2005] *La semaine juridique* 771, 777. The standard of proof applicable in civil matters bears little difference with that applied in criminal matters: Clermont and Sherwin (n 102 above) p 250.

[149] Clermont and Sherwin (n 102 above) p 246.

[150] A similar standard applies in front of the administrative courts: *ibid*, p 246.

[151] Clermont and Sherwin (n 102 above) p 266.

[152] *Ibid*, p 267.

[153] Flour and Aubert (n 3 above) para 133; XY Li-Kotovtchikhine, 'Le certain en droit civil' (1999) 133 *Petites Affiches* 12, 13; Legeais (n 105 above) p 174.

[154] G Marty and P Raynaud, *Droit civil: Introduction générale à l'étude du droit* t I, 2nd edn, (Paris, Sirey, 1972) para 213; L Neyret, 'Vaccination contre l'hépatite B: fin de débat judiciaire?' [2003] *Dalloz* 2579, 2580; YM Serinet and P Mislawski, note under Cass civ 1st, 23 September 2003 (n 147 above) p 899.

finding of a 'sufficient degree' of probability[155] or the 'objective foreseeability' of the damage.[156] In practice, a very high probability will suffice.[157] The notion of probability therefore occupies a greater place in the French law of evidence than one might first be led to believe. In addition, even if in principle French courts adhere to the all-or-nothing approach, they have shown no scruples in calculating damages in proportion to the probability of their causal relationship with the fault.[158]

3. *The Risk of Error*

Where the burden lies and the severity of the standard of proof reveal a choice as to who should bear the burden of evidential uncertainties and the risk of error in the adjudication process. The burden and standard of proof are therefore primarily concerned with risk allocation.[159] This significant expression indicates that the law must make a choice as to which party bears the risk of absence or insufficiency of the evidence. Admitting the proof of a fact in the absence of certainty necessarily entails that errors will be made and demonstrates that the law is, to some extent, ready to accept this risk.[160] There is, however, clear concern, when choosing the applicable rules, to keep this risk of error to the minimum and allocate it as far as possible equally between the parties.[161]

Given the above, any relaxation of the rules of evidence must be at least partly the result of a policy concern to modify the allocation of the risk of uncertain evidence and judicial error. For instance, it may reflect the law's decision to burden the creator of specific types of risk more heavily or mitigate the inequality between the parties with regard to evidence in certain types of cases. In these exceptional instances, the main concern may no longer be to distribute the risk of uncertainty between the parties, but rather to respond to a policy choice.[162]

[155] Jourdain (n 95 above) p 14; Starck, *et al* (1991) (n 44 above) para 1441; Legeais (n 105 above) p 174. Eg, Angers 1st ch B, 30 March 2005, Juris-Data No 273651. See also: ch 5, text between fn 8 and 16.

[156] Viney and Jourdain (n 4 above) paras 362–69. On the judges' discretion to appreciate the probative weight of the evidence: Ghestin and Goubeaux (n 97 above) para 609.

[157] Clermont and Sherwin (n 102 above) 256, or a *degré suffisamment élevé de vraisemblance:* CAA Marseille 3rd ch, 10 June 2004 (administrative law).

[158] Ch 4 below.

[159] England: Emson (n 122 above) p 419; Uglow (n 105 above) p 65; Dennis (n 117 above) p 370; France: Legeais (n 105 above) p 170; Carbonnier (n 98 above) para 175; Lagarde (n 105 above) p 206; Lagarde (n 148 above) p 776.

[160] Against: Porat and Stein (n 99 above) p 17: Unavailability of certainty is not a justification for the doctrinal allocation of the risk of error.

[161] *Ibid*, pp 37–38.

[162] *Ibid*, p 17: allocation of the risk of error is the result of a moral and political decision.

Without entailing reconsideration of the rules regarding the burden and standard of proof, however, the law of evidence affords a tool for rebalancing the parties' positions *vis-à-vis* proof in cases involving uncertain evidence or the absence of direct evidence of the facts they seek to prove. This tool consists of inferences in common law and factual presumptions in civil law.

B. Inferences in Common Law

1. *Principle*

The law of evidence grants much to plaintiffs who are faced with uncertainties surrounding causation. Circumstantial or indirect evidence allows the plaintiff to bridge gaps in the evidence by attempting to convince the judge to draw a reasonable inference from the facts that are demonstrated.[163] For an inference to be drawn, there must be some evidence in support of it,[164] and no evidence that negatives it.[165] If a positive or negative conclusion can be reached on the basis of the direct evidence available, however, the inquiry should stop there and recourse to inferences or factual presumptions is unwarranted.[166]

Inferences are related to the process of thinking about a piece of evidence and are based on the judge's common sense.[167] This thinking process may or may not

[163] *Parfitt v Lawless* (1872) LR 2 P & D 462, 472 adopted by the Supreme Court of Canada in *Canadian Pacific Railway Company v Murray* [1932] SCR 112; [1932] 2 DLR 806. See also: England: *Husain v Bank of Credit & Commerce Intl SA* (CA, 31 January 2002) para 15; Emson (n 122 above) pp 353 and 458; Anderson and Twinning (n 145 above) p 61; Australia: Heydon (n 105 above) p 16; Canada: *Westco Storage Ltd v Inter-City Gas Utilities Ltd* (1989) 59 Man R (2d) 37 (CA) 51.

[164] *Duffy v St Joseph* (n 58 above) para 14; *Grass v Women's College Hospital* (n 58 above) para 94.

[165] Canada: *Duffy v St Joseph* (n 58 above) para 15, which would more correctly be treated as a case where there was direct evidence of absence of causation; *Smith v Grace* (n 58 above) paras 8 and 67.

[166] England: *Barkway v South Wales Transport Co Ltd* [1950] AC 185 (HL); *Ratcliffe v Plymouth and Torbay Heath Authority* (1998) 42 BMLR 64 (CA) 83; Canada: *Wipfli v Britten* (1984) 13 DLR (4th) 169 (BCCA) 178; *Torrison v Colwill* (1987) 42 CCLT 51 (BCSC), 62–63; *Westco Storage* (n 163 above) p 57; *Oiom v Brassington* (1990) 52 BCLR (2nd) 240 (BCCA) 257; *Lawrence v Smith* (1991) 84 Alta LR 26 (QB) 39; *Grant Estate v Mathers* (1991) 100 NSR (2nd) 363 (SC) 395; *McGowan v King* (n 107 above); *Sigouin (Guardian ad litem of) v Wong* (1991) 10 CCLT (2nd) 236 (BCSC) 275; *Geffen v Goodman Estate* (n 121 above) p 399 (Sopinka J); *Egedebo v Windermere District Hospital Assn* (1993) 78 BCLR (2nd) 63 (CA) 68; *Mumford (Next Friend of) v Health Sciences Centre* (1993) 85 Man R (2nd) 271 (CA); *Davies v Gabel Estate* [1995] 2 WWR 35 (QB); *Stewart v Pettie* (1995) 121 DLR (4th) 222; [1995] 1 SCR 131, 154 (Major J); *Dixon Estate* (n 3 above) p 136; *Suchorab v Urbanski* (1997) 156 Sask R 46 (QB) 56; *Meloche v Hotel Dieu Grace Hospital/Villa Marie* (1999) 179 DLR (4th) 77 (OntCA) 89–90; *Duffy v St Joseph* (n 58 above) para 15; *Smith v Grace* (n 58 above) paras 8 and 67; *O'Grady v Stokes* (n 58 above) para 203; Québec: *St-Jean v Mercier* [2002] 1 SCR 491; (2002) 209 DLR (4th) 513, para 115. See also: *Hollis v Dow Corning* (n 130 above) p 697: Sopinka J applies the same rule to the possibility of reversing the burden of proof.

[167] With regard to medical causation: *McGowan v King* (n 107 above); *Webster v Chapman* (n 58 above) p 93; *Husain v BCCI* (n 163 above) para 15; *Robinson v Sydenham District Hospital Corp* (2000) 130 OAC 109 (OntCA).

result in a belief (and proof),[168] especially considering that inferences may be weak, medium, or strong.[169] Wigmore explains that the inferential process is analagous to pushes given to a wheelchair the thinker is seated in and which is pointed towards a door. No one push suffices to get the chair to the door, and possibly not all three could achieve the goal. Pushes are also given away from the door. The movement of the chair at each single push is like an inference and the final position of the chair is like proof.[170]

A closely related concept, that of presumptions, generally provides that if a party proves a certain fact (the *primary fact*), then another fact (the *presumed fact*) will be taken to be proven unless evidence is adduced by the opponent to rebut, ie, contradict, the presumption.[171] The party who benefits from a presumption is not completely relieved of his burden of proof, since he still has to demonstrate the existence of the facts grounding it.[172]

There exist both legal and factual presumptions.[173] Legal presumptions are defined as rules of substantive law that have certain consequences directly annexed to the proof of a particular fact.[174] Unlike legal presumptions, factual presumptions do not compel the court to draw the inference in question.[175] They are described as deductions of fact that may logically and reasonably be drawn from a fact or a group of facts found or otherwise established;[176] or as 'provisional inferences that we are willing to make unless and until there is further evidence which makes it necessary to reassess.'[177] A key difference between inferences and factual presumptions would appear to have to do with frequency of occurrence:

> Inasmuch as it is the usual function of the trier of fact to draw inferences from other facts, one may well wonder why certain facts or a combination of them should be called a presumption. The most plausible explanation is that there are certain circumstances

[168] JH Wigmore, *The Science of Judicial Proof*, 3rd edn, (Boston, Little Brown, 1937).
[169] *Ibid*, pp 3–8; Keane (n 134 above) p 636.
[170] Wigmore (n 168 above) pp 9–10.
[171] Unless the presumption is irrebuttable in which case no evidence to the contrary is admissible.
[172] Dennis (n 117 above) p 371. There exist, however, presumptions which do not necessitate the proof of any basic facts, *eg*: The presumption of innocence in criminal law. See also: Elliott (n 115 above) p 77; Sopinka, *et al* (n 105 above) p 95.
[173] Sopinka, *et al* (n 105 above) p 105. The classification of the different types of presumptions, as well as whether all presumptions are 'true' presumptions, is the subject of debate. These debates are ignored for the purpose of this study, however.
[174] Heydon (n 105 above) p 276. There are irrebuttable presumptions of law (when a conclusion must be drawn from a given premise and no rebutting is permitted) and rebuttable ones (where the persuasive or evidential burden is on the other party to disprove or rebut—depending on the theory adopted it).
[175] Sopinka, *et al* (n 105 above) p 105; Heydon (n 105 above) p 276.
[176] Sopinka, *et al* (n 105 above) p 97; Bayne (n 130 above) para 4.510.
[177] Uglow (n 105 above) p 690.

> or combinations of facts which recur frequently. It has been found that whenever these circumstances or facts are present, it may safely be inferred that the presumed fact also exists. In order to assist the trier of fact, these recurring circumstances of combination of facts are said to give rise to a presumption of fact.[178]

Thus factual presumptions are 'merely frequently recurring examples of circumstantial evidence.'[179] The assimilation of factual presumptions and circumstantial evidence has encouraged some to argue that they are not presumptions in the technical sense, since they involve only the normal process of discretionary inferential thought[180] without any modification of the allocation of risk or greater weight attributed to it.[181] Nevertheless, the tendency to treat as set doctrines repetitive circumstantial inferences drawn in similar circumstances is worth bearing in mind and will assume importance in this text.

2. *Type of Evidence Required*

The tribunal's power to draw an inference or a factual presumption is discretionary.[182] The facts adduced in support of the presumption may demonstrate that the inference should logically be drawn, but they can never impose this conclusion.[183] How to determine the type of evidence necessary to justify an inference of causation in the absence of positive proof is not an easy question to answer, however. By its fact based nature, this mode of reasoning depends greatly on the individual circumstances of each case. Some cases have nevertheless attempted to provide guidelines. In *Jones v Great Western Railway Co,* Lord Macmillan distinguished inferences from conjectures:

> The dividing line between conjecture and inference is often a very difficult one to draw. A conjecture may be plausible but it is of no legal value, for its essence is that it is a mere guess. An inference in the legal sense, on the other hand, is a deduction from the evidence, and if it is a reasonable deduction it may have the validity of legal proof. The

[178] Sopinka, *et al* (n 105 above) p 98. See also: Emson (n 122 above) pp 457–58; Elliott (n 115 above) p 89; Keane (n 134 above) pp 634 and 636.

[179] Elliott (n 115 above) pp 89–90; Keane (n 134 above) pp 633 and 652 and ff; Howard, Bagshaw and Phipson (n 104 above) pp 69 and 75 and ff; Heydon (n 105 above) p 275. Eg, in England: The presumption that a normal person intends the natural consequences of his acts; the presumption of continuance; the presumption of intention; the doctrine of recent possession; and *res ipsa loquitur*. See also for Australia: Ligertwood (n 105 above) para 6.16: reliance upon extraneous policies to determine the incidence of the burdens of proof distinguishes presumptions from inferences of fact.

[180] Uglow (n 105 above) pp 689–90; Howard, Bagshaw and Phipson (n 104 above) p 69.

[181] Sopinka, *et al* (n 105 above) p 99. See also: The criticism of R Bagshaw, *Cross and Wilkins: Outline on the Law of Evidence*, 7th edn, (London, Butterworths, 1996) 39; and Keane (n 134 above) p 636.

[182] Emson (n 122 above) p 458; Elliott (n 115 above) pp 78 and 89; Stockdale and McAlhone (n 130 above) p 40; Howard, Bagshaw and Phipson (n 104 above) p 69; Sopinka, *et al* (n 105 above) p 97.

[183] Sopinka, *et al*, p 97.

> attribution of an occurrence to a cause is, I take it, always a matter of inference. The cogency of a legal inference of causation may vary in degree between practical certainty and reasonable probability. Where the coincidence of cause and effect is not a matter of actual observation there is necessarily a hiatus in the direct evidence, but this may be legitimately bridged by an inference from the facts observed and proved.[184]

To draw a valid inference, the court's finding must thus be based on something stronger than assumption, conjecture, supposition, hypothesis, or surmise.[185] Inferences may be based on only one fact,[186] but they must be reasonable and supported by the evidence adduced and, if believed, they must render their conclusion more probable than any other.[187] It is not sufficient for the plaintiff to merely argue that the defendant's hypothesis is not probable.[188]

3. The Impact

Inferences can be rebutted. The strength of the inference determines the kind of proof needed for the defendant to rebut it, or whether he needs to rebut it at all.[189] More complicated questions, however, are whether he has to demonstrate the exact cause of the damage or whether raising alternative hypotheses to explain what happened is sufficient. Canadian sources situate the answer somewhere in the middle. Raising a hypothesis or suggesting the existence of other possible causes is not sufficient,[190] but it is not required that the defendant show exactly what happened. It is sufficient that he raise an alternative cause which is at least equally probable and supported by the expert and factual evidence.[191] If the opponent succeeds in rebutting the inference, the normal burden of proof applies.[192] If he does not attempt to rebut it, the court still has the discretion to conclude or not that causation has been proven.

The opportunity granted to the defendant to rebut the inferences does not mean that the burden of proof is placed on his shoulders.[193] The ultimate burden

[184] (1930) 47 TLR 39, 45 noted in *CC Raworth & Sons Ltd v Moncton* [1957] 8 DLR (2nd) 478 (NBSC) 485.

[185] *McLaren v Canadian Pacific Railway* [1938] 4 DLR 620 (SaskCA) 623; *Westco Storage* (n 163 above) p 46 and ff.

[186] Sopinka, *et al* (n 105 above) p 97.

[187] *McLaren v CPR* (n 185 above) pp 623 and 627, *Westco Storage* (n 163 above) p 46 and ff.

[188] *Westco Storage* (n 163 above) p 57.

[189] Sopinka, *et al*, argue that consequently factual presumptions allocate neither the evidential burden nor the legal burden: *ibid*, p 97.

[190] *British Columbia Electric Railway Co v Clarke* [1950] 3 DLR 161 (SCC) 164 (not reported in SCR).

[191] *United Motors Service Inc v Hutson* [1937] 1 DLR 737; [1937] SCR 294, 304.

[192] Murphy (n 104 above) p 79.

[193] Reminded in Canada: *Grass v Women's College Hospital* (n 58 above) para 94, citing *Snell, Lurtz v Duchesne* (n 58 above) para 346. Murphy (n 104 above) p 79. Against: Morgan's theory commented on at Murphy (n 104 above) p 79.

remains with the plaintiff, but the inference simply casts a *tactical* or *evidential* burden upon the other party to adduce evidence to the contrary.[194] Drawing an inference may, however, lead in practice to the same results as reversing the burden of proof. This is especially the case if the defendant has no evidence to offer to displace the inference, or when all other possible causes have been considered and eliminated by the court.[195]

It is not only in the common law of evidence that an unknown fact about which the direct evidence is silent may be proven indirectly. Civil law similarly allows indirect evidence through reliance on factual presumptions.

C. Factual Presumptions in Civil Law

1. *Principle*

In Québec and French civil law, the standard of proof of causation can also be met by the presentation of indirect evidence of causation,[196] more specifically through presumptions. Presumptions allow the indirect demonstration of unknown contentious facts with the assistance of inferences drawn from facts that are in evidence before the court.[197] These presumptions result either from statute (legal presumptions)[198] or from the judge's discretionary powers (factual presumptions).[199] French commentators however suggest that legal presumptions can be established by a *jurisprudence constante* (unbroken line of authority), allowing the courts to impose a presumption even in the absence of a text, if this responds to a necessity for equity.[200]

In instances in which testimony is admissible,[201] courts are allowed to deduce from proven facts (also called *indices,* clues) the existence of unknown ones.[202] The assessment of factual presumptions is carried out on a case-by-case basis and depends on a close examination of the facts in evidence.

[194] Sopinka J in *Snell v Farrell* (n 9 above) pp 329–30 (full citation above) at text to n 127). See also: Emson (n 122 above) p 458; Murphy (n 104 above) p 78; Keane (n 134 above) p 636. Against: Howard, Bagshaw and Phipson (n 104 above) p 69.

[195] Eg: *BC Electric R Co v Clarke* (n 190 above) p 164; *Henderson v Henry E Jenkins & Sons* (n 107 above) p 302.

[196] CcQ, Arts 2846 and 2849.

[197] CN, Art 1349 and CcQ, Art 2846 and Kélada (n 107 above) p 292.

[198] CN, Arts 1350 and 1352, CcQ, Art 2847.

[199] CN, Art 1353 and CcQ, Art 2849. Factual presumptions also exist in French administrative law, but administrative courts are not bound by the 'serious, precise and concordant' condition: JM Auby, note under CE, 3rd and 5th sub-s, 22 December 1976, JCP.1978.G.II.18792.

[200] Discussed more fully at ch 5, text between fn 324 and 349.

[201] CN, Art 1353; Royer (n 102 above) para 841.

[202] CN, Arts 1349 and 1353 and CcQ, Art 2849; B Starck, H Roland and L Boyer, *Introduction au droit*, 5th edn, (Paris, Litec, 2000) paras 1635–36.

2. The Serious, Precise, and Concordant Requirement

The drawing of factual presumptions is left to the court's discretion.[203] The French and Québec civil codes provide some guidance, however, by indicating that only serious, precise, and concordant presumptions can be taken into consideration.[204] In Québec, Larombière's 1857 definition of these three requirements is sometimes referred to by the courts when evaluating this condition:

> *Les présomptions sont graves, lorsque les rapports du fait connu au fait inconnu sont tels que l'existence de l'un établit, par une induction puissante, l'existence de l'autre. ...*
>
> *Les présomptions sont précises, lorsque les inductions qui résultent du fait inconnu tendent à établir directement et particulièrement le fait inconnu et contesté. S'il était également possible d'en tirer les conséquences différentes et mêmes contraires, d'en inférer l'existence de faits divers et contradictoires, les présomptions n'auraient aucun caractère de précision et ne feraient naître que le doute et l'incertitude.*
>
> *Elles sont enfin concordantes, lorsque, ayant toutes une origine commune ou différente, elles tendent par leur ensemble et leur accord, à établir le fait qu'il s'agit de prouver.... Si, au contraire, elles se contredisent et se neutralisent, elles ne sont plus concordantes, et le doute seul peut entrer dans l'esprit du magistrat.*[205]

This signifies that the judge should exclude clues which are vague and arbitrary conjectures, pure hypotheses, speculation, or vague suspicions, as well as clues that contradict, counterbalance, or neutralise each other. Some civil law judges have recognised that presumptions may vary in degree of probative weight between 'practical certainty' and 'reasonable probability' or, as Planiol puts it, may render '*la chose probable à un degré plus ou moins fort.*'[206]

Even though the serious, precise, and concordant criterion appears to imply that a plurality of clues is necessary, the judge may rely on a single element if it is sufficient to establish the unknown element.[207] Moreover, factual presumptions

[203] Starck, *et al* (n 202 above) para 1638; Kélada (n 107 above) p 305.

[204] CC, Art 1353 and CcQ, Art 2949.

[205] L Larombière, *Traité pratique des obligations*, t 5 (Paris, Durand, 1857) 381 approved in, eg: *Longpré v Thériault* [1979] CA 258; and *Lavergne v Aubry* [1984] RL 336 (CP). See also: Kélada (n 107 above) p 305; Royer (n 102 above) para 842; *Montreal Tramways Co v Léveillé* [1933] SCR 456, 466, 474 and Lamont J's circular definition at 469: 'presumptions in which the connection between the facts established in evidence and the facts to be proved is such that the existence of the known facts establishes by inference or deduction the fact in dispute.'

[206] *Montreal Tramways v Léveillé* (n 205 above) p 474 (Lamont J).

[207] Ghestin and Goubeaux (n 97 above) para 651; Marty and Raynaud (n 154 above) para 244*bis*; Larombière (n 205 above) p 383; Starck, *et al* (n 202 above) para 1638. This is admitted by the Cour de cassation: Cass civ 3rd, 28 November 1972, Bull civ 1972.III.n636; Cass civ 3rd, 12 April 1972, Bull civ 1972.III.n218, 156; Cass civ 1st, 5 February 1991, D 1991.456 (note Massip); G Bourgeois, P Julien and M Zavaro, *La pratique de l'expertise judiciaire* (Paris, Litec, 1999) 89. The ancient rule, probably originating from the Roman law rule *testis unus, testis nullus*, according to which one clue was not sufficient to draw a presumption, is now abandoned: R Decottignies, *Les présomptions en droit privé* (Paris, LGDJ, 1950) para 113.

can rest on proof by exclusion based on the fact that no other cause than the one alleged can explain the damage. Such evidence is fragile, however, and some contend it is valid only if the exclusion is total.[208]

The question of whether serious, precise, and concordant presumptions exist and that of their probative weight lie within the judge's discretion.[209] Québec doctrine has expressed the view that the judge's discretion is not absolute and is limited by these requirements, however.[210] By contrast, French commentators and cases have argued the serious, precise, and concordant criterion does not restrict the judge's discretion[211] and that these words are meant only to urge the judge to exercise caution in drawing presumptions.[212]

3. *The Effects of Factual Presumptions*

Once the basic facts—or *indices*—are established and the court is prepared to presume the unknown fact,[213] it is up to the other party to rebut the presumed elements of evidence with a contrary proof.[214] In Québec, the rebuttal of a presumption of causation succeeds if it is shown that the occurrence of the harm is as consistent with lack of fault as with the existence of fault.[215] In France, evidence closer to certainty is required.[216] Again, the possibility of rebutting a factual presumption does not mean that it effects a reversal of the burden of proof, even though judges and commentators often state that it does.[217]

[208] P le Tourneau and Cadiet (n 4 above) para 818; Lalou (n 43 above) p 205; Baudouin and Deslauriers (n 4 above) para 605. Against: the HIV-HCV case law, ch 5, text between fn 206 and 275.

[209] Decottignies (n 207 above) para 106; and G Aron, *Théorie générale des présomptions légales en droit privé* (Paris, Pedone, 1895) 14. But see: R Barraine, *Théorie générale des présomptions en droit privé* (Paris, LGDJ, 1942) para 349: Judges are demanding before they admit a factual presumption. The case law studied in ch 5 tends to confirm this view.

[210] Royer (n 102 above) para 842; Nadeau (n 84 above) para 843. See also. *Therrien v Launay* (2005) WL 434762, Carswell Que 486 (SC, 4 March 2005) para 548.

[211] Decottignies (n 207 above) para 113; Barraine (n 209 above) paras 229 and 349; Ghestin and Goubeaux (n 97 above) para 651; Marty and Raynaud (n 154 above) para 244; Larombière (n 205 above) p 382.

[212] Aron (n 209 above) p 14; Barraine (n 209 above) para 232 referring to Planiol and Ripert and Josserand.

[213] But Bernardot and Kouri (n 3 above) pp 67–68: Once a presumption of fault or causation is drawn, fault or causation is *proven*, not presumed.

[214] Marty and Raynaud (n 154 above) para 215.

[215] Jutras (n 90 above) p 906, fn 24, approved in *St-Jean v Mercier* (n 166 above) para 112. See also : *Montreal Tramways Co v Léveillé* (n 205 above) p 466 (Lamont J); Royer (n 102 above) para 852; L Ducharme, *Précis de la preuve*, 5th edn, (Montréal, Wilson & Lafleur, 1996) para 601.

[216] Ghestin and Goubeaux (n 97 above) para 649; Legeais (n 105 above) p 175: *probabilité suffisamment grande*; T Faict et P Mistretta, note under Cass civ 1st, 23 September 2003 (n 147 above) para 9.

[217] Eg: *Parent v Lapointe* [1952] 3 DLR 18; [1952]1 SCR 376, 381 (implicitly); *Gburek v Cohen* (n 120 above) pp 2429 and 2439–40; *Stéfanik v Hôpital Hôtel-Dieu de Lévis* [1997] RJQ 1332 (CS) 1354; *Prat v Poulin* [1997] RJQ 2669 (CA) 2693; *Mainville v Cité de la Santé de Laval* [1998] RJQ 2083 (CS) 2099; Baudouin and Deslauriers (n 4 above) paras 600 and 603; A Bernardot, 'Le médecin et les présomptions de fait' (1971) 2 *Revue de droit de l'Université de Sherbrooke* 75, 84; Mazeaud (n 1 above) p 811.

Conclusion to Section 2

Theoretically, all the rules above seem to form a perfect set of principles affording some leeway for the parties and judges in cases where the evidence does not afford direct proof of causation. The examination of medical cases involving such uncertainty reveals that matters are not so simple. The situations of uncertainty analysed in this text feature evidence that is scarce, controversial, or non-existent, to the point that even the approaches to causation and the rules of evidence presented above do not appear adequate for dealing with them in a fair manner. Thus while most cases may be addressed on the basis of the existing rules of evidence, some are more difficult and have necessitated readdressing these rules. The next section gives a brief overview of the types of scientific uncertainties that have prompted the re-evaluation of the approach to causation which is the subject of the next chapters.

Section 3

The Impact of Scientific Uncertainties on the Proof of Causation

Ce que nous appelons le hasard n'est et ne peut être que la cause ignorée d'un effet connu
Voltaire

Developments in medical knowledge have given great assistance in establishing causal relationships that could not be assessed in the past, but they also 'reveal increasingly complex interactions which would heighten the problems of proving causation in the individual case.'[218] The absence of scientific evidence with respect to the cause of the damage, or its controversial nature, is certainly one of the most acute problems courts and parties must face when dealing with medical malpractice claims. The difficulties faced by patients attempting to prove factual causation

See also: *Leroux v Hôtel-Dieu d'Arthabaska* [1990] RRA 378 (CQ-PC) 380. On this question: Royer (n 102 above) para 847; *Gouin-Perreault v Villeneuve* (n 120 above) pp 9–10 (Owen J) (with regard to factual presumptions of fault); *St-Jean v Mercier* (n 166 above) para 111.

[218] Great Britain Report: *Royal Commission on Civil Liability and Compensation for Personal Injury (The Pearson Report)* (London, Cmnd 7054, Her Majesty's Stationery Office, 1978) para 1364 citing the Medical Research Council.

have often been stressed in the doctrine and cases of the four jurisdictions under study.[219] These hurdles also affect the decision-maker who must reach a conclusion despite causal uncertainty.

Scientific uncertainty must be distinguished from factual uncertainty, which is excluded from our field of study. True, this distinction may be legitimately contested as artificial, since scientific uncertainty necessarily involves elements of factual uncertainty.[220] For the purpose of this study, scientific uncertainty is nevertheless distinguished from uncertainty that is *purely* factual, ie, that does not involve any scientific elements.[221] Acknowledging the limitations of this dichotomy leads us to limit its purpose, however. First, it sets boundaries to the field of our study. Second, it emphasises the fact that cases of scientific uncertainty involve a special kind of uncertainty, to address which the tribunal of fact needs knowledge going beyond common general knowledge. In such instances, an additional problem flows from the tribunal's difficulty in relying on its common sense to reach a decision that is truly legal *and* rests on scientific findings. It is arguable that cases involving scientific uncertainty call more compellingly for a special approach to causation, since the facts known to the tribunal are much more difficult to assess than those involved in pure factual inquiries, for which common sense applied to the lay evidence may often be sufficient to resolve gaps in evidence.

Scientific uncertainty must also be distinguished from scientific *controversy.* In medical liability cases, courts are unavoidably faced with conflicting experts' opinions, which normally rest on an important body of lay and scientific evidence. Cases where the scientific evidence regarding causation is controversial, with the experts defending different schools of thought, are not true cases of uncertainty. In such situations, the difficulty facing the court flows not from the

[219] England: *Gregg v Scott,* para 23; Grubb and Laing (n 14 above) para 7.02; Jones (n 12 above) pp 5–2 and 5–15; Canada: *Rothwell* v *Raes* (1988) 54 DLR (4th) 193 (OntHCJ) 219; (1990) 76 DLR (4th) 280 (OntCA); *Snell v Farrell* (n 9 above) p 322; *McGowan v King* (n 107 above) p 527; *Briffett v Gander and District Hospital Board* (n 134 above) p 301; *Hock v Hospital for Sick Children* (n 31 above) p 345; *Meyers v Stanley* (n 8 above) para 54; Picard and Robertson (n 17 above) p 220; McInnes (n 8 above) p 446; France: Boyer-Chammard and Monzein (n 3 above) pp 110–11; Québec: *Dodds v Schierz* (n 6 above) p 2627 (Monet J); PA Crépeau, 'La responsabilité civile du médecin' (1977) 8 *Revue de droit de l'Université de Sherbrooke* 25, 38; P Deslauriers and SE Chebin, 'Perspectives québécoises sur la responsabilité médicale' (1999) 101 *Revue du notariat* 299, 306; AT Mécs, 'Medical Liability and the Burden of Proof' (1970) 16 *McGill Law Journal* 163, 165; Jutras (n 90 above) pp 897 and 899; Giesen (n 3 above) p 694. But see: *Ratcliffe v Plymouth and Torbay HA* (n 166 above) p 85.

[220] Eg: *Bystedt v Hay* (n 58 above) the causal issue was whether lack of appropriate medical care when the infant plaintiff was diagnosed with herpes simplex virus type II caused or materially contributed to her condition as a spastic quadriplegic. Underlying this question was a factual uncertainty as to the exact moment when the infant was infected with the virus, *intrapartum* (during labour and delivery) or *in utero.*

[221] Eg: *Fitzgerald v Lane* [1987] 1 QB 781, 810–11 (aff'd: [1989] 1 AC 328 (HL)).

absence or the uncertainty of the scientific evidence, but from the fact that the assessment of that evidence is rendered more complex because of its controversial nature. It is the task of the court to resolve the controversy in one way or another.[222] Whether these cases involve causal uncertainty is questionable, as the hurdle is not different from the typical evidential inquiries in front of the courts.[223] We have therefore excluded from our study cases in which the *prima facie* uncertainty was resolved through a careful assessment of the evidence, which usually leads the court to prefer one set of expertise over another, not necessarily based on the content of the expertise itself, but rather on the quality of the expertise and the expert's testimony. This, of course, is the main approach to analysing medical causation; courts must first do their best to resolve the apparent uncertainty on the basis of the evidence available.

This section examines the different kinds of scientific uncertainties encountered in the area of medical liability litigation. Even though the process of classification undertaken here serves no normative function, it may provide a better understanding and afford greater mastery of the problems for which solutions are sought in cases of scientific uncertainty.

A. Scientific Uncertainties affecting Causation

In the judicial context, scientific uncertainty may arise at different levels of the causal inquiry. It may flow either from objective limitations in scientific medical knowledge about a particular biological process (abstract, or general, causation) or from the difficulty of providing a scientific explanation for the sequence in a concrete case (personal causation).[224] Whether the uncertainty affects abstract or personal causation, it results in the experts' inability to provide an answer to the causal inquiry or in scientific dispute amongst them. In both situations, if the uncertainty is not resolved, this inevitably prevents the plaintiff from discharging his burden of proving causation.

[222] On the distinction between uncertainty and controversy: *Gregg v Scott*, para 44 (Lord Nicholls, diss).

[223] As courts, especially in Canada, have insisted: Ch 5, text to fn 19.

[224] Eg, England: *Gardiner v Motherwell Machinery and Scrap Co Ltd* [1961] 1 WLR 1424 (HL) (the House of Lords addresses only the abstract possibility of causation without verifying whether it was consistent with the plaintiff's particular situation); *Stokes v Guest Keen and Nettlefold (Bolts and Nuts) Ltd* [1968] 1 WLR 1776 (BAss); *Loveday v Renton* [1990] 1 Med LR 117 (QBD); *Reay v British Nuclear Fuels Plc* [1994] 5 Med LR 1; *Gates v McKenna* (1998) 48 BMLR 9 (QBD); Grubb and Laing (n 14 above) para 7.02 and Jones (n 12 above) pp 5–16; Australia: *Seltsam Pty Ltd v McGuiness* (2000) 49 NSWLR 262 (NSWSC) 271; Canada: *Rothwell v Raes* (n 219 above) pp 201 (HC) and 282 (CA); France: Cass civ 1st, 5 April 2005, Pet Aff 2005.n122.p9 (note Henin), Pet Aff 2005.n137.p16 (note Rebeyrol) where causation is addressed under these two steps and found proven.

1. Abstract Causation

Uncertainty may first affect *abstract causation*. This assesses whether causation between the plaintiff's injury and its alleged cause is scientifically demonstrated from an abstract and objective point of view in the population as a whole. In this category may be found, for instance, all cases in which the uncertainty or controversy flows from limitations in the medical knowledge about the origin or mechanism of development of medical conditions (*aetiology*). This level of inquiry normally involves minimal reference to the facts of the case, save to the extent that one must first identify the agent and type of injury concerned.

Cases involving uncertainty at the abstract level are often voluminous and give rise to impressive reviews of medical, statistical, epidemiological and genetic evidence.[225] In several, the plaintiff fails in the difficult task of overcoming uncertainty at the abstract scientific causation level.[226] For instance, in *Rothwell v Raes* (1988), there was evidence that upon rare occasions, severe and permanent brain damage resulted from the administration of DPTP vaccine (against diphtheria, pertussis (whooping cough), tetanus, and poliomyelitis). The court nevertheless found it was unlikely that DPTP vaccine caused or contributed to irreversible brain damage in young infants.[227] A central consideration was that encephalopathy is likely to occur, in any event, during the first 6 months of life, the usual period of administration of the vaccine.[228]

Although some cases, such as *Rothwell v Raes,* insist that the abstract possibility of scientific causation be assessed on the balance of probabilities,[229] we suggest

[225] Extreme examples include *Rothwell v Raes* (n 219 above); *Loveday v Renton* (n 224 above); *Berthiaume v Val Royal Lasalle Ltée* [1992] RJQ 76 (CS); *Reay v British Nuclear Fuels Plc* (n 224 above); *Seltsam Pty Ltd v McGuiness* (n 224 above).

[226] Eg, England: *Kay's Tutor v Ayrshire and Arran Health Board* [1987] 2 All ER 417 (HL) 420: No evidence that an overdose of penicillin can cause deafness; *Loveday v Renton* (n 224 above): No link between brain damage in young children and pertussis vaccine; *Vadera v Shaw* (1999) 45 BMLR 162 (CA): Link between stroke and contraceptive pill not proven on the balance of probabilities, despite expert evidence of an increased risk; *Lee v Clark,* first instance decision reviewed and aff'd at (CA, 24 April 1998): No scientific demonstration that the type of head injury suffered by plaintiff can cause schizophrenia; *Reay v British Nuclear Fuels Plc* (n 224 above): No link between irradiations of men in the course of their work and leukaemia suffered by their children; *Gates v McKenna* (n 224 above) p 22: No neurophysiologic link between hypnosis and schizophrenia; Canada: *Rothwell v Raes* (n 219 above): Pertussis vaccine not scientifically shown to cause serious neurological damage; France: Cass civ 1st, 23 September 2003 (n 147 above): No scientific proof of a link between hepatitis B vaccine and multiple sclerosis. See also: F Maury, 'Victimes du VHB (vaccin contre l'hépatite B): Faut-il attendre une certitude scientifique pour les indemniser?' (2004) *Médecine et droit* 125, 126.

[227] (N 219 above) pp 247 and 251 (HC), aff'd 334–35 (CA). Compare with Versailles, 2 May 2001, D 2001.IR.1592.

[228] In obiter, the Court added that, had it found post-pertussis encephalopathy theoretically possible, the infant plaintiff would have nevertheless failed at the personal level, as his case fell into the relatively large number of neurological damage cases that are idiopathic in origin: (CA) (n 219 above) 335.

[229] See also: *Berthiaume v Val Royal Lasalle Ltée* (n 225 above). But see: *Kay v Ayrshire* (n 226 above) (only required the demonstration of an increase of risk at the abstract level); *Loveday v Renton* (n 224 above) (Stuart-Smith LJ); *Lee v Clark* (first instance) (n 226 above).

the abstract causation inquiry should be strictly limited to assessing a *possible* causal *association* between the damage and its alleged cause.[230] Statistics and epidemiological surveys can in fact be misleading and may not be meaningful[231] in light of the particularities of individual cases[232] taken into account at the personal causation stage.[233] Any uncertainty existing in relation to abstract causation may, however, thereafter be taken into account in assessing the probability of causation or attributable risk in respect of the individual.[234] This requirement would not only render the assessment of abstract causation a less burdensome enterprise for the court, but would also limit the importance assigned to objective medical statistics and allow for fuller concentration on the plaintiff's particular situation.

The fact that the requirement in the first step is met does not guarantee that personal causation will be assumed, although it constitutes a prerequisite to such finding.[235] It may in fact be impossible to show that causation was present in the individual situation.

2. *Personal Causation*

The second step is referred to as *personal causation* and requires that the court confront the abstract possibility of causation against the possibility that the damage was caused by other factors in the individual case under study. While a causal relationship may exist between an agent and a particular condition in a certain percentage of cases, it may in fact be impossible to say whether it caused the condition in the case at hand.[236] This evidential problem may emerge from difficulties in accurately reconstructing the sequence of past events because there exist a

[230] See also: Spigelman CJ in *Seltsam Pty Ltd v McGuiness* (n 224 above) para 79, citing *Fernandez v Tubemakers of Australia Ltd* (1975) 2 NSWLR 190, 197 (industrial disease). In France, Gossement has pleaded in favour of using factual presumptions to overcome uncertainty at this level: note under Cass civ 1st, 23 September 2003 (n 147 above). See also: Versailles 3rd, 12 September 2003: Resp civ et ass 2004.n11.comm.344 (note Radé).

[231] *Rothwell v Raes* (n 219 above) p 226.

[232] *BC Electric R Co v Clarke* (n 190 above); *Laferrière v Lawson* (n 134 above) pp 606 and 609; *Suchorab v Urbanski* (n 166 above); Versailles, 2 May 2001, D 2001.IR.1592. See also: MJ Powers and NH Harris, *Clinical Negligence*, 3rd edn, (London, Butterworths, 2000) 915.

[233] Eg: *Vadera v Shaw* (1998), up-held in appeal: (1999) (n 226 above): Causation between the taking of an oral contraceptive and the stroke suffered by the plaintiff was not established (in obiter) based on objective scientific knowledge, namely epidemiological studies. Goldberg argues that Alliott J failed to particularise the evidence to the individual patient by not taking into account factors that made the causal relationship more probable in her case, ie, that she 22 years old, Asian, had no history of health problems and suffered the stroke six weeks after the administration of the contraceptive pill: R Goldberg, 'The Contraceptive Pill, Negligence and Causation: Views on *Vadera v Shaw*' (2000) 8 *Medical Law Review* 316, 331.

[234] Suggested in *Reay v British Nuclear Fuels Plc* (n 224 above) p 24. See also: *Seltsam Pty Ltd v McGuiness* (n 224 above) paras 79 and 89.

[235] G Demeyere (n 62 above).

[236] Cane (n 23 above) p 93.

multiplicity of possible explanations of the patient's damage and, in the particular instance, facts with which to identify its exact cause are lacking.[237] This may lead the experts to conclude that there is no explanation for the plaintiff's situation because it does not fit with any known medical pattern.[238] More frequently, the experts may be able to identify possible causes of the damage but incapable of choosing between them, or their choices may be disputed by colleagues.

It is noteworthy that these uncertainties or disputes do not always flow from lack of medical knowledge. Often the information exists, but it is not available to the parties or the decision-maker for some reason. The unavailability of the information may be owing to the fact that medical acts take place before a limited number of witnesses, with a patient under either medication or anaesthesia;[239] the complexity and technicality of medicine make it difficult for the patient, as well as for the courts, to fully understand the issues at stake;[240] or the parties and tribunal of fact may have to handle incomplete or silent medical records, as well as lack of clarity in the lawyers' questions and witnesses' answers.[241] Moreover, the solidarity existing between medical professionals may, even with honest expert witnesses, complicate the search for truth and introduce special problems for the plaintiff attempting to find an expert willing to give testimony in his favour.[242] The result of these factors is that one of the parties, the physician, is often in a better position to know the injury's cause.[243] Many cases examined in the following chapters have evolved against the background of these factors, which, while not always tangible, are nevertheless real.

Cases involving several possible causes amongst which a choice cannot be made are particularly difficult. Some diseases are the result of a complex combination of factors which interact in an unknown way, and one may not always be able to

[237] Eg: *Bryce v Swan Hunter Group Plc* [1988] 1 All ER 659 (QB); *Berthiaume v Val Royal Lasalle Ltée* (n 225 above); *Fairchild v Glenhaven* (n 50 above).

[238] Eg: *Kirschenbaum-Green v Syrchin* (n 90 above) pp 827 (CS) and 423 (CA); *Ratcliffe v Plymouth and Torbay Health Authority* (n 166 above) p 72.

[239] *Ratcliffe v Plymouth and Torbay HA* (n 166 above) p 83; R Savatier, 'La responsabilité médicale en France (Aspects de droit privé)' (1976) *Revue internationale de droit comparé* 493, 499.

[240] D Jacotot, 'Vers la généralisation de l'obligation de sécurité dans le domaine de la responsabilité médicale' (1997) *Petites Affiches* 25, 28; Savatier (n 239 above) p 499.

[241] *Gburek v Cohen* (n 120 above) p 2442 (Beauregard J); *Gray v Southampton and South West Hampshire Health Authority* (2000) 57 BMLR 148 (QBD) 149 (Toulson J).

[242] These hurdles are aggravated by many patients' lack of financial means to retain an expert witness: M Brazier, *Medicine, Patients and the Law*, 3rd edn, (Harmondsworth, Penguin, 2003) 188.

[243] England: *Ratcliffe v Plymouth and Torbay HA* (n 166 above) p 83; Canada: *Snell v Farrell* (n 9 above) p 322; *Briffett v Gander and District Hospital Board* (n 134 above) p 301; *Hock v Hospital for Sick Children* (n 31 above) p 345. In addition, delays and particularities in the judicial process may also limit the evidence available to both parties and the court, eg: *Sindell v Abbott Laboratories* 26 Cal 3d 588; 2 ALR 4th 1061; 163 Cal Rptr 132; 607 P 2d 924 (Cal, 1980); *Bull v Devon Area Health Authority* (1989) 22 BMLR 79 (CA) 91–92 and 116; *Reay v British Nuclear Fuels Plc* (n 224 above); *Gray v Southampton* (n 241 above) p 149.

point to an individual particular causal factor. Moreover, when the possible causes include the defendant's negligence alongside other, non-faulty, factors it may indeed be impossible to assess whether the defendant participated in the creation of the injury and, if he did, to what extent. This typical problem is illustrated by the Canadian case of *Snell v Farrell* (1990).

> Nine months after an operation to remove a cataract, it was discovered that the plaintiff had lost her eyesight as a result of optic nerve atrophy. The experts could not, however, agree on the cause of the damage: it could have flowed from the doctor's negligence in continuing with the surgery despite the presence of a retrobulbar bleed which could be indicative of a haemorrhage; or it could have been the result of a stroke in the eye, likely to occur in a patient suffering, as the plaintiff did, from high blood pressure or diabetes. Moreover, the plaintiff was also suffering from severe glaucoma, which can, over a long period, also produce optic nerve atrophy.[244]

A particular species of uncertainty at the personal level, which brings about acute difficulties, consists of cases in which *inherent risks*, also called *therapeutic risks*,[245] are involved. Medical science provides no certainty of success, only probabilities which may vary according to cases. Risks are an integral part of medical acts, and their realisation can lead to serious damage. The central problem of therapeutic risks is that they may arise even though medical procedures are performed with impeccable accuracy and skill. The risk provoked by the defendant's fault must therefore always be measured against the background risk, and it may in many cases be impossible to determine whether the injury was a result of the inherent risk or the doctor's fault, as exemplified by *Gburek v Cohen* (1988).

> A patient suffering from a severe infection was treated over a long period with a toxic antibiotic that can affect the ear and the kidney. Normally, the treatment's duration should not exceed 7 to 10 days but, in this plaintiff's case, it lasted 40 days. He thereafter became deaf. There existed two possible causes of the plaintiff's deafness: the doctor's negligence in not carrying out the tests that could have allowed for detection of excess accumulation of antibiotic in the plaintiff's ear or blood; or an inherent risk of deafness that can arise even in the presence of normal dosage of antibiotic. The absence of tests themselves made it impossible to determine whether they would have allowed for avoiding the damage and consequently the exact cause of the damage remained unknown.[246]

[244] (N 9 above). See also: England: *Wilsher v Essex Area HA* (n 58 above); Canada: *Grant Estate v Mathers* (n 166 above) p 384; Québec: *St-Jean v Mercier* (n 166 above).

[245] *Aléas thérapeutiques.* They can be defined as the rare realisation of a known risk not due to any fault on the medical practitioner's part.

[246] (N120 above). A situation which may be complicated by other causes, such as a patient's predisposition, a negative personal reaction to a treatment that has otherwise been successful, or unknown causes.

A second type of difficulty frequently encountered at the personal level arises from the fact that plaintiffs are often already involved in a negative process which the defendant may thereafter negligently omit to interrupt. It may be impossible to determine whether the damage is the result of the doctor's fault or the normal outcome of the pre-existing condition, however, as illustrated by *Laferrière v Lawson* (1991).

> The plaintiff consulted with the defendant, a breast cancer specialist, about the presence of an abnormal lump in her breast. The defendant performed a biopsy and removed the lump, which was found to be cancerous. He did not inform his patient of the cancerous condition, nor did he arrange any follow-up treatment. Four years after the biopsy, the patient was diagnosed with generalised cancer. She underwent surgery and various treatments but died three years later, after bringing an action against the defendant for damages. It was impossible to determine whether the deceased patient would have survived had the appropriate treatment been carried out in time, however. The damage could have been caused by two alternative events: the absence of treatment or the plaintiff's condition itself (cancer).[247]

The last two examples demonstrate that shedding light on an unknown sequence of events when addressing uncertain causation in medical liability may necessitate both explanatory and hypothetical inquiries, as they are designated by Hart and Honoré.[248] According to these authors, an explanatory causal difficulty occurs when it is not clear how a certain harm came about.[249] A hypothetical causal problem is encountered when, to determine whether a wrongful act was a necessary condition of the harm, the court inquires whether compliance with the law would have averted the harm.[250] This text questions whether the explanatory-hypothetical inquiry distinction should be given weight in medical litigation, however. Asking what happened or which events produced the plaintiff's damage must necessarily involve asking 'What would have happened had the defendant not acted negligently?' Further, answering this question may also necessitate explanatory inquiries such as 'What was the stage of the plaintiff's cancer at the time of the commission of the fault?' The explanatory-hypothetical inquiry distinction is consequently given limited weight here.[251]

The distinction between abstract causation and personal causation has also limited practical importance, since in many cases abstract causation is proven and most of the uncertainty revolves around the question of the existence of causation

[247] (N 134 above). See also: Cass civ 1st, 14 December 1965, D 1966.jur.453, Bull civ 1965.I.541, Bull civ 1966.I.128, JCP 1966.G.II.14753 (note Savatier).
[248] Hart and Honoré (n 4 above) p 407.
[249] *Ibid*, pp 408–11.
[250] *Ibid*, pp 411–18.
[251] See also: ch 4, text between fn 202 and 205.

in the specific case at hand. One must nevertheless be alert to the differences that exist between the two. First, they do not involve the examination of the same kinds of evidence. The first step is a pure scientific question which depends on the scientific, statistical, epidemiological, and genetic evidence presented before the court and assessed by it. The second step involves a more personal analysis and greater attention to the specific circumstances of the case and elements of lay evidence, as well as the exercise of the judge's common sense. Moreover, it is at the personal level of the inquiry that courts have been most intensely concerned to ensure fairness to the plaintiff by rendering the rules of causation more flexible.[252]

All the cases described above involve a further distinction between two causal processes: cumulative and alternative. This distinction[253] proves determinative of the courts' substantive and evidential responses to scientific causal uncertainties in some of the jurisdictions studied. Consequently, it is of more than academic interest.

B. Cumulative and Alternative Causal Mechanisms

Both mechanisms are found in situations in which a person has been exposed to more than one source of risk, each independently able to produce a type of outcome, and then suffers that outcome. The mechanism at work may have been that the total outcome was entirely produced by one of the sources alone (alternative cause mechanism).[254] It may also have been that both sources caused an effect and the total gravity of the outcome is an aggregate of these two effects (cumulative cause mechanism).[255] In either context, when uncertainty prevails, the plaintiff is unable to show factual causation: either the damage may have occurred anyway but for the defendant's fault; or the defendant's fault alone was not sufficient to provoke it. Consequently, while the two causal mechanisms are conceptually different, they bring about the same result: under traditional principles of causation, the plaintiff fails.

In cumulative causal processes, evidential problems more precisely arise from the impossibility of determining the exact extent of the contribution made by the defendant. The paradigm example of this difficulty is the English industrial disease case *Bonnington Castings v Wardlaw* (1956), already described above.[256] This difficulty has been to a great extent solved by the material contribution test in common law, and does not present major problems in civil law.[257]

[252] *Kay v Ayrshire* (n 226 above) pp 421 (Lord Keith) and 422 (Lord Griffiths): Alternative approaches to the traditional assessment of causation apply only if abstract causation is first demonstrated; *Lee v Clark* (n 226 above).

[253] Described by Stapleton (n 134 above) p 401.

[254] See also: Hart and Honoré (n 4 above) p 249.

[255] Stapleton (n 134 above) p 401.

[256] *Bonnington* (n 53 above), see above, text to n 53–54.

[257] (N 88 above).

In alternative cause cases, difficulties occur where two or more possible causes could each on their own have produced the whole of the damage, but where scientific uncertainty renders impossible the determination of which of the different factors has in fact done so. In these cases, the question does not revolve around the extent of the contribution since the *existence* of contribution itself is unknown. All that can be said is that the defendant increased the risk of the outcome by adding one possible cause of the damage. Interesting examples are found in the Canadian cases of *Snell v Farrell* (1990) and *Laferrière v Lawson* (1991).[258]

The alternative/cumulative distinction is not absolved from any criticism, however, and it often breaks down in cases of causal uncertainty. Uncertainty as to the scientific causal mechanisms may go indeed as far as preventing the categorisation of a case as one of cumulative or alternative causation.[259] In some cases, while the origin of the disease may be identifiable, ignorance as to the process by which it develops makes it impossible to determine whether the damage originates from a faulty or non-faulty event or both.[260]

Conclusion to Chapter 1

Whatever the type of process involved, the consequence of causal uncertainty is invariably the same: the victim of the damage is generally unable to prove causation on the traditional evidential standards. In light of this result, an insistence on the application of the orthodox rules has been considered unjust and as leading to serious under-deterrence of the harmful activity in question.[261] The courts have therefore challenged it in a series of cases and thereby created more uncertainty on this subject, despite their obvious aim of not letting uncertainty of evidence prevent an innocent victim from recovering from a negligent defendant.

[258] Already summarised above: text to nn 244 and 247. See also: *Wilsher v Essex Area HA* (n 58 above).

[259] M Jones, *Medical Negligence* (London, Sweet & Maxwell, 1996) para 5–27. This difficulty is illustrated by the debates concerning the mechanism involved in *McGhee v National Coal Board* (n 8 above) and triggered by the unknown aetiology of dermatitis. Some insist the process was cumulative: AM Dugdale and KM Stanton, *Professional Negligence*, 3rd edn, (London, Butterworths, 1998) 389. Against: *Fairchild v Glenhaven* (n 50 above) para 93 (Lord Hutton). Others hold the causal mechanism was unknown but contribution was inferred: J Stapleton (n 134 above) pp 403–4. Indeed, it was unclear whether the disease was caused by *both* the fault of the defendant (in allowing the dust to remain on the plaintiff's skin) and an innocent cause (the fact of the exposure to brick dust at work), or by one of these *alone*. See also: *Fairchild v Glenhaven* (n 50 above) para 7 (Lord Bingham).

[260] England: *Fairchild v Glenhaven* (n 50 above) paras 7 (Lord Bingham), 46 (Lord Hoffmann), 78 (Lord Hutton) and 120 (Lord Rodger); Canada: *Webster v Chapman* (n 58 above) p 89; *Logozar v Golder* (1994) 21 CCLT (2nd) 203 (AltaCA) 205; Québec: *Dussault v Hôpital Maisonneuve* [1976] CS 791, 805–6; *Kirschenbaum-Green v Syrchin* (n 90 above) p 827 (CS).

[261] Fleming (n 134 above) p 663.

This confusion may be the result of the courts' difficult dilemma in cases involving uncertainty. Enforcing the traditional and fundamental rules of proof of causation could mean letting an innocent victim of a proven wrong go uncompensated. On the other hand, ordering compensation despite the uncertainty could mean holding the defendant doctor or hospital liable for the whole loss in cases where it is impossible to identify their exact contribution. One also observes a willingness not to depart from the strict application of the normal principles related to the traditional standard and burden of proof of causation without articulate justification. Judicial efforts have therefore been centred on reaching a just balance between justice for the plaintiff and fairness to the defendant by means which, while giving the courts flexibility, could also ensure respect for the fundamental rules on which the law of negligence and *responsabilité civile* are based. A difficult reconciliation to effect . . . .

Having reviewed the different rules at play in the judicial assessment of causation and the various situations in which uncertainty may prevent the plaintiff from meeting his burden of proof to the appropriate standard, this text will now undertake a thorough examination of the courts' different reactions to causal scientific uncertainty in the four jurisdictions under study. More precisely, it examines some courts' advocacy of greater flexibility in the assessment of causation and the way the need for flexibility has been translated into concrete judicial means.

2

Flexibility

> The traditional approach to causation has come under attack in a number of cases in which there is concern that due to the complexities of proof, the probable victim of tortious conduct will be deprived of relief.
>
> Sopinka J in *Snell v Farrell*

The difficulties of proof specific to the field of medical malpractice have prompted challenges to the strict application of the traditional rules of evidence in a series of medical malpractice cases.[1] These challenges have led to affirmation of the need for flexibility in the assessment of the causal link in cases involving scientific uncertainty. The mechanisms through which flexibility is expressed by the courts vary according to the jurisdictions, however, and are not always clearly set out. This chapter examines the judicial affirmation of this need for flexibility. The chapters that follow will study the different legal mechanisms through which this desire for flexibility has been expressed by the courts in order to respond to the different causal uncertainties reviewed in chapter 1: reversal of the burden of proof (chapter 3), loss of chance (chapter 4), and inferential reasoning (chapter 5).

Some courts have reacted to the results of a strict application of the rules regarding causation and the burden and standard of proof by emphasising the need for more flexibility in applying the rules of evidence of causation. This approach has led them to find concrete ways of injecting this flexibility into the assessment of causation. Before reviewing the solutions devised by the courts, this chapter considers how agreement on the need for flexibility has been expressed by the judiciary in the field of medical liability: by emphasising the flexibility inherent in the burden and standards of evidence (section 1); by affirming the judiciary's independence *vis-à-vis* the expert evidence (section 2); and by giving concrete meaning to this independence in dealing with expert controversies on causation (section 3).

[1] Sopinka J in *Snell v Farrell* [1990] 72 DLR (4th) 222; [1990] 2 SCR 311, 320; F Maury, 'Victimes du VHB (vaccin contre l'hépatite B): Faut-il attendre une certitude scientifique pour les indemniser?' (2004) *Médecine et droit* 125, 127.

Section 1

Importance and Mutability of the Traditional Standards

While acknowledging the need for flexibility in assessing causation, courts insist on the importance of the traditional principles of evidence in its demonstration.[2] Emphasising the importance of the traditional approach to causation in the landmark case of *Snell v Farrell* (1990), the Supreme Court of Canada nonetheless trenchantly recognised that the courts' dissatisfaction with the traditional approach to causation stems to a large extent from its too rigid application in many cases.[3] This finding led the Supreme Court of Canada to express more openly and clearly than any other court the need for flexibility in the assessment of causation and the possibility of departing from the traditional rules of evidence, especially when confronted with scientific uncertainty. It also insisted that the burden and standard of proof of causation are flexible concepts:

> [I]t has long been recognised [in common law countries] that the allocation of the burden of proof is not immutable. The legal or ultimate burden of proof is determined by the substantive law 'upon reasons of experience and fairness'. . . . This court has not hesitated to alter the incidence of the ultimate burden of proof when the underlying rationale for its allocation is absent in a particular case. . . . This flexibility extends to the issue of causation.[4]

It is generally agreed that this decision is supportive of a less onerous standard of proof of causation applicable to cases of medical malpractice where there is some inherent difficulty in proving causation with scientific accuracy.[5] The flexibility

[2] *Lapointe v Hôpital Le Gardeur* [1989] RJQ 2619 (CA) 2643 and 2647 (rev'd on another point: [1992] 90 DLR (4th) 7; [1992] 1 SCR 351); *Snell v Farrell* (n 1 above) 327; *Laferrière v Lawson* [1991] 78 DLR (4th) 609; [1991] 1 SCR 541, 609; *Grant Estate v Mathers* (1991) 100 NSR (2nd) 363 (SC) 374–75; *Athey v Leonati* [1996] 140 DLR (4th) 235; [1996] 3 SCR 458, 466; *St-Jean v Mercier* [1999] RJQ 1658 (CA) 1667, *aff'd* [2002] 1 SCR 491; [2002] 209 DLR (4th) 513. See also: *Fairchild v Glenhaven Funeral Services* [2002] 3 All ER 305 (HL) para 43 (Lord Nicholls): to preserve fairness to the defendant, considerable restraint must be exercised in any relaxation of the threshold but-for test of causal connection. Such relaxation should not be resorted to indiscriminately whenever a plaintiff has difficulty in discharging the requirement to meet the test: there must be good reasons for departing from the but-for test. In *Fairchild* and *Chester v Afshar* [2005] 1 AC 134; 3 WLR 927; 4 All ER 587 (HL), the House of Lords adopted a very liberal attitude to the proof of causation, however: ch 5, text between fns 67–103.

[3] (N 1 above) 328.

[4] *Ibid*, p 321 referring to *Cook v Lewis* [1951] 1 DLR 1 SCR 830. See also: AM Linden, *Canadian Tort Law*, 7th edn, (Markham, Butterworths, 2001) 111; *McGhee v National Coal Board* [1973] 1 WLR 1 (HL) 6–7 (Lord Wilberforce).

[5] Confirmed by the Supreme Court of Canada itself in *Stewart v Pettie* [1995] 121 DLR (4th) 222; [1995] 1 SCR 131, 154. See also: *Taylor v Hogan* (1994) 119 Nfld & PEIR 37 (NfldCA) 47; *Pauluik v*

advocated in *Snell v Farrell* was reaffirmed in Québec law thereafter.[6] Some English sources have also recognised that a more generous judicial attitude may be adopted in some circumstances.[7] The same need for flexibility is expressed by a small section of the French doctrine, which observes that the courts tend, when there is doubt with regard to causation, to relax the burden and standard of proof.[8] More particularly, Viney and Jourdain have pleaded in favour of such generosity in the medical context:

> *Cette nouvelle orientation, encore timide et discrète, de la jurisprudence, mérite d'être encouragée. L'assouplissement de preuve du lien de causalité qu'elle postule se justifie pleinement en matière médicale où la victime se trouve en proie à des difficultés de preuve souvent insurmontables liées aux mystères du corps humain et aux imperfections de la science médicale.*[9]

How can flexibility be granted to judges when the assessment of causation in medical malpractice involves complex scientific issues on which scientists themselves do not agree? It may in fact be asked whether dependence on medical expertise does not curtail the flexibility aimed at by the courts. In order to give a fair account of the interplay between the courts' flexibility and the complexities of medical causation, one must first study the role of science in the judicial determination of causation and its impact on the courts' expression of flexibility.

Section 2

Flexibility and Independence of the Judiciary

In the judicial assessment of causation, science loses some of its usual prestige, being placed on the same level as other considerations and factors, such as

Paraison and Hart (1995) 107 Man R (2nd) 145 (ManCA) 154; *Meloche v Hotel Dieu Grace Hospital/Villa Marie* [1999] 179 DLR (4th) 77 (OntCA) 88; *Williamson v Kozak* (2003) AJ no 1467; ABQB 953 (AltaQB, 21 November 2003) para 64; and *Michener v Doris* (2003) BCJ No 2301; BCSC 1541 (BCSC, 8 October 2003) para 175 (obiter), both citing *Snell.*

6 *Laferrière v Lawson* (n 2 above); *Chouinard v Robbins* (QuéCA, 10 December 2001) para 58 (Rochette J, dissenting on another question); *Laforce v Dumont* (2003) JQ no 4945 (QuéCA, 5 May 2003) para 9 (Baudouin J).

7 Eg, *McGhee v National Coal Board* (n 4 above) 4 (Lord Reid).

8 G Viney and P Jourdain, J Ghestin, (dir), *Traité de droit civil: Les conditions de la responsabilité,* 2nd edn, (Paris, LGDJ, 1998) 191–92, 200–1, 203; J Flour and JL Aubert, *Droit civil: Les obligations 2) Le fait juridique* (Paris, Armand Colin, 1997) para 163.

9 (N 8 above) para 373, commenting on the concept of *creation of an unjustified risk*: Ch 5, text between fns 159 and 163.

common sense. As the courts of England, Canada, Australia, and Québec have strongly insisted on assessing causation on the basis of common sense rather than scientifically,[10] courts should benefit, at least in theory, from some independence from the scientific evidence. Yet in medical liability cases, especially those involving uncertainty, the expert evidence necessarily has a prominent role to play, since it is often impossible for the judge to exercise his common sense without relying on the medical experts' explanations.

A. Judicial Independence from Experts' Opinions[11]

The assistance of scientific experts in confronting causal uncertainty in medical matters is indispensable. The expert plays an important role *vis-à-vis* the plaintiff, who, confronted with the complexities and technicalities of medical science, as well as his lack of information with regard to the medical act performed on his person, needs assistance in shedding light on the different possible causes of his damage. The expert also provides assistance to the judge, who faces similar hurdles, as well as being confronted with the supplementary difficulty of taking a legal decision on the basis of scientific evidence. Science and law do not, however, always make a happy couple and courts' stands on scientific issues in civil matters may depart from strict scientific opinions.

In common law and Québec, witnesses' opinions are admissible in civil matters whenever, in order to decide a case, the court needs to be informed on facts, scientific or technical, which are not within its competence and for the understanding of which the lay evidence is not sufficient.[12] In almost every medical liability case, the expert opinion therefore is required for the tribunal to understand the evidence and to come to an independent opinion.[13]

[10] See above, ch 1, text between fns 8 and 11.

[11] See generally: L Khoury, 'L'incertitude scientifique en matière civile et la preuve d'expert' in P Patenaude, (dir), *L'interaction entre le droit et les sciences experimentales:* Actes du colloque, 15 May 2001 (Sherbrooke, RDUS, 2001).

[12] England: *Davie v Magistrates of Edinburgh* (1953) SC 34; MN Howard, R Bagshaw and SL Phipson, *Phipson on Evidence,* 15th edn, (London, Sweet & Maxwell, 2000) 921; A Keane, *The Modern Law of Evidence,* 5th edn, (London, Butterworths, 2000) 496; R Emson, *Evidence,* 2nd edn, (London, MacMillan, 2004) 353–55; Canada: J Sopinka, SN Lederman and AW Bryant, *The Law of Evidence in Canada,* 2nd edn, (Toronto, Butterworths, 1999) 616–17 and 620; Australia: I Freckelton and H Selby, *Expert Evidence: Law, Practice, Procedure and Advocacy,* 2nd edn, (Pyrmont, NSW, Law Book, 2002) 11; France: NCPC, Art 144; Québec: *Donolo Inc v St Michel Realties Inc* [1971] CA 536, 537–38; *Roberge v Bolduc* [1991] 78 DLR (4th) 666; [1991] 1 SCR 374, 429; JC Royer, *La preuve civile,* 3rd edn, (Cowansville, Yvon Blais, 2003) para 466; L Ducharme, *Précis de la preuve,* 5th edn, (Montréal, Wilson & Lafleur, 1996) 151.

[13] *Davie v Edinburgh Magistrates* (n 12 above); *Webster v Chapman* [1997] 155 DLR (4th) 82 (ManCA) 90. On the expert witness's role: *National Justice Cia Naviera SA v Prudential Assurance Co Ltd, The Ikarian Refer* [1993] 2 Lloyd's Rep 68 (QBD, Comm Ct) 81–82; *Bureau v Sakkal* [1994] RRA 893 (CS) 904.

The expert's mission is restricted to his field of expertise, recognised by the tribunal.[14] Moreover, he is not entitled to give an opinion on matters which are within the experience of lay people generally or within the general knowledge and understanding of the tribunal of fact.[15] This rule forbids him more specifically to give an opinion on legal questions.[16] The probative value of the expert's opinion depends on whether it is serious, independent, objective, unbiased, and within the expert's field of expertise.[17] It also depends on the authority, experience, and qualifications of the expert[18] and whether it rests on his personal observations and the existing evidence or on the evidence eventually adduced at trial by the parties,[19] rather than on general and abstract scientific theories.[20]

[14] Sopinka, *et al* (n 12 above) 623; JD Heydon, *Cross on Evidence (Australia)*, 7th edn, (Sydney, Butterworths, 2004) 926; A Ligertwood, *Australian Evidence,* 2nd edn, (Sydney, Butterworths, 1993) para 7.44; DA Bellemare, 'L'homme de science devant les tribunaux' (1977) 37 *Canadian Bar Review* 465, 472 and 482.

[15] Howard, Bagshaw and Phipson (n 12 above) 925; Keane (n 12 above) 499; P Murphy, *Evidence and Advocacy,* 5th edn, (London, Blackstone, 1998) 147; Emson (n 12 above) 355–56.

[16] England: Howard, Bagshaw and Phipson (n 12 above) 924; Australia: Ligertwood (n 14 above) para 7.34; Heydon (n 14 above) 947; Freckelton and Selby (n 12 above) 251 and ff about the cautionary rule prohibiting experts to give their opinions on ultimate issues, which is largely ignored in practice: J Gans and A Palmer, *Australian Principles of Evidence,* 2nd edn, (Sydney, Cavendish, 2004) 253. §80(a) of the Uniform Evidence Acts (referring to the Evidence Act 1995 (Cth) www.austlii.edu.au/au/legis/cth/consol_act/ea199580 (23 August 2005) and the mirror legislation of New South Wales, Tasmania and Norfolk Island) however states that such evidence is not inadmissible: P Bayne, *Uniform Evidence Law: Text and Essential Cases* (Leichhardt, NSW, Federation Press, 2003) para 8.480; Canada: Sopinka, *et al* (n 12 above) 624; France: NCPC, Art 238; Cass civ 1st, 7 July 1998, Bull civ 1998.I.n239; Québec: *Villemaire-Grenier v Lachapelle* [1989] RRA 38 (CQ) 44; Royer (n 12 above) para 475; and CD Gonthier, 'Le témoignage d'experts: à la frontière de la science et du droit' (1993) 53 *Canadian Bar Review* 187, 193. This includes the question of whether or not the standard of proof has been met: HLA Hart and T Honoré, *Causation in the Law,* 2nd edn, (Oxford, Clarendon Press, 1985) 411. But see: J Bell, S Boyron and S Whittaker, *Principles of French Law* (Oxford, OUP, 1998) 100–1: In practice, they are often asked questions which require the application of legal concepts; G Bourgeois, P Julien and M Zavaro, *La pratique de l'expertise judiciaire* (Paris, Litec, 1999) 90 and 109.

[17] England: *The Ikarian Refer* (n 13 above); Canada: *Meyers (Next Friend of) v Stanley* (2003) AJ No 685, ABQB 468 (AltaQB, 27 May 2003) para 79; Australia: Heydon (n 14 above) 926; and ff Freckelton and Selby (n 12 above) 22–23 and 28; France: NCPC, Art 237; Bourgeois, *et al* (n 16 above) 90; P Vayre and F Vayre, 'Le médecin expert judiciaire. Mission pour responsabilité professionnelle' *Gazette du Palais* 2001.doctr.425; Québec: Royer (n 12 above) para 485; P Lesage-Jarjoura and S Philips-Nootens, *Éléments de responsabilité médicale: Le droit dans le quotidien de la médecine* (Cowansville, Yvon Blais, 2001) 51. See also: *Whitehouse v Jordan* [1980] 1 All ER 650 (CA) 655 (Lord Denning MR), *aff'd* [1981] 1 WLR 246 (HL); *Mackell v Moulson* (BCSC, 5 December 2001) para 84; *Chouinard v Robbins* (n 6 above) para 58.

[18] *Davie v Edinburgh Magistrates* (n 12 above).

[19] *Westco Storage Ltd v Inter-City Gas Utilities Ltd* (1989) 59 Man R 2d 37 (CA) 57; *Mackell v Moulson* (n 17 above) para 88.

[20] England: Howard, Bagshaw and Phipson (n 12 above) 921–22; Canada: *Westco Storage* (n 19 above) 57; *Oiom v Brassington* (1990) 52 BCLR (2nd) 240; (BCCA) 255 and 257. Australia: *Adelaide Stevedoring Co Ltd v Forst* (1940) 64 CLR 538 (AustHC) 568 (Dixon J, dissenting); *Black v Tomislav Lipovac BHNF* (1998) Lexis 467 (AustFC, 4 June 1998) para 80; *Naxakis v Western General Hospital* (1998) 197 CLR 269 (AustHC) 280–81; Québec: *Dame Ducharme v Royal Victoria Hospital* (1940) 69 BR 162, 169; *Dodds v Schierz* [1986] RJQ 2623 (CA) 2628; *Garantie (La), Cie d'Assurance de l'Amérique du Nord v Massicotte* [1988] RRA 16 (CA) 20; *Bureau v Sakkal* (n 13 above) 903; Royer (n 12 above) para 477 and 485.

The observations above are subject to several qualifications as regards the French expert. Because of the inquisitory nature of the French judicial system, French judges take a more active part in the search for truth, themselves investigating and questioning the witnesses during the hearing.[21] The parties nevertheless have primary responsibility for gathering and presenting the evidence before the court. The judge can assist the parties in their search for evidence but must not take their place.[22] The mechanisms for the collection of evidence, called *mesures d'instruction,*[23] can be ordered by the judge when there are not sufficient elements of evidence available to one party to prove a fact, but cannot make up for the deficiencies of a party in the administration of the evidence.[24] When a claim introduces technical aspects which the judge is not able to assess on his own,[25] he has the discretion to appoint the expert of his choice.[26] Although judges have the power to appoint several experts,[27] they usually appoint only one.[28] Consequently, French expertise is generally not contradictory.[29]

Nelken states that inside the court, law enslaves science to correspond to its own norms.[30] The image is exaggerated[31] but illustrates the status of scientific proof in court. Even though it is of valuable help to the judiciary and usually given great weight, scientific opinion does not limit the judge's complete autonomy in assessing the evidence and deciding whether the plaintiff has met his burden of proof.[32] It is the judge's responsibility to arrive not at a medical diagnosis but at a 'legal

[21] D Giesen, *International Medical Malpractice Law: A Comparative Law Study of Civil Liability Arising from Medical Care* (Boston, Martinus Nijhoff, 1988) 713.

[22] NCPC, Art 146.

[23] Bell, *et al* (n 16 above) 96.

[24] NCPC, Art 146 al 2.

[25] NCPC, Arts 256 and 263; W Bobleter, *Le lien de causalité entre un traumatisme et ses conséquences corporelles probables* (Paris, Mémoire DESS, Paris II Assas, 1990) 21.

[26] NCPC, Arts 143–78. The appointment can be requested by one or several parties. The expert is usually taken from a national list of *experts judiciaries.*

[27] NCPC, Art 264. When several experts are appointed, they write only one report which expresses one view only: NCPC, Art 282 al 2. If their views are not unanimous, divergences can be expressed in the report.

[28] NCPC, Art 264. In England, Australia, Canada and Quebec, courts also have the power to appoint a court expert, although this procedure is seldom used: England: Howard, Bagshaw and Phipson (n 12 above) 8; Australia: Ligertwood (n 14 above) para 7.37; Freckelton and Selby (n 12 above) 608 and ff; Canada: R Delisle, D Stuart and D Tanovich, *Evidence: Principles and Problems,* 7th edn, (Toronto, Carswell, 2004) 773–74; Québec: Cpc, Art 414; Royer (n 12 above) 280.

[29] The expert must nonetheless hear all the interested parties and provide the parties with all the documents at the basis of his opinion. Moreover, the expert can ask for the opinion of another expert, but not on a question related to his speciality: NCPC, Art 278.

[30] D Nelken, 'A Just Measure of Science' in M Freeman and H Reece, (eds), *Science in Court* (Dartmouth, Ashgate, 1998) 11, 16. See also: Gonthier (n 16 above) 196.

[31] We prefer Jasanoff's description of science as the 'indispensable ally [of law] in a shared project of truth finding': S Jasanoff, *Science at the Bar* (Cambridge, MA, Harvard University Press, 1995) 42.

[32] NCPC, Art 246; *Roberge v Bolduc* (n 12 above) 430; *State Electricity Commission of Victoria v Johnson* (1995) VIC Lexis 1345 (VicSC, 31 October 1995); *Brouillet v Brouillet* (QuéSC, 1 October 2002) para 35, A Bernardot and RP Kouri, *La responsabilité civile médicale* (Sherbrooke, RDUS, 1980) 17.

diagnosis'[33] and the expert only assists him in this task.[34] The expert's testimony has the same value, and is assessed in the same manner as any other element of testimonial evidence.[35] The judge is free to attach to it such weight as he thinks fit or even disregard it altogether.[36] It has even been argued that merely following the path pointed out by the expert evidence without critical consideration of it and the other evidence would be equivalent to an abdication of the court's duty to decide.[37] Thus in theory it is open to the court to reach a conclusion different from that of the expert, even when the expertises are unanimous.[38] The courts do sometimes prefer the lay evidence to that of the experts[39] or decide, on the basis of their own common sense, to disregard expert opinion.[40]

Yet in general judges tend to follow impartial, relevant, and credible expert opinions which find adequate support in the evidence adduced by the parties. The image of objectivity and certainty that science projects enhances the authority of the parties' and judge's conclusions.[41] In practice, this is reflected in the greater importance that judges often give expert testimony in comparison to that of lay witnesses.[42] This phenomenon is more prevalent in France, where

[33] *Fincham v Anchor Insulation Co Ltd*, The Times, 16 June 1989 (QBD).

[34] Bobleter (n 25 above) 21.

[35] England: Emson (n 12 above) 367; France: J Penneau, *Faute et erreur en matière de responsabilité médicale* (Paris, LGDJ, 1973) para 99; Québec: CcQ, Art 2845 and Cpc, Art 423 al 2; *Shawinigan Engineering Co v Naud* [1929] 4 DLR 57; [1929] SCR 341, 343; *Donolo v St Michel Realties* (n 12 above) 538; *Laferrière v Lawson* (n 2 above) 606, *Brouillet v Brouillet* (n 32 above) para 35; Royer (n 12 above) para 484; H Kélada, *Notions et techniques de preuve civile* (Montréal, Wilson & Lafleur, 1986) 271 and cases cited at fn 822.

[36] England: Emson (n 12 above) 366–67; Keane (n 12 above) 496 and 507–8; Howard, Bagshaw and Phipson (n 12 above) 924–25; Australia: Ligertwood (n 14 above) para 7.48; *Lipovac v Hamilton Holdings Pty Ltd* (1996) Aust ACTSC Lexis 52 (Aust Cap Terr SC, 13 September 1996) text to fn 149; Québec: *Boothman v Poirier* (2005) WL 546105, Carswell Que 601 (Qué SC, 2 February 2005) para 37; France: Cass civ 1st, 13 February 1985, JCP 1985.G.II.20388; J Vincent and S Guinchard, *Procédure civile*, 27th edn, (Paris, Dalloz, 2003) 853; Bourgeois, *et al* (n 16 above) 90.

[37] Giesen (n 21 above) 695; *Joyce v Merton Sutton and Wandsworth Health Authority* [1996] PIQR 121 (CA); P Deschamps, 'L'obligation de moyens en matière de responsabilité médicale' (1990–91) 58 *Assurances* 575, 589.

[38] *Davie v Edinburgh Magistrates* (n 12 above); *Gardiner v Motherwell Machinery and Scrap Co Ltd* [1961] 1 WLR 1424 (HL) 1429 (Lord Reid); Cass civ 1st, 23 May 1973, Gaz Pal 1973.2.885 (note Doll), JCP 1975.G.II.17955 (note Savatier), Bull civ 1973.1.n181, JCP 1974.G.II.17643 (note Savatier); Metz 1st, 21 January 2004, Juris-Data No 234287; *Dodds v Schierz* (n 20 above) 2628 and 2636 ; J Ghestin and G Goubeaux, *Traité de droit civil: Introduction générale*, 3rd edn, (Paris, LGDJ, 1990) para 650.

[39] Eg, *Montreal Tramways Co v Léveillé* [1933] SCR 456; *Masson v Jutras* [1955] BR 173, 174; Dame *Tremblay v Audet* [1973] CS 693, 694; *Canadian Pacific Railways v Blais* [1969] CS 446, 450.

[40] Eg, Cass civ 1st, 13 February 1985 (n 36 above); *Snell v Farrell* (n 1 above); *Naxakis v Western General Hospital* (n 20 above) 280–81.

[41] D Jutras, 'Expertise médicale et causalité' in *Congrès du Barreau du Québec* (SFPBQ Montréal 1992) 897, 900.

[42] Sir R Cross, *Cross and Tapper on Evidence*, 10th edn, (London, Butterworths, 2003) 570; Royer (n 12 above) para 486. Eg, *Sunne v Shaw* [1981] CS 609, 619; *Bédard v Lavoie* [1987] RRA 83 (CA) 84; *Labrosse v Hydro-Québec* [1989] RRA 739 (CA) 743–44 (non medical).

judges tend to follow the experts' conclusions and hesitate before deciding otherwise.[43]

The judge's theoretical independence from the expert evidence takes on a particular aspect with regard to uncertain causation in medical malpractice. Because parties to these cases often rely on scientific, mathematical, and statistical evidence to make their demonstration of the causal link, courts have had to reaffirm their independence *vis-à-vis* this type of evidence.

B. Independence from Scientific, Mathematical, and Statistical Evidence

The judicial distancing from abstract theories of causation and the affirmation that the assessment of causation should be done on the basis of common sense have led the courts of England, Australia, Canada and Québec to draw a distinction between legal and scientific causation in dealing with medical malpractice cases.[44] Assessment of causation in this field is grounded on the principle that causation should not be assessed on the basis of mathematical calculations[45] and does not require mathematical, scientific, or medical certainty or accuracy.[46] The

[43] Bourgeois, *et al* (n 16 above) 90; Bell, *et al* (n 16 above) 361 and 101–2; YM Serinet and P Mislawski, note under Cass civ 1st, 23 September 2003, D 2004.898, 901 (case also found at Pet Aff 2004.n12.p14 (note Gossement), Pet Aff 2004.n81.p9 (note Mémeteau), JCP 2003.Entreprise et Affaires.II.1749 (note Faict et Mistretta), JCP 2003.G.II.10179 (note Jonquet, Maillols, Mainguy, Terrier), D 2004.1344 (note Mazeaud)).

[44] Australia: *March v E & MH Stramare Pty Ltd* (1991) 171 CLR 506 (non-medical), 508 (Mason CJ), 522 (Deane J); *Naxakis v Western General Hospital* (n 20 above) 280–81; *Seltsam Pty Ltd v McGuiness* (2000) 49 NSWLR 262 (NSWSC) para 142 (Spigelman CJ) (non-medical); *Finch v Rogers* (2004) NSWSC 39 (NSWSC, 13 February 2004) para 133; Canada: *Mackell v Moulson* (n 17 above) para 109, *Levitt v Carr* [1992] 4 WWR 160 (BCCA) 177; Québec: *Laferrière v Lawson* (n 2 above) 609; *Camden-Bourgault v Brochu* [2001] RRA 295 (CA); *Brouillet v Brouillet* (n 32 above) para 36; *Lacombe v Hôpital Maisonneuve-Rosemont* (2004) para 31.

[45] *Yorkshire Dale Steamship Co Ltd v Minister of War Transport* [1942] AC 691 (HL) 706; *Athey v Leonati* (n 2 above) 467; *Seltsam Pty Ltd v McGuiness* (n 44 above) paras 136–37; *Mackell v Moulson* (n 17 above) para 109.

[46] England: *Alphacell Ltd v Woodward* [1972] AC 824 (HL) (Lord Salmon); *Elvicta Wood Engineering Ltd v Huxley* (CA, 19 April 2000) para 4; Canada: *Snell v Farrell* (n 1 above) 328 (Sopinka J); *Lankenau Estate v Dutton* [1991] 79 DLR (4th) 705 (BCCA) 57; *Levitt v Carr* (n 44 above) 177; *Taylor v Hogan* (n 5 above) 50–51; *Heidebrecht v The Fraser-Burrard Hospital Society* (BCSC, 10 October 1996) para 107–8; *Meyers v Stanley* (n 17 above) para 54, citing *Snell*; *Lurtz v Duchesne* (2003) OJ no 1540 (OntSCtJ, 16 April 2003) para 346; *McNeil v Easterbrook* (2004) WL 213 1088, Carswell Ont 3926 (OntSCtJ, 29 September 2004) para 15; *Adair Estate v Hamilton Health Sciences Corp* (2005) WL 1244381, CarswellOnt 2180 (OntSCtJ, 25 April 2005) para 111; Australia: Ligertwood (n 14 above) para 1.25 and 2.39: Australian courts have rejected mathematical analysis of the evidence outside medical negligence in *TNT Management Pty Ltd v Brooks* (1979) 23 ALR 345 (AustHC) and *State Government Insurance Commission (South Australia)* (1984) 37 SASR 31 (SASC); France: Cass civ 1st, 9 May 2001, Bull civ 2001.I.n130, D 2001.2149 (rap Sargos); Cass civ 1st, 17 July 2001, Bull civ 2001.I.n234; Québec: *Partanen v Commission de Transport de Montréal* [1964] SCR 231, 235 (not reported in DLR); *Martel v Hôtel-Dieu de St-Vallier* [1969] 14 DLR (3rd) 445; [1969] SCR 745, 749; *Donolo v St Michel Realties* (CS) cited in the CA's judgment: (n 12 above) 538; *Dame Cimon v Carbotte*

distinction is less prominent in France where it is nevertheless insisted that *legal certainty* is not equivalent to *medical certainty.*[47]

This rule can be justified by the differences in the respective aims pursued by the two disciplines which has an impact on the legal and scientific interpretation of concepts which seem *a priori* to reflect the same reality. Jurists and scientists give a distinct meaning to concepts such as causal link, certainty, proof, and probability. At least in the common law jurisdictions, as well as in Québec, the law reasons in terms of balance of probability, which does not necessitate mathematical or scientific certainty.[48] By contrast, science requires something closer to certainty before allowing itself to speak in absolute terms.[49] It consequently fluctuates between two extremes until scientific developments make it possible to opt decisively for one side or the other. In fact, science progresses over time, and scientific truth can only be situated on a continuum. It is therefore usual for a scientist to exercise caution before making categorical affirmations about the aetiology of an ailment, for example.

Unlike the scientist, the judge cannot wait for the scientific developments to render an issue less uncertain before taking a decision in a particular litigation.[50] The *hesitations* or *uncertainties* of science do not automatically constitute a hurdle for the jurist since the requirement for legal *certainty* is satisfied with a probability greater than 50 per cent, at least in common law and Québec[51]:

> It is not therefore essential that the medical experts provide a firm opinion supporting the plaintiff's theory of causation. Medical experts ordinarily determine causation in terms of certainty whereas the law demands a lesser standard. As pointed out in Louisell, *Medical Malpractice*, vol 3, the phrase 'in your opinion with a reasonable degree of medical certainty', which is the standard form of question to a medical expert, is often misunderstood. The author explains, at p 25–57:

[1971] CS 622; *Sunne v Shaw* (n 42 above) 612; *Dodds v Schierz* (n 20 above) 2627 (Monet J, partly diss) 2636 (L'Heureux-Dubé J); *Houde v Côté* [1987] RJQ 723 (CA) 728; *Laferrière v Lawson* (n 2 above) 609; *Lapointe v Hôpital Le Gardeur* (n 2 above) 2643; *Desormeaux v Centre Hospitalier St Mary's* [1992] RRA 516 (CS) 519 and 520; *Ami v Stephenson* [2000] RRA 781 (CS) 781 and 784; PA Crépeau, 'La responsabilité médicale et hospitalière dans la jurisprudence québécoise récente' (1960) 20 *Revue du Barreau* 433, 474; PA Crépeau, 'La responsabilité civile du médecin' (1977) 8 *Revue de droit de l'Université de Sherbrooke* 25, 29.

[47] P Jourdain, 'Imputabilité d'une contamination virale à une transfusion sanguine: la preuve par exclusion du lien de causalité érigée en présomption de droit' (2001) *Revue trimestrielle de droit civil* 889, 892; Viney and Jourdain (n 8 above) para 333; YM Serinet and P Mislawski, note under Cass civ 1st, 23 September 2003 (n 43 above).

[48] Canada: *Briffett v Gander and District Hospital Board* (1996) 137 Nfld & PEIR 271 (CA) 288 and 301; *Strichen v Stewart* (2005) Carswell Alta 556 (AltaCA, 28 April 2005) para 35; Québec: *Sunne v Shaw* (n 42 above) 612; *Houde v Côté* (n 46 above) 728. On the distinction between the goals of law and science: *March v Stramare* (n 44 above) 509 (Mason CJ).

[49] Canada: *Meyers v Stanley* (n 17 above) para 55.

[50] Ligertwood (n 14 above) para 1.26.

[51] For a discussion of the French standard, see ch 1, text between fns 147 and 158.

> Many doctors do not understand the phrase . . . as they usually deal in 'certainties' that are 100% sure, whereas 'reasonable' certainties which the law requires need only to be more probably so, ie, 51%.[52]

In his search for the probable explanation of the events, the judge therefore applies a criterion that falls below the certainty the scientific community requires before reaching a similar conclusion.[53]

In appropriate circumstances, common sense may even be relied on to draw inferences of causation in the absence of evidence to the contrary although positive or scientific proof has not been adduced.[54] This principle has been expressed most clearly by the Supreme Court of Canada in *Snell v Farrell* (1990). As will be recalled, the Court had to analyse the claim of a patient who had been the victim of an optic nerve atrophy following a surgery to remove a cataract.[55] Despite the fact that none of the medical experts had been able to establish the cause of damage, the Court inferred that it resulted from the surgeon's fault. It did not matter that the experts were not able to identify the exact cause of the plaintiff's damage, since it was not essential that positive scientific evidence provide a firm opinion supporting the plaintiff's theory of causation.[56] Moreover, the Court emphasised that the application of common sense may allow an inference of causation when circumstances other than a positive medical opinion permit it.[57] This opinion was

[52] *Snell v Farrell* (n 1 above) 330. See also: England: WT Tsushima and KK Nakano, *Effective Medical Testifying: A Handbook for Physicians* (Oxford, Butterworth-Heinemann, 1998) 5; Australia: *Seltsam Pty Ltd v McGuiness* (n 44 above) paras 93–94 (Spigelman CJ) (non-medical); Canada: *Sigouin (Guardian as litem of) v Wong* (1991) 10 CCLT (2nd) 236 (BCSC) 271; *Heidebrecht v Fraser-Burrard Hospital Society* (BCSC, 10 October 1996) para 108; R Meeran, 'Problems of Causation in Environmental Personal Injury' (1992) *Solicitors' Journal* 804, 805; France: Bobleter (n 25 above) 27. See also: WS Malone, 'Ruminations on Cause-in-Fact' (1956) 9 *Stanford Law Review* 60, 64.

[53] K Lippel, *et al*, 'La preuve de la causalité et l'indemnisation des lésions attribuables au travail répétitif: rencontre des sciences de la santé et du droit' (1999) 17 *Windsor Year Book Access Justice* 35, 37. On the danger of confusing the scientific and legal burdens of evidence: Lippel, *et al* (above) 76 and ff and K Lippel, 'L'incertitude des probabilités en droit et en médecine' (1991–92) 22 *Revue de droit de l'Université de Sherbrooke* 445, 449.

[54] Canada: *Snell v Farrell* (n 1 above) 330; *Robinson v Sydenham District Hospital Corp* (2000) 130 OAC 109 (OntCA) 119; *Dybongco-Rimando Estate v Jackiewicz* (2001) CarswellOnt 3219 (OntSC, 28 August 2001) para 35; *Lurtz v Duchesne* (n 46 above) paras168 and 346; *Aristorenas v Comcare Health Services* (2004) WL 1938380, Carswell Ont 3599 (OntSCtJ, 7 September 2004) para 68; *Fournier v Wiens* (2004) 33 Alta LR (4th) 114 (AltaQB) para 97; *Bear (Litigation Guardians of) v Lambos* (2005) CarswellSask 232 (Sask QB, 28 March 2005) para 45; *O'Grady v Stokes* (2005) ABQB 247, Carswell Alta 578 (AltaQB, 26 April 2005) para 202; *Miller v Budzinski* (2005) BCD Civ J 516; (2004) BCD Civ J Lexis 1530 (BCSC, 24 December 2004) para 469; Australia: *Naxakis v Western General Hospital* (n 20 above) 280–81; *Seltsam Pty Ltd v McGuiness* (n 44 above) paras 93 and 143 (Spigelman CJ) (non-medical).

[55] Summarised at ch 1, text to fn 244.

[56] Canada: *Snell v Farrell* (n 1 above) 335–36; *Meringolo (Committee of) v Oshawa General Hospital* (1991) 46 OAC 260 (CA) 272; *Taylor v Hogan* (n 5 above) 50; *Logozar v Golder* (1994) 21 CCLT (2nd) 203 (AltaCA) 225–26 (Harradence JA, diss) (non-medical); Québec: *Kirschenbaum Green v Syrchin* [1997] RRA 39 (CA) 45. Against: *McGhee v National Coal Board* (n 4 above) 7 (Lord Wilberforce), approved recently by the House of Lords in *Fairchild v Glenhaven* (n 2 above).

[57] *Snell v Farrell* (n 1 above) 335–36.

reiterated by the Supreme Court of Canada shortly afterwards in *Laferrière v Lawson* (1991), a civil law case:

> Cases in which the evidence is scarce or seemingly inconclusive present the greatest difficulty. It is perhaps worthwhile to repeat that a judge will be influenced by expert scientific opinions which are expressed in terms of statistical probabilities or test samplings, but he or she is not bound by such evidence. Scientific findings are not identical to legal findings. Recently, in *Snell v Farell* . . ., this court made clear . . . that '[c]ausation need not be determined by scientific precision' and that '[I]t is not . . . essential that the medical experts provide a firm opinion supporting the plaintiff's theory of causation' . . . . Both this Court and the Quebec Court of Appeal have frequently stated that proof of the causal link must be established on the balance of probabilities taking into account all the evidence which is before it, factual, statistical and that which the judge is entitled to presume.[58]

The principles stated by the Supreme Court of Canada have since become the basis of judicial assessment of causation in medical malpractice cases in both Québec civil law and Canadian common law.[59]

Hence, according to Canadian and Québec, as well as to lesser extent, English and Australian, sources, the tribunal is not bound by scientific debates or absence of scientific conclusions on causation. This rule extends to the statistical evidence inevitably presented by the parties in cases involving uncertain causation.[60] Despite the assistance this type of evidence may provide to the judge, the doctrine and case law in England, Canada, and Québec warn against the undue use of statistics, mathematics, and epidemiological studies to prove causation[61] by issuing reminders that courts must not be paralysed by them.[62] In *Laferrière v Lawson*, the Supreme Court of Canada indicated that statistical evidence may be helpful as

[58] (N 2 above) 606 (reference omitted). See also, Canada: *Lankenau Estate v Dutton (*n 46 above) 717; *Heidebrecht v Fraser-Burrard Hospital* (n 46 above) paras 107–9; *McNeil v Easterbrook* (n 46 above) para 15; Québec: *Hôtel-Dieu d'Amos v Gravel* [1989] RJQ 64 (CA) 71.

[59] Canada: *Pierre (Next Friend of) v Marshall* [1994] 8 WWR 478 (AltaQB) 505–6; *Briffett v Gander and District Hospital Board* (n 48 above) 291; *Athey v Leonati* (n 2 above) 467; *Elliott v Nicholson* (1998) 171 NSR (2nd) 252 (NSSC) 269; *Wilson v Byrne* (2004) WL 1201437, Carswell Ont 2314, OJ No 2360 (OntSCtJ, 4 June 2004) para 83; Québec: *St-Jean v Mercier* (CA) (n 2 above) 1666. But see: Mongeon J in *Therrien v Launay* (2005) WL 434762, Carswell Que 486 (SC, 4 March 2005) paras 76–77. The Supreme Court of Canada acts as a court of both civil law and common law in the field of private law, depending on whether it hears appeals from Québec or the common law provinces.

[60] S Uglow, *Evidence: Text and Materials* (London, Sweet & Maxwell, 1997) 61; T Anderson and W Twining, *Analysis of Evidence: How to Do Things with Facts* (London, Weidenfeld & Nicolson, 1991) 386–87. The question of the use of statistical probabilities in court, for instance through reliance on Bayes Theorem, is not reviewed in this text. On this question: R Goldberg, *Causation and Risk in the Law of Torts* (Oxford, Hart Publishing, 1999).

[61] *Laferrière v Lawson* (n 2 above) 609; *Judge v Huntingdon Health Authority* (1994) 27 BMLR 107 (QB) 122; *Elvicta Wood v Huxley* (n 46 above); Uglow (n 60 above) 61.

[62] *Brooks v J & P Coates (UK) Ltd* [1984] 1 All ER 702 (QBD) 711. See also: *Seltsam Pty Ltd v McGuiness* (n 44 above) para 78.

indicative but is not determinative, adding that 'where statistical evidence does not indicate causation on the balance of probabilities, causation in law may nonetheless exist where evidence in the case supports such a finding.'[63]

A ground for caution is the fact that while general statistics give indications as to a specific situation in the general population, they say nothing about the individual situation of the particular plaintiff, which should remain the court's main concern.[64]

This does not signify that courts refuse to look at statistical, mathematical, or epidemiological evidence and take it into account in their assessment of causation. Many courts do so to a greater or lesser extent:[65] a 'clinical epidemiological study cannot in itself prove causation but it may justify an inference that a statistical association reflects a causal link.'[66] Where there is evidence about a particular plaintiff, however, that evidence must be preferred.[67] Keeping distances from mathematical and statistical evidence may, however, prove difficult for the judge dealing with scientific causal uncertainty as this may be the only evidence available to him.[68]

The fact that causation is not determined by the expert but by an independent judge who must not take dictation from the scientific evidence implies that he is free to take into account other considerations when assessing causation. These consist of lay evidence and the judge's common sense. They may also, admittedly or not, include policy considerations.

[63] *Laferrière v Lawson* (n 2 above) 606 and 609; *SFP v MacDonald* (1999) 234 AR 273 (AltaQB) 281. Eg, *Yates v Rockwell Graphic Systems Ltd* [1988] 1 ICR 8 (QB) 16; Cass civ 1st, 9 July 1996, Bull civ 1996.I.n306, Resp civ et ass 1996.comm.385; *Suchorab v Urbanski* (1997) 156 Sask R 46 (QB) 57. See also the criminal law case of *R v Adams*, The Times, 9 May 1996 (CA): statisticians' expert evidence referring to Bayes' Theorem trespassed on an area peculiarly and exclusively within the jury's province, namely the way in which they assess the relationship between one piece of evidence and another. Jurors assess evidence and reach conclusions not by means of a formula, mathematical or otherwise, but by the joint application of their individual common sense and knowledge of the world to the evidence before them.

[64] *Hotson v East Berkshire Area Health Authority* [1987] 2 WLR 287 (CA) 303 (Croom-Johnson LJ): To be a figure in statistics does not by itself give the plaintiff a cause of action; *Gregg v Scott* [2005] 2 AC 176 (HL) para 28 (Lord Nicholls), para 111 (Lord Hope). See also: *Van Dyke v Grey Bruce Regional Health Centre* (2005) OJ No 2219; ONC Lexis 2415 (OntCA, 3 June 2005) para 49; D Gerecke, 'Risk Exposure as Injury: Alleviating the Injustice of Tort Causation Rules' (1990) 35 *McGill Law Journal* 797, 813–14. Gerecke questions the requirement of focussing on the particular plaintiff's situation, however, on the basis that all evidence is, ultimately, probabilistic.

[65] Eg, of extensive analyses of statistical, epidemiological, mathematical evidence, England: *Loveday v Renton* [1990] 1 Med LR 117 (QBD); *Reay v British Nuclear Fuels Plc* [1994] 5 Med LR 1 (QB); *Griffiths v British Coal Corporation* [1998] EWJ No 4656 (QB, 23 January 1998); Canada: *Rothwell* v *Raes* (1988) 54 DLR (4th) 193 (OntHCJ); (1990) 76 DLR (4th) 280 (OntCA); Québec: *Berthiaume v Val Royal Lasalle Ltée* [1992] RJQ 76 (CS).

[66] Osler J in *Rothwell v Raes* (n 65 above) 210. See also: *Laferrière v Lawson* (n 2 above) 608–9.

[67] *Pauluik v Paraison* (n 5 above) 151 (Helper JA) and 154 (Kroft JA) (non-medical); *SFP v MacDonald* (n 63 above) 281.

[68] Eg, *The CJD Litigation: Group A and C Plaintiffs* (1998) 54 BMLR 100 (QBD) 103.

C. Common Sense, Lay Evidence and Policy

The importance of common sense and of the whole of the evidence in the general assessment of causation has already been stressed.[69] In the medical liability context, it is invoked in advancing the view that expert evidence is not conclusive; causation must be ultimately decided on the basis of the uninitiated judge's common sense.[70] Judicial common sense must rest not just on the scientific proof but on the whole of the evidence. The expert opinions consequently enjoy no special status in court, but must be put in context and assessed in the light of the other evidence adduced by the parties.[71] Judges are therefore allowed to rest their decisions on considerations which would never be taken into account in a purely scientific analysis. Such considerations may relate to concerns about economic, social, or moral values that the law pursues.[72] More frequently, they relate to lay elements of proof introduced in evidence by the parties.

In Canada, Australia and Québec, courts have indeed recalled that the judge may find causation proven on the basis of his common sense, despite a inconclusive scientific opinion, if the *other elements of the evidence* supports such a conclusion.[73] This has been emphasised even in France by Penneau, who stresses that the judge's latitude to take into account considerations other than purely scientific ones allows him to affirm his independence *vis-à-vis* scientific evidence:

> *La véritable signification de la liberté d'appréciation du juge apparaît alors, en présence de l'information technique que représente l'expertise normalement et objectivement conduite. Si le juge n'est pas tenu de suivre l'avis des experts, ce ne peut être parce qu'il peut nier techniquement un avis qu'il demande précisément en raison de son incompétence. C'est parce qu'au cours de la transposition qu'il est obligé d'opérer, le plus souvent, du domaine technique au domaine juridique, d'autres éléments sont intervenus, qu'il doit prendre en considération sur le terrain du droit où lui seul est compétent.*

[69] See ch 1, text between fns 8 and 11, and text at fn 91 and 144. For a discussion of the common sense justification for relaxing rules of proof of causation, see ch 5, text between fns 291 and 313.

[70] *Edmison v Boyd* (1987) 77 AR 321 (AltaCA) 322; *Hock (Next Friend of) v Hospital for Sick Children* (1998) 106 OAC 321 (OntCA) 347; T Ward, 'Law's Truth, Lay Truth and Medical Science' in H Reece, (ed), *Law and Science* (Oxford, OUP, 1998) 243, 260: although it is a priori difficult to admit that common sense be relied on to deal with a purely scientific question. Against: A Beever, 'Cause-in-Fact: Two Steps out of the Mire' (2001) 51 *University of Toronto Law Review* 327, 364.

[71] Eg, Canada: *Hock v Hospital for Sick Children* (n 70 above) 347; Québec: *Montreal Tramways v Léveillé* (n 39 above) 480; *Kirschenbaum Green v Syrchin* [1993] RRA 821 (CS) 836, *aff'd*, (n 56 above); *Stéfanik v Hôpital Hôtel-Dieu de Lévis* [1997] RJQ 1332 (CS) 1352; *Zanchettin v DeMontigny* [2000] RRA 298 (CA) 305. See also, in England: Emson (n 12 above) 367–69. But see: Cross and Tapper (n 42 above) 570: the expert's testimony is likely to carry more weight than that of an ordinary witness.

[72] Below, text between fns 75 and 86.

[73] *Snell v Farrell* (n 1 above) 336; *Laferrière v Lawson* (n 2 above) 606–7; *St-Jean v Mercier* (CA) (n 2 above) 1666 and Kélada (n 35 above) 275. See also, in Australia: *Black v Tomislav Lipovac BHNF* (n 20 above) para 97; *Naxakis v Western General Hospital* (n 20 above) 281 and 314.

> *On mélange autrement le fait et le droit. Il faut entendre que sur le terrain particulier du fait technique, où il est en règle générale radicalement incompétent, la compétence de l'expert s'impose au juge. Mais sur le terrain du droit, la compétence du juge reprend toute sa plénitude, et le rapport d'expertise ne devient qu'*un élément particulier de l'ensemble *sur lequel le juge fondera sa décision* (emphasis added).[74]

Despite efforts made by courts of both traditions to justify their conclusions on grounds of principle,[75] departures from traditional principles of causation in cases involving evidentiary gaps have also been repeatedly justified on the basis of policy, especially in common law jurisdictions.[76] Such influence is harder to identify in civil law, which, in theory, is subject to a body of pre-existing rules dictating the solution to the judge in a particular case.[77] Nevertheless, in practice, policy factors also play a significant part in this tradition's courts' decisions.[78] Such policy motivations are not always clearly expressed, however, prompting pleas for clearer appeals to policy.[79]

Still, cases involving uncertain causation have been the occasion, especially in the common law, for interesting discussions of policy considerations for assisting plaintiffs, as well as overt departures from the orthodoxy in order to pursue

[74] Penneau (n 35 above) para 99.

[75] England: MJ Powers and NH Harris, *Clinical Negligence*, 3rd edn, (London, Butterworths, 2000) 895; F Cownie, 'Medical Negligence—A Question of Policy?' (1987) *Professional Negligence* 95, 97; EI Picard, *Legal Liability of Doctors and Hospitals in Canada*, 2nd edn, (Toronto, Carswell, 1994) 185 and 189 and the 1996 edition: EI Picard and GB Robertson, *Legal Liability of Doctors and Hospitals in Canada*, 3rd edn, (Toronto, Carswell, 1996) 221; MA Jones, *Textbook on Torts*, 8th edn, (Blackstone, London, 2002) 253. But see Stapleton who stresses that she has yet to hear a compelling account of the difference between principle and policy: J Stapleton, 'The Golden Thread at the Heart of Tort Law: Protection of the Vulnerable' (2003) 24 *Australian Bar Review* 1, 2.

[76] J Stapleton, 'Scientific and Legal Approaches to Causation' in I Freckelton and D Mendelson, *Causation in Law and Medicine* (Hampshire, Ashgate Darmouth, 2002) 18; G Edmond and D Mercer, 'Rebels without a Cause? Judges, Medical and Scientific Evidence and the Uses of Causation' in I Freckelton and D Mendelson, *Causation in Law and Medicine* (Hampshire, Ashgate Darthmouth, 2002) 93, EJ Weinrib, 'A Step Forward in Factual Causation' (1975) 38 *MLR* 518, 532–33. The importance of policy in medical negligence cases is also insisted upon: Cownie (n 75 above) 96. But see M McInnes, 'Causation in Tort Law: A Decade at the Supreme Court of Canada' (2000) 63 *Saskatchewan Law Review* 445, 457: Policy is used only to supplement basic causal tests.

[77] CC Emanuelli, 'Le droit comparé selon une perspective canadienne' (1980) 40 *Revue du Barreau* 75, 84. The style of judgments in France also precludes exhaustive references to considerations of policy: K Zweigert and H Kötz, T Weir, (tr), *Introduction to Comparative Law*, 3rd edn, (Oxford, Clarendon Press, 1998) 19.

[78] France: G Boyer-Chammard and P Monzein, *La responsabilité médicale* (Paris, PUF, 1974) 98 and 102; Dorsner-Dolivet, note under Cass civ 1st, 17 November 1982; C Potier, *Les présomptions de causalité* (Paris, Mémoire de DEA Paris I Panthéon Sorbonne 1996) 16 and 21; Flour and Aubert (n 8 above) 162. Concessions of this kind are, not surprisingly, rare in Québec, given its courts' orthodox approach to the assessment of causation in medical liability. This section, however, avoids discussing the legitimacy of policy considerations in the civil law.

[79] J Stapleton (n 76 above) 21, Cownie (n 75 above) 97. See also: NJ Mullany, 'Common Sense Causation—An Australian View' (1992) 12 *OJLS* 431, 436; R Travers 'Medical Causation' (2002) 76 *Australian Law Journal* 258, 268; Cownie (n 75 above) 97, expressing, however, the need for legislation in this area.

policy goals.[80] A common justification is that the assessment of causation may and should vary according to the purpose for which the causal question is asked.[81] Another is the concern not to leave such cases without a remedy, thereby rendering useless a legal duty that has been breached.[82] Other policy factors invoked include the need for compensation[83] and deterrence; the unavailability of evidence because of the defendant's fault; the relationship between the parties and their respective social status; and the fact that all the alternative causes are culpable.[84] More generally, there are often direct or implicit references to the desire to assist the victim of a proven wrong the cause of which is difficult to demonstrate.[85] Counterbalancing the above, the desire to protect the medical profession against extensive liability is also expressed.[86]

Words of caution are however voiced. Honoré has warned that causal principles should not without good reason be swept aside on grounds of legal policy 'in favour of imposing the risk of harm on a party who has not caused it' in order to avoid dispensing 'palm tree justice'.[87] In the landmark English decision in *Wilsher v Essex* (1988), Lord Bridge was of the opinion that we would do society nothing but disservice 'if we made the forensic process still more unpredictable and hazardous by

[80] Eg, *Chester v Afshar* (n 2 above) paras 17–18, 24–25 (Lords Steyn), 81, 85, 87 (Lord Hope) and 101 (Lord Walker). Against: Lords Bingham and Hoffmann, dissenting in *Fairchild v Glenhaven* (n 2 above); T Honoré, 'Medical Non-Disclosure, Causation and Risk: *Chappel v Hart*' (1999) 7 *Torts Law Journal* 1, 20–21.

[81] *Fairchild v Glenhaven* (n 2 above) paras 48–49 and 54 (Lord Hoffman). See also: *Chappel v Hart* (1998) 195 CLR 232 (Aust HC) 256 (para 63) (Gummow J); 276 (para 96) (Kirby J); 285 (para 122) (Hayne J); *Rosenberg v Percival* (2001) 205 CLR 434 (Aust HC) paras 85–86 (Gummow J); *Chester v Afshar* (n 2 above), especially the reasons of Lord Hope, paras 83–84; all three judgments dealt with the medical duty to inform however. Outside medical liability: *Environment Agency v Empress Car Co* [1999] 2 AC 22 (HL) 29: adding that answers will depend upon the rule by which responsibility is being attributed. The House of Lords seems to restrict this comment to questions of causation arising for the purpose of attributing responsibility, however, which makes it more relevant to legal rather than factual causation; *Kuwait Airways Corporation v Iraqi Airways Co (Nos 4 and 5)* [2002] 2 WLR 1353 (HL) para 128 (Lord Hoffmann).

[82] *Chester v Afshar* (n 2 above) para 87 (Lord Hope), in the context of the medical duty to inform. See also: Lord Hoffmann in *Fairchild v Glenhaven* (n 2 above) paras 62 and 69.

[83] *Gavalas v Singh* (2001) 3 VR 404 (VicCA) 417.

[84] JG Fleming, 'Probabilistic Causation in Tort Law' (1989) 68 *Canadian Bar Review* 661, 671. Compare: *Fitzgerald v Lane* [1987] 1 QB 781, 810, *aff'd* [1989] 1 AC 328 (HL) and *Wilsher v Essex Area Health Authority* [1988] 1 AC 1074 (HL) in England.

[85] Lambert JA in *Haag v Marshall* (1989) 61 DLR (4th) 371 (BCCA) 379; *Briffett v Gander and District Hospital Board* (n 48 above) 301. (Marshall JA); Klar, appendix to *SFP MacDonald* (n 63 above) 303, Boyer-Chammard and Monzein (n 78 above) 102. Against: *Lévesque v Hôpital Notre-Dame de Sainte-Croix* [1993] RRA 93, 104. A desire to favour the victim over the solvable and usually insured defendant is also raised: *Vyner v Waldenberg Brothers Ltd* [1946] 1 KB 50, 55; Potier (n 78 above) 25; *Sindell v Abbott Laboratories* 26 Cal 3d 588; 2 ALR 4th 1061; 163 Cal Rptr 132; 607 P 2d 924 (Cal, 1980).

[86] *Lalumière v X* [1946] CS 294 (Qué) 295; *Whitehouse v Jordan* [1980] 1 All ER 650 (CA), 658–59 and 662; R Savatier, 'Le droit des chances et des risques dans les assurances, la responsabilité civile dans la médecine et sa synthèse dans l'assurance de responsabilité médicale' (1973) 44 *Revue générale des assurances terrestres* 457, 478 and 480.

[87] Honoré (n 80 above) 6–7.

distorting the law to accommodate the exigencies of what may seem hard cases'.[88] Despite these warnings, it is hard to ignore the fact that causal uncertainty confronts the judge with social choices as to which party should be made to bear the burden of the uncertainty.[89] The following chapters will demonstrate that these choices have often been made in favour victims of proven negligence by not letting scientific uncertainty burden their attempts to seek compensation.

The judge's autonomy and independence towards scientific evidence and the impact of common sense and lay elements of facts on his decisions, as well as that of policy, can therefore lead courts to conclusions that may be scientifically incorrect although totally legally defensible.[90] It may justify the court in departing from the experts' assessment of causation[91] or in choosing amongst divergent expert medical opinions with regard to causation.

Section 3

Flexibility in Light of Expert Controversies

All the principles above are tested when experts disagree. In these circumstances, one may ask whether the courts are allowed to invoke their autonomy and rely on common sense and lay evidence in order to choose between divergent expert opinions. Although we have argued that such a situation does not strictly involve pure scientific uncertainty, it deserves special attention, since causal uncertainty is often thought to be the result of medical controversies, and the solutions described in chapters 3 to 5 have been invoked by judges in such situations.

When assessing fault, the tribunal cannot substitute its own opinion for that of specialists or attempt to settle scientific debates or divergent medical opinions.[92]

[88] *Wilsher v Essex* (QB) (n 75 above) 883. See also: *Fitzgerald v Lane* (n 84 above) (non medical): Slade J warns that '[b]road considerations of justice may be potentially misleading guides where questions of causation arise' but nevertheless takes a decision admittedly based on policy; L'Heureux-Dubé J in *Lapointe v Hôpital Le Gardeur* (1992) 90 DLR (4th) 7; [1992] 1 SCR 351, 380: '*la sympathie est un mauvais guide*'; *Bureau v Dupuis* [1997] RRA 459 (QuéCS); Lord Phillips in *Gregg v Scott* (n 64 above) para 172; Power and Harris (n 75 above) 895.

[89] A Gossement, note under Civ 1st, 23 September 2003 (n 43 above).

[90] An oft-cited example is the case of Charlie Chaplin, who in 1946 was ordered to pay child support even though blood tests had revealed he was not the father of the child in question: *Berry v Chaplin* 74 Cal App 2d 652; 169 P 2d 442 (Cal, 1946).

[91] Cass civ 1st, 13 February 1985 (n 36 above).

[92] England: *Clark v MacLennan* [1983] 1 All ER 416 (QB) 424, *Newbury v Bath District Health Authority* (1999) 47 BMLR 138 (HCJ QBD) 5; Canada: *ter Neuzen v Korn* (1995) 127 DLR (4th) 577;

This is true of all the jurisdictions studied herein, except for Australia.[93] As long as the defendant has complied with a practice recognised as reasonable by the medical profession, he cannot be held liable even if the technique he used is not unanimously approved[94] or even if a different, equally or more reasonable, technique exists.[95] Save in exceptional cases where the court finds that the practice accepted by the profession is itself unreasonable,[96] the judge must refuse to take sides on scientific controversies involving different but equally defensible schools of thought because he lacks competence to make a judgment on the appropriateness of a medical practice. In France, Penneau stresses how illogical it is for the judge to seek experts' conclusions on fault because of his own technical lack of competence and then reserve the option of not following them: '*Il y a dans cette dernière démarche un risque de contresens pouvant même aboutir à faire méconnaître au juge, obnubilé par sa pseudo-connaissance livresque, les véritables problèmes juridiques qui sont pourtant seuls de sa véritable compétence*'[97]

The above rule does not prevent the judge from weighing the objectivity and credibility of the different opinions; the expert's experience and competence to render the opinion in question; or the harmony of the opinion with the rest of the factual evidence. If the different opinions are of equal value, however, the controversy leads to the rejection of the plaintiff's claim on the ground that he has not discharged his burden of proof with regard to fault.

[1995] 3 SCR 674, 696–97; France: M Planiol and G Ripert, *Traité pratique de droit civil français: Les obligations*, t6 (Paris, LGDJ, 1925–34) para 525; Québec: *Ducharme v Royal Victoria Hospital* (n 20 above) 168; *Coulombe v Lemieux* [1945] CS 435, 438; *Fafard v Gervais* [1948] CS 128, 129; *Savoie v Gaudette* [1976] CA 127, 129–30; *Stacey v Plante* [1979] CS 665, 668; *Dodds v Schierz* (n 20 above) 2635 (L'Heureux-Dubé J); *Blass v Antoniou* [1989] RRA 816 (CS) 816; *Weiswall v Gordon* [1998] RRA 31 (CA) 821; Jarjoura and Nootens (n 17 above) 52.

[93] *Rogers v Whitaker* (1992) 175 CLR 479: The test for negligence is *not* to be determined solely and even primarily by reference to the practice followed or respected by a responsible body of opinion in the medical profession.

[94] *Stacey v Plante* (n 92 above) 668; *Lapointe v Hôpital Le Gardeur* (n 2 above) 363; *Bolitho v City and Hackney Health Authority* [1998] AC 232 (HL) 778–79; JL Baudouin and P Deslauriers, *La responsabilité civile*, 6th edn, (Cowansville, Yvon Blais, 2003) paras 1452 and 1490; Jarjoura and Nootens (n 17 above) 254–55.

[95] *ter Neuzen v Korn* (n 92 above) 695.

[96] England: *Bolitho v City and Hackney Health Authority* (n 94 above) 242–43 (Lord Browne-Wilkinson); Canada: *ter Neuzen v Korn* (n 92 above) 696–98 and 701: allowed where the practice is '"fraught with obvious risks" such that anyone is capable of finding it negligent, without the necessity of judging matters requiring diagnostic or clinical expertise' or if the matter falls within the 'ordinary common sense of juries'; *Walker Estate v York Finch General Hospital* (2001) 198 DLR (4th) 193; [2001] 1 SCR 647, para 82; Québec: *G v C* [1960] BR 161, 167 and 171; *Roberge v Bolduc* (n 12 above) 437; *Prat v Poulin* [1997] RJQ 2669 (CA) 2693; *Weiswall v Gordon* (n 92 above) 824, *rev'd* [1998] RRA 31 (CA).

[97] Penneau (n 35 above) 54–55. See also: Rivard J in *Létourneau v R* [1965] BR 77, 78.

Can this rule be literally transposed to the assessment of causation?[98] For some, the answer to this is in the affirmative.[99] This opinion tends to ignore that the assessment of causation must equally be based on the judge's common sense and on the whole of the evidence, lay and scientific, and that expert opinions on causation are in theory not determinative of the tribunal's conclusions. This principle has led English courts to distinguish between the judicial attitude to controversial medical expert opinion with regard to fault and causation.[100] They have also insisted on judges not resorting to the rules regarding the burden of proof to abdicate their responsibility for resolving a difference in medical opinion with regard to causation.[101] Finally, doctrinal writers have stressed the necessity for the judge to decide for himself which view is to be preferred, since it is his responsibility to decide whether the standard of proof is satisfied.[102]

Canadian and Québec cases also agree that a choice must be made amongst the controversial medical expertises, as long as the choice is based on acceptable evidence. This position was unanimously confirmed by the Supreme Court of Canada in the civil law case of *St-Jean v Mercier* (2002):

> A trial judge must reach a legal conclusion based on the scientific evidence and other evidence presented. Not to come to a definitive conclusion on a balance of probabilities amounts to an undue advantage granted to the defendant, who might simply need to come up with a plausible but contrary scientific theory in order to negative the plaintiff's claim. Such an approach is tantamount to an alteration of the standard of proof since the trial judge is no longer looking at which scientific theory is most probable. It is an error of law in the analysis of causation for a trial judge to conclude that he or she does not have the authority to make a final legal determination in the face of competing theories.
>
> There is room for the principle of judicial neutrality in the analysis of fault. It is appropriate for the courts not to take a position when there are competing but recognized medical theories on what is competent professional practice or an appropriate diagnosis. . . . However, it is not appropriate to be similarly neutral on matters of causation and

[98] The absence of French cases and commentaries on this issue is perhaps explained by the fact that medical evidence is usually offered by a single court-appointed expert.

[99] England: Peter Pain J in *Clark v MacLennan* (n 92 above) 425; T Hodgkinson, *Expert Evidence: Law and Practice* (London, Sweet & Maxwell, 1990) 15; Québec: *Labrosse v Hydro-Québec* (CS) cited at (n 42 above) 741 (CA); *St-Jean v Mercier* (CS, 27 January 1998) (rev'd on this point by the CA: (n 59 above) 1666 and the Supreme Court of Canada: [2002] 1 SCR 491; (2002) 209 DLR (4th) 513, paras 56–57); Giesen (n 21 above) 1056.

[100] Ebsworth J in *Newbury v Bath District HA* (n 92 above).

[101] *Sewell v Electrolux*, The Times, 7 November 1997 (CA). See also: *Loveday v Renton* (n 65 above) 123–24. But see *Bolitho v City and Hackney HA* (n 94 above) 779: the *Bolam test* may be relevant to causation in some cases and reintroduce deference towards the medical opinions, Emson (n 12 above) 369, MA Jones, *Textbook on Torts*, 8th edn, (London, Blackstone, 2002) 228–29. See also, in Québec: *Aubin v Moumdjian* (QuéSC, 5 April 2004) paras 29–30.

[102] Hart and Honoré (n 16 above) 411.

thereby refrain from determining whether causation has been established on the legal standard of balance of probabilities.[103]

Controversies with regard to causation are solved in some cases by putting the emphasis on the *whole* of the evidence[104] rather than on a strict attachment to the scientific evidence. More frequently, they are resolved by assessing the relative value of the experts' testimony and weighing the experts' credibility,[105] independence,[106] experience and authority,[107] objectivity,[108] and reliance on scientific literature and the case's facts.[109] Finally, conflicts are also resolved by paralleling the expert evidence with the facts of the case adduced in evidence which the tribunal finds proven.[110] Scientific evidence which is in harmony with the whole of the evidence must be preferred to expert evidence which is not.[111] Even though it may at first sight appear scientifically erroneous for a layperson to choose amongst divergent valid scientific opinions, the rules that causation does not have to be shown with scientific accuracy, that the judge is the sole person competent to assess whether the standard of proof of causation has been met, and that common sense, the whole of the evidence, and policy considerations must be the basis for its assessment, can justify such a choice.

[103] (N 99 above) paras 56–57 relying on Jutras (n 41 above) 902. Compare: *Bigcharles v Dawson Creek and District Health Care Society* [2001] 91 BCLR (3rd) 82 (BCCA). See also: *Pelletier v Roberge* [1991] RRA 726 (CA) 730; *Aslin v Otto* (1997) 151 DLR (4th) 176 (BCCA) 178–79; *Brazel v Nicholls* (2003) NSWCA 387 (1 December 2003) para 71.

[104] *Briffett v Gander and District Hospital Board* (n 48 above) 302; *Burke-Pietramala v Samad* (2004) BCD Civ J 1579; BCD Civ J Lexis 485 (BCSC, 5 April 2004) para 111, which does not make a sophisticated analysis of this rule when addressing causation, however; and, *Boothman v Poirier* (n 36 above) para 37.

[105] *Davies v Gabel Estate* [1995] 2 WWR 35 (QB) 47.

[106] *Rehman v University College London Hospitals NHS Trust* (2004) All ER (D) 435 (May) (QB, 20 May 2004) paras 78 and 82; *Burke-Pietramala v Samad* (n 104 above) paras 108–9.

[107] *Rothwell v Raes* (n 65 above) 282–83; *Bull v Devon Area Health Authority* (1989) 22 BMLR 79 (CA): See the trial judge's reasons at 106, *aff'd* at 108; *Pierre v Marshall* (n 59 above) 507; *Taylor v Hogan* (n 5 above) 257; *Taylor v West Kent* [1997] 8 Med LR 251 (QBD) 257; *Scott v Northern Devon Healthcare Trust* (QB, 31 July 2000) 8.

[108] *Elvicta Wood v Huxley* (n 46 above); *Mackell v Moulson* (n 17 above) para 84.

[109] *Bauer v Seager* (2000) 147 Man R (2nd) 1 (ManQB) 19. See generally: England: *Gates v McKenna* (1998) 48 BMLR 9 (QBD) 256; *Gray v Southampton and South West Hampshire Health Authority* (2000) 57 BMLR 148 (QBD); *Milkhu v North Western Hospitals NHS Trust* (2003) EWHC 94 (QB, 30 January 2003); Canada: *Brown (Nest Friend of) v University of Alberta Hospital* (1997) 145 DLR (4th) 63 (AltaQB); *Bigcharles v Dawson Creek* (n 103 above) para 71 (Hollinrake JA); Québec: *St-Jean v Mercier* (SCC) (n 2 above) paras 95–96.

[110] England: *Gray v Southampton and South West Hampshire Health Authority* (n 109 above) 154–55; *Elvicta Wood v Huxley* (n 46 above); Canada: *Bauer v Seager* (n 109 above) 19; *Jenkins v Knickle* (2003) PEIJ No 65, PESCTD 49 (PEISC, 23 June 2003) paras 58 and 83; Québec: *Miller v Brues* [1973] CA 902, 907; *Michaud v Bergeron* [1980] CA 246, 247 (non-medical); *La Garantie v Massicotte* (n 20 above) 18–19 (non-medical); *Hôtel-Dieu D'Amos v Gravel* (n 58 above).

[111] *Houde v Côté* (n 46 above) 728; *Zanchettin v Demontigny* (n 71 above) 301; *Jenkins v Knickle* (n 110 above) para 149.

Conclusion to Chapter 2

The review above has shown that judges working in the two legal traditions under study, and especially those of common law Canada, have found it crucial to insist on the necessity of introducing more flexibility into the assessment of causation in cases affected by scientific uncertainty. In the area of medical malpractice, this concern has led some of them to stress the mutability of the burden and standard of proof. Flexibility is also validated through reminders, not just of judges' independence from medical experts, but also of the fact that legal and scientific notions of causation are not symmetrical. Finally, the exercise of flexibility was observed in judges' expression of their independence from expert evidence when addressing expert controversies.

Scientific uncertainties have not only led to a challenge to the traditional rules of evidence and the affirmation of the need for flexibility and judicial independence in the assessment of causation. In fact, these have proven insufficient to meet the objective of assistance to the plaintiff. The courts of the five jurisdictions have consequently also sought to find means in the substantive law of civil liability and evidence to attain this flexibility concretely and efficiently. They have thus experimented with different concepts and tools in an attempt, in cases in which they thought just to do so, to bypass the effects of the traditional requirements of the burden and standard of proof of causation and assist victims who, through no fault of their own, are unable to prove causation.[112]

Despite the obvious aim of not letting uncertainty of evidence prevent an innocent victim from recovering from a negligent defendant, the courts have introduced a fair measure of uncertainty as to when and how strict adherence to the traditional rules of evidence can be departed from. Nevertheless, one may generalise by saying that in the field of medical malpractice, French courts tend to rely mainly on the concept of loss of chance (chapter 4), while the courts of Canada, England, and Québec reach this flexibility through inferences and factual presumptions (chapter 5). Australia is situated in the middle, with its courts having relied on both loss of chance and inferences to deal with uncertain causation in medical cases. In very limited circumstances, reversal of the burden of proof has also been resorted to in some jurisdictions (chapter 3).

[112] See also: MA Jones, *Medical Negligence*, 3rd edn, (London, Sweet & Maxwell, 2003) 5–20.

3

Reversal of the Burden of Proving Causation

After some attempts at imposing this solution in England, Canada, and, on very rare occasions, Québec, the current state of the law is now clear: the burden of proving causation is and shall remain with the plaintiff.[1] Exceptions are provided for in very limited circumstances, particularly in cases involving factual rather than scientific uncertainty. This chapter very briefly sets out the cases in which reversal is accepted as a solution to causative uncertainties in each legal tradition. It also reviews the diverse attempts at extending this solution beyond these cases and describes the current impact of reversal of the onus of proof as a solution to scientific causal uncertainties.

Section 1

Common Law

A. Reversal Prior to *McGhee*

The Canadian Supreme Court recently recalled in *Snell v Farrell* (1990) that the burden of proof of causation is not immutable. One of the instances in which this has long been recognised in Canada is illustrated by *Cook v Lewis* (1951),[2] which was concerned with the problem of the indeterminate defendant, namely, the difficulty of identifying the author of the fault which caused the damage. Even though this question is essentially one of factual uncertainty, it is nevertheless interesting for our purpose, as it demonstrates the courts' readiness to relax the traditional standard and burden of proof of causation when they lead to unjust

[1] England: *Bonnington Castings Ltd v Wardlaw* [1956] AC 613 (HL) 619–20 (Lord Reid) and 625 (Lord Keith); *Wilsher v Essex Area Health Authority* [1988] 1 AC 1074 (HL) 1090; Canada: *Snell v Farrell* (1990) 72 DLR (4th) 222; [1990] 2 SCR 311, 321, 326–27; and *Davies v Gabel Estate* [1995] 2 WWR 35 (QB).

[2] *Cook v Lewis* [1951] 1 DLR 1; SCR 830.

results. Moreover, the underlying principles and justifications for doing so are relevant to a greater variety of cases fraught with uncertainty.

The claimant was shot in the face while hunting. A party of three hunters admitted discharging their guns in the vicinity almost simultaneously. At trial, the jury found the plaintiff had been shot by one of the three hunters but was not able to say which one and consequently rejected the claim. Presented with this difficulty, the Supreme Court of Canada resolved it with the assistance of the California Supreme Court decision in *Summers v Tice* (1948),[3] which involved similar facts. As in *Summers*, the defendants in *Cook v Lewis* were held jointly and severally liable and it was up to them to prove that their individual act was not the cause of the harm.[4]

At first sight, this solution appears burdensome to the defendants, on whom is imposed full compensation of a damage some of them may not have caused.[5] It also seems to overlook the fact that the different defendants may be facing the same evidential difficulty as the plaintiff.[6] Various justifications have been suggested for adopting a more severe attitude towards the defendants, however. The first rests on the fact that all the defendants have been negligent and consequently it is clear the injury was not caused by neutral conduct, ie, by factors unconnected to the defendant or which are the fault of no one.[7] In these circumstances, it is considered unjust that the entire loss should be borne by the innocent victim rather than the negligent defendants.[8] The law prefers a *50 per cent chance of doing justice to the certainty of doing injustice*[9] and refuses to let the victim fall between two tortfeasors.[10] Indeed, the fact that there are a limited number of possible defendants is also argued to justify reversal, since it limits the possibility of error. The fewer faulty defendants there are, the greater are the odds that each of them individually caused the damage.[11] It is also argued that in these cases partial causal connection is established, since the damage obviously flows from a risk that all of the defendants created. Finally, it is contended that allowing defendants to exploit the inherent difficulty as a defence of their breach of duty in such cases could render the duty in effect unenforceable.[12]

[3] *Summers v Tice* 33 Cal 2d 80, 199 P 2d 1; 5 ALR 2d 91 (Cal, 1948), embodied in the Restatement of Torts: Rest.2d Torts, §433B, sub-s (3).

[4] *Summers v Tice* (n 3 above) 4; *Cook v Lewis* (n 2 above) 833.

[5] P Cane, *Atiyah's Accidents, Compensation and the Law*, 6th edn, (London, Butterworths, 1999) 94.

[6] Cane (n 5 above) 94.

[7] *Snell v Farrell* (n 1 above) 327; PH Osborne, *The Law of Torts*, 2nd edn, (Toronto, Irwin Law, 2003) 57; HLA Hart and T Honoré, *Causation in the Law*, 2nd edn, (Oxford, Clarendon Press, 1985) 424 (discussing *Summers*).

[8] EJ Weinrib, 'A Step Forward in Factual Causation' (1975) 38 *MLR* 518, 524.

[9] GL Williams, 'Case and Comment' (1953) 31 *Canadian Bar Review* 315, 317.

[10] See also: *McGhee v National Coal Board* [1973] 1 WLR 1 (HL) 6 (Lord Wilberforce); Weinrib (n 8 above) 528.

[11] This leads some to argue that *Cook v Lewis* should apply only to cases in which the number of potential defendants is small: GHL Fridman, *The Law of Torts in Canada*, vol 1 (Toronto, Carswell, 1989) 342; Osborne (n 7 above) 57. In Australia, *Wintle v Conaust* agreed and refused to extend *Cook v Lewis* in a case involving five potential tortfeasors: [1981] VR 951 (CA).

[12] Weinrib (n 8 above) 529.

A second justification rests on the fact that the defendants' negligence has caused the impairment of the plaintiff's means of proof and it is believed unfair that the plaintiff should have to bear an onus which the defendant has rendered impossible to satisfy.[13] In *Cook v Lewis*, Rand J partly justified his decision on this basis; the defendants had not only violated the victim's substantive right to security but had also culpably impaired his remedial right of establishing liability.[14]

Even though the *Cook v Lewis* exception is still recognised,[15] subsequent Canadian cases have rejected its application to medical malpractice cases.[16] Moreover, reliance on the undermining of the plaintiff's means of proof as a justification for reversing the burden of proof in medical malpractice was also explicitly rejected.[17]

Cook v Lewis has no equivalent in the English case law.[18] English law has nevertheless been known to concede that reversal of the burden of proof can solve causal uncertainty, particularly in the context of industrial diseases.[19] This possibility was repudiated in *Bonnington Castings v Wardlaw* (1956),[20] a stand confirmed by a House of Lords majority in *McGhee v National Coal Board* (1973) and unanimously in *Wilsher v Essex Health Authority* (1988). Following Lord Wilberforce's minority opinion in *McGhee*, however, the possibility of extending this solution was hung in the balance for almost a decade in England and Canada, while it attracted limited attention in Australia.

[13] England: Hart and Honoré (n 7 above) 424–25 (discussing *Summers*); Canada: *Snell v Farrell* (n 1 above) 327; Osborne (n 7 above) 57; Weinrib (n 8 above) 525.

[14] *Cook v Lewis* (n 2 above) 832–33. See also: Cartwright J, p 842, *Summers v Tice* (n 3 above); Hart and Honoré (n 7 above) 424; Fridman (n 11 above) 342.

[15] *Snell v Farrell* (n 1 above) 327.

[16] *Joseph Brant Memorial Hospital v Koziol* (1977) 77 DLR (3rd) 161; [1978] 1 SCR 491, 500–1; *Bigcharles v Dawson Creek and District Health Care Society* (BCCA, 16 May 2001) paras 62–64 (Hollinrake JA). But see: *Hollis v Dow Corning Corp* (1995) 129 DLR (4th) 609; [1995] 4 SCR 634, 682: LaForest J relied on *Cook v Lewis* to reverse the burden of proof of causation onto a breast implants manufacturer's shoulders (analogy criticised at p 693 by Sopinka J on the basis of *Wilsher* and *Snell v Farrell*). The application of the rule of *Hollis* was subsequently restricted: *Lange v Bennett* [1964] 1 OR 233 (HC) 237–38; *Walker Estate v York Finch General Hospital* (2001) 198 DLR (4th) 193; [2001] 1 SCR 647, para 86 (Major J). It was also rejected in medical liability: *Bigcharles v Dawson Creek* (n 16 above) para 62–64. For a criticism: Fridman (n 11 above) 342.

[17] *Joseph Brant Memorial Hospital v Koziol* (1977) 77 DLR (3rd) 161; [1978] 1 SCR 491; *Bigcharles v Dawson Creek* (n 16 above) paras 62–64 (Hollinrake JA) (on the basis of *Snell v Farrell*).

[18] Some doctrinal writers accept it as affording a just solution, however: S Deakin, A Johnston and BS Markesinis, *Tort Law*, 4th edn, (Oxford, Clarendon Press, 2003) 192. But see: WVH Rogers, *Winfield and Jolowicz on Torts*, 16th edn, (London, Sweet & Maxwell, 2002) 222–23; JF Clerk, *Clerk and Lindsell on Torts*, 16th edn, (London, Sweet & Maxwell, 1989) 2–13. The indeterminate defendant problem is rather solved by the joint tortfeasors doctrine which requires that the defendants joined together to commit the wrongful act. It may now be dealt with, under some conditions, by the simple demonstration that the defendants have materially increased the plaintiff's risk of damage: *Fairchild v Glenhaven Funeral Services* [2002] 3 All ER 305 (HL) reinterpreting *McGhee v National Coal Board* (n 10 above): discussed at ch 5, text between fns 67 and 101.

[19] *Vyner v Waldenberg Brothers Ltd* [1946] KB 50, 55.

[20] (N 1 above) 619 (Lord Reid) and 625 (Lord Keith). This rejection was adopted in medical liability: *Barnett v Chelsea Hospital* [1969] 1 QB 428, 438 (Neil J).

B. *McGhee v National Coal Board* (1973)

1. *Lord Wilberforce's Position*

The plaintiff contracted dermatitis from exposure to brick dust at work and claimed against his employer for omitting to provide a shower on the work premises. His employer admitted negligence but pleaded absence of causation on the ground that the plaintiff was exposed to this risk in any event. The experts were in fact unable to say how exactly the process of dermatitis worked and, consequently, could not determine whether the possibility of showering after work could have permitted him to avoid the disease. At the time it was not certain whether dermatitis developed as a result of one single abrasion on the skin (here provoked by dust) or an accumulation of abrasions. It was only if the latter were the case that the court could find that the presence of a shower on the work premises would have allowed the plaintiff to avoid his damage. The Court of Appeal nevertheless held that causation was established. The majority of the House of Lords confirmed this decision by inferring causation on the ground that by his breach, the defendant employer had materially increased the plaintiff's risk of suffering from the damage.[21]

Lord Wilberforce went further, emphasising that the special facts of the case called for a special approach. He criticised the inferential solution as being a fiction drawn for policy reasons, since it was not supported by the medical experts' conclusions.[22] In his opinion, where a breach of duty and a loss which could be caused by such a breach are shown, it is up to the defendant as a 'matter of policy' to show that his breach did not cause the loss. The onus of proving causation could therefore be shifted onto the defendant's shoulders if it was shown that the defendant, by breaching his duty of care, had created a risk and injury occurs within the area of that risk.[23] In reaching this conclusion, Lord Wilberforce added that it is the employer not the worker who should suffer from such an inherent evidential difficulty, since the former is the creator of the risk and must be taken to have foreseen the possibility of damage.[24] Lord Wilberforce's reversal thus went beyond the justifications on which *Cook v Lewis* was grounded. The two alternative causes did not both flow from negligent conduct, even though they related to the same source of risk, which was under the defendant's control.[25] Moreover, the uncertainty was created not by the defendant's negligence but by the state of science, which was unable to explain the development process of dermatitis.[26]

[21] Discussed ch 5, text between fns 23 and 31.

[22] *McGhee v National Coal Board* (n 10 above) 7, now supported by *Fairchild v Glenhaven* (n 18 above). Against: ch 2, text between fns 44 and 68.

[23] *McGhee v National Coal Board* (n 10 above) 6–7.

[24] *Ibid*, p 6. Also a consideration of Lord Salmon at 12, who placed the burden of proof on the plaintiff, however.

[25] JG Fleming , 'Probabilistic Causation in Tort Law' (1989) 68 *Canadian Bar Review* 661, 670.

[26] Weinrib (n 8 above) 526.

Despite the fact that it was a minority opinion, Lord Wilberforce's view was adopted in Canada[27] and England[28] and was extended to Canadian medical malpractice instances.[29] Concurrently, other decisions rejected McGhee as an authority for shifting the burden of proving causation to the defendant's shoulders,[30] some relying rather on it to infer causation when the defendant materially increased the risk of damage and damage arose within the area of risk.[31] By the end of the eighties, Lord Wilberforce's reversal of the burden of proof had fallen into disfavour in both England and Canada, a disfavour intensified following the English House of Lords decision in *Wilsher*.

2. *Rejection of Lord Wilberforce's Opinion*

The clear rejection of Lord Wilberforce's position came from the House of Lords in *Wilsher v Essex Health Authority* (1988).[32] In this case, Lord Bridge noted *McGhee* laid down no new principle of law and the majority opinions in *McGhee* had reaffirmed the principle that the onus of proving causation lies with the

[27] *Dalpe v Edmundston (City of)* (1979) 25 NBR (2nd) 102 (CA); *Nowsco Well Service Ltd v Canadian Propane Gas & Oil Ltd* (1981) 122 DLR (3rd) 228 (SaskCA) 248; *Letnik v Metropolitan Toronto (Municipality)* (1988) 49 DLR (4th) 707 (FCA) 721 and 724. On this question: *Snell v Farrell* (n 1 above) 323–26; Osborne (n 7 above) 55; R Roth, 'Causation and the Burden of Proof: An Age Old Dilemma and a New Age Approach' (1992) 14 *Advocates' Quarterly* 70, 70; M McInnes, 'A Decade at the Supreme Court of Canada' (2000) 62 *Saskatchewan Law Review* 445, 447 and cases cited at fn 8; Fridman (n 11 above) 343 and cases cited at fn 780; AM Linden, *Canadian Tort Law*, 7th edn, (Markham, Butterworths, 2001) 111 and cases cited at fn 70; G Robertson, 'Overcoming the Causation Hurdle in Informed Consent Cases: The Principle in *McGhee v NCB*' (1984) 22 *University of Western Ontario Law Review* 75, 86.

[28] *Clark v MacLennan* [1983] 1 All ER 416 (QB) 427. In Australia, little influence is noticed in medical liability cases and beyond. But see the comments of Gaudron J in *Bennett v Minister of Community Welfare* (1992) 176 CLR 408 (AustHC) 420–21 (non-medical); and Kirby J in *Chappel v Hart* (1998) 195 CLR 232 (AustHC) 273, para 93 (Kirby J). See also: *Van Den Heuven v Tucker* [2003] 85 SASR 511 (SASC) para 96 which notes that this proposition has been controversial.

[29] *Powell v Guttman* (1978) 89 DLR (3rd) 180 (ManCA) 192 (it is not completely clear whether O'Sullivan JA intended to reverse the burden of proof or accept *McGhee* as introducing a new test for causation); *Clark v MacLennan* (n 28 above) 427. See also: MA Jones, *Medical Negligence*, 3rd edn, (London, Sweet & Maxwell, 2003) 5–24.

[30] *Hotson v East Berkshire Area Health Authority* [1987] 1 AC 750, 300 (Croom-Johnson LJ). In 1978, the Pearson Report (Great Britain, Report: *Royal Commission on Civil Liability and Compensation for Personal Injury*, Cmd 7054 (London, Her Majesty's Stationery Office, 1978)) para 1336 rejected a proposal to reverse the onus of proof of negligence in medical malpractice. This suggestion had been based on the fact that doctors are in a better position than patients to prove absence of negligence.

[31] England: *Bryce v Swan Hunter Group Plc* [1988] 1 All ER 659 (QB); Canada: *Dalpe v Edmundston (City of)* (n 27 above); *Haag v Marshall* (1989) 61 DLR (4th) 371 (BCCA) 378–79. This last interpretation has generally been considered as the more consistent one in Canada: EI Picard, *Legal Liability of Doctors and Hospitals in Canada*, 2nd edn, (Toronto, Carswell, 1984) 188 (also see the 1996 edition: EI Picard and GD Robertson, *Legal Liability of Doctors and Hospitals in Canada*, 3rd edn, (Scarborough, Carswell, 1996) 226); Roth (n 27 above) 77 and ch 5, text between fn 39 and 40. It also appears to be the predominant interpretation in Australia: ch 5, fn 109.

[32] (N 1 above). See also: *Seyfert v Burnaby Hospital Society* (1986) 27 DLR (4th) 96 (BCSC).

plaintiff while adopting a robust and pragmatic approach to the undisputed facts by being prepared to infer causation:[33]

> [T]o attempt to extract from [*McGhee*] some esoteric principle which in some way modifies, as a matter of law, the nature of the burden of proof of causation which a plaintiff or pursuer must discharge once he has established a relevant breach of duty is a fruitless one. . . .
>
> But, whether we like it or not, the law, which only Parliament can change, requires proof of fault causing damage as the basis of liability in tort. We should do society nothing but disservice if we made the forensic process still more unpredictable and hazardous by distorting the law to accommodate the exigencies of what may seem hard cases.[34]

Wilsher's rejection of the reversal option was adopted by the Supreme Court of Canada in *Snell v Farrell* (1990).[35] *Snell* reaffirmed the burden of proof must remain with the plaintiff throughout the case, save in exceptional circumstances illustrated by *Cook v Lewis*, ie, when it is clear that the injury has not been caused by neutral conduct:

> I have examined the alternatives arising out of the *McGhee* case. They were that the plaintiff simply proves that the defendant created a risk that the injury which occurred would occur. Or, what amounts to the same thing, that the defendant has the burden of disproving causation. If I were convinced that defendants who have a *substantial connection* to the injury were escaping liability because plaintiffs cannot prove causation under currently applied principles, I would not hesitate to adopt one of these alternatives. In my opinion, however, properly applied, the principles relating to causation are adequate to the task. Adoption of either of the proposed alternatives would have the effect of compensating plaintiffs where a substantial connection between the injury and the defendant's conduct is absent (emphasis added).[36]

In this statement, Sopinka J appears to open the door to reversal more generally in cases where the defendant is closely connected to the injury and is escaping

[33] (N 1 above) 1090. Interpretation confirmed in eg, *Best (An Infant) v Wellcome Foundation Ltd* [1993] ECC 342 (Sup Ct Irl) (manufacturer's liability); *Fairchild v Glenhaven* (n 18 above) paras 94–109 (Lord Hutton, dissenting on this point) (industrial disease). Against: *Fairchild v Glenhaven* (n 18 above) paras 21 and 35 (Lord Bingham), 45 (Lord Nicholls), 46 and 65 (Lord Hoffman) and 142 and 144 (Lord Rodger).

[34] (N 1 above) 569 and 571.

[35] Facts summarised ch 1, text to fn 244. This position was approved or emphasised in several cases thereafter, eg, *Briffett v Gander and District Hospital Board* (1996) 137 Nfld & PEIR 271 (CA) 287; *Hock (Next Friend of) v Hospital for Sick Children* (1998) 106 OAC 321 (CA) 346; *Meloche v Hotel Dieu Grace Hospital/Villa Marie* (1999) 179 DLR (4th) 77 (OntCA) 89. See also: *Couillard and Labutis v Waschulewski's Estate* (1988) 87 AR 161 (QB) 171. Outside medical malpractice: *Gallant v Fialkov* (1989) 69 OR (2nd) 297 (HCJ) 317; *Westco Storage Ltd v Inter-City Gas Utilities Ltd* (1989) 59 Man R (2nd) 37 (CA) 45; *Haag v Marshall* (n 31 above) 378; *Oiom v Brassington* (1990) 52 BCLR (2nd) 240 (BCCA) 254.

[36] *Snell v Farrell* (n 1 above) 326–27. See also: *Lawrence v Smith* (1991) 84 Alta LR 26 (QB) 38; *Walker Estate v York Finch* (n 16 above) para 99 (Major J).

liability because the plaintiff cannot prove causation. The numerous cases that have referred to *Snell* since 1990 have not, however, relied on this part of Sopinka J's opinion to justify reversing the burden of proof in medical malpractice cases.[37]

Another door was arguably opened by *Snell v Farrell.* After a reminder that the burden of proof in civil cases is not immutable, Sopinka J states, relying on Wigmore, that one of the broad principles concerning the burden of proof is that 'where the subject matter of the allegation lies particularly within one party's knowledge, that party may be required to prove it.'[38] He adds further:

> Proof of causation in medical malpractice cases is often difficult for the patient. The physician is usually in a better position to know the cause of the injury than the patient. On the basis of the second basic principle referred to above, there is an argument that the burden of proof should be allocated to the defendant. In some jurisdictions, this has occurred to an extent by operation of the principle of *res ipsa loquitur*. . . . In Canada, the rule has been generally regarded as a piece of circumstantial evidence which does not shift the burden of proof. . . .[39]

Sopinka J's statement is ambiguous. It is uncertain whether he meant to restrict his comment to the effect of *res ipsa loquitur* on the burden of proving fault,[40] or *causation,* or to allow for the general possibility of reversing the burden of proof of causation where the defendant has particular knowledge of the causal information. Even though Sopinka ultimately relied on this element to infer causation, the comment above shows a willingness to accept this last possible avenue, as of principle. In *Hollis v Dow Corning Corp* (1995), a case involving manufacturers' duty to inform, Sopinka J in fact reiterated this opinion in a dissenting decision and added:

> As a result, the burden of proof is properly reversed where the defendant has somehow participated in *destroying* the means of proving the case against it *or* where the defendant somehow *controls* the relevant evidence. Only within this limited sphere of cases is the plaintiff partially relieved of the burden of proving causation (emphasis added).[41]

[37] Sopinka J did not explain what he meant by *substantial connection.* One may speculate that he was referring to the *Cook v Lewis* situations and not necessarily to a more extensive application of the reversal of the onus of proving causation. Against: *Grant Estate v Mathers* (1991) 100 NSR (2nd) 363 (SC) 374–75.

[38] (N 1 above) 321. See also pp 328–29 and *Hollis v Dow Corning* (n 16 above) 694 (Sopinka J, diss).

[39] (N 1 above) 322.

[40] One school of thought holds *res ipsa loquitur* to reverse the burden of proof of fault: P Atiyah, '*Res Ipsa Loquitur* in England and Australia' (1972) 35 *MLR* 337, 337. The majority view in Canada, which Sopinka J confirms in the above statement, is that it operates as an inference.

[41] (N 16 above) 695. This possibility was thereafter restricted to manufacturer's liability: *Lange v Bennett* (n 18 above); *Walker Estate v York Finch* (n 16 above) para 86 (Major J); *Bigcharles v Dawson Creek* (n 16 above) paras 62–64.

After *Snell*, however, the Canadian,[42] as well as English,[43] courts unanimously reiterated their support for keeping the burden of proof with the plaintiff in medical malpractice cases. This stand has also been taken by Australian courts.[44]

Section 2

Civil Law

A. The Indeterminate Defendant

French and Québec cases have also allowed reversal of the burden of proof to solve the causative problems linked to the indeterminacy of the author of the damage. The Québec legislator codified in 1991 the case law[45] holding that, where the defendants have committed separate faults, each of which may have caused the

[42] *Davies v Gabel Estate* (n 1 above) 54; *Briffett v Gander and District* (n 35 above) para 60; *Gallant v Fialkov* (n 35 above) 317; *McGowan v King* (OntCtJ, 25 April 1991) 5; *Jourdain (Litigation Guardian of) v Hogg* (OntCtJ, 3 November 1993) para 45; *Bauer v Seager* (2000) 147 Man R (2nd) 1 (ManQB) 31; *Martin v Inglis* (SaskQB, 17 April 2002) paras 125–26 (obiter); *O'Grady v Stokes* (2005) ABQB 247, Carswell Alta 578 (AltaQB, 26 April 2005) para 202, relying on *Snell.*

[43] *Bull v Devon Area Health Authority* (1989) 22 BMLR 79 (CA) 87 and 114; *Stockdale v Nicholls* [1993] 4 Med LR 198 (QB) 199; *Bolitho v City and Hackney Health Authority* [1998] AC 232 (HL) 239; *The CJD Litigation: Group A and C Plaintiffs* (1998) 54 BMLR 100 (QBD) 102; *Tahir v Haringey Health Authority* [1998] Lloyd's Rep Med 104 (CA) 107; *Brown v Lewisham and North Southwark Health Authority* [1999] Lloyd's Law Rep Med 110 (CA) 116; *Smith v National Health Service Litigation Authority* [2001] Lloyd's Rep Med 90 (HCJ QBD) 11.

[44] *Chappel v Hart* (n 28 above) 273 (para 93) (Kirby J) and, outside medical liability: *Wintle v Conaust* (n 28 above) text accompanying fn 38 (referring to *Wilsher*); *Trust Company of Australia Ltd v VIP Medical Centres of Excellence Pty Ltd* (1994) NSW Lexis 13278, BC9403046 (23 September 1994); *Bendix Mintex PTY Ltd v Barnes* (1997) 42 NSWLR 307 (NSWSC) 318 (Mason P) and 339 (Beazley JA) (referring to *Wilsher*); *EM Baldwin & Son Pty Ltd v Plane* (1998) NSW Lexis 2503 (NSWCA, 23 December 1998) text to, and cases cited at, fn 67; *TC v The State of New South Wales* [2001] WL 1383033, [2001] NSWCA 380, 31 October 2001, paras 58–59 and 62–63 (Mason P) (referring to *Wilsher* at fn 23); *Van Den Heuvel v Tucker* (n 28 above) para 96. See also: J Gunson, 'Turbulent Causal Waters: The High Court, Causation and Medical Negligence' (2001) *Tort Law Review* 53, 77–79. This was confirmed in 2002 in the Ipp Report: DA Ipp, Commonwealth of Australia, *Review of the Law of Negligence, Final Report* (Canberra, September 2002), Part 7, para 7.34 and put in legislative form in most states: Civil Liability Act 2002 (NSW) §5E; Civil Liability Act 2003 (Qld) §12; Civil Liability Act 1936 (SA) §35; Civil Liability Act 2002 (Tas) §14; Civil Liability Act 2002 (WA) §5D; Civil Law (Wrongs) Act 2002 (ACT) §46; Wrongs Act 1958 (Vic) §52. Against: *Bennett v MCW* (n 28 above) 420–21 (Gaudron J) (employment context), referred to in the medical negligence case of *Boehm v Deleuil* (2005) WL 1444518, WADC 55 (WADC, 30 March 2005) 115.

[45] Perhaps influenced by *Cook v Lewis* (n 2 above), eg, *Gauthier v Bérubé* [1960] CS 23; *Massignani v Veilleux* [1987] RRA 541 (CA) 543 (Crête J) and 544 (Montgomery J); *Leroux v Hôtel-Dieu d'Arthabaska* [1990] RRA 378 (CQ-PC) 380–81. For a critique: A Bernardot and RP Kouri, *La responsabilité civile médicale* (Sherbrooke, RDUS, 1980) 375–76. This reversal is *partial* because the plaintiff must still show that his damage arose within the scope of the risk created by the defendants.

injury, they may be held liable *in solidum* where the exact identity of the culpable member cannot be identified.[46] This clear stand contrasts with the French approach, which assists plaintiffs through complex developments of which we will only provide a general picture here.

For a long time, French courts refused compensation in these cases on the basis that causation was not demonstrated. In response to the doctrinal criticisms that this solution was contrary to equity,[47] the judiciary finally imposed *in solidum* liability on all the faulty members of a group, thereby imposing on the defendants the task of showing individually that they have not caused the damage.[48] To do so, the French courts have not used the tools provided by the law of evidence; rather they have created imaginative concepts which provide conceptual justification for placing the burden of the uncertainty on the defendants' shoulders.[49] Their reasoning has rested mainly on substantive legal notions such as *faute collective*, *fautes connexes*, *garde collective*, and *garde en commun*.[50] The relaxation of the rules of evidence afforded by these approaches has been defended on the basis that the plaintiff has partially proven causation by demonstrating that the agent of his damage can originate only from one of the defendants. Because he has shown all that he would have to if there was only one defendant, it is considered contrary to equity to dismiss his claim on the sole basis that his damage may have

[46] CcQ, Art 1480 (this article was added to the civil code during the 1991 reform). The rule is admittedly imposed for the protection of victims unable to establish causation: Québec, Ministère de la Justice, *Commentaires du ministre de la Justice: Le Code civil du Québec*, t I (Québec, Publications du Québec, 1993) 906. See also: *Stéfanik v Hôpital Hôtel-Dieu de Lévis* [1997] RJQ 1332 (CS) 1354–55 and *St-Jean v Mercier* [2002] 1 SCR 491; (2002) 209 DLR (4th) 513, para 119. Art 1480 CcQ can be paralleled with similar provisions in European civil codes, *eg*, BGB, §830I and Burgerlijk Wetboek (BW) Art 6:166I and 6:99.

[47] G Viney and P Jourdain, J Ghestin, (dir), *Traité de droit civil: Les conditions de la responsabilité*, 2nd edn, (Paris, LGDJ, 1998) para 375.

[48] Eg, Cass civ 2nd, 19 May 1976, JCP 1978.G.II.18773 (note Dejean de la Bâtie). Some treat it rather as a presumption of accountability (*imputabilité*), since causation between the damage and its suspected agent has to be proven: H Aberkane, 'Du dommage causé par une personne indéterminée dans un groupe determiné de personnes' (1958) *Revue trimestrielle de droit civil* 516, 530 discussing Art 1384 al 1 CN. Others interpret the decisions as imposing a presumption of causation: Viney and Jourdain (n 47 above) para 380; P Jourdain, *Droit à la réparation: Lien de causalité*, Jurisclasseurs, Fasc 160 (Paris, Éditions techniques, 1993) 20.

[49] These were introduced inter alia in the context of hunting accidents, collective games, children play and sports.

[50] See generally: Viney and Jourdain (n 47 above) 204–14, and criticism: 211 and ff; IE Postacioglu, 'Faits simultanés et le problème de la responsabilité collective' (1954) 52 *Revue trimestrielle de droit civil* 438; Aberkane (n 48 above); D Mayer, 'La "garde" en commun' (1975) *Revue trimestrielle de droit civil* 197; H Mazeaud, L Mazeaud and J Mazeaud, *Traité théorique et pratique de la responsabilité civile délictuelle et contractuelle*, tII, 6th edn, (Paris, Montchrestien, 1965); G Durry, 'Jurisprudence française en matière de droit civil' (1971) *Revue trimestrielle de droit civil* 377; H Lalou, *Traité pratique de la responsabilité civile*, 6th edn, (Paris, Dalloz, 1962) 197–98; Jourdain (n 48 above) 19–21; P le Tourneau and L Cadiet, *Droit de la responsabilité civile* (Paris, Dalloz, 1998) para 829–39; P Conte and P Maistre du Chambon, *La responsabilité civile délictuelle*, 2nd edn, (Grenoble, Presses universitaires de Grenoble, 2000) 140–42.

been caused by several persons specifically identified, with no one individual being able to be singled out.[51]

It is not necessary to go over the debate that these techniques have prompted. Suffice it to say that they are widely criticised.[52] Inter alia, they are described as a posteriori justifications for the policy decision of not leaving the victim without redress and more fairly balancing the burden of poof in cases in which the identification of the author of the damage is impossible, and as *purs artifices* invented by the judges in order to meet the needs of these cases.[53] Some French scholars have therefore pleaded for the resolution of the indeterminate defendant on the evidential level, by creating a presumption of causation.[54] Others have suggested grounding *in solidum* liability on the basis of the fact that the damage lies not only in the physical injury suffered by the plaintiff but also in the disappearance of his means of proof caused by the group members' negligent actions, which can be considered worthy of compensation in itself.[55] These points are well taken. The French law on indeterminate defendants may provide support to an argument defending the inability of the substantive rules of law to solve what is essentially an evidential problem.[56]

B. Reversal in Medical Malpractice

In France, scientific uncertainties in medical liability are not solved by shifting the burden of proof of causation onto the defendant's shoulders, perhaps because most of these cases are dealt with through the loss of chance theory.[57] In Québec, this solution has been regularly resorted to by Beauregard J of the Court of Appeal, however. The main decision in this respect is *Gburek v Cohen* (1988). In a

[51] Viney and Jourdain (n 47 above) 212–13; Jourdain (n 48 above) 20.

[52] Viney and Jourdain (n 47 above) 211 and ff; le Tourneau and Cadiet (n 50 above) paras 838–39; Conte, *et al* (n 50 above) 141; Aberkane (n 48 above) 522; Bernardot and Kouri (n 45 above) 374–85.

[53] Viney and Jourdain (n 47 above) 211–12.

[54] P Azard, note under Grenoble, 16 May 1962, D 1963.137. Based on works by Mayrand in Québec and Postacioglu in France, he also suggests that, where the defendants' faults render the demonstration of causation impossible, the plaintiff should be granted damages for the loss of his chance to obtain compensation. See also: Dejean de la Bâtie (n 48 above) and Conte, *et al* (n 50 above) 142.

[55] Postaciolgu (n 50 above) 441. See also: Riom, 5 February 1964, JCP 1964.G.II.13640 (note Esmein). Against: Aberkane (n 48 above) paras 27–28. Aberkane recognises one of its advantages, however, ie, that it acknowledges the problem is one of evidence, not exclusively of civil liability.

[56] Aberkane (n 48 above) 532.

[57] Compare with German law where courts are ready to reverse the onus of proof against a doctor in case of serious treatment errors (C von Bar, *The Common European Law of Torts*, vol 1 (Oxford, Clarendon Press, 1998) para 416) or when his conduct has prevented the plaintiff from proving causation (D Giesen, *International Medical Malpractice Law: A Comparative Law Study of Civil Liability Arising from Medical Care* (Boston, Martinus Nijhoff, 1988) 419) and cases cited at fns 32 and 36, 521 and cases cited at fn 51; W van Gerven, J Lever and P Larouche, *Cases, Materials and Text on National, Supranational and International Tort Law* (Oxford, Hart Publishing, 2000) 460; Fleming (n 25 above) 671).

minority opinion, Beauregard J reversed the burden of proof of causation upon the demonstration that the defendant had increased the plaintiff's risk of damage, a solution admittedly inspired by *McGhee*.[58]

It will be recalled that this case involved an uncertain causal link between the plaintiff's deafness and the omission of blood tests and audiograms that are recommended in the treatment of meningitis with gentamycine, a toxic antibiotic.[59] In a minority opinion, Beauregard J found the defendant negligent only for omitting to prescribe the tests necessary to detect a possible abnormal blood concentration of the antibiotic.[60] In his opinion, deafness could equally have resulted from an abnormal concentration of antibiotic in the blood or in the ear, however, and the negligently omitted tests would have possibly only revealed the former.[61] It was therefore impossible to single out one cause over another precisely because of the absence of tests.

Beauregard J nevertheless justified the plaintiff's compensation by shifting the burden of proving causation to the defendant.[62] The absence of testing was the reason for the impossibility of determining whether the blood concentration of antibiotic had been abnormal.[63] Beauregard J solved this uncertainty by presuming the risk of damage had been increased by the defendant. This presumption was grounded on the fact that the causal uncertainty had been caused by the defendant's faulty omission to carry out tests. On the basis of this presumed increase of risk, he then shifted to the defendant the burden of proving causation.[64]

Beauregard J had also previously relied on this concept in *Houde v Côté* (1987) to impose onto the defendant's shoulders the burden of explaining the events that preceded the occurrence of the injury. Despite expert controversy on this issue, the trial judge and a unanimous Court of Appeal had found the defendant anaesthetist's fault had caused the partial paralysis in which his patient had woken following general anaesthesia. In a minority opinion, Beauregard J noted that he found the determination of the cause of the plaintiff's damage difficult due to the absence of relevant information in the patient's file. Nevertheless, he agreed with the positive finding of causation of the majority of the Court of Appeal's judges,

58 *Gburek v Cohen* [1988] RJQ 2424 (CA). See also: *Beausoleil v La Communauté des Soeurs de la Charité de la Providence* [1965] BR 36, 43 and *Kulczycky v Rafferty* [1989] RRA 582 (CS) (rev'd on this point: [1994] RJQ 1792 (CA) 1800).

59 Ch 1, text to fn 246.

60 The doctor was not found at fault for omitting to carry out audiogram tests, since they had only a relative usefulness in preventing sudden loss of hearing, which Beauregard J believed was what had affected the plaintiff. The majority found the defendant at fault for omitting these tests, however.

61 (N 58 above) 2444–45.

62 This case is a good illustration of the relatively rare situation where position of the burden is significant.

63 (N 57 above) 2444–46.

64 *Ibid*, p 2447, citing *McGhee*.

since, because of the doctor's *obligation de rendre compte,* he believed the defendant bore the burden of proving precisely what happened during the anaesthesia.[65] He further added that because of the incomplete records kept by the defendant, the court could presume the plaintiff's injury resulted from the defendant's negligence.[66]

These isolated judgments are not authoritative in Québec law, not only because they are minority opinions, but because they were decided before the Supreme Court of Canada decisions in *Snell v Farrell* (1990) and *Laferrière v Lawson* (1991), in which the highest court reaffirmed that the burden of proving causation in medical malpractice rests on the plaintiff's shoulders. Nevertheless, they provide an interesting illustration of the common law influence over Québec decisions in this area, in particular through the concepts of risk and negligent undermining of the plaintiff's means of proving causation.

Section 3

Critical Analysis

The current general judicial reluctance to reverse the onus of proof of causation in medical liability cases prompts us to believe that it is not an immediate realistic judicial avenue, even though it might be an interesting option for legislative reform in special cases.[67] It is nevertheless interesting to look at the values the systems rely on to justify recourse to reversal of the onus of proving causation in cases that are thought deserving. Moreover, placing these justifications in parallel with the cases that interest us here provides compelling reasons to hesitate before extending this solution to medical liability.

A central consideration lies in whether there are 'strong' reasons to depart from the normal allocation of the burden of proof in medical liability cases affected by uncertainty.[68] A parallel between the French and Canadian approaches to uncertainty about the identity of the defendant is particularly enlightening to answer this question. The justifications relied on by the courts to shift the burden of proof

[65] *Houde v Côté* [1987] RJQ 723 (CA) 729–30.

[66] For a critique: *Zanchettin v DeMontigny* [2000] RRA 298 (CA) 312. See also: *Kulczycky v Rafferty* (CA) (n 58 above) 1793–94, 1800 and 1803–4; *Therrien v Launay* (2005) WL 434762, Carswell Que 486 (QuéSC, 4 March 2005) paras 473–74.

[67] Eg, where the defendant's negligence undermined the plaintiff's means of proof, although this option was rejected in England and Canada: discussed generally ch 5, text between fns 404 and 415.

[68] Respectful of Viscount Maugham's warnings in *Joseph Constantine Steamship Line Ltd v Imperial Smelting Corporation Ltd* [1942] AC 154 (HL) 174.

in these cases are of particular interest. As we saw, the generous attitude of the courts is motivated by the fact that the defendants, limited in number, are all authors of culpable behaviour and have, through their negligence, created similar risks of damage, within the scope of which the injury has clearly fallen, thereby proving partially causation. This coupled with the fact that the defendant's negligence has had the effect of undermining the plaintiff's means of proving causation provides a compelling policy argument for modifying the normal assignment of the burden of proof.

Most of these considerations cannot generally be transposed to the typical medical liability cases in which uncertainty prevails. In these instances, the alternative cause of the damage is frequently a non-faulty event. Alongside the doctor's fault, there may be risks that have not emanated from the defendant's culpable actions, such as inherent risks associated with medical treatment or a pre-existing situation resulting from sickness or accident. In addition, the uncertainty in such cases usually prevents determining which of the alternative risks was fulfilled, the faulty or the non-faulty, not who is the author of an identified risk already shown to be causal of the damage. In medical cases, keeping the burden of demonstrating causation with the plaintiff thus seems fair, since otherwise the risk of error has greater implications; it can impose full liability for damage which may originate from events unconnected to fault.[69] However, the weight given in the indeterminate defendant case law to the undermining of the plaintiff's means of proof is an interesting policy motivation for generosity which could have more general application to medical liability instances—a point to which we will return in chapter 5.

Besides this possible parallel, the French indeterminate defendant case law also provides a useful warning against recourse, in order to address pure problems of proof, to legal concepts that are not designed to solve evidential uncertainties. In Canadian law, *Cook v Lewis* (1951) provided a good example of decisiveness in situating the problem as one of evidence, not of causation. Moreover, part of the French doctrinal critique of the judicial responses to the indeterminate defendant problem has centred on the fact that such evidential problem deserves an evidential solution. Consequently, while reversal of the burden of proof of causation does not constiute an acceptable avenue in the current state of medical malpractice, it nevertheless encourages the search for an evidential solution to problems of causal uncertainty.

[69] *Snell v Farrell* (n 1 above) 327. Similarly, the additional policy motivation which led to the introduction of market-share liability in the United States, ie, the desire to assist victims of large enterprises in facing the difficulties that flow from these enterprises' liberty to keep proper records of their actions and explain the negative outcomes of the marketing of their products, are difficult to transpose to the area of medical malpractice: Giesen (n 57 above) 610.

Conclusion to Chapter 3

The instances in which reversal is clearly admitted do not concern the issue of causation between fault and damage, but rather the linking of the damage to the particular author of the fault, at least in Canada, Québec, and France.[70] Thus they do not address the question of uncertain causation caused by the impossibility of scientifically assessing the physical origin of the damage. The courts' reluctance to reverse the burden of proof must nevertheless be taken into account when one assesses the realistic judicial avenues to the solution of the problem of scientific uncertainty. The serious limitations to this solution imposed by English, Canadian, Australian, French, and Québec case law make it unlikely to be retained by the courts of these jurisdictions. It is worth noting, however, the interesting albeit isolated tendency in the Canadian and Québec case law to rely on the idea of the negligent undermining of the plaintiff's means of proof of causation to justify reversal.

What links the reversal of the burden of proof to the next solution, the probabilistic assessment of damages, is that they both necessitate a modification of existing substantive legal rules. While reversal modifies a substantive rule of evidence, probabilistic assessment of damages forces reconsideration of the way liability is traditionally assessed in the tort of negligence, as well as in *responsabilité civile.*

[70] *St-Jean v Mercier* (SCC) (n 46 above) para 118.

4

Probabilistic Assessment of Damages

Probabilities lie at the heart of the assessment of causation. Nothing is certain in this world and one can often assess only the probability of existence of facts and events. This reality has led to the common law and Québec fiction that when evidence to satisfy the requirements of liability, including causation, show probability, it is deemed 100 per cent certain. While causal certainty is in theory required in France, the courts are also often satisfied with a high probability of existence of causation. This fiction is reflected in what is called in common law the *all-or-nothing* rule, according to which, when the requirement of proof of causation is met, the plaintiff can recover the whole of his damage even if there remains a possibility that the defendant has not caused it. Either the defendant's fault caused the damage or it did not.[1] Damages are in theory not calculated in proportion to the judge's conviction that the defendant caused the loss, ie, on the basis of its causative probability.[2]

This brings about the following situation where the balance of probabilities applies. Whenever the background risk[3] is greater than that added by the defendant, a partial award is not made to account for the possibility that the defendant's fault may have caused the damage even if he has negligently doubled the risk faced by the plaintiff.[4] For instance, if the plaintiff demonstrates that the defendant's fault increased the possibility of injury arising by 40 per cent, the defendant does not have to compensate even 40 per cent of the damage, since the balance of probabilities requirement is not met. On the other hand, if the plaintiff shows that there is a 60 per cent probability that the defendant caused his loss, he can recover his whole damage. The award is not discounted, at the causation stage, for the

1 *Athey v Leonati* (1996) 140 DLR (4th) 235; [1996] 3 SCR 458, 475; T Honoré, 'Causation and Remoteness of Damage' in A Tunc, (ed), *Encyclopaedia of Comparative Law*, vol XI (The Hague, Tübingen, 1971) 34; S Chapman, 'Apportionment of Liability between Tortfeasors' (1948) 64 *LQR* 26, 27–28.

2 R Savatier, 'La responsabilité médicale en France (Aspects de droit privé)' (1976) *Revue internationale de droit comparé* 493, 501.

3 The sum of other sources of risk operating at the same time as the defendant's fault and which might have also caused the outcome: J Stapleton, 'The Gist of Negligence, Part II: The Relationship between "Damage" and "Causation"' (1988) 104 *LQR* 389.

4 Stapleton (n 3 above) 390.

possibility that part of the loss might have been caused by another factor.[5] The law thus admits the possible commission of an error each time it grants or refuses compensation.

In principle, this rule also exists in France, even though the extent of the probability that must be demonstrated before the court deems causation proven with certainty is less clear, but certainly much higher than 50 per cent.[6] Savatier has expressed it with vigour by arguing that the judge should not 'calculate his reservations':

> *La mission du juge est de juger, et non de doser ses hésitations. Si son intime conviction est faite en faveur des preuves exigées du demandeur, il doit lui donner entièrement raison. Mais si la preuve de la causalité du dommage reste à ses yeux incertaine, son doute doit avoir pour effet le rejet de la demande. C'est une règle de sécurité! Comment, dans le doute qui l'assiège, pourrait-il d'ailleurs évaluer sérieusement de prétendues chances de causalité?*[7]

The all-or-nothing rule has been criticised, however, as leading in every case to an unfair result[8] by either under-deterring or over-deterring defendants.[9] In medical cases, this rule generally applies to the plaintiff's disadvantage in situations of uncertainty,[10] as courts tend to be cautious to avoid imputing to the doctor damage which is the direct consequence of events he could not prevent.[11] Some have therefore suggested that the all-or-nothing rule be departed from to allow, as a matter of principle and fairness to both parties, for compensation of damage in proportion to its causative probability.[12]

Under such a system, known as *proportional recovery*,[13] if it is established that there is a 40 per cent probability that the defendant's negligence was the cause of

[5] Compare with the common law *thin skull rule*: at the causation stage, the plaintiff's particular susceptibility is not taken into account and loss of chance reasoning is inapplicable. Thus one cannot argue that the fault deprived the plaintiff of only the chance of maintaining his health.

[6] Ch 1, text between fns 147 and 158.

[7] (N 2 above) 502.

[8] England: N Jansen, 'The Idea of a Lost Chance' (1999) 19 *OJLS* 271, 274; France: G Durry, 'La faute du médecin diminuant les "chances de guérison" du malade' (1969) *Revue trimestrielle de droit civil* 797, 798 ; Dorsner-Dolivet, note under Cass civ 1st, 17 November 1982, D 1984.jur.305, 308 (Case also reported at Bull civ 1982.I.n333; D 1983.380; JCP 1983.G.IV.41; JCP 1983.G.II.20056 (note Saluden)); Québec: S Gaudet, *L'application de la notion de perte de chances en droit médical* (Paper presented to the CIAJ's Conference: 'Responsabilité médicale et hospitalière: Aspects juridiques et éthiques' Montréal, 29 October 1990) 38–39.

[9] Stapleton (n 3 above) 390. She concedes that this result is avoided by the deduction made at the valuation stage, however. See also: D Gerecke, 'Risk Exposure as Injury: Alleviating the Injustice of Tort Causation Rules' (1990) 35 *McGill Law Journal* 797, 807.

[10] G Durry, 'Sur un probable revirement de jurisprudence en matière de réparation de la perte d'une chance de guérison ou de survie' (1983) *Revue trimestrielle de droit civil* 547, 548; Dorsner-Dolivet, note under Cass civ 1st, 17 November 1982 (n 8 above) 308.

[11] Eg, natural process or the act of a third party or of the plaintiff himself.

[12] Stapleton (n 3 above) 406.

[13] Also called probabilistic assessment of damages, or probabilistic increased-risk concept.

the plaintiff's damage, the plaintiff may recover compensation for 40 per cent of this damage. This amount reflects the risk created by the defendant and the damage suffered by the plaintiff through that risk, or, in other words, the proportion of the chance of avoiding the damage that the defendant deprived the plaintiff of. *Loss of chance* is the best known expression of the principle of proportional recovery. According to this theory, if, before the defendant's fault intervened, a plaintiff possessed a chance to make a gain or to avoid a loss, and the fault destroyed that chance, the plaintiff can obtain compensation for the value of that lost chance instead of claiming for the negative situation in which he has been left. This concept has the clear advantage of allowing the plaintiff to recover at least part of his damage despite the uncertainties surrounding causation, while holding the defendant liable only for a portion of the loss, based upon the extent of his causal responsibility for it.

The popularity of the notion of loss of chance obscures the fact that it has a twin sister sometimes called *liability for risk* or *risk-based liability.*[14] Discussed mainly in common law, this doctrine views exposure to risk as an actual injury worthy of redress.[15] Despite differences existing between the two approaches,[16] the discussion of loss of chance can generally be applied equally to risk-based liability.

Section 1

Loss of Chance

A. Statement of the Problem

The loss of chance concept was originally applied in cases now called *classic*[17] and subsequently has been extended to medical cases. While reliance on loss of chance is a necessary part of the assessment of damage in classic cases, it is far more controversial in medical negligence cases.

[14] T Weir, 'Loss of a Chance—Compensable in Tort? The Common Law' in O Guillod, (ed), *Développements récents du droit de la responsabilité civile* (Genève, Centre d'études juridiques européennes, 1991) 117; JG Fleming, *The Law of Torts*, 9th edn, (London, Sweet & Maxwell, 1998) 229.

[15] Gerecke (n 9 above) 801.

[16] The main one is that, while the term *loss* of chance implies that some tangible damage has been suffered, liability for exposure to risk implies that the risk does not have to be fulfilled for the claim to be admissible: Jansen (n 8 above) 281. Nothing inherent in the loss of chance doctrine prevents it from being applied to claims based on the increase of a risk that has not materialised, however. On this question: Stapleton (n 3 above) 395 and 409.

[17] It has been relied on since the 19th century in France: Cass req, 17 July 1889, §1891.I.399. See also: G Viney and P Jourdain, J Ghestin, (dir), *Traité de droit civil: Les conditions de la responsabilité*, 2nd edn, (Paris, LGDJ, 1998) para 280.

1. The Classic Loss of Chance Cases

There is little doctrinal and judicial resistance to the acceptability of loss of chance reasoning in the so-called classic loss of chance cases,[18] even though this head of damage is by definition hypothetical.[19] In these cases, often argued in contract, the defendant's negligent action or omission crystallises the plaintiff's situation, and the plaintiff is thereby altogether prevented from taking the chance. Consequently, the hoped-for end result remains forever hypothetical.[20] One must therefore wonder, when assessing damages, what position the plaintiff would have occupied if the contract had been performed.[21] Classic examples are the cases in which a lawyer has allowed the limitation period of his client's claim to lapse;[22] a person has failed to buy a lottery ticket for a friend after agreeing to do so; a commercial opportunity has been lost;[23] a woman has been prevented from taking her chance in a beauty contest[24] or a horse from participating in a race; etc.[25] Chance is also referred to in extra-contractual[26] cases involving personal injury in order to assess the eventuality of future hypothetical damage such as whether the plaintiff would have supported his family, would have obtained employment, would

[18] France: J Penneau, *La responsabilité médicale* (Paris, Sirey, 1977) para 104; J Penneau, note under Cass civ 1st, 27 March 1973, D 1973.jur.595, 596; L Dubouis, 'Perte d'une chance de survie. Indemnisation' (1971) *Revue Trimestrielle de Droit Sanitaire et Social* 66, 67; F Bouvier, 'La responsabilité médicale' *Gazette du Palais* 1984.doctr.284, 288; Viney and Jourdain (n 17 above) para 370; J Boré, 'L'indemnisation pour les chances perdues: une forme d'appréciation quantitative de la causalité d'un fait dommageable' *La semaine juridique* 1974.I.2620, para 6; R Savatier, 'Une faute peut-elle engendrer la responsabilité d'un dommage dans l'avoir causé?' *Dalloz* 1970.chr.123, 124; C Müller, *La perte d'une chance* (Berne, Staempfli, 2002) paras 38 and ff (France) and 177 and ff (England) 213 and ff (Canada and Québec); Québec: JL Baudouin and P Deslauriers, *La responsabilité civile*, 6th edn, (Cowansville, Yvon Blais, 2003) para 323.

[19] Baudouin and Deslauriers (n 18 above) para 323; J Pineau and M Ouellette, *Théorie de la responsabilité civile*, 2nd edn, (Montréal, Thémis, 1980) 20. Some also describe it as future damage. This view is contradicted by the fact that the damage called loss of chance occurs as soon as the chance is lost: S Philips-Nootens, 'La perte de chance: détournement du lien de causalité ou dommage distinct?' (1990) 50 *Canadian Bar Review* 611, 612; and C Larroumet, *Réflexions sur la responsabilité civile: Évolution et problèmes actuels en droit comparé* (Montréal, Institute of Comparative Law, McGill University Press, 1983) para 656. In civil law, as long as the damage is certain, it does not matter whether or not it is a future event.

[20] Boré (n 18 above) para 29; Penneau (1977) (n 18 above) para 104; Penneau (1973) (n 18 above) 595–96.

[21] SM Waddams, 'Damages: Assessment of Uncertainties' (1998) 13 *Journal of Contract Law* 1, 5.

[22] *Kitchen v Royal Air Force Association* [1958] 1 WLR 563 (CA). See also: G Masel, 'Damages in Tort for Loss of Chance' (1995) *Torts Law Journal* 1, 1. Against: Baudouin and Deslauriers (n 18 above) para 323.

[23] *Commonwealth v Amann Aviation Pty Ltd* (1991) 174 CLR 64; *Sellars v Adelaide Petroleum NL* (1994) 179 CLR 332 (AustHC); *Rufo v Hosking* (2004) NSWCA 391 (1 November 2004) para 4.

[24] *Chaplin v Hicks* [1911] 2 KB 786.

[25] For other examples: Nootens (n 19 above) 613; and JG Fleming, 'Probabilistic Causation in Tort Law' (1989) 68 *Canadian Bar Review* 661, 674. For a review of classic cases in Australian law: H Luntz, 'Loss of Chance' in I Freckelton and D Mendelson, (eds), *Causation in Law and Medicine* (Hampshire, Ashgate Dartmouth, 2002) 157 and ff; D Hamer, 'Chance Would Be a Fine Thing: Proof of Causation and Quantum in an Unpredictable World' (1999) 23 *Melbourne University Law Review* 557.

[26] Ie, in tort cases and extra-contractual *responsabilité civile.*

have continued playing tennis had he not suffered injury, or whether the plaintiff will suffer some ailment in the future as a result of the wrongdoing.[27]

In all of these cases, the language of chance allows one to assess the plaintiff's hypothetical damage by calculating not the value of the end result expected but that of the plaintiff's chance of achieving that end result, gain the advantage, or avoid the loss. When doing so, it is sufficient to show that there was a reasonable chance or, in civil law language, a *real and serious* chance that the hoped-for result would have been achieved.[28] The chance is calculated on the basis of the probability of realisation of the expected result,[29] and consequently the plaintiff receives compensation for only a portion of his injury.[30] French commentators insist, however, that the chance must be capable of being assessed objectively, independent of the value of the hoped for benefit.[31] Moreover, the lost chance must be causally related to the defendant's fault.[32] In both contractual and extra-contractual situations, the loss of chance reasoning thus involves either attempting to define what would

[27] Waddams (n 21 above) 15; Masel (n 22 above) 5. Eg, *Malec v JC Hutton Pty Ltd* (1990) 169 CLR 638 (AustHC) 642–43: damages for loss of earning capacity resulting from the development of a psychiatric condition caused by a disease, brucellosis, were discounted on the grounds that because of a back condition the plaintiff may have developed a similar neurotic condition independently of the defendant's negligence, thus using the concept of chance solely in order to consider future contingencies when assessing damages (Deane and Dawson JJ dissenting). On the distinction between the use of chance within the discount for vicissitudes and its use to account for the fact that the defendant's tort might not be the cause of the plaintiff's loss: F Trindade and P Cane, *The Law of Torts in Australia*, 3rd edn, (Victoria, OUP, 1999) 479, fn 23.

[28] The chance must not be minimal or a mere speculative possibility. England: *Kovats v Ogilvie* (1970) 17 DLR (3rd) 343 (BCCA) 346; *Davies v Taylor* [1974] AC 207 (HL); Canada: *Schrump v Koot* (1977) 82 DLR (3rd) 553 (OntCA) 556; France: Couturier, note under Cass civ 1st, 7 June 1989, D 1991.Jur.158, 159 (also reported at D 1991.somm.323; JCP 1989.G.IV.294; D 1991.somm.323); J Flour and JL Aubert, *Droit civil: Les obligations 2) Le fait juridique* (Paris, Armand Colin, 1997) paras 133–34; P Jourdain, 'Responsabilité civile, conditions de la responsabilité' (1989) *Revue trimestrielle de droit civil* 81, 82; Viney and Jourdain (n 17 above) paras 202–03, B Starck, H Roland and L Boyer, *Obligations 1, La responsabilité délictuelle*, 5th edn, (Paris, Litec, 1996) para 109; P Jourdain, 'Sur la perte d'une chance' (1992) *Revue trimestrielle de droit civil* 109, 113. See also: CcQ, Art 1611.

[29] Flour and Aubert (n 28 above) para 134; Boré (n 18 above) para 7; I Vacarie, 'La perte d'une chance' (1987) 3 *Revue de la recherche juridique* 903, 924; J Huet, 'Perte d'une chance: du plus ou moins classique' (1986) *Revue trimestrielle de droit civil* 117; V Tacchini-Laforest, 'Réflexions à propos de la perte de chance' (1999) 142 *Petites Affiches* 7, 8; Viney and Jourdain (n 17 above) para 282.

[30] Boré (n 18 above) para 7; Viney and Jourdain (n 17 above) para 284.

[31] P Conte and P Maistre du Chambon, *La responsabilité civile délictuelle*, 2nd edn, (Grenoble, Presses universitaires de Grenoble, 2000) 43–45; Starck, *et al* (n 28 above) para 110; Flour and Aubert (n 28 above) para 134.

[32] R Savatier, 'Le droit des chances et des risques dans les assurances, la responsabilité civile dans la médecine et sa synthèse dans l'assurance de responsabilité médicale' (1973) 44 *Revue générale des assurances terrestres* 457, 472; Jourdain (1992) (n 28 above) 113; Viney and Jourdain (n 17 above) para 282. Classic cases must be distinguished from cases where, through the defendant's fault, the chance is not taken but the event nevertheless takes place. In such cases, it is possible to assess what the result of the chance would have been. For example, the defendant omits to place a bet on a particular horse for the plaintiff and this horse wins the race. In such scenario, there is no loss of chance but an identifiable damage suffered by the plaintiff, ie, not getting the prize money. Chance intervenes solely in the identification of the defendant's fault: *not taking the chance as mandated*.

be, hypothetically, the present if the past had been different (*hypothetical prognostic*), or imagining a hypothetical future based on the present (*simple prognostic*).[33]

2. *The Debated Use: Medical Loss of Chance Cases*

The doctrine's extension to cases involving medical faults in which the causal link between the final damage—death, sickness or disability—and the doctor's fault is uncertain is more controversial and has provoked a very active debate in all of the jurisdictions studied. In the context of medical liability, the concept is most useful when, even though causation between the doctor's fault and the plaintiff's damage is not established on the basis of the traditional standards, it allows the plaintiff to plead that before the medical act was undertaken, he had a chance of cure or of survival which the defendant's fault destroyed.[34] Hence, losing a chance of recovery is considered a form of legal damage in its own right, independent of the final outcome suffered by the patient. Consequently, the plaintiff is not required to make the impossible demonstration of the exact cause of the final damage (X). He has to prove only that the physician's fault caused a distinct damage, the loss of chance (Y) (Figures 1 and 2).

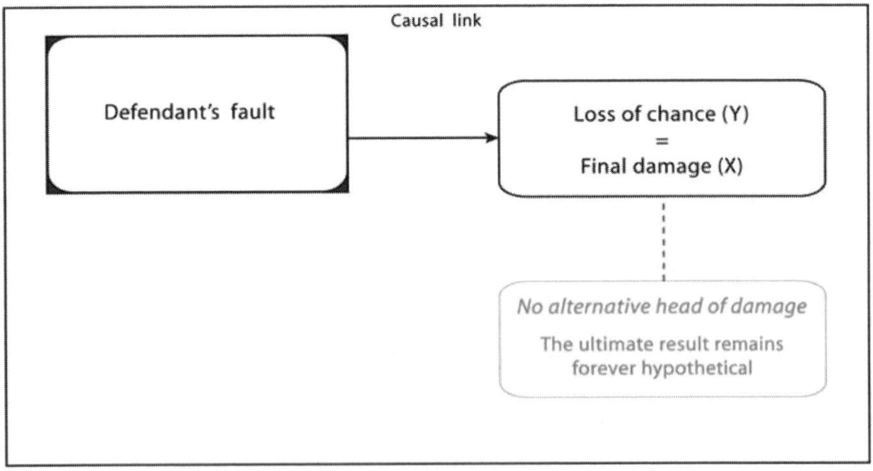

FIGURE 1: Loss of Chance in the Classic Cases

[33] *Prognostic hypothétique* and *prognostic simple:* Müller (n 18 above) 49. See also Müller's distinction between *actual* loss (chance definitively lost without any consequence for the future) and *future* loss (chance definitively lost with consequences in the future): 56 and 69.

[34] Eg, *Hotson v East Berkshire Area Health Authority* [1987] 1 AC 750; *Laferrière v Lawson* (1991) 78 DLR (4th) 609; [1991] 1 SCR 541; *Allied Maples Group Ltd v Simmons & Simmons (a firm)* [1995] 1 WLR 1602 (CA).

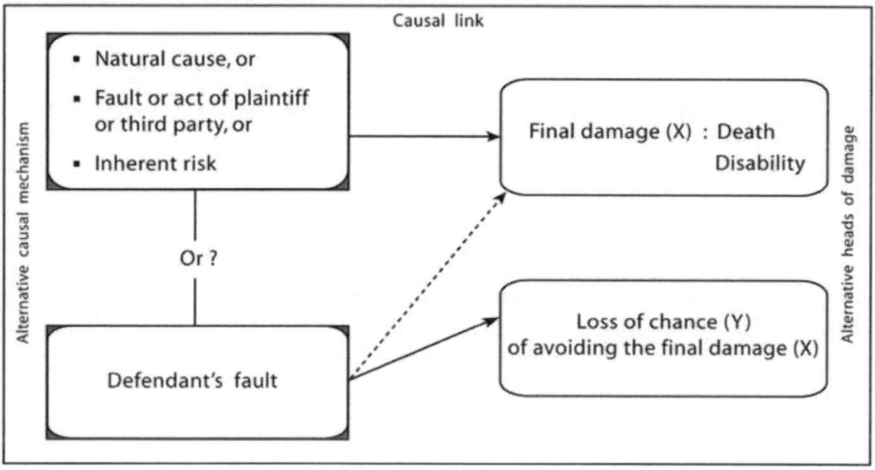

FIGURE 2: Loss of Chance in Medical Cases

The reception of the loss of chance argument in medical malpractice cases has differed depending on the jurisdiction concerned. The French judiciary has widely incorporated the loss of chance concept in its decisions, while the other jurisdictions have generally eschewed it, with the exception of some Australian lower courts.

B. Position of the Judiciary[35]

Only the French judiciary currently unequivocally agrees to compensate patients for their loss of chance of survival or recovery; generally, it does not treat loss of chance as controversial. In complete contrast, the Québec and Canadian case law has strictly rejected the application of the doctrine to medical negligence cases. Finally, the English judiciary is positioned somewhere in the middle, albeit closer to its Canadian than its French counterpart. Though no firm position has been voiced on the subject, one can interpret the English decisions as an effective rejection of the doctrine. Finally, Australian developments have also not resolutely settled their attitude to loss of chance, which differs depending on the level of court concerned.

[35] This section does not look at the use of loss of chance in cases involving the medical obligation to inform, since in this context loss of chance would be used to face a factual uncertainty, ie deciding whether or not the patient would have undergone the medical treatment had he known about the undisclosed risk. On this question: Waddams (n 21 above). See also: *Chester v Afshar* (2004) 1 AC 134; [2005] 3 WLR 927; [2005] 4 All ER 587 (HL) and, generally, the French case law on the medical obligation to inform, in which loss of chance is relied on almost without fail.

1. England

Long before it became an issue in England, the Scottish case of *Kenyon v Bell*[36] had rejected the applicability of loss of chance in medical negligence, considering the argument extravagant and contrary to principle. Thirty-five years later, the question came before the English House of Lords in *Hotson v East Berkshire Area Health Authority* (1987),[37] which constitutes the landmark English case on the question even though it did not directly address it.

A 13-year-old boy fell out of a tree in his school playground, injuring his hip. A few hours later, he was brought to a hospital, where, for unknown reasons, his hip was not x-rayed. He was sent home without treatment. The pain in his left leg persisted to such an extent that five days later he was taken to the hospital again, x-rayed, and found to be suffering from a displacement of the left epiphysis, which was operated on the next day. The plaintiff nevertheless developed avascular necrosis in his left hip. The medical evidence showed that it was likely the disability would have resulted from the fall anyway but that there was a 25 per cent chance the plaintiff would have recovered had he been treated promptly. The plaintiff argued that a substantial, as opposed to a speculative, chance of benefit or advantage is an asset, the loss of which could be compensated in tort provided the plaintiff proves on balance of probabilities that the fault caused the chance to be lost and that the lost chance was foreseeable. The defendant insisted that the case was concerned not with the possible future contingencies of an injury proven to have been caused by negligence but with whether there was proof at all that the relevant injury was so caused, a question that had to be decided on the balance of probability. No recovery for loss of chance could be granted because, had all care been taken, the plaintiff would still have suffered from the same result.

The trial judge and the Court of Appeal agreed with the plaintiff's contention and awarded 25 per cent of the full damages and a small amount for pain and suffering for the five days' delay in treatment.[38] The House of Lords disagreed, albeit without directly addressing the loss of chance issue. The Law Lords preferred to focus on what they believed was a preliminary question, whether the plaintiff had shown a causal connection on the balance of probabilities between the avascular necrosis and the defendant's fault. Since there was a 75 per cent chance of the

[36] [1953] SC 125.

[37] *Hotson v East Berkshire AHA* (n 34 above). Damages had previously been calculated on the basis of causative probability in other cases, eg, *Clark v MacLennan* [1983] 1 All ER 416 (QB) 432–33; *Bagley v North Herts Health Authority* (1986) 136 NLJ 1014 (QB).

[38] On the basis of an analogy with the classic cases of *Chaplin v Hicks* (n 24 above); *Mallett v McMonagle* [1970] AC 166 (HL); *Davies v Taylor* (n 28 above). But see: Croom-Johnson LJ: loss of chance can ground an action in tort but only where the chance is one personal to the plaintiff. To be a figure in statistics does not by itself give a cause of action. He nevertheless confirms the trial judge's findings, however, as the plaintiff was asking only for 25% of his damage.

disease developing independent of any fault on the defendant's part, the disease was caused by the fall, not the hospital's negligence. Lord Ackner and Lord Bridge insisted it is only once causation is established on the balance of probabilities that the question of valuation of damages arises and the loss of chance debate becomes relevant.[39]

On the basis of famous English classic cases,[40] Lord Ackner, Lord Mackay, and Lord Bridge distinguished the determination of past events from the determination of contingent future events. Lord Ackner stated that the assessment of damage which depends upon the courts' view as to what happened in the past must be decided on the balance of probabilities.[41] The Law Lords agreed that *Hotson* involved a question of past facts.

As for the question of applicability of loss of chance in medical malpractice, Lord Bridge and Lord Mackay left the issue open. Lord Bridge qualified the analogy made with the classic cases as superficially attractive while believing there were formidable obstacles to its acceptance.[42] He rejected any probabilistic approach by stressing that if the plaintiff had proven on a balance of probabilities that the defendant's negligent failure to diagnose and treat his injury promptly had materially contributed to the development of avascular necrosis, there is no principle of English law which would have entitled the defendant to a discount from the full measure of damage to reflect the chance that, even given prompt treatment, avascular necrosis might still have developed. He admitted, however, that in some cases, and perhaps particularly in medical negligence cases, *causation* may be so shrouded in mystery that the court can only measure statistical chances; but that was not the case here.[43] As for Lord Mackay, he found it would be unwise to rule that a plaintiff could never recover for pure loss of chance.[44] In the present case, however, the plaintiff had no chance of avoiding the necrosis, since, by the time he first presented himself at the hospital, he was 'doomed'.[45]

Loss of chance was therefore not conclusively addressed by the House of Lords.[46] Yet commentators have expressed the opinion that it is unlikely the

[39] (N 34 above) 782 (Lord Bridge), 793 (Lord Ackner). See, on the standard of proof: 785 (Lord Mackay).

[40] *Chaplin v Hicks* (n 24 above); *Mallett v McMonagle* (n 38 above); *Davies v Taylor* (n 28 above).

[41] Lord Ackner (n 34 above) 792–93. See also: Lord Mackay at 785.

[42] Without explaining which: *ibid*, p 782.

[43] *Ibid.*

[44] *Ibid*, p 786 (Lord Mackay). He emphasises that materially increasing the risk of dermatitis is equivalent to materially decreasing the chance of escaping dermatitis. He was thus ready to accept that loss of chance could ground a successful claim in damages until the time *McGhee* was departed from.

[45] Compare: Gaudron J in *Naxakis v Western General Hospital* (1998) 197 CLR 269 (AustHC) 280 (awarded a small sum was granted for the avoidable pain suffered during the delay between the misdiagnosis and the treatment), Cass civ 1st, 17 November 1982 (n 8 above).

[46] *Laferrière v Lawson* (n 34 above) 608, relied on in England in *Smith v National Health Service Litigation Authority* [2001] Lloyd's Rep Med 90 (QB) 17 (noted to WL). See also: Stapleton (n 3 above) 393.

English courts will adopt the theory of loss of chance after *Hotson*.[47] Fairgrieve has rightly gone further by noting that:

> Their Lordships did not specifically reject the possible acknowledgment of loss of chance as a head of damage, but surely their refusal to apply it in *Hotson*, where the facts constituted a paradigm example of loss of chance in a medical context, transforms an ostensibly open decision into what is effectively a rejection.[48]

The subsequent English case law expressed objections to reliance on loss of chance in personal injury[49] and medical malpractice cases.[50] It also insisted that causation has to be proven on the balance of probabilities,[51] often justifying this position on the basis of the past facts–future contingencies dichotomy[52] or generally on the ratio of *Hotson*.[53] One exception is found in *Judge v Huntingdon* (1994), a case involving the misdiagnosis of a breast cancer. The judge, having found that the chances of success of timely treatment would have stood at 80 per cent, stated that the assessment of damages should proceed on the finding of an 80 per cent chance of full expectation of life, likening this case to some of the classic instances which he found were not contradicted by the House of Lords in *Hotson*.[54] This result is in fact surprising, considering that such a probability clearly met the balance of probabilities.[55]

The balance of probability rule was reaffirmed by the Court of Appeal in *Allied Maples Group Ltd v Simmons & Simmons (A Firm)* (1995), a case concerned with solicitors' liability. The court accepted, however, that the percentage of chance of an outcome could be relied on in very limited cases, namely when the causative

[47] S Deakin, A Johnston and BS Markesinis, *Tort Law*, 4th edn, (Oxford, Clarendon Press, 2003) 187; Weir (n 14 above) 123.

[48] D Fairgrieve, *An Anglo-French Comparative Law Study of the Loss of Chance Doctrine in Medical Negligence Cases* (MJur Thesis, Oxford University, 1997) 13.

[49] *R v Secretary of State for the Home Department, ex p Gallagher* [1996] 2 CMLR 951 (CA), on the basis of *Hotson v East Berkshire AHA* (n 34 above); *Davies v Wyre Forest District Council* [1998] PIQR P58 (QB).

[50] *Stockdale v Nicholls* [1993] 4 Med LR 198 (QB) 199; *Mellor v Sheffield Teaching Hospitals NHS Trust* (2004) EWHC 780; (2004) All ER (D) 195 (QB, 22 April 2004) para 228.

[51] *Tahir v Haringey Health Authority* [1998] Lloyd's Rep Med 104 (CA) 107.

[52] *Husain v Bank of Credit & Commerce Intl SA* (CA, 31 January 2002) para 63. In accordance with *Mallett v McMonagle* (n 38 above) 176 (Lord Diplock); *Davies v Taylor* (n 28 above) 212–13 (Lord Reid); *Judge v Huntingdon Health Authority* (1994) 27 BMLR 107 (QB) 118–20.

[53] *Tahir v Haringey HA* (n 51 above) 108.

[54] (N 52 above) 123. The Court refers to *Mallett v McMonagle* (n 38 above); and *Davies v Taylor* (n 28 above). It adds, at 119–20, that for the purpose of assessing chances in personal injury claims, medical negligence claims are not placed in a separate category.

[55] See also: The ambiguous reasons in *Tahir v Haringey HA* (n 51 above) 108–9; and *Webb v Barclays Bank plc* referred to in CA's judgment: [2001] Lloyd's Rep Med 500 (CA) para 18. *Webb* was subsequently reversed at the agreement of both parties who recognised that damages for the loss of chance of complete or better recovery cannot be compensated.

question necessitates the assessment of what a third party would have done in the absence of the defendant's negligence. In these cases, showing that there was a substantial chance the loss would have been avoided by the third party's action was considered sufficient to entitle the plaintiff to recover, albeit in proportion to that chance.[56] The extension of *Allied Maples Group* to medical malpractice cases has led to questionable results, such as those in *Smith v National Health Service Litigation Authority* (2000). In this decision, *Allied Maples Group* was relied on to conclude there was a substantial chance the claimant's congenitally displaced hip would have been avoided had proper examination been carried out on the plaintiff in the early neo-natal period. It was argued that, since this examination would necessarily have been carried out by a third party to whom the defendant doctor should have referred the plaintiff, *Allied Maples Group* applied.[57]

A similar argument had been previously rejected in a case involving scientific uncertainty, however. In *The CJD Litigation, Straddlers Groups A and C v Secretary of State* (1998), the plaintiffs, having contracted Creutzfeldt-Jakob Disease (CJD), were claiming against the State because of its alleged negligence in not informing their physicians of the risk of transmission of the sickness through receipt of cadaveric Human Growth Hormone. Morland J found the claimants could succeed, since they had demonstrated, on the balance of probabilities, that had they been informed, their physicians would have discontinued the therapy. Even if the assessment of causation depended on what third parties would have hypothetically done had the defendant acted diligently, the Court rejected an argument based on *Allied Maples*.[58] It therefore awarded damages without any discount in respect of any percentage chance that the clinician might not have stopped the treatment. In doing so, the Court emphasised discount for chance could arise only at the quantification stage when one attempts to assess a future hypothetical outcome, for example whether a plaintiff would have received a promotion had he not had CJD.[59]

The House of Lords recently revisited this issue in *Gregg v Scott* (2004). The defendant had negligently diagnosed as innocuous a cancerous lump under the claimant's left arm. This misdiagnosis led to a nine-month delay in the claimant receiving treatment, allowing his condition to deteriorate, the tumour to enlarge, and the disease to spread elsewhere. As a result, his prospects of disease-free survival

[56] *Allied Maples Group Ltd v Simmons & Simmons (A Firm)* (n 34 above). *Substantial chance* was not defined, however. See also: M Lunney, 'Chances of Recovery in Tort: *Allied Maples Group v Simmons & Simmons*' (1996–97) 7 *King's College Law Journal* 101, 103.

[57] (N 46 above) 22. This was clearly obiter since not only did the trial judge, despite the uncertainty of the factual evidence in this regard, find on the balance of probabilities that such an examination had been carried out, but he also found the omission to detect the condition did not in itself suggest negligence because of the test's unreliability.

[58] On the basis of *Hotson v East Berkshire AHA* (n 34 above).

[59] *The CJD Litigation: Straddlers Group A and C Plaintiffs* (1998) 54 BMLR 104 (QBD) 107–8.

for 10 years were reduced from 42 per cent, when he first consulted the defendant, to 25 per cent at the date of the trial.[60] On such facts, *Gregg* was quite distinct from *Hotson* in the sense that the final outcome (X) was still prospective at the moment of the trial. The trial judge nevertheless dismissed the claim on the basis of the reasoning in *Hotson v East Berkshire Area Health Authority*,[61] concluding that Gregg had not established on the balance of probabilities that the negligence had any effect on the outcome of the disease since the prospect of cure was less than 50 per cent at the moment of the doctor's breach of duty. The Court of Appeal agreed, although it emphasised that *Hotson* had left the question open.[62] This position was confirmed by the House of Lords, albeit with two dissenting opinions from Lord Nicholls and Lord Hope.

Distinguishing *Hotson*,[63] Lords Hope and Nicholls would have granted damages for loss of chance. Lord Nicholls believed that a remedy was essential in this case and strongly criticised as irrational and indefensible the all-or-nothing rule flowing from the balance of probabilities criterion;[64] whether the prospect of recovery was above or below 50 per cent, the patient had lost something of importance and value, and denying him recovery in the second case would empty the doctor's duty of content.[65] While he agreed that events that happened in the past were matters to be established on the balance of probability, Lord Nicholls believed that proof of future possibilities called for an assessment of the likelihood of that event happening.[66] The same approach should also apply when deciding what would happen in the future, but for something which happened in the past,[67] as well as when assessing hypothetical events which did not happen in the past, nor will happen in the future because the defendant's wrong precluded them from ever materialising.[68]

[60] *Gregg v Scott* [2005] 2 AC 176 (HL). See also: Jansen who objects to the application of loss of chance if a chance subsists, qualifying these cases as mere instances of exposure to risk: (n 8 above) 281–82; Müller (n 18 above) paras 402–3.

[61] The plaintiff did not ask damages for pain and suffering, only for diminished prospects of survival.

[62] With an interesting dissent from Latham LJ who argued that the claimant could succeed on conventional grounds since he had suffered physical injury, namely the enlargement of his tumour, which in turn caused his chances of survival to be reduced, thereby relying on chance solely as a means to quantify the consequences of the physical injury. Such reasoning was specifically rejected by Mance and Simon Brown LJJ, however.

[63] *Gregg v Scott* (n 60 above) para 38 (Lord Nicholls): in *Hotson*, contrary to *Gregg*, once the patient's condition at the time of the negligence was identified, there was no significant medical uncertainty about what would have happened to the plaintiff if he had been treated promptly; paras 109–10 (Lord Hope): *Hotson* involved a question of past facts ('what happened?') to be answered on the balance of probabilities, whereas *Gregg* involved the question 'what would have happened if?', ie proving hypothetical prospects of a successful outcome that still lay in the future on the date of the alleged negligence.

[64] *Ibid* para 1.

[65] *Ibid*, paras 3–4.

[66] *Ibid*, paras 9–10, citing Lord Diplock in *Mallett v McMonagle* [1970] AC 166 (HL) 176.

[67] *Ibid*, para 10.

[68] *Ibid*, paras 14 and 17.

Beyond classic cases, Lord Nicholls would extend the application of loss of chance to cases involving true medical uncertainty, as it reflects fairly and rationally the loss suffered by a patient,[69] namely the diminution of his prospects of recovery which the doctor had a legal duty to promote by exercising due skill and care in diagnosing and treating his condition.[70] To counter floodgate arguments and the fear of substantially increasing the financial burden of the National Health Service, he suggested limiting its application to cases where the patient's prospects of recovery, notwithstanding negligence, are fraught with a significant degree of medical uncertainty; where the patient was already suffering from illness or injury at the time of the negligence;[71] and where the patient had a reasonable prospect of recovery and the diminution was a significant one.[72]

The majority of the House disagreed. Lord Hoffmann believed that the loss of chance principle had no application to this case since it can only apply to damage that is clearly attributable to the defendant's wrongful act, which was not the case here, as the trial judge had found that the deprivation of survival had not been caused by the delay in treatment.[73] A wholesale adoption of possible rather than probable causation as the criterion of liability would be so radical a change of the law as to amount to a legislative act. Because of this, and the consequences it could have for insurance companies and the National Health Service, Lord Hoffmann, with whom Lord Phillips and Baroness Hale agreed, thought such change should be left to Parliament.[74]

For Lord Phillips, resolving issues of causation on the balance of probabilities will always be easier than identifying in terms of percentage the effect that clinical negligence has on the chances of a favourable outcome: 'A robust test which produces rough justice may be preferable to a test that on occasion will be difficult, if not impossible, to apply with confidence in practice.'[75] He also worried about the possible destruction of the coherence of the common law 'if special tests of causation are developed piecemeal to deal with perceived injustices in particular factual situations.'[76] He however conceded the application of loss of chance once the adverse outcome that the exercise of due care might have averted has

[69] *Ibid*, para 46.

[70] *Ibid*, para 24. See also: Lord Hope, para 100.

[71] By opposition to claims based simply on negligent exposure to noxious substances, which carry a risk of developing disease in years to come.

[72] Paras 48–53. The argument to the effect that the loss of chance approach could encourage doctors to practice defensive medicine was also rejected. See also: Lord Hope: paras 115–16.

[73] Paras 67–68 and 71. Lord Hoffmann cites the Québec civil law decision of *Laferrière v Lawson* in support of is conclusions: para 81. He also rejected the distinction between cases in which inability to prove causation is a result of lack of medical knowledge of the causal mechanism (*Wilsher*) rather than lack of knowledge of the facts (*Hotson*), as proof of causation is difficult in both cases: para 88.

[74] Para 90.

[75] *Ibid*, para 170.

[76] *Ibid*, para 172, referring to *Fairchild's* special approach to causation: see ch 5, text to fns 67 ff.

occurred, but not where it is still prospective,[77] such as in this case where Gregg's prospects of survival were good and the long-term result of the treatment was still uncertain.[78]

Baroness Hale distinguished this case from *Hotson*, which she described as an instance in which the 'die was already cast' by the time the claimant got to the hospital, the claimant having already suffered the adversed outcome, avascular necrosis, and therefore having no chance to lose. By contrast, *Gregg* was a case where the claimant's chance of a favourable outcome were 'wiped out' while in the air before being able to land, or were significantly reduced by the negligence.[79] She was however still concerned with the consequences of adopting the loss of chance argument in such cases since almost any claim for loss of an outcome could be reformulated as a claim for loss of a chance of that outcome. Moreover, retaining both loss of chance and the all-or-nothing rule as alternatives would have substantial implications; the claimant would theoretically still have the prospect of 100 per cent recovery if he could show that it is more likely than not that the doctor's negligence caused the adverse outcome, while also having, in the alternative, the prospect of lesser recovery for loss of a chance.[80]

Gregg v Scott thus confirms the House of Lords' reluctance to accept loss of chance, although this stand is still not a firm one. Similarly, in Australia, while the lower courts have admitted medical loss of chance, the High Court has predominantly positioned itself against this principle, although there have been some dissenting voices and the door has therefore been left ajar.

2. *Australia*

The application of loss of chance in Australian medical liability cases was originally rejected,[81] but has now been accepted[82] in some lower court's decisions

[77] *Ibid*, para 188.

[78] *Ibid*, paras 190–91. He seemed open to granting compensation for the fact that the delay involved more intrusive treatment and more pain, if that question had been in front of the House.

[79] *Ibid*, paras 211–12. According to this distinction, *Laferrière v Lawson* can be distinguished from *Gregg v Scott* (n 60 above), although their facts are very similar. While in the first case, the plaintiff had died by the time the judgment was rendered, in the second, he still had prospects of recovery: see text between n 107 and n 113.

[80] *Ibid*, para 224. She was also concerned that nothing would prevent this approach from being extended to medical negligence: para 225. See generally: C Foster, 'Last Chance for Lost Chances' (2005) *New Law Journal* 248.

[81] *Stacey v Chiddy* (1993) 1993 NSW Lexis 7679 (NSWSC, 23 April 1993) 38 (Cripps JA); *Sullivan v Micallef* (1994) Aust Torts Reps 81–308 (NSWCA); *Anasson v Koziol* (1996) Aust ACTSC Lexis 68 (ACTSC, 20 December 1996): Damages were granted for the additional distress caused by the doctor's negligence: paras 48–49. See also: Luntz (n 25 above) 187.

[82] *Tran v Lam* (1997) NSW Lexis 1435 (NSWSC, 20 June 1997) 50 and 77; *Tamworth Base Hospital v Durant* (2000) NSW Lexis 225 (NSWSC, 8 August 2000) 30–31 (Priestley JA), accepting the trial judge's assessment; *Mouratidis v Brown* (2002) WL 31481229, FCAFC 330 (AustFC, 7 November 2002) para 70. But see the critique of D Hamer (n 25 above) 600. See also: *O'Shea v Sullivan* (1994) NSW Lexis 12783 (NSWSC, 6 May 1994) 59, *aff'd*: *Sullivan v Micallef* [1994] Aust Torts Reports 81–308; (1994) WL 16185812 (NSWCA, 16 August 1994) 16): Full damages granted because the plaintiff 'lost more than a chance of being cured'.

when the chance is real and substantial,[83] and proven on the balance of probabilities to be caused by the fault.[84]

For instance, in *Gavalas v Singh* (2001), the Victoria Court of Appeal dealt with the failure to diagnose the plaintiff's brain tumour, which led to delay in its treatment. One of the major issues was whether and to what extent complete eradication of the tumour would have been achieved had the surgery to remove it been carried out earlier, assuming that the smaller the tumour when detected, the better the anticipated result of the removal. Smith AJA[85] stressed: 'It is difficult to see any reason in principle why a plaintiff should not be compensated in appropriate circumstances for a lost opportunity if it flows from the alleged negligence.'[86] There was a strong case for recognising lost opportunity as a head of damage in light of the policy of compensating the injured and promoting reasonable conduct, as well as the fact that the defendant's negligence had caused the unavailability of critical evidence—here the size of the tumour at the moment the diagnosis should have been made.[87] Smith AJA thus insisted that if the relationship between the defendant and the plaintiff involved the defendant giving the plaintiff the opportunity to seek timely treatment and, as a result, a more favourable outcome, one could speak of a lost chance or a lost opportunity.[88] Nevertheless, he warned that he was not laying down a general rule as to the applicability of loss of chance in medical cases, and that courts should proceed 'in the traditional incremental common law way.'[89]

Most recently, in *Rufo v Hosking* (2004), Hodgson JA of the New South Wales Court of Appeal also accepted the argument. In this case, the plaintiff had suffered spinal microfractures as a result of heavy dosage treatment with corticosteroids. It was held sufficient for her to prove on the balance of probabilities that she had been deprived of a 'valuable' chance to avoid this loss, although that chance was of less than 50 per cent.[90] Hodgson JA limited the application of loss of chance to cases in which the best that medical science can say is that the treatment had a quantifiable chance of success. In the court's view, loss of chance could not apply where the uncertainty arises merely from imperfections in the evidence, such as contradictory expert views.[91] Cambell and Santow JJA agreed.[92] For Santow JA,

[83] *Stacey v Chiddy* (n 81 above) (Mahoney JA and Cripps JA), although not applicable in this case; *Brown v Willington* (2001) ACTSC 100 (24 October 2001) *Rufo v Hosking* (n 23 above) paras 39 (Santow JA), 410 (Campbell J).

[84] *Rufo v Hosking* (n 23 above) para 40 (Santow JA). See generally: *Quantock v Australian Capital Territory Health and Community Care Service* (2003) ACTSC 98 (28 November 2003) para 28; *Finch v Rogers* (2004) NSWSC 39 (NSWSC, 13 February 2004) para 119; D Hamer (n 25 above) 610–13.

[85] *Gavalas v Singh* (2001) 3 VR 404 (VicCA). Smith AJA dealt with loss of chance solely to provide indications in the event the case was returned to the County court for the *assessment of damages*.

[86] *Gavalas v Singh* (n 85 above) 417.

[87] *Ibid*, p 417.

[88] *Ibid*, p 418.

[89] *Ibid*. See also: Callaway JA, 409.

[90] On the basis of *Malec v JC Hutton Pty Ltd* (n 27 above); and *Sellars v Adelaide Petroleum NL* (n 23 above).

[91] *Rufo v Hosking* (n 23 above) para 10.

[92] See also: *Ibid*, paras 52–53 (Santow J) and 410 (Campbell J): chance must be 'of substance'.

loss of chance was a remedy for the injustice caused by the 'all-or-nothing' rule. He also believed it consistent with the medical duty of care since the latter aims to achieve the best chance of a successful medical outcome[93].

The Australian High Court has shown more reluctance to admit medical loss of chance, although some cases have expressed, in *obiter*, support for the idea.[94] In *Chappel v Hart* (1998), a case concerned with the breach of a medical duty to inform,[95] the plaintiff complained that had she been informed of the risk of infection associated with the removal of a pharyngeal pouch in her oesophagus, she would not have had the surgery when she did. She would rather have taken steps to have it performed by 'the most experienced [surgeon] with a record and a reputation in the field.' The majority agreed that, in such case, the procedure would have been subject to a similar but reduced risk.[96] For Gaudron J, however, the damage sustained by the plaintiff was not the loss of a chance but the physical injury which she did in fact, sustain.[97] McHugh J, dissenting on another issue, agreed, adding that because no part of the relationship between the plaintiff and the defendant involved her being given the opportunity to seek a higher standard of care or better treatment from another surgeon or an opportunity to have the procedure carried out without injury.[98] Only Kirby J was favourable to the

[93] Paras 24, 45–46 and 52. See also: *Sturch v Willmott* (QdlSC, 13 April 1995) referred to in the court of appeal's judgment of Davies JA: *Sturch v Willmott* (QdlCA, 22 November 1995) www.courts.qld.gov.au/qjudgment/QCA%201995/QCA95-521.pdf (3 October 2005); *Talbot v Lusby* [1995] QSC 143 (QdlSC, 14 July 1995) www.austlii.edu.au/cgibin/disp.pl/au/cases/qld/QSC/1995/143.html?query=%22talbot%22+and+%22lusby%22 (3 October 2005) text between fns 15 and 20: Fryberg J relied on the balance of probabilities to decide the issue of past fact, ie the stage of the plaintiff's cancer at the moment of the doctor's negligence, then relying on loss of chance to assess the chance of a cure at that time as 90%; *Veivers v Connolly* [1995] 2 Qd R 326 (QSC) 335; *Board of Management of Royal Perth Hospital v Frost* (WAFCSC, 26 February 1997); *Kite v Malycha* (1998) 71 SASR 321 (SASC) 339. Australian case law refuses the loss of chance reasoning where the chance lost is a chance that the plaintiff may have acted in such a way as to receive a benefit or avert a detriment, however: *Sellars v Adelaide Petroleum NL* (n 23 above) 353 (non medical); *Tran v Lam* (n 82 above) 50; D Hamer (n 25 above) 605–6 and cases cited.

[94] RP Balkin and JLR Davis, *Law of Torts*, 3rd edn, (Chatswood, NSW, LexisNexis Butterworths, 2004) 322. See generally: I Freckelton, 'Editorial' (1999) 7 *Journal of Law and Medicine* 5.

[95] And, thus, involving factual uncertainty which explains its brief treatment in this text.

[96] *Chappel v Hart* (1998) 195 CLR 232 (AustHC) para 97 (Kirby J). See also: MA Jones, *Medical Negligence*, 3rd edn, (London, Sweet & Maxwell, 2003) para 6–160; P Cane, 'A Warning about Causation' (1999) 115 *LQR* 21, 23–24; and T Honoré, 'Medical Non-disclosure, Causation and Risk: *Chappel v Hart*' (1999) 7 *Torts Law Journal* 1, para 10.

[97] *Chappel v Hart* (n 96 above) para 5. McHugh J agreed: para 50. See also: paras 75–76 (Gummow J), seemingly approving Gonthier J's decision in the Québec civil law case of *Laferrière v Lawson*, and paras 134–44 (Hayne J, dissenting on another issue). This is a classical argument against the loss of chance technique, eg, *Laferrière v Lawson* (n 34 above). Kirby J adds that if, independent of the breach on the part of a defendant, the evidence shows that the plaintiff would have suffered loss, the damages may be reduced by reference to the estimate of the chances that this would have occurred: para 93. But see the critique of Luntz (n 25 above) 183–84.

[98] *Chappel v Hart* (n 96 above) para 50.

argument which he thought was 'a more rational and just way of calculating damages caused by established medical negligence.'[99]

A year later, in *Naxakis v Western General Hospital* (1999), a case involving delay in the diagnosis of a burst aneurysm, loss of chance was dealt with in obiter dictae by Gaudron and Callinan JJ, who adopted opposite stands. Callinan J accepted there was room for loss of chance when the chance is lower than 51 per cent. In the contrary case, he believed the balance of probabilities standard should apply and that the plaintiff should recover in full.[100] On the other hand, Gaudron J objected to the application of loss of chance on the facts of the case, although she did not close the door completely to its application in medical malpractice instances:

> In cases involving the failure to diagnose or treat a pre-existing condition, there is no philosophical or logical difficulty in viewing the loss sustained as the loss of a chance to undergo treatment which may have prevented some or all of the injuries or disabilities sustained. Indeed, in such cases, philosophical or logical analysis would lead to the conclusion that characterisation of the loss as the loss of a chance is strictly correct. It would also lead to the conclusion that the all or nothing approach involved in allowing damages for the actual harm suffered on the basis that it was more likely than not that the harm would have been prevented by proper treatment is, at best, rough justice.[101]

Nevertheless, she emphasised difficulties in valuing the chance, an exercise depending on speculation and statistical analysis, which could not inform as to what the personal chance of the patient was.[102] She also believed that loss of chance will not necessarily work for the benefit of the individual plaintiff in cases where the chance lost is 51 per cent or greater.[103] Finally, she expressed the opinion that where the risk inherent in a pre-existing but undiagnosed or untreated condition eventuates, there is no loss of chance since the factors have played themselves out and all that is at issue are past uncertain events.[104]

[99] *Ibid*, para 93, referring to his judgment in *CES v Superclinics (Australia) Pty Ltd* (1995) 38 NSWLR 47 (CA) 56–57. See also: Priestley JA, paras 27–28. The reluctance of the High Court may be explained by its willingness to resort to presumptions of causation where the defendant's breach increased the risk of the plaintiff's injury and the plaintiff suffers that injury. See also: I Freckelton and K Petersen, *Controversies in Health Law* (Sydney, Federation Press, 1999): 'the presumption that the injuries actually sustained shortly after the negligence were caused by the negligence makes the loss of chance analysis unhelpful': 128. See ch 5, text between fns 282 and 283.

[100] *Naxakis v Western General Hospital* (n 45 above) paras 129–30. See also: I Callinan, 'Legal Rules Governing the Requirement of Causation in Tort Law' in I Freckelton and D Mendelson, (eds), *Causation in Law and Medicine* (Hampshire, Ashgate Dartmouth, 2002) 133.

[101] *Naxakis v Western General Hospital* (n 45 above) 278.

[102] *Ibid*, p 280.

[103] *Ibid*, p 279.

[104] *Ibid*, pp 280–81, citing the Québec case of *Laferrière v Lawson*. She also saw little practical significance for the loss of chance approach applied in conjunction with the balance of probabilities: p 280. Compare: *Hotson*, 786 (Lord Mackay).

The ambivalent positions of the English and Australian courts are a notable contrast to the clear stand that Québec and Canadian courts have taken in the last ten years.

3. *Québec and Canada*

Québec courts generally assess causation in medical liability instances without recourse to the loss of chance analysis, preferring to focus on the actual damage which has occurred. While the *intermediate* damage represented by the loss of chance may be mentioned in the course of analysis, the courts' preference is to satisfy themselves not only that a chance was lost but that on the balance of probabilities that chance would have been realised.[105] In 1991, this approach to loss of chance was confirmed by the Supreme Court of Canada in *Laferrière v Lawson*. The Court not only rejected the argument that loss of chance constitutes a redefinition of the damage, but also believed that, used in the medical context, the idea artificially bypasses the causation requirement. This position did not, however, constitute a revolution; it had already been largely adopted by the doctrine[106] and most of the case law on the subject.[107] Interestingly, Canadian common law courts consider this judgment as authoritative despite the fact that it was judged according to the rules of Québec civil law.[108]

As we saw,[109] the case arose from the defendant's omission to inform the plaintiff of her cancerous condition, which eventually led to her death. The trial judge dismissed the claim because there was no proof that the treatment the patient lost the chance to undertake would have had a positive effect on her health. The

[105] *Laferrière v Lawson* (n 34 above) 586. See also p 591.

[106] Nootens (n 19 above); Gaudet (n 8 above); I Parizeau, 'Le lien de causalité . . . au bord du gouffre' (1989) 49 *Canadian Bar Review* 514.

[107] *Gburek v Cohen* [1988] RJQ 2424 (CA) 2445 (Beauregard J); *Lapointe v Hôpital Le Gardeur* [1989] RJQ 2619 (CA) 2637 (Lebel J), 2629 and 2631 (Jacques J, diss); *Laferrière v Lawson* [1989] RJQ 27 (CA) 29–34 (Vallerand, dissenting); *Lachambre v Perreault* [1990] RRA 397 (CA) 399. There are a few exceptions, however: *Tardif v Laverrière* [1976] CS 1803, 1804; *Zuk v Mihaly* [1989] RRA 737 (QuéSC) 738, *Laferrière v Lawson* (CA) (above) 35–36 (Jacques J) and 39–40 (Moisan J); *Tremblay v Barrette* [1990] RRA 319 (CS) 329.

[108] *Cabral v Gupta* [1993] 1 WWR 648 (CA) 651; *Cottrelle v Gerrard* (2003) OJ No 4194; (2004) CarswellOnt 1623 (CA, 22 April 2004) paras 25 and 36 (relying on *Laferrière, St-Jean v Mercier* and *Hotson*); *Fournier v Wiens* (2004) 33 Alta LR (4th) 114 (AltaQB) para 98; *Lindahl Estate v Olsen* (2004) 360 AR 310 (AltaQB) paras 33 and 416; *O'Grady v Stokes* (2005) ABQB 247, Carswell Alta 578 (AltaQB, 26 April 2005) para 200; *Armstrong v Centenary Health Centre* (2005) WL 1331599, Carswell Ont 2366 (OntCA, 13 June 2005) para 93; *Georghiades v MacLeod* (2005) WDFL 2826 (OntSCtJ) para 130; *McPherson v Bernstein* (2005) WL 1231377, Carswell Ont 2165 (OntSCtJ, 27 May 2005) paras 205–6 (also relying on *St-Jean v Mercier* and *Gregg v Scott,* CA). Against: *Lindahl Estate v Olsen* (above) para 147 seems willing to accept the argument for the part of the claim framed in breach of the medical contract: paras 430, 434 and 437.

[109] See: ch 1, text to fn 247.

Québec Court of Appeal reversed the decision and found that the defendant's fault resulted in the loss of a real and serious chance for the plaintiff to benefit from proper medical care.[110] This decision was ultimately reversed by the Supreme Court of Canada. While granting damages for anguish and frustration,[111] it refused to compensate the plaintiff for the loss of chance of getting treatment at an earlier stage.[112]

Gonthier J, giving the Court's majority judgment, believed that recourse to loss of chance is admissible in exceptional cases in which the damage can be understood only in probabilistic and statistical terms and where it is impossible to evaluate sensibly whether or how the chance would have been realised in a given case, as when someone is negligently deprived of the chance to participate in a lottery. To transform these exceptional cases into the theoretical basis for recovery in all loss of chance situations would, in his opinion, be unnecessarily abstract and give the impression that the court is more interested in the certainty of statistical chances than the probable result which those chances represent. Consequently, the Supreme Court rejected the introduction of loss of chance into Québec medical liability:

> I am inclined to favour an approach which focuses on the actual damage which the doctor can be said to have caused to the patient by his or her fault, and to compensate accordingly. First, as I have said, I can see no basis for treating acts and omissions differently. Accordingly, there is no theoretical imperative directing courts to abandon traditional causal analysis and to adopt instead an essentially artificial loss of chance analysis. Secondly, while I concede that loss of chance analysis is less objectionable when used to evaluate damages in cases where the defendant's responsibility is otherwise clearly established or, perhaps, where no other causal factor can be identified, this type of analysis must be viewed with extreme caution in cases where there are serious doubts as to the defendant's causal role in the face of other identifiable causal factors. Even though our understanding of medical matters is often limited, I am not prepared to conclude that particular medical conditions should be treated for purposes of causation as the equivalent of diffuse elements of pure chance, analogous to the non-specific factors of fate or fortune which influence the outcome of a lottery. Thirdly, as has been pointed out frequently, in the medical context the damage has usually occurred, manifesting itself in sickness or death. In Savatier and Penneau's terms, the chance is not

[110] (CA) (n 107 above) (Vallerand J dissented).

[111] Compare with *Farrese v Fichman* (2005) WL 679018; [2005] Carswell Que 775 (CS, 25 Feberuary 2005) paras 236–37, 240.

[112] *Laferrière v Lawson* (n 34 above) 609–12 (LaForest J dissented). See also: *Massinon v Gys* [1996] RJQ 2258 (CS) 2273; *Labonté v Tanguay* (2001) para 49, confirmed by the Court of Appeal: (2003) paras 17–18; *Therrien v Launay* [2005] WL 434762, Carswell Que 486 (QuéSC, 4 March 2005) para 579. Compare: *Montpellier*, 29 May 1934, D 1934.453 and the Australian decision to grant full damages in *Tai v Hatzistavrou* (1999) NSWCA 306 (15 August 1999). As it was the case in *Laferrière*, other cases achieve compensation by focusing on a different type of injury, eg, *Fournier v Wiens* (n 108 above) para 125: an earlier diagnosis of cancer would have resulted in less invasive surgery.

> suspended or crystallized as is the case in the classical loss of chance examples; it has been realized, and the morbid scenario has necessarily played itself out. It can and should be analyzed by means of the generally applicable rules regarding causation.[113]

By restricting in such fashion the application of loss of chance,[114] the Supreme Court of Canada confirmed Québec's distinctiveness *vis-à-vis* the French judicial approach.

4. *France*

(a) Civil Courts[115]

Several civil cases in France have addressed the question of loss of chance based on the premise that it is first and foremost an independent type of damage which results from the loss of an opportunity either to realise a benefit or to avoid an injury.[116] Yet since civil law courts are as of principle hesitant to award damages which are hypothetical and future, they have required that the chance lost be real and serious. Moreover, the degree of likelihood that the chance would have been realised must be taken into account when evaluating the damage.

As early as 14 December 1965, the Cour de cassation granted a claim for loss of chance in a medical context very similar to the facts of *Hotson*.[117] After falling, an 8-year-old boy was diagnosed by the defendant doctor with a fracture of the humerus. Following the defendant's treatment, the child was still suffering when moving his elbow; other physicians later consulted found a dislocation of the elbow. Damages were consequently claimed against the first doctor who saw the child. The Court's experts expressed doubts as to the results of a proper timely treatment, however. The Court of Appeal, with whom the Cour de cassation agreed, nevertheless granted the claim on the ground that serious, precise, and concordant presumptions showed that the boy's damage was the direct consequence of the defendant's fault. It then found that the defendant's fault deprived the plaintiff of a chance of recovery for which they granted compensation.[118]

[113] (N 34 above) 605.

[114] Baudouin and Deslauriers (n 18 above) para 326 argue that the Supreme Court of Canada restricted the application of loss of chance to cases which fit the classic analysis. In the excerpt cited, Gonthier J appears to limit further the scope of application of loss of chance, however.

[115] Because of the amount of French decisions on this question, only the main cases of the Cour de cassation are discussed.

[116] Couturier, note under Cass civ 1st, 7 June 1989 (n 28 above) 159.

[117] Bull civ 1965.I.541, para 707; D 1966.jur.453; JCP 1966.G.II.14753 (note Savatier), (1967) *Revue trimestrielle de droit civil* 181 (note Durry). See also: Viney and Jourdain (n 17 above) para 280. Compare with Cass civ 1st, 7 March 1966, Bull civ 1966.I.128: Full compensation could be granted for a delay in the treatment of a fracture.

[118] Since sufficient factual presumptions were found, causation between fault and damage was proven and full recovery should have been allowed: Savatier, note under Cass civ 1st, 14 December 1965 (n 117 above).

Since this time, and despite some ferocious criticisms expressed in the doctrine, many cases have compensated lost chances in instances involving medical malpractice.[119] In fact, French courts have not paid much attention to the doctrine's objections and loss of chance still enjoys their support. Some judgments have even applied it while expressly acknowledging the uncertainty surrounding the existence of a causal link between the fault and the final injury.[120] In these cases, compensation is justified, expressly or implicitly, by the fact that the lost chance is independent of the final damage,[121] and is in a direct relationship with the fault.[122] The compensation awarded always covers only a fraction of the final injury, however. Decisions granting full recovery of the final damage on the basis of the theory have been criticised by the Cour de cassation.[123] Nevertheless, the courts do not believe that they are *partially* compensating the plaintiff's damage. On the contrary, because damage is redefined as the lost chance, recovery is considered entire.[124] Not surprisingly, loss of chance is rejected in favour of full recovery in cases in which the final damage was in direct relation to the fault.[125]

Without repudiating the theory as such, some decisions have also condemned judgments based on loss of chance when causation between the fault and the final

[119] Cass civ 1st, 18 March 1969 and 27 January 1970, JCP 1970.G.II.16422; Cass civ 1st, 25 May 1971 (*1ère et 2e espèces*), Bull civ 1971.I.n170, D 1972.534 (note Penneau), JCP 1971.G.II.16859; Cass civ 1st, 17 November 1970, D 1971.46; Cass civ 1st, 9 May 1973 (2 cases), JCP 1974.G.II.17643 (note Savatier), Gaz Pal 1973.Jur.631 (note Doll), D 1973.116; Cass civ 1st, 27 March 1973, JCP 1974.G.II.17643 (note Savatier), D 1973.Jur.595 (note Penneau); Cass civ 1st, 2 May 1978, Gaz Pal 1978.2.somm.251, JCP 1978.G.II.18966 (note Savatier); Cass civ 1st, 24 March 1981, D 1981.jur.545 (note Penneau), JCP 1981.G.IV.212, Bull civ 1981.I.n98; and cases cited at n 135 below.

[120] Cass civ 1st, 18 March 1969 and 27 January 1970 (n 119 above); Cass civ 1st, 8 January 1985, D 1986.jur.39 (note Penneau); Cass civ 1st, 24 March 1981 (n 119 above); Cass civ 1st, 12 November 1985 (n 119 above); Cass civ 1st, 16 July 1991 (n 135 above); Cass civ 1st, 4 November 2003, D 2004.n9.p601; Rennes 7th, 29 September 2004, Juris-Data No 255649. See also: F Descorps Declère, 'La cohérence de la jurisprudence de la Cour de cassation sur la perte de chance consecutive a une faute du medecin' (2005) *Dalloz* 742.

[121] Cass civ 1st, 18 March 1969 and 27 January 1970 (n 119 above); Cass civ 1st, 25 May 1971 (n 119 above); Cass civ 1st, 21 November 1978, JCP 1979.G.II.19033 (note Savatier); Cass civ 1st, 2 May 1978 (n 119 above); Cass civ 1st, 24 March 1981 (n 119 above); Cass civ 1st, 17 November 1982 (n 8 above); Cass civ 1st, 8 January 1985 (n 120 above); Cass civ 1st, 12 November 1985 (n 119 above); Cass civ 1st, 10 January 1990, D 1991.somm.358, Gaz Pal 6–7 June 1990, D 1990.IR.31; Montpellier 1st div, 21 January 1993, JCP 1993.G.IV.283.

[122] Paris 1st B, 18 September 2003, Juris-Data No 228790.

[123] Cass civ 1st, 27 March 1973 (n 119 above); Cass civ 1st, 9 May 1973 (n 119 above); Cass civ 1st, 18 January 1989 D 1989.somm.315.

[124] Cass civ 1st, 1 June 1976, JCP 1976.II.18483 (note Savatier); Montpellier, 21 January 1993 (n 121 above). See also: G Mémeteau, 'Perte de chance et responsabilité médicale' (1997) *Gazette du Palais* 1367, 1370.

[125] Cass civ 1st, 1 June 1976 (n 124 above) (note Savatier); Cass civ 1st, 26 March 1996, Bull civ 1996.I.n155, RTDC 1996.623, JCP 1996.G.I.3985 (note Viney), D 1997.jur.35 (note Roche Dahan) (breach of the duty to inform); Cass civ 1st, 13 May 1997, Resp civ et ass 1997.comm.n274; Paris 1st B, 12 November 2004, Juris-Data No 254352. Loss of chance is sometimes used, after the causal link between the plaintiff's injury and the fault is proven, to operate a discount for vicissitudes of life, eg, Pau 1st, 11 October 2004, Juris-Data No 256842.

damage has not been shown.[126] They contend that this automatically excludes the possibility of causation between the fault and the loss of the chance.[127] The Cour de cassation decision of 17 November 1982 is the most famous instance of this. The defendant doctor injected air into his patient's nose while carrying out sinus surgery. This was negligent, since it created a risk of embolism because of the presence of a non-faulty cut revealed by a haemorrhage. Air did penetrate the blood vessels and embolism followed, leading to the patient's permanent disability. The embolism could not be linked to the defendant's fault, however, because it could also have been caused by air normally contained in the sinus. The Court of Appeal nevertheless compensated the plaintiff for his lost chance of avoiding embolism. This decision was condemned by the Cour de cassation on the basis that loss of chance could be used only to assess damages.

This decision was described as a *coup d'état,*[128] a reconsideration of the case law on loss of chance,[129] and a reversal of it.[130] It was also more reasonably interpreted as limiting the function of loss of chance to the definition of the damage[131] and as a reminder that the argument should not be used to bypass the absence of causation.[132] Thus it was argued that the Court was merely reaffirming that for a finding of causation between the fault and the alleged lost chance, the doctor's fault must have played some role in producing the damage.[133] These positions contradict the view of loss of chance as an autonomous head of damage and the argument that causation must be proven only between that head of damage (not the final outcome) and the fault. Another interpretation which responds more logically to this criticism is that this case illustrates the rule that loss of chance cannot be relied on to counteract the absence of causation and can apply only if there were *strong chances* of avoiding the damage. Consequently, loss of chance cannot be resorted to when alternative causes of the damage exist, as in this case.[134]

Notwithstanding the diverse interpretations of the 17 November 1982 case, which constitutes but one example of the confusion loss of chance can lead to in

[126] Cass civ 1st, 16 July 1991, JCP 1992.G.II.21947.

[127] Cass civ 1st, 2 May 1978 (n 119 above); Cass civ 1st, 17 November 1982 (n 8 above); Cass civ 1st, 12 November 1985, Bull civ 1985.I.n299 (*Germain v Estragnat*); Cass civ 1st, 11 October 1988, Bull civ 1988.I.n281; Cass civ 1st, 10 January 1990 (n 121 above); Viney and Jourdain (n 17 above) para 372 and cases cited at fn 193.

[128] Dorsner-Dolivet (n 8 above).

[129] Viney and Jourdain (n 17 above) para 372.

[130] Saluden, note under Cass civ 1st, 17 November 1982 (n 8 above); Durry (1983) (n 10 above) 548; Penneau, note under Cass Civ 1st, 17 November 1982, *Dalloz* 1983.IR.380.

[131] G Mémeteau, 'Perte de chance en droit médical français' (1986) 32 *McGill Law Journal* 125, 141; Mémeteau (1997) (n 124 above) 1370; Durry (1983) (n 10 above) 548; Müller (n 18 above) para 108.

[132] Durry (1983) (n 10 above) 547.

[133] Penneau, note under Cass civ 1st, 8 January and 27 March 1985, D 1986.392 commenting on Cass civ 1st, 17 November 1982 (n 8 above).

[134] Dorsner-Dolivet and Saluden's respective notes under Cass civ 1st, 17 November 1982 (n 8 above).

medical negligence, loss of chance was not yet dead. After 1982, the French courts repeatedly agreed to compensate for lost chances, even in cases in which there was uncertainty as to the causal link between the fault and the final damage.[135] More than any other solution discussed in this study, loss of chance remains the French judiciary's preferred tool for dealing with causative difficulties caused by scientific uncertainty in medical malpractice. This preference has also been expressed by the administrative courts.[136]

(b) Administrative Courts

French administrative courts have applied the concept of loss of chance to the assessment of damages in medical liability cases at least since 1964.[137] This has been the case, for instance, in the context of injury resulting from delay in treatment,[138] errors in diagnosis leading to the wrong treatment,[139] negligent treatment,[140] and absence of diagnosis tests.[141] Reliance on loss of chance allows the administrative

135 Cass civ 1st, 12 November 1985, Bull civ 1985.I.n298, JCP 1986.G.IV.42 (*Konstantinow v Manrique*); Cass civ 1st, 8 January 1985 and 27 March 1985 (n 133 above); Cass civ 1st , 7 June 1989 (n 28 above); Cass civ 1st, 18 January 1989, D 1989.somm.315; Cass civ 1st, 10 January 1990 (n 121 above); Cass civ 1st, 16 July 1991, JCP 1992.G.II.21947 (involving breach of the duty to inform); Paris 1st B, 27 novembre 2003, Juris-Data No 227819; Cass civ 1st, 4 November 2003 (n 120 above). See also: Tacchini-Laforest (n 29 above) 10 and cases cited at fn 34 and 35; Viney and Jourdain (n 17 above) para 372 and cases cited at fn 190.

136 Loss of chance is also resorted to in French penal law: Müller (n 18 above) paras 117–20. Because of the large number of decisions on this question, only the main cases of the Conseil d'État and the Cours administratives d'appel are cited.

137 CE 24 April 1964, Rec CE.259 (*Hôpital civil de Thann*) cited and commented on by Müller (n 18 above) paras 111 and 113; CE contentieux, 18 November 1966, Juris-Data No 63783. See generally: Müller (n 18 above) paras 111–16.

138 CE 5th and 3rd sub-s, 6 May 1985, Juris-Data No 40705 (no %); CE 5th and 3rd sub-s, 6 July 1988: Juris-Data No 40025 (25%) (facts similar to those of *Wilsher*); CAA Paris plenière, 20 June 1989, Juris-Data No 47256; CAA Bordeaux, 6 June 1989, Juris-Data No 047620 (no %), CE 5th and 3rd sub-s, 20 March 1991, Juris-Data No 042039, Gaz du Pal 1991.438 (no %); CAA Lyon 3rd, 11 May 1994, Juris-Data No 046740 (serious chances: 100%); CAA Nantes 2nd, 20 June 1991, Gaz Pal 1992.pan.99, Juris-Data No 051226 (no %); CE contentieux, 19 December 1984, Rec CE.433, Juris-Data No 29047 (*Mlle Boehrer*); CAA Paris plénière, 9 June 1998, Juris-Data No 050723; CE, 1 June 1998; Trib adm Poitiers 1st, 3 June 1999: Juris-Data No 100723 (60%).

139 CE contentieux, 9 July 1975, Rec CE.421, Juris-Data No 93206 (*Sieur Grandclément*); CE 5th and 3rd sub-s, 6 May 1985 (n 138 above); CE 5th and 3rd sub-s, 6 May 1988, Gaz Pal 1989.pan.20; CAA Lyon 3rd, 11 May 1994 (n 138 above) (serious chances: 100%).

140 CE 3rd and 5th sub-s, 4 August 1982, Juris-Data No 27727; CAA Paris 1st, 2 October 1990, Juris-Data No 046825; CE 5th and 3rd sub-s, 20 March 1991 (n 138 above); CE 5th and 3rd sub-s, 11 December 1991, Gaz Pal 1992.pan adm.115, Juris-Data No 048768 (no %); CAA Nantes 1st, 10 April 1991, Juris-Data No 050697 (loss of 100% chance of survival); Trib adm Rennes 3rd, 30 December 1992, Juris-Data No 048620; CAA Nantes 3rd, 16 November 2000, Juris-Data No 147205; CAA Paris 3rd A, 25 January 2000, Juris-Data No 130880 (no %); CAA Douai 2nd, 17 June 2003, No 01DA00951 (loss of chance appears to be used to qualify both the injury and the fault).

141 CE 5th and 3rd sub-s, 6 May 1985 (n 138 above) (no %); CAA Paris 1st, 2 October 1990 (n 140 above) (no %); CE 5th and 3rd sub-s, 18 October 1989, Gaz Pal 1990.pan adm.11; CE, 1 June 1998 (n 138 above); CAA Paris, 3rd B, 20 October 1998, Juris-Data No 045752. See also: CAA Nantes 3rd, 29 December 2000, Juris-Data No 145991 (defective diagnosis equipment).

courts to grant compensation in cases where the causal link between the fault and the final injury is only 'probable'.[142] To be compensated, the loss of the chance must not remain solely hypothetical;[143] it must be real.[144] As in front of the civil jurisdictions, loss of chance is discarded for full recovery where, in the absence of fault, the final injury would not have arisen,[145] or where the plaintiff lost a *serious* chance of recovery.[146] Conversely, if the evidence demonstrates that the final injury would have arisen regardless of the defendant's negligence, recovery for lost chances is refused.[147] It is noteworthy that in many of the cases allowing recovery for lost chances, the percentage of the chance lost is not assessed by the court.[148]

Both the civil and administrative courts have thus approached medical causal uncertainty mainly through loss of chance, which explains the relative lack of importance of other methods, such as presumptive reasoning, in addressing this problem in French law.

Section 2

Market-share Liability

This section would be incomplete without brief comments on the American doctrine of *market-share liability*. However, we will dispense with discussion of its subtleties and analysis of its soundness because, first, market-share liability

[142] CAA Paris 3rd B, 9 May 2001, Juris-Data No 158818.

[143] CAA Lyon 1st, 20 March 2001, Juris-Data No 163535.

[144] CAA Douai 2nd, 23 March 2004, No 03DA00440.

[145] CAA Nancy plénière, 21 December 2000, Juris-Data No 137233; CAA Nancy 3rd, 26 October 2000, Juris-Data No 147224; CAA Nancy 3rd, 5 February 2004, No 97NC02374. However, some decisions conclude that all of the plaintiff's chances were destroyed by the defendant's fault: CAA Nantes 1st, 10 April 1991 (n 140 above).

[146] Trib adm Nantes 4th, 11 February 1993, Juris-Data No 046763; CAA Lyon 3rd, 11 May 1994 (n 138 above).

[147] CAA Nantes 3rd, 27 May 2004, No 02NT01100; CAA Lyon 3rd, 6 November 2001, Juris-Data No 182201.

[148] CE 5th and 3rd sub-s, 6 May 1985 (n 138 above); CAA Paris plenière, 20 June 1989 (n 138 above); CAA Bordeaux, 6 June 1989 (n 138 above); CE 5th and 3rd sub-s, 20 March 1991 (n 138 above); CAA Nantes 2nd, 20 June 1991 (n 138 above); CE, 1 June 1998 (n 138 above); CAA Paris 3rd B, 20 October 1998 (n 141 above); CAA Paris, plénière, 9 June 1998 (n 138 above). Against: CE 5th and 3rd sub-s, 6 July 1988 (n 138 above) (25%); Trib adm Rennes 3rd, 30 December 1992 (n 140 above) (2/3); CAA Lyon 3rd, 11 May 1994 (n 138 above) (serious chances: 100%); Trib adm Poitiers 1st, 3 June 1999 (n 138 above) (60%); CAA Paris 3rd ch, 9 May 2001 (n 142) (50%). The percentage may be established by taking into account the chance that the injury might have arisen in any case, due to the plaintiff's state of health (CAA Douai 2nd, 17 June 2003 (n 140 above): 1/3) or other inherent risks linked to the treatment (CE 5th and 3rd sub-s, 6 July 1988 (n 138 above) (25%).

[148] CE contentieux, 9 July 1975, (n 139 above); CE 5th and 3rd sub-s, 6 May 1985 (n 138 above); CE 5th and 3rd sub-s, 6 May 1988 (n 139 above); CAA Lyon 3rd, 11 May 1994 (n 138 above) (serious chances: 100%).

mainly concerns the attribution of liability for damage caused by defective pharmaceutical products. Second, it is unlikely that this option will be followed, especially in Canadian and English common law.[149] This view is confirmed by the cold reception given to proportional recovery in these countries, as well as the independence their judiciaries seek to maintain from mathematical and statistical approaches to the determination of causation, especially in Canada.[150] Finally, market-share liability was developed to deal with a purely factual uncertainty, namely the impossibility of identifying the author of the damage. Saying a few words on the reasoning behind this technique is nevertheless of interest, since it bears resemblances to, and is inspired by, two of the solutions examined in this book, reversal of the burden of proof and probabilistic assessment of damages. Moreover, it has developed interesting justifications for its plaintiff-friendly approach and the limits imposed on it, which may have an impact on other instances of uncertain causation.[151]

The idea of market-share liability was developed in *Sindell v Abbott Laboratories* (1980).[152] This case arose from a defect in diethylstilbestrol (DES), a drug which expectant mothers took during their pregnancy to prevent miscarriage. These women's daughters suffered as a result from a type of cancer, as well as other conditions, a fact which was not discovered until their puberty. By the time the plaintiffs became aware of their damage, it was impossible to identify the precise manufacturer of the drug their mothers had ingested. A claim was nevertheless brought against eleven pharmaceutical companies, all of which had been in the business of manufacturing, promoting, and marketing DES from a single formula.

In order to deal with the impossibility of identifying the author of damage, the Supreme Court of California refused recourse to *Summers v Tice* (1948),[153] the application of which it found unfair in this specific instance. In *Sindell*, the defendants were not at fault for the difficulty or impossibility of identifying causation, since this was due rather to the passage of time. Furthermore, they had not possessed more information than the plaintiffs in this respect.[154] Finally, there were 200 possible defendants in *Sindell*, whereas in *Summers v Tice* there were only two who were both called before the Court. Consequently, while in *Summers* there was a 50 per cent chance that one of the two defendants was responsible for the plaintiff's injuries, the probability was much lower in *Sindell*.

The Court nevertheless recognised that in an area of mass production and complex marketing methods some adaptation of the rules of causation and liability

[149] Jones (n 96 above) 8–60.

[150] Ch 2, text between fns 44 and 68.

[151] For a review of its advantages and disadvantages: Fleming (n 25 above) 668.

[152] *Sindell v Abbott Laboratories* 26 Cal 3d 588; 2 ALR (4th) 1061; 163 Cal Rptr 132; 607 P 2d 924 (Cal, 1980).

[153] 33 Cal 2d 80; 199 P 2d 1; 5 ALR 2d 91 (Cal, 1948). See ch 3, text to fn 3.

[154] *Sindell v Abbott* (n 152 above) 930.

might be appropriate.[155] Where liability would otherwise be found against several manufacturers save for the fact that the plaintiff could not identify which of them had marketed the pharmaceutical product which has caused him injury, each manufacturer was to be held liable in proportion of its *market-share* of the loss, unless it could show that it did not cause it.[156] On that basis, not only could liability be allocated proportionally to each defendant's causative chance of having been the cause of the plaintiff's damage, but the burden of disproving causation was automatically shifted to the defendant's shoulders. To diminish the injustice of shifting the burden of proof, it was necessary, however, to prove possession by the defendant of a *substantial share* of the market for the drug at the time of the events.[157] Since, in practice, the defendants were unable to show that their respective product did not cause the harm in the individual case at hand, the plaintiffs were thus effectively dispensed from proving causation.[158]

The decision was admittedly based on policy factors, *inter alia* that defendants are better able to bear the cost of injury than the plaintiff, consumer, or patient; that they were in the best position to discover and guard against defects in their products and warn of harmful effects; that liability could provide an incentive to enhance product safety; that as between an innocent plaintiff and negligent defendants, the last should bear the cost of the injury; and even though the absence of evidence of causation was not due to the defendants, their conduct in marketing a drug the effects of which are delayed for many years played a significant role in creating the unavailability of proof. Richardson J dissented vigorously on the basis that this approach did violence to long established traditional tort principles by imposing liability on manufacturers that are not shown to have played any part whatever in causing the injury;[159] it was 'an unreasonable overreaction for the purpose of achieving what is perceived to be a socially satisfying result.'[160]

The post-*Sindell* American case law has not approached the problem uniformly[161] and *Sindell* seems not to have been followed beyond the DES cases even in

[155] *Ibid*, p 936.

[156] *Ibid*, p 937.

[157] *Ibid.* The case, admittedly, did not resolve practical problems in defining the market and in determining whether a defendant holds a *substantial* part of it.

[158] HLA Hart and T Honoré, *Causation in the Law*, 2nd edn, (Oxford, Clarendon Press, 1985) 424. For an interesting comparative review: Van Gerven, J Lever and P Larouche, *Cases, Materials and Text on National, Supranational and International Tort Law* (Oxford, Hart Publishing, 2000) 447–52.

[159] *Sindell v Abbott* (n 152 above) 938–39.

[160] *Ibid*, p 943.

[161] A Porat and A Stein, *Tort Liability under Uncertainty* (Oxford, OUP, 2001) 63–64. Some courts followed and expanded on it, eg, *Martin v Abbott Laboratories* 102 Wn 2d 581; 689 P2d 368 (Wash, 1984); *McCormack v Abbott Laboratories* 617 F Supp 1521 (DC Mass, 1985). Others criticised or rejected it: AM Linden and LN Klar, *Canadian Tort Law: Cases, Notes and Materials,* 11th edn, (Toronto, Butterworths, 1999) 277; Gerecke (n 9 above) 816 and 819. The South Australian Law Reform Committee rejected it in 1985: *87th Report Relating to Claims for Injuries from Toxic Substances and Radiation Effects*, No 87 (1985).

the United States.[162] It has been criticised as seeking to achieve not corrective but distributive justice, as lacking precedent, and as being incompatible with the traditional notion of tort as a system of individual responsibility.[163]

Section 3

Critical Analysis (Loss of Chance)

A critical discussion of loss of chance may at first sight appear superfluous, given the positions of the courts towards this concept. It is justified, however, by the prominence of this solution in the French medical malpractice cases, as well as by the existence of some English and Australian cases that, despite *Hotson v East Berkshire Area HA* (1987), have been willing to rely on the notion. In this section, we wish to argue for complete closure of the loss of chance door *until* agreement is reached on the need to reassess the rules of proof and civil liability.

Particular examination of the judicial application of the French concept of loss of chance and the critique of the associated doctrine cannot but be illuminating, for the French experience with this concept in the field of medical negligence has lasted for 40 years. Despite its extensive application by the French courts, the doctrine remains highly divided on this issue. Loss of chance thus should not be supposed an attractive option without a close analysis of French developments, as the Supreme Court of Canada did in *Laferrière v Lawson* (1991).[164] Québec's clear positioning on this issue also sets an admirable example of decisiveness. While rejecting the loss of chance option, the Supreme Court of Canada pleaded in favour of flexibility in the assessment of causation in the confidence that such flexibility was attainable by other means. This makes the Québec position an interesting model.

At first sight, the concept of loss of chance appears to be an attractive alternative to the all-or-nothing rule. Not only does it give the courts the flexibility they desire; it also achieves apparent fairness to both parties. By ensuring the award of damages is calculated according to the probability that the defendant caused the plaintiff's damage, it allows victims to obtain damages despite causal uncertainties,

[162] Gerecke (n 9 above) 821–22.

[163] Fleming (n 25 above) 668. Conversely, in The Netherlands, it was considered not generous enough towards victims: Hoge Raad der Nederlanden (Dutch Supreme Court), HR 9 October 1992, Rvdw 1992, nr219 translated in Van Gerven, *et al* (n 158 above) 447–49. It was also found unnecessary in light of Art 6:99 BW. See on this article: C Von Bar, *The Common European Law of Torts*, vol 1 (Oxford, Clarendon Press, 1998) 60–61.

[164] *Laferrière v Lawson* (n 34 above).

but without compensating them unduly. On the other hand, it does not impose an unfair burden on the defendant, since it holds him liable only to the extent that he is shown to have caused the damage.[165] In addition, the concept appears conceptually sound, as it focuses on a simple redefinition of the damage and maintains the traditional fault and causation requirements. But a careful look below the surface reveals difficulties that prevent an adoption of this approach without a broader and deeper analysis of its conceptual framework and all its implications.

In France as elsewhere, this solution has led to fierce doctrinal controversies which have had a clear influence on the positions adopted by the courts. This section begins with an overview of the different arguments developed by the doctrine in favour of and against this concept; next it argues further against the concept by emphasising its general implications and the fact that this solution is not required by the need to assess causation with flexibility, a aim that can be attained through other, conceptually sounder, means. The doctrinal discourse is analysed irrespective of jurisdictional frontiers, since the similarity amongst the arguments developed in the four jurisdictions makes a strict comparative review unnecessary. Moreover, the logic of loss of chance is similarly expressed conceptually in both civil law and common law, further justifying an integrated treatment of the debates.

These involve mainly two schools of thought. According to the first, loss of chance in medical cases is viewed as merely a type of damage, as in the classic cases. The second objects to it, contending that its true impact on medical liability cases is the undermining of the causation requirement.

A. Doctrinal Debate: Arguments in Favour

Besides the positive impact of avoiding the unfairness of the traditional all-or-nothing approach,[166] the strongest argument in favour of loss of chance is the contention that it is a valid type of damage independent of the actual *future* damage, ie, the benefit missed or the injury that was not avoided.[167] This simple reformulation of the nature of the injury allows for recourse to the classic cases reasoning and the contention that loss of chance solely seeks the calculation of the loss. By requalifying

[165] On the fairness of the approach: R Goldberg, 'The Role of Scientific Evidence in the Assessment of Causation in Medicinal Product Liability Litigation' in H Reece, (ed), *Law and Science* (Oxford, OUP, 1998) 55, 59.

[166] England: *Hotson v East Berkshire Area Health Authority* [1987] 2 WLR 287 (CA) 294 (Donaldson MR) 298 (Dillon LJ); J Stapleton, 'The Gist of Negligence, Part II: The Relationship Between "Damage" and "Causation"' (1988) 104 *LQR* 389, 390–91; Canada: Gerecke (n 9 above) 802.

[167] Defended in England and Scotland: Stapleton (n 166 above) 392–93 and 396–97; N Jansen, 'The Idea of a Lost Chance' (1999) 19 *OJLS* 271, 274 and 282; M Hogg, 'Lost Chances in Contract and Delict' (1997) *Scots Law Times* 71, 71; in France: G Durry, 'Faute médicale et perte de chances de survie' (1972) *Revue trimestrielle de droit civil* 408, 410 ; G Durry, 'La faute du médecin diminuant les "chances de guérison" du malade' (1967) *Revue trimestrielle de droit civil* 181, 182; A Tunc, 'Perte d'une chance de guérison par suite d'une erreur de diagnostic' (1963) *Revue trimestrielle de droit civil* 334, 335;

the loss of the chance as a type of injury (Y), different from the ultimate loss that is suffered in many medical cases (X),[168] the inquiry becomes essentially, as in the classic instances, concerned with identifying an hypothetical hoped-for result that still layed in the future at the moment of the wrongdoing.

Such an argument adequately fits the traditional analysis, since causation must still be proven between the lost chance and the fault, whether on the balance of probabilities or with certainty. Moreover, once causation is shown, the loss (ie, the loss of chance) is payable in full and there is no discount to allow for the possibility that the chance might have been lost through the operation of other causes. Finally, one must ensure that the chance lost is not a speculative or hypothetical one or, in civil law terms, that it is real and serious, by demonstrating a certain level of probability of fulfilment of the chance. This approach is *prima facie* compelling because it confirms the apparent conceptual validity of the notion and its conformity with the rules of civil liability.

Other arguments in favour of the concept include the following. A substantial chance of a cure is something of considerable value to which plaintiffs are entitled and for which people will give money, as is the case with economic opportunity.[169] It is also argued that loss of chance better accounts for the fact that statistical chances do not necessarily reflect the plaintiff's personal chance, ie, the fact that even if, statistically, a patient has only a 25 per cent chance of surviving, *this* plaintiff may himself have been one of the 25 per cent who would have escaped but for the defendant's action.[170] Some also plead that when statistics are available, they provide a better and easier way of assessing causal responsibility than the vague traditional balance of probabilities standard.[171] In addition, in lightening the plaintiff's burden of proof, loss of chance helps him deal with the imbalance of knowledge and financial resources between him and the defendant doctor. In doing so, it also contributes to making the medical profession more responsible and consequently helps ensure quality of practice.[172] Loss of chance consequently

J Boré, 'L'indemnisation pour les chances perdues: une forme d'appréciation quantitative de la causalité d'un fait dommageable' (1974) I *La semaine juridique* 2620, para 38; P Sargos, Report under Cass civ 1st, 8 July 1997, JCP.1997.G.II.22921, para 18; Couturier, note under Cass civ 1st, 7 June 1989, D 1991.jur.158, 160 (also reported at D 1991.somm.323, JCP 1989.G.IV.294, D 1991.somm.323); L Dubouis, 'Perte d'une chance de survie. Indemnisation' (1971) *Revue trimestrielle de droit sanitaire et social* 66, 69. In Canada, Gerecke (n 9 above) 802 develops the same argument with regards to risk.

[168] The 'X' injury exists in most medical liability cases reviewed in this work, except for *Gregg v Scott* (n 60 above) where, interestingly, it was still prospective at the moment of the trial.

[169] Waddams (n 21 above) 21, 33 and 36, adapting the words of *Chaplin v Hicks;* Masel (n 22 above) 20.

[170] Stapleton (n 166 above) 394.

[171] M Stauch, 'Causation, Risk and Loss of Chance in Medical Negligence' (1997) 17 *OJLS* 205, 206; C Müller, 'La perte d'une chance médicale en droit comparé et suisse' (2003) 9 *Revue générale de droit médical* 105, 120.

[172] England: Stapleton (n 166 above) 399; Hogg (n 167 above) 72; Gerecke (n 9 above) 808; France: G Durry, 'La faute du médecin diminuant les "chances de guérison" du malade' (1969) *Revue trimestrielle de droit civil* 797, 798. See also: Fleming (n 25 above) 679–80.

allows for the policy objectives of compensation of the injured and the promotion of reasonable conduct (deterrence).[173] Finally, in answer to objections that loss of chance could impose overwhelming liability on the medical profession, it is argued that the disadvantage of having to grant damages for lost chances in most cases is counterbalanced by the fact that under the all-or-nothing rule, 100 per cent of the injury is compensated even when the causal probability is less.[174]

Even supporters impose limitations on the application of loss of chance, however. Chabas has argued that loss of chance reasoning can apply only in the presence of a pre-existing chance. This requirement is met when the plaintiff's situation is reduced to *only* a chance before the fault is committed and the defendant's fault makes the plaintiff lose this chance.[175] For instance, if a patient, through no fault of the defendant, is already engaged in a process capable by itself of producing a negative outcome, death or disability (eg, cancer),[176] all he possesses is a chance of avoiding the outcome. The doctor's fault, a wrong diagnosis, an improper treatment, or a delayed intervention, may increase his pre-existing risk of death or disability, or in other words make him lose a chance of avoidance. If the patient subsequently dies of cancer or is left disabled, it may be uncertain whether the patient's damage flows from the pre-existing risk ('He would have died in any event') or from the aggravation of the risk due to the doctor's fault ('He would not have died if treated promptly'). According to Chabas, loss of chance is admissible to solve this type of uncertainty. The damage becomes the loss of the pre-existing chance, which is assessed by taking into account the reasonable possibilities of the treatment ('With proper treatment, the patient would have had a 25 per cent chance of cure or survival'). Hence the choice between the two alternative causes is avoided. Only one possible cause remains: the doctor's fault.

Conversely, if the plaintiff possesses all his chances with regard to the particular risk that arose when the fault was committed, or if he has none, loss of chance has no relevance.[177] For instance, the patient consults the doctor with a pre-existing

[173] *Gavalas v Singh* (n 85 above).

[174] Müller (n 171 above) 119–20.

[175] F Chabas, 'La perte d'une chance en droit français' in O Guillod, (ed), *Développements récents du droit de la responsabilité civile* (Genève, Centre d'études juridiques européennes, 1991) 131. See also: J Penneau, note under Cass civ 1st, 4 November 2003 (n 120 above); Müller (n 18 above) paras 365 and 369.

[176] Eg, England: *Hotson v East Berkshire Area Health Authority* [1987] 1 AC 750; France: Cass civ 1st, 17 November 1982, D 1984.jur.305, 308 (note Dorsner-Dolivet), Bull civ 1982.I.n333, D 1983.380, JCP 1983.G.IV.41, JCP 1983.G.II.20056 (note Saluden); Versailles, 27 January 1994, D1994.jur.83; Chabas (n 175 above) 133–35, 153 and 156; Québec: *Laferrière v Lawson* (n 34 above).

[177] Cass civ 1st, 25 May 1971 (*3e espèce*), Bull civ 1971.I.n170, D 1972.534 (note Penneau), JCP 1971.G.II.16859.

ailment involving a risk of damage, (eg, a back problem necessitating surgery). Because the surgeon (or hospital) negligently omits to secure the assistance of an anaesthetist throughout the operation, the patient dies from anoxia.[178] Before the fault was committed with regard to the specific damage which arose, the patient retained all his chances save those affected by inherent medical risks. The only relevant question in such a case is whether the defendant's fault caused the final damage.

Chabas' distinction may simply turn on the dichotomy between cases in which the defendant's fault increases a pre-existing risk and cases in which it creates a new risk, loss of chance having meaning only in the former.[179] This distinction is rarely made in the case law, however.[180] Moreover, it has its drawbacks. Because of the invariable existence of inherent medical risks, one can almost always argue the doctor's fault increased a risk rather than created a new one solely by modifying the definition of the risk.[181] For instance, in the above example, one could contend that there are generally no guarantees but only chances that one will survive anaesthesia.

Despite this and other criticisms,[182] we agree that if loss of chance is to be accepted, it is only when the patient's situation is *reduced to no more than chance* with regard to the damage that arose that chance can be identified as an autonomous asset in the plaintiff's patrimony. Even in such cases, loss of chance is an unacceptable avenue, however. Indeed, despite the favourable arguments mentioned above, the doctrinal debates in the four main jurisdictions have brought several objections to light which make a compelling case against the concept of loss of chance.

[178] See also, eg, Cass civ 1st, 27 January 1970, JCP 1970.G.II.16422; Cass civ 1st, 1 June 1976, JCP 1976.G.II.18483 (note Savatier); Cass civ 1st, 17 November 1982 (n 176 above); Cass civ 1st, 8 January 1985, D 1986.jur.39 (note Penneau).

[179] This distinction may actually explain the rejection of loss of chance in the Cass civ 1st, 17 November 1982 (n 176 above) case: 186 above (ch 2). See also: Vacarie's distinction between actions and omissions; in her opinion, loss of chance is admissible only in the latter: I Vacarie, 'La perte d'une chance' (1987) 3 *Revue de la recherche juridique* 903, 908–13. Often, cases involving positive action are instances in which the defendant created a new risk rather than increased an existing one, however, eg, Cass civ 1st, 17 November 1982 (above); Cass civ 1st, 8 January 1985 (n 178 above). See also D Hamer's critique of the distinction: (n 25 above) 603.

[180] It was overlooked in Cass civ 1st, 27 March 1973, JCP 1974.G.II.17643 (note Savatier), D 1973.jur.595 (note Penneau): Chabas (n 175 above) 140. See also: Cass civ 1st, 27 January 1970 (n 178 above); Cass civ 1st, 17 November 1982 (n 176 above); Viney and Jourdain (n 17 above) para 372. The distinction was made by the Québec Court of Appeal in *Lapointe v Hôpital Le Gardeur* where a loss of chance argument was rejected on this basis: (N 107 above) 2643 (Lebel J) and 2647 (Mailhot J) (not discussed on appeal: (1992) 90 DLR (4th) 7; [1992] 1 SCR 351).

[181] See also: P Jourdain, 'Sur la perte d'une chance' (1992) *Revue trimestrielle de droit civil* 109, 111.

[182] *Ibid*, p 111; V Tacchini-Laforest, 'Réflexions à propos de la perte de chance' (1999) 142 *Petites Affiches* 7, 10.

B. Doctrinal Objections

In general, academic writings, especially in France and Québec, reveal unease with the extension of the loss of chance theory to medical cases. The objections revolve around the following elements: medical loss of chance cannot be assimilated to the classic cases; loss of chance opens the door to speculative claims, is assessed arbitrarily, and gives an undue role to statistics; it prompts unjust results and its real effect is to allow the judge to ignore the absence of causation between the fault and the actual damage; and finally it may lead to a revolution in the systems of civil liability.

1. Distinction from the Classic Cases

Opponents to medical loss of chance have attempted to destroy the analogy drawn by its supporters between these cases and the classic ones.[183] The most interesting contrasting elements revolve around the division between tort and contract loss of chance cases in common law; the identification of the type of uncertainty the court must deal with in the two situations; whether or not the fault prevented the chance from being taken and the expected end result from being achieved; the chance's dependence on the final result; and the state of the plaintiff when the fault was committed.

(a) The Contract–Tort Divide

It has been argued that, in English law, the contract–tort distinction can explain the reluctance to allow these claims in medical cases,[184] since the origins of the classic loss of chance cases lie in contract law.[185] The loss of chance argument may indeed seem more compelling in the case of a breach of contract, when the aim is to provide the creditor with a chance (for instance, a financial opportunity).[186] Moreover, as Fairgrieve explains, this distinct treatment may be justified by the fact that proof of loss is not *per se* a requirement for contractual liability which rather rests on the proof of breach of contract entitling the plaintiff to, at the very least, nominal damages; the question of loss actually arises only at the moment of

[183] See especially: Savatier, note under Cass civ 1st, 14 December 1965 JCP 1966.G.II.14753 (also reported at Bull civ 1965.I.541, par707, D 1966.jur.453).

[184] Fairgrieve (n 48 above) 3; Müller (n 18 above) para 187.

[185] Müller (n 18 above) para 177.

[186] Masel (n 22 above) 15 commenting on *Sellars v Adelaide Petroleum NL* (n 23 above) 349, although this case confirmed the possibility to recover in a tort action for the loss of a commercial opportunity; GHL Fridman, *The Law of Contract in Canada*, 4th edn, (Scarborough, Carswell, 1999) 795; JW Carter and DJ Harland, *Contract Law in Australia*, 4th edn, (Chatswood, NSW, Butterworths, 2002) 864–65.

the assessment of damages.[187] By contrast, under tort law, loss and its causal relationship with the defendant's fault are two strict conditions for liability which have to be proven on the balance of probabilities.[188] The use of chance language when assessing the existence of these conditions is consequently much more controversial than when it is solely used at the level of quantum assessment.

This divide can today hardly justify drawing the line between recoverable and non-recoverable loss of chance, however.[189] It has indeed long been recognised that damages in tort can also be assessed, in some cases, by reference to chance.[190] Moreover, the tort–contract distinction does not adequately explain the reluctance to allow medical loss of chance, since nothing precludes plaintiffs from bringing their claims against doctors in contract,[191] although one would have to argue that a term of the contract contained a promise to provide the patient with a chance of cure or survival, an element likely to be controversial.[192]

(b) Taking of the Chance

A second ground for distinguishing between the medical and classic situations resides in whether or not the plaintiff had the possibility of taking the chance. In the typical classic cases the defendant halts, through his fault, the progress of a series of developments which could have been the source of gains.[193] In these cases, the chance is destroyed and the hoped for result will never be obtained and therefore remains contingent.[194] Loss of chance analysis allows the courts to assess the damage despite the fact that it has not yet been made real.

Medical cases fall into another category, however. The medical fault decreases the plaintiff's chances of recovery; but the plaintiff is not prevented from taking his chance. He has done so, albeit in conditions made different by the fault, and

[187] Fairgrieve (n 48 above) 3; H Reece, 'Losses of Chances in the Law' (1996) 59 *MLR* 188, 190.

[188] Discussed in *Sellars v Adelaide Petroleum NL* (n 23 above) 351.

[189] WVH Rogers, *Winfield and Jolowicz on Torts*, 16th edn, (London, Sweet & Maxwell, 2002) 220; Reece (n 187 above) 189–91; MA Jones, *Textbook on Torts*, 8th edn, (London, Blackstone, 2002) 244 and (n 96 above) 5–40; C Von Bar, *The Common European Law of Torts*, vol 1 (Oxford, Clarendon Press, 1998) para 445.

[190] See above, text to n 26. The distinction is rejected based on this exact reasoning in *Sellars v Adelaide Petroleum NL* (n 23 above) 351.

[191] Reece (n 187 above) 190. This is possible in all cases in Canada and Australia, but only against private doctors in England.

[192] By relying upon an implied contractual term: *Rufo v Hosking* (n 23 above) para 34 (Santow JA). This was the exact argument of the plaintiff in *Lindahl Estate v Olsen* (n 108 above) paras 36 and 146.

[193] S Gaudet, *L'application de la notion de perte de chances en droit médical* (Paper presented to the CIAJ's Conference: 'Responsabilité médicale et hospitalière. Aspects juridiques et éthiques' Montréal, 29 October 1990) 14 citing H Mazeaud, L Mazeaud and J Mazeaud, *Traité théorique et pratique de la responsabilité civile délictuelle et contractuelle*, t II, 6th edn, (Paris, Montchrestien, 1965) para 219.

[194] J Penneau, note under Cass civ 1st, 27 March 1973 (n 180 above) 597; Tacchini-Laforest (n 182 above) 8. There will never be a *X* damage (See Figures 1 and 2).

has lost. The chance is exhausted and the result is no longer hypothetical:[195] '*[L]e destin a tranché.*'[196] The plaintiff suffers an identifiable and known damage and the loss of the chance is only a step leading to this final damage, which must occur in order for the compensation question to become relevant.[197] This final damage is a past accomplished event, the cause of which is uncertain.[198] It is the difficulties flowing from this uncertainty that the judge must overcome.[199] Consequently, the concept of loss of chance has no role to play where the chance has been taken and the final outcome fulfilled.[200]

(c) Type of Uncertainty

The above distinction can be paralleled with another grounded on the past facts–future contingencies dichotomy. The reasoning is the following. When the chance has been taken and the outcome is realised, the court's task is to retrace the historical facts which led to the plaintiff's loss ('What did happen'). This question must be answered on the balance of probabilities.[201] In cases where the taking of the chance has been halted and the resulting damage remains contingent, the

[195] J Penneau, *La responsabilité médicale* (Paris, Sirey, 1977) para 106. Eg, Cass civ 1st, 17 May 1988, Bull civ 1988.I.n148, D 1988.IR.160 discussed by P Jourdain 'Responsabilité civile: Conditions de la responsabilité' (1989) *Revue trimestrielle de droit civil* 81, 83. See also: France: Savatier, note under Cass civ 1st, 23 March 1973, JCP 1974.G.II.17643; Penneau, note under Cass civ 1st, 27 March 1973 (n 180 above) 596; Québec: S Philips-Nootens, 'La perte de chance: détournement du lien de causalité ou dommage distinct?' (1990) 50 *Canadian Bar Review* 611, 614; Gaudet (n 193 above) 17–19, 27.

[196] R Savatier, 'Une faute peut-elle engendrer la responsabilité d'un dommage sans l'avoir causé?' [1970] *Dalloz* 123, 124. See also: Penneau, note under Cass civ 1st, 27 March 1973 (n 180 above) 597 and Penneau (1977) (n 195 above) para 107.

[197] Penneau, note under Cass civ 1st, 27 March 1973 (n 180 above) 596.

[198] Savatier (n 196196 above) 123–24; J Huet, 'Perte d'une chance: du plus ou moins classique' (1986) *Revue trimestrielle de droit civil* 117, 119; Vacarie (n 179 above) 931; Dorsner-Dolivet, note under Cass civ 1st, 17 November 1982 (n 176 above) 306; Penneau, note under Cass civ 1st, 27 March 1973 (n 180 above) 597.

[199] Savatier (n 196 above) 124. Australia: Masel (n 22 above) 6: The 'approach to events that allegedly would have occurred, but cannot now occur, or that allegedly might occur, is different from (the) approach to events that allegedly have occurred'.

[200] Nootens (n 195 above) 614; A Porat and A Stein, *Tort Liability under Uncertainty* (Oxford, OUP, 2001) 72. This would tend to exclude *Gregg v Scott* (n 60 above) from this critique since the final outcome was still unknown at the moment of the trial. Such cases present another difficulty, however: whether the reduction of a chance, or the increase of a risk, can be compensated when the final outcome is still prospective: See ch 5, text to fns 373–74

[201] *Mallett v McMonagle* [1970] AC 166 (HL) 176; *Davies v Taylor* [1974] AC 207 (HL) 212–13; *Doyle v Wallace* [1998] PIQR 146 (CA) Q148; T Hill, 'A Lost Chance for Compensation in the Tort of Negligence by the House of Lords' (1991) 54 *MLR* 511, 514. In Australia, a distinction between proof of historical facts, future possibilities and past hypothetical situations is also made, the civil standard of proof applying in the first category only: *Malec v JC Hutton Pty Ltd* (n 27 above) 639–40 (Brennan and Dawson JJ) 642–43 (Deane, Gaudron and McHugh JJ); *Sellars v Adelaide Petroleum NL* (n 23 above) 350; *Norris v Blake (by his Tutor Porter) (No 2)* (NSWSC, 11 February 1997). Against: Couturier, note under Cass civ 1st, 7 June 1989 (n 167 above) 159.

question to be decided is one of damage and depends on future hypothetical events ('What would have happened if . . .?'). The question can be answered only by assessing the chance of a favourable outcome.

This distinction is difficult to apply because it is possible to reformulate every case as one of uncertainty about either past facts or hypothetical future events.[202] For example, *Laferrière v Lawson* (1991)[203] can be understood as a case in which how the chance turned out is known, the patient died, and the case is just a question of explaining how this outcome arose (past facts). It could also be redefined as a case involving the determination of future contingent events, ie, whether the plaintiff would have fallen in the category of patients who would have benefited from prompt treatment.[204] Moreover, in order to further determine what would have happened had the defendant not omitted to diagnose the plaintiff's breast cancer, a question of past fact is determinative, ie, the stage of the plaintiff's cancer and her chances of recovery at the time of the omission.[205] This demonstrates that the future contingencies–past facts dichotomy can be manipulated to make each case fall within one category or the other, and that both may involve a hypothetical inquiry that requires a difficult assessment of probabilities, similar to the one inherent to the application of the *causa sine qua non* test.

An alternative way to separate legitimate loss of chance cases from illegitimate ones is to concentrate on whether the uncertainty affects the existence of *causation* or *damage*. In the classic cases, there are usually no alternative competing causes of the damage involved and the causal link is clearly established between the fault and the injury. Yet the precise final damage, ie, whether or not the hoped for result would have been obtained, remains uncertain because it depends on a hypothetical set of events: would the plaintiff have won the race, the contest, or the lottery? Would he have been successful in court? Since the uncertain loss can be assessed only by referring to the chances of achieving this hypothetical result, such a probabilistic approach is acceptable.[206]

On the other hand, in the medical loss of chance cases, the fault and the damage are usually well identified. The damage is the final result which has already occurred, the death, sickness or disability. The uncertainty thus flows not from the hypothetical nature of the loss but rather from the fact that it is unknown whether the plaintiff would in fact have fallen into the lucky category of those who would

[202] Fairgrieve (n 48 above) 18; Jones (n 189 above) 244; and MA Jones, *Medical Negligence* (London, Sweet & Maxwell, 1996) (n 96 above) 5–42 (no equivalent in the 2003 edition). See also: Müller (n 18 above) paras 422–23.

[203] The facts of this case were summarized at ch 1, text to fn 247.

[204] Dillon J did in *Hotson* (CA) (n 166 above) 298; AM Dugdale and KM Stanton, *Professional* Negligence, 3rd edn, (London, Butterworths, 1998) 399.

[205] On this: Reece (n 187 above) 191–92; Jones (n 189 above) 244 and (1996) (n 202 above) 5–42.

[206] See Figure 1: 98 above.

have benefited from a positive outcome; ie, it affects causation.[207] Based on this distinction, loss of chance in medical cases is hard to justify, since it artificially prevents the facing of this uncertainty and the making of the necessary choice between alternative causes. In accordance with the courts' position in the classic cases, chance should only be used to clear up uncertainties about assessment of damages, not causation.[208]

The distinction between uncertainty with regard to damage or to causation is not without flaws however. Through intellectual techniques, classic loss of chance cases can easily be analysed from the point of view of uncertain causation[209] (eg it is uncertain whether being able to attend the beauty contest would have made any difference because the contestant might have lost in any event for some reason unrelated to the wrongdoing). Moreover, the proponents of medical loss of chance have shown that these cases can be argued as cases in which quantification damage is uncertain (eg what kind of situation would the plaintiff have been in if she could have run the chance under different conditions?).

More sophisticated (and potentially restrictive) is Helen Reece's distinction between indeterministic and deterministic situations.[210] In her opinion, recovery of loss of chance should be allowed only in the presence of indeterministic events. A phenomenon is *deterministic* when its past solely determines its future, when one is able to predict whether an event will occur or not. In deterministic situations, probability is relative to beliefs and knowledge and hence only epistemological interpretations of probabilities exist. Every proposition being either true or false, probability is only a means of managing lack of knowledge.[211]

On the other hand, *indeterministic* situations are found when an event has a random component, ie, if it could not have been predicted at any point in the past, it cannot be predicted in the present even given unlimited time, resources and evidence, and we cannot imagine how it would become predictable in the future. These are solved through both epistemological and objective interpretations of probability. According to the latter probability is a property of the external world, similar to mass or volume, independent of human knowledge or belief. In indeterministic cases, there is therefore an objective probability of the occurrence of

[207] See Figure 2: 98 above and Penneau, note under Cass civ 1st, 27 March 1973 (n 180 above) 597. See also: Chabas (n 175 above) 133: '[A]u lieu d'avoir perdu, indiscutablement par la faute du médecin, des chances de survie, il y avait des chances pour que ce fût par la faute du médecin qu'il avait perdu la vie.'

[208] A Bénabent, *Droit civil: Les obligations*, 4th edn, (Paris, Montchrestien, 1999) para 563; C Larroumet, *Droit civil: Les obligations, Le contrat*, tIII, 5th edn, (Paris, Economica, 2003) para 656. The *CJD Litigation, Straddlers Groups A and C v Secretary of State* (1998) 54 BMLR 100 (QBD) 107–8 draws this distinction.

[209] Waddams (n 21 above) 23–24.

[210] Reece (n 187 above) 188, approved by C Miller, 'Coal Dust, Causation and Common Sense' (2000) 63 *MLR* 763, 764. Compare: A Bénabent, *La chance et le droit* (Paris, LGDJ, 1973) 177.

[211] Reece (n 187 above) 193.

an event which may be known or unknown, and an epistemological probability of the occurrence of the event representing the degree to which we believe that the event will occur. This epistemological degree of belief is set to the same value as the objective probability if one knows the objective probability and is rational.[212]

Reece's submission is that the traditional burden and standard of proof of causation are irrelevant in indeterministic situations because neither side can prove or disprove causation on the balance of probabilities. The purpose of the orthodox rules becomes important in deterministic situations, however, since the legal system is founded on a fundamental epistemological assumption that present knowledge about past events is in principle possible.[213] Yet the risk of 'non-persuasion' which it is reasonable for the plaintiff to bear is the risk of 'uncertainty in evidence, not uncertainty in the world' which is found in indeterministic situations.[214] In these, a plaintiff can recover without proving but-for causation if he can show on the balance of probabilities the loss of a significant chance.[215]

The closest example of a truly indeterministic case is, in Reece's opinion, that, mentioned by Gonthier J in *Laferrière v Lawson* (1991) of the lottery ticket which is not placed in the draw due to the negligence of the tickets' seller. In such a case, Gonthier J was of the opinion that: 'The judge has no factual context in which to evaluate the likely result other than the realm of pure statistical chance. Effectively, the pool of factual evidence regarding the various eventualities in the particular case is dry in such cases, and the plaintiff has nothing other than statistics to elaborate the claim in damages.'[216]

Reece's argument attracted the eye of Lord Hoffmann in the recent case of *Gregg v Scott* (2004), where he argued that everything has a determinate cause, even if we do not know what it is:

> There is no inherent uncertainty about what caused something to happen in the past or about whether something which happened in the past will cause something to happen

[212] *Ibid*, p 193.
[213] *Ibid*, p 205.
[214] *Ibid*, p 204.
[215] *Ibid*, p 194.
[216] *Laferrière v Lawson* (n 34 above) 603. See also: *Hotson v East Berkshire AHA* (n 176 above) 782 (Lord Bridge). Reece also exemplifies the indeterministic category with some of the classic cases: *Chaplin v Hicks* [1911] 2 KB 786; and *Kitchen v Royal Air Force Association* [1958] 1 WLR 563 (CA); *Davies v Taylor* (n 201 above). She also includes *Allied Maples Group Ltd v Simmons & Simmons (a firm)* [1995] 1 WLR 1602 (CA), as well as cases involving human decisions ('hypothetical conduct cases'): (n 205 above) 197–98 and 203. She adds, at 195–96, that *Hotson* was a deterministic case: there was a time in the past when the cause of the necrosis could have been humanly determined, for example if the blood vessels had been examined after the fall. See also: 194 and 206 where she recognises her classification's inherent difficulties and the fact that there might not be two categories, deterministic and indeterministic, but rather a spectrum along which each case may be fitted.

> in the future. Everything is determined by causality. What we lack is knowledge, and the law deals with lack of knowledge by the concept of the burden of proof.[217]

Reece's approach, coupled with the distinction based on the identification of the *real area of uncertainty*, damage or causation, afford a stronger basis for identifying whether a case falls within the acceptable realm of loss of chance than the past facts–hypothetical events dichotomy. The revealing aspect of both suggestions is that they confirm the vast majority of medical cases fall within the category of inadmissible loss of chance cases.

(d) State of the Plaintiff when Fault Committed

Another element of distinction is the different situation the plaintiff is in when the defendant commits his fault. In many of the classic cases, the plaintiff is usually engaged in a positive process leading to the obtaining of a benefit and the defendant's fault makes him lose the chance of attaining this positive outcome: win the race, contest, or trial; obtain a job or promotion; etc. By contrast, when the doctor enters the scene, the plaintiff in medical loss of chance cases is usually on his way to suffering damage.[218] Yet he has a chance of avoiding this negative outcome and the defendant's role is to attempt to realise this chance. If he fails, the damage suffered remains primarily the result of a process foreign to the defendant. Consequently, compensation, even partial, appears unjust, since it places on the doctor's shoulders a risk for which he is not primarily responsible.[219]

(e) Dependence of the Chance

The independent nature of loss of chance as a head of damage is one of the main contentions in favour of the validity of loss of chance. In the classic cases, the disappearance of the chance can easily be distinguished from the hoped for advantage, which is so hypothetical and intangible that it can never be compensated.[220] Thus the assessment of the lost chance does not depend upon the occurrence of the outcome of the chance.

[217] Para 79. One exception to this would be the actions of human beings, which may explain in part why loss of chance is accepted in these cases, as per *Allied Maple Group*, although Lord Hoffmann rather believes that the real reason justifying the exception is one of policy: Paras 82–83.

[218] Unless, the chance of recovery is higher than 50% (or of a higher probability in France) in which case it is taken for granted that he will recover.

[219] R Savatier, 'Le droit des chances et des risques dans les assurances, la responsabilité civile dans la médecine et sa synthèse dans l'assurance de responsabilité médicale' (1973) 44 *Revue générale des assurances terrestres* 457, 470.

[220] Jourdain (n 182 above) 109.

Opponents to loss of chance in medical cases contest its independent nature in these instances, however.[221] This argument finds support in the fact that the lost chance is always calculated on the basis of the final outcome itself, by applying to it the percentage of the lost chance.[222] This has led some commentators to contend that the *distinct* or *intermediate* injury called loss of chance does not exist in reality and is absorbed in the final damage once the latter has occurred.[223] When calculating the loss of chance by applying a percentage probability to the value of the ultimate consequence, the courts are not compensating for a lost chance but are in reality compensating for a portion of the underlying physical injury.[224] Some add that if it were truly independent, the doctrine would oblige the doctor to indemnify the patient for this lost chance even if he is cured or survives.[225] Although the autonomy of the lost chance is often pleaded, some French judgments have expressly acknowledged this close relationship between the lost chance and the final damage.[226]

2. *Problems in the Evaluation of the Chance*

Loss of chance has also been objected to as allowing claims for damage that has not yet occurred and remains speculative.[227] Nothing in the doctrine prevents the plaintiff from claiming compensation solely for having lost a chance, been subjected to risk, or having incurred increased risk of suffering the final outcome.[228] This consequence can in practice be avoided, however, by simply restricting the application of the doctrine to cases where the final outcome has occurred or where it is certain that it will occur in the near future.[229] While this restriction ensures the avoidance of speculative claims, it also provides additional arguments

[221] F Bouvier, 'La responsabilité médicale' [1981] *Gazette du Palais* 281, 288; Penneau, note under Cass civ 1st, 27 March 1973 (n 180 above) 597; Dorsner-Dolivet, note under Cass civ 1st, 17 November 1982 (n 176 above) 306; G Mémeteau, 'Perte de chance en droit médical français' (1986) 32 *McGill Law Journal* 125, 145; G Mémeteau, 'Perte de chance et responsabilité médicale' [1997] *Gazette du Palais* 1367, 1371; Jourdain (n 182 above) 114; P Sargos, report under Cass civ 1st, 8 July 1997 (n 167 above) para 27; Penneau, note under Cass civ 1st, 27 March 1973 (n 180 above) 597; Gaudet (n 193 above) 29. Against: Gerecke (n 9 above) 807 and Stapleton (n 166 above) 395 and 409.

[222] But see: Fairgrieve (n 48 above) 25.

[223] Gaudet (n 193 above) 29.

[224] Hill (n 201 above) 518.

[225] Gaudet (n 193 above) 30–31. Stapleton (n 166 above) 392 argues that it ought to be so. See also: 409.

[226] Cass civ 1st, 7 June 1989 (n 167 above). See also: JL Aubert, 'Responsabilité civile: dommage, perte d'une chance: Aggravation du préjudice, réparation complémentaire' (1990) *Répertoire du Notariat Defrénois* 746, 747 and G Mémeteau, *La responsabilité civile médicale en droit comparé français et québécois* (Montréal, CRDPCQ, 1990) 609.

[227] Stapleton (n 166 above) 395; Fleming (n 25 above) 673; Nootens (n 195 above) 620.

[228] Admitted by Stapleton (n 166 above) 392. See also: Gerecke (n 9 above) 832.

[229] Stapleton (n 166 above) 395: a convincing rationale for this restriction would have to be found, however.

to loss of chance opponents who insist on the lack of autonomy of this head of damage.

The identification of the exact nature of the interest which the defendant's fault destroyed can be achieved by resorting to statistics.[230] The opponents to loss of chance denounce the arbitrary nature of the assessment of lost chances; Savatier in particular believes the judge evaluates the chance 'with the number of his choice',[231] describing this power as inaccurate and subjective.[232] One cannot help noticing that the French cases on loss of chance rarely undertake a thorough assessment of the causal probability between the fault and the damage; and it is sometimes hard to assess what type of evidence forms the basis for their measure of the chance.[233]

Even adherents of loss of chance admit the difficulty of assessing statistical chances when uncertainty makes it impossible to assess both the background risk to which the plaintiff is already exposed and the risk added by the defendant's fault.[234] For instance, Lord Nicholls, dissenting in *Gregg v Scott* (2004), admits some of the drawbacks of statistical analysis while nonetheless maintaining that when there is nothing better, courts should be able to use statistical figures:

> Statistical evidence, however, is not strictly a guide to what would have happened in one particular case. Statistics record retrospectively what happened to other patients in more or less comparable situations. They reveal trends of outcome. They are general in nature. The different way other patients responded in a similar position says nothing about how the claimant would have responded. Statistics do not show whether the claimant patient would have conformed to the trend or been an exception from it. They are an imperfect means of assessing outcomes even of groups of patients undergoing treatment, let alone a means of providing an accurate assessment of the position of one individual patient.[235]

[230] *Ibid*, p 399.

[231] R Savatier, 'La responsabilité médicale en France (Aspects de droit privé)' (1976) *Revue internationale de droit comparé* 493, 502.

[232] Savatier (n 196 above) 123 and (n 219 above) 473. Over thirty years ago, Savatier's objection was grounded on the belief that chances of success in medical matters cannot be mathematically evaluated by a probability calculation, that serious statistics are lacking in this respect, and that the infinite diversity of medical faults, pathologies, and individual biological states renders statistical assessment impossible. Today, this position must be nuanced. See also: Viney and Jourdain (n 17 above) para 371; Penneau (1977) (n 195 above) paras 105–6. The arbitrary nature of the assessment is admitted by some judges, eg, Jacques J in *Lapointe v Hôpital Le Gardeur* (n 107 above) 2632 (CA); Badgery-Parker J in *Tran v Lam* (1997) NSW Lexis 1435 (NSWSC, 20 June 1997) 76 (this question was not discussed on appeal, but the appeal was allowed and the matter was remitted to district court for rehearing on the ground that trial judge gave inadequate reasons for his decision on causation: [2003] WASCA 318, WL 23002582 (18 December 2003)); Wilcox and Higgins JJ in *Mouratidis v Brown* (n 82 above) paras 70 and 72.

[233] Text between fns 272 and 277 below, although this can be explained by the style of French judgments.

[234] Stapteton (n 3 above) 407.

[235] Para 28. See also: Lord Hope at para 111.

One must indeed remain wary of the over-use of statistics. It is easy to forget the many other variables coming into play in each individual case.[236] Some indeed insist statistical chances of a disease's progress and the individual chances of the patient in question must be distinguished from one another.[237] In England, Hill has based his objections to loss of chance on this distinction, insisting that the loss of a personal chance must be shown in cases where the courts assess the chance of future hypothetical outcome.[238] Statistical chances are not necessarily determinative of the chance an individual patient would have had;[239] a patient who has lost a 15 per cent statistical chance of survival may have in fact personally lost nothing if he is one of those patients who would have died anyhow. Moreover, each of the patients who in fact fall in the 15 per cent should be compensated in full, not just for 15 per cent of the damage. In Hill's opinion, it is the courts' task to assess which group the plaintiff falls into.[240]

To the extent, then, that the doctrine of loss of chance unduly encourages the use of pure statistics in assessing causation, without necessarily ensuring they are linked to the specific case at hand, it is subject to criticism. Yet one must acknowledge that personal chances are often difficult to assess and that pure statistical chances may be the only tangible element in the hands of the judge.

3. *General Implications of Loss of Chance*

There exists more compelling objections to loss of chance. The main one is that loss of chance may denature the traditional requirements of causation and evidence and even lead to a complete revolution in the rules of civil liability in two ways. First, it provides a conceptual justification for by-passing the fundamental requirement of showing causation. Second, it theoretically allows recourse to proportional liability in every case.

(a) By-passing the Causation Requirement

The initial attractiveness of the concept of loss of chance fails in fact to meet the main objection to this doctrine. This is that, in medical malpractice cases, it allows

[236] The same argument could be made in the classic cases.

[237] Hill (n 201 above) 512–14; Penneau (1977) (n 195 above) para 110; Penneau, note under Cass civ 1st, 27 March 1973 (n 180 above) 598; Savatier, note under Cass civ 1st, 2 May 1978, JCP 1978. G.II.18966. Against: Saluden, note under Cass civ 17 November 1982 (n 176 above).

[238] Hill (n 201 above) 512–14. Hill adds the plaintiff in *Hotson* lost only a statistical chance; he had no personal chance to lose as he was doomed when he reached the hospital. See also: Hill's example at 216 and Croom-Johnson LJ in *Hotson v East Berkshire AHA* (CA) (n 166 above) 303.

[239] Against: W Scott, 'Causation in Medico-Legal Practice: A Doctor's Approach to the "Lost Opportunity" Cases' (1992) 55 *MLR* 521, 524–25.

[240] Hill (n 201 above) 512.

for obviating the absence of a causal link between the fault and the final damage by affording partial compensation in cases in which causation is not proven. True, the strict requirement of proof of causation appears to be maintained because recovery is allowed only if the link between the fault and the lost chance is shown. Once it is the case, this loss is payable in full and no discount is made for the possibility that this chance was lost due to some other cause.[241] This reasoning does not refute the objection which looks beyond the doctrine's superficial attractiveness to concentrate on its real practical effect in the area of medical negligence, however. The real impact of the concept is still that the judge can ignore his doubts with respect to causation and grant partial recovery despite uncertainty remaining as to the causal link between the fault and the final and concrete damage. Some supporters of medical loss of chance recognise the argument seeks to bypass the traditional effects of the causation test.[242] Its opponents push the argument further. They argue that substituting loss of chance not to die or to be cured for the actual damage allows compensation to be granted even if the defendant's negligence is not shown, under the traditional principles, to have caused the death or absence of cure.

Loss of chance offers an apparently coherent conceptual device with which to justify avoiding the difficult task of choosing between alternative causes of the final damage. When granting recovery on the basis of loss of chance in medical cases where the causal link between the fault and the final outcome is not proven, the extent of compensation becomes in fact the expression of the extent of the judge's uncertainty about causation: '*[Le juge] confond le degré de la prétendue chance perdue avec le degré de son doute propre sur la causalité*.'[243] For Savatier, loss of chance creates a paradise for indecisive judges,[244] who can use it to evade the difficult task of assessing whether the final damage is the result of the defendant's fault.[245] Savatier insists that the judge must judge and that if he is not able to overcome his doubts, his decision must be in the defendant's favour:[246] '*Toute intime conviction repose sur un choix. Le juge est maître de ce choix. C'est une haute et*

[241] Stapleton (n 166 above) 396–97.

[242] *Ibid*, p 392; Jansen (n 167 above) 283. See also: Descorps Declère (n 120 above) 742 who, although defending the concept, insists that it should never be used to palliate for a doubtful causal link; Müller (n 18 above) para 329, who acknowledges that whether loss of chance concerns causation or the assessment of damages is one of the most delicate questions of the loss of chance theory.

[243] Savatier (1973) (n 219 above) 473. See also: Mémeteau (1986) (n 221 above) 136–37; Mémeteau (1997) (n 221 above) 1367; Tacchini-Laforest (n 182 above) 10.

[244] Savatier (1970) (n 196 above) 125.

[245] Savatier (1973) (n 219 above) 463, 474–76.

[246] Savatier (1970) (n 196 above) 125; Savatier, note under Cass civ 1st, 27 March and 9 May 1973, JCP 1974.G.II.17643; Penneau, note under 27 March 1973 (n 180 above) 597; Boré (n 167 above) para 40; Penneau (1977) (n 195 above) para 109.

lourde responsabilité! Mais il ne saurait l'esquiver en traduisant ses doutes par une 'moyenne'. Il n'est pas arbitre amiable compositeur!'[247]

This objection has been adopted by several French[248] and Québec writers,[249] as well as by the Canadian and Québec courts.[250] It is in fact feared this position may extend to other areas of civil liability and lead to the abandonment of the traditional standard of proof of causation altogether.[251]

(b) Proportional Liability in Every Case

Another crucial problem lies in the fact that loss of chance, if applied logically, could potentially lead to a complete revolution in the traditional rules of evidence and civil liability.[252] In most medical cases, it is in fact possible, in theory, to plead that the patient had some chance of cure, survival, or improvement in his condition before the defendant's fault was committed;[253] partial recovery could thus be allowed every time negligence is proven.[254] Recognising this problem, some advocates of the loss of chance approach have attempted to restrict its application to cases involving true uncertainty,[255] without however defining which cases will qualify as such.

Moreover, the admission of loss of chance has been criticised as creating injustice for the defendant, since the argument is used only when it benefits the plaintiff. But if the plaintiff is allowed to re-identify the damage as his lost chance of avoiding the final outcome, what prevents the *defendant* from doing the same?

[247] Savatier, note under Cass civ 1st, 14 December 1965 (n 183 above). In England, Weir agrees: 'Now, in this world nothing is certain except the views of law professors and communists, and certainly the law has to deal with incertitudes. [T]hat is why our judges are paid a lot. They have difficult decisions to make': T Weir, 'Loss of a Chance—Compensable in Tort? The Common Law' in O Guillod, (ed), *Développements récents du droit de la responsabilité civile* (Genève, Centre d'études juridiques européennes, 1991) 150–51.

[248] Viney and Jourdain (n 17 above) paras 370–71; Tacchini-Laforest (n 182 above) 9; Boré (n 167 above) para 2; Jourdain (n 182 above) 110; Dorsner-Dolivet, note under Cass civ 1st, 17 November 1982 (n 176 above) 307; P le Tourneau and L Cadiet, *Droit de la responsabilité civile* (Paris, Dalloz, 1998) para 876; Rabut, note under Cass civ 1st, 18 March 1969 and 27 January 1970 (n 178 above). Against: G Boyer-Chammard and P Monzein, *La responsabilité médicale* (Paris, PUF, 1974) 101.

[249] Nootens (n 195 above) 618; Gaudet (n 193 above) 6; I Parizeau, 'Le lien de causalité . . . au bord du gouffre' (1989) 49 *Canadian Bar Review* 514, 517.

[250] *Laferrière v Lawson* (n 34 above).

[251] France: Savatier (n 196 above) 124–25; Savatier (n 219 above) 476; Dorsner-Dolivet, note under 17 November 1982 (n 176 above) 307; Québec: Gaudet (n 193 above) 7; Nootens (n 195 above) 618; Parizeau (n 249 above) 514 and 517. It could also undermine rules such as the thin-skull rule and its civil law equivalent. For instance, in *Smith v Leech Brain* [1962] 2 QB 405, the defendant could have argued that the plaintiff was deprived of only a chance of living, since he already had a pre-cancerous condition. Such argument was rejected in Canada on the basis of *Hotson*: *Briffett v Gander & District Hospital Board* (1996) 137 Nfld & PEIR 271 (NfldCA).

[252] Hogg (n 167 above) 74.

[253] Bouvier (n 221 above) 289; Penneau, note under Cass civ 1st, 27 March 1973 (n 180 above) 598.

[254] Savatier (n 219 above) 479.

[255] Descorps Declère (n 120 above) 743.

Indeed, the defendant might wish to plead that he deprived the plaintiff only of a chance of recovery and nothing in the doctrine prevents him logically from doing so. For example, a patient with an 80 per cent chance of survival consults a doctor. Following the commission of a medical fault, the patient does not recover. The court finds that even if it was not certain the plaintiff would have recovered, the probability of 80 per cent favoured the plaintiff's full recovery. No discount is made for the 20 per cent chance that the patient would not have recovered in any event.[256] This creates a peculiar theoretical contradiction, since, while the argument is welcomed in cases where the plaintiff is not able to show causation, it is foreclosed when he is able to prove it.[257] There is nothing in the theory to preclude its use by the defendant, however, especially if the aim of loss of chance is solely to redefine the damage. Admitting that the theory should logically be equally available to the defendant may, however, lead to a complete shift from the traditional all-or-nothing balance of probabilities approach to causation, to one in which damages would in every case be calculated on a purely mathematical basis, according to causative probability.

Decisions admitting the concept of loss of chance, as well as the doctrine pleading in its favour, cannot rationally sustain their position without addressing this crucial question. The only coherent position that accepts the loss of chance solution also accepts a reassessment of the traditional rules of civil liability and evidence law. As long as the systems stay faithful to these rules, the question of loss of chance should not occur, as it cannot logically coexist with them.[258] If the introduction of loss of chance reveals dissatisfaction with the results yielded by the traditional rules of evidence, this dissatisfaction must be addressed, and the advisability of reforming the rules should be discussed openly and not achieved indirectly through concepts such as loss of chance. If the systems are willing to reconsider the way they address liability altogether, then loss of chance becomes an alternative which may deserve further analysis necessitating taking into account broad social, economic, political, and legal considerations.[259]

This, and the other doctrinal objections discussed above, lead us to take the position that loss of chance should be inapplicable in medical malpractice, as well as in any case in which it has the effect of obviating the absence of evidence of causation between the defendant's fault and the final damage. Considering the distinct position of French law with respect to loss of chance, however, it may be asked

[256] Such argument was made by the defendant, and rejected, in Cass civ 1st, 1 June 1976 (n 178 above).

[257] Lord Bridge mentions the anomaly in *Hotson v East Berkshire AHA* (n 176 above) 783.

[258] See also: Gaudron J in *Naxakis v Western General Hospital* (n 45 above) 280.

[259] Such as whether admitting proportional recovery could cause greater damage to patients than the refusal of it, by leading to over-deterrence. Possible reactions include fear and the taking of fewer risks, the practice of defensive medicine, and the refusal to treat certain types of patient.

whether there are compelling reasons to treat this concept differently in France than in the other jurisdictions?

4. *The French Standard of Proof: A Justification?*

The question is especially interesting considering that, while Québec and French rules of civil liability share many similarities, their respective treatment of the loss of chance question in medical malpractice cases is radically different. In *Laferrière v Lawson*, Gonthier J partly explained this difference on the basis of the two jurisdictions' different attitudes to the standard of proof of causation.[260] This interesting avenue deserves greater attention, since it may not only explain why French courts have relied to such a great extent on loss of chance, but also provide material for assessing the general value of loss of chance as an instrument for relaxing the rules of evidence. Further, it may afford additional arguments for common law and Québec courts to eschew this reasoning.

(a) Probabilities and Certainty

The rules of proof regarding causation are in theory less rigid in Québec and the common law than in France, since the balance of probabilities requirement is fundamentally more generous than the strict French certainty standard. In Québec, since a probability of more than 50 per cent is sufficient to meet this standard, cases falling below this threshold are treated strictly and rejected. Conversely, because the French starting point, certainty, lacks flexibility, the courts must ground their generosity on something else than their evaluation of the evidence, ie, on the redefinition of the traditional substantive conditions for liability. French courts perhaps believe that the causal link is 'more safely anchored where the certain loss of the chance [is] itself considered the damage.'[261] One thing is certain: through loss of chance, French courts are looking for the flexibility their traditional requirements of evidence seemingly do not provide.[262]

This is all well in theory. In spite of the theoretical certainty requirement and perhaps in reaction to it, French courts have been willing, however, to presume the certainty of the causal link when 'sufficient' probabilities of causation exist.[263] The fact that French courts do sometimes in practice grant themselves the flexibility they lack in theory shows a flaw in the above distinction based on the two juris-

[260] (N 164 above) 601–3.
[261] *Ibid*, p 602.
[262] Viney and Jourdain (n 17 above) para 371. This aim is admitted by Durry (n 172 above) 798. Eg, CAA Paris 3rd ch, 9 May 2001 (n 142) where damages for loss of chance were granted because the causal link with the final injury was *only* probable. See also: Descorps Declère (n 120 above) 746.
[263] Viney and Jourdain (n 17 above) para 347 and 368. See also: ch 5, text between fns 8 and 16.

dictions' different standard of proof. It also puts in doubt the necessity for French courts to seek flexibility in the loss of chance theory, since arguably the judiciary is ready to introduce it in the traditional assessment of evidence.

Contradictions in the Court of Appeal's and the Cour de cassation's treatment of cases involving significant reductions in the patients' chances of recovery provide support for this view. While the Court of Appeal has proven ready to presume causation in some of these instances, the Cour de cassation has often disagreed on appeal and insisted on treating the same cases strictly as loss of chance instances. Two decisions of the Cour de cassation dated 27 March 1973,[264] and 9 May 1973,[265] afford interesting examples.

In the first, the Court of Appeal found the defendant's negligent omission to verify whether his deceased patient had an empty stomach before the operation he conducted 'considerably reduced' his chances of survival. On this basis, the plaintiff was fully compensated for his prejudice. In the 9 May case, the Court of Appeal reached a similar conclusion. The plaintiff gave birth in a private clinic to a stillborn child who was resuscitated but with residual brain damage. The defendant doctor was found at fault for not attending to his patient and for leaving her in the care of nurses who were not midwives and did not possess the knowledge necessary to detect signs of anoxia. The experts were of the opinion that observation of the contractions, the foetal heartbeat, and the amniotic fluid would have allowed for the detection of and the taking of a therapeutic decision before the baby's health was placed in jeopardy. The Court of Appeal therefore held the defendant doctor fully liable for the plaintiff's damage, on the grounds that his fault caused her to lose 'significant' chances of seeing her son escape the damage he now suffered from.

In both cases, the Cour de cassation disagreed with the Court of Appeal on the ground that loss of chance could lead only to partial compensation. These conclusions were reached despite the fact that once causation is proven through factual presumptions, and the damage well identified and demonstrated, loss of chance becomes superfluous and full damages should be granted unless the presumption is rebutted by the defendant.[266] Moreover, both patients' risk of damage had been substantially increased by the defendant's fault. Thus, arguably, the probabilities

[264] Cass civ 1st, 27 March 1973 (n 180 above).

[265] Cass civ 1st, 9 May 1973, (2 cases) JCP 1974.G.II.17643 (note Savatier), Gaz Pal 1973.Jur.631 (note Doll), D 1973.116.

[266] Savatier, note under Cass civ 1st, 14 December 1965 (n 183183 above). See also: Paris, 10 March 1966, D 1966.jur.662: The four-in-five chance of surviving the patient would have had if treated immediately was sufficient to presume causation. The Court thereafter granted only partial recovery, measured according to the patient's lost chance of survival; see Durry's comments on this case: (n 167 above) 182.

were high enough for the Court, in exercising its discretion, to presume the certainty of causation and thereby grant full recovery.[267]

On 1 June 1976, the Cour de cassation seems to have adopted this view in another case of unattended foetal distress. The experts believed the baby's injury would have 'normally' been avoided by appropriate therapeutic care had the foetal distress been diagnosed sooner. Consequently, the doctor was held liable for not attending his patient when informed that she was having uterine spasms, as was the clinic for employing nurses who were unqualified to deal with this kind of situation. The Cour de cassation was of the opinion that full award of damages should be granted. It rejected the defendant's argument that causation was not proven because the plaintiff did not make a precise demonstration of the medical acts the doctor should have carried out. Moreover, it was of the opinion that the defendant could not benefit from his omission by arguing that only the baby's lost chances should be compensated.

These cases show a contradiction between the French case law's attachment to loss of chance and its willingness to presume causation in certain cases, as where a risk has been created or increased or on the presence of sufficient probabilities of causation, as will be demonstrated in chapter 5.[268] These cases also demonstrate that it is the courts' rigidity in applying the certainty evidential requirement, and in particular the Cour de cassation's refusal in some cases to equate high probabilities of causation with certainty, which leads them to resort to the loss of chance solution. One may question this reluctance, in a medical malpractice context, to adopt an attitude they have resorted to in other contexts. As dicussed in chapter 5, French courts are ready to admit indirect proof of causation through factual presumptions, as has been strikingly the case when dealing with claims from victims of contaminated blood transfusions.[269] They are also willing to relax the certainty requirement in order to infer causal certainty from sufficient probabilities or on the basis of the creation or increase of a risk. If this is so, loss of chance becomes useless except to the extent that it restricts the doctors' liability. Full recovery to which presumptions lead can, however, be counterbalanced by the fact that recovery is not granted in every case, as is possible in theory with loss of chance. French courts' decisions would probably find a more logical and fair conceptual justification and better doctrinal acceptance if they

[267] Savatier, note under Cass civ 1st, 9 May 1973, JCP 1974.G.II.17643. A second claim flowing from the May 9 case, this time against the private clinic, led to an apparently contradictory judgment. The Cour de cassation considered causation was proven between the plaintiff's damage and the nurses' insufficient qualifications to detect foetal anoxia. In the opinion of the Court, the defendant's fault had contributed to the damage suffered and, on that basis, full recovery of the damage could be granted: Cass civ 1st, 9 May 1973 (n 265 above). See also: Durry (1967) (n 167 above) 181 and Cass civ 1st, 14 December 1965 (n 183 above).

[268] Ch 5, text between fns 159 and 172.

[269] In the HIV/HCV cases, the courts' generosity appears obviously motivated by the particular nature of the fault and the extent of the damage suffered by the victims: ch 5, text to fns 217 ff.

were ready to find presumptions based on high probabilities in instances of medical negligence.

This opinion is echoed in the French doctrine. For instance, Huet observes that the loss of chance cases often involve clues and factual presumptions which could have allowed causation to be proven and hence full damages to be recovered.[270] In the same vein, Boré asks 'what is a chance but the expression of a probability excluding certainty?' He wonders whether one should not elevate this probability to the level of a factual presumption and order full compensation or, on the contrary, deny this probative weight and reject compensation because the damage is not certain.[271]

The contention that factual presumptions would afford an interesting alternative to loss of chance would gain credibility if one could demonstrate that French courts generally require that the chance be of a certain percentage in order to be compensated in medical malpractice cases. If loss of chance is admitted only when the probability of causation is high, this could confirm the possibility of addressing these cases alternatively on the basis of discretionary presumptions of causation based on 'sufficient' probability. Moreover, should a higher than 50 per cent chance be required by the French courts to allow compensation for lost chances, this would confirm that the French line of reasoning lacks relevance for Québec, Canada, Australia, and England, since the French loss of chance cases would simply fit within the balance of probabilities requirement.

(b) Degree of Chance Required

To address this question adequately, one must determine the kind of statistical chance courts find acceptable for applying a loss of chance analysis. Unfortunately, attempts to test this hypothesis have yielded uncertain results.[272] There are few indications in the French cases as to the level of probability of fulfilment of the chance needed to comply with the *real and serious* criterion, and judges possess broad discretion on this head.[273] A few decisions are nevertheless revealing. On 10 March

[270] Huet (n 198 above) 119. One could in fact argue this was so in the 27 March and 9 May 1973, cases, and in the 14 December 1965 case (n 183 above).

[271] Boré (n 167 above) para 12. An argument first made by Savatier (n 196 above) 126 and (1974) (n 180 above) para 12. See also: Bénabent (n 210 above) 179; Flour and Aubert (n 28 above) para 163 who generally refer to the possibility of relaxing the burden and standard of proof by relying on factual presumptions.

[272] Gonthier J in *Laferrière v Lawson* (n 34 above) 564 notes, however, the loss of chance debate in France has not really concerned weak chances, but rather mainly cases in which the chance was probable, though not certain. Müller (n 18 above) para 390, is of the opinion that the majority of the French and Belgian doctrine requires a probability of over 50%, but that the case law ignores this requirement.

[273] Viney and Jourdain (n 17 above) para 284. Outside medical malpractice, some cases refer to the necessity of 'very serious chances': Cass civ 2nd, 20 December 1966, Bull civ II.n979; Cass civ 2nd, 8 June 1983, Bull civ 1983.II.n124; 'reasonable chances': Cass civ 1st, 8 December 1981, D 1982.IR.212; 'sufficient probability': Angers, 5 February 1970, D 1970.538. In medical liability, Boré and Charaf-Eldine mention the necessity of 'sufficient probabilities': Boré (n 167 above) para 37; A Charaf Eldine, 'La théorie de la perte d'une chance sanitaire (devant la Cour de cassation et le Conseil d'État)' (1983) 19 *Revue trimestrielle de droit sanitaire et social* 48, 63.

1966, the Court of Appeal of Paris judged a chance of four-fifths to be high enough. On 8 July 1997, the Cour de cassation granted a claim for lost chances because the experts believed that if the treatment had been undertaken sooner, the chance of avoiding the damage, amputation, would have been 'much higher'. On 5 February 1991, the Cour de cassation rejected a loss of chance claim because the experts believed the x-rays received during a woman's pregnancy may have very 'slightly' increased the normal probability of the child's being born deaf. In addition, in the 27 March and 9 May 1973 cases already commented on, the Cour de cassation granted recovery for the loss of 'serious' chances and for the reduction of the plaintiff's chances 'in considerable proportions'. Finally, the rejection by the Cour de cassation in the 17 November 1982 case already examined, of the loss of chance argument in a case where a non-faulty alternative cause of the damage had been demonstrated in addition to the defendant's fault, tends to confirm the necessity of proving the loss of a substantial chance by the plaintiff.[274] However, in the administrative case law, we note percentages ranging from 25 per cent to 50 per cent.[275]

As for the doctrine, it has stated that only a 'sufficient' probability is taken into account when compensation is granted for lost chances.[276] On the other hand, Chabas, after recalling that certainty does not exist in matters of evidence and that the proof of causation rests on very high probabilities, notes that, in loss of chance cases, this 'very high' probability does not exist and the generous conditions of the *causa sine qua non* theory are not even met.[277] Vacarie is of a different opinion and states that the loss of a chance may be regarded as a direct and certain damage whenever the chance of survival or recovery is greater than the risks of death or disability.[278]

Although inconclusive, these instances give some indication that it is realistically possible for the French courts to legitimately solve causal uncertainties through the existing evidential means of factual presumptions based on high probabilities of causation instead of indirectly modifying substantive law through loss of chance.

5. *From Substance to Evidence*

Even in France, some decisions prefer a more direct liberalisation of the causal link to loss of chance,[279] as will be analysed in chapter 5, but this solution remains

[274] (N 176 and n 186 above).

[275] CE 5th and 3rd sub-s, 6 July 1988 (n 138 above); Trib adm Rennes 3rd, 30 December 1992 (n 140 above); CAA Paris ch 3, 9 May 2001 (n 142 above); CAA Douai 2nd, 17 June 2003 (n 140 above).

[276] Bénabent (n 210 above) 180; N Lesourd, 'La perte d'une chance' (1963) 2 *Gazette du Palais* 49, 50; Durry (1969) (n 172 above) (RTDC 1969.778); Angers, 5 February 1970, JCP 1970.G.II.16308.

[277] F Chabas, 'Vers un changement de la nature de l'obligation médicale' (1973) I *La semaine juridique* 2541, para 4.

[278] Vacarie (n 179 above) 916–17.

[279] Presuming causation on the basis of the concept of faulty creation of a dangerous situation or of a risk: ch 5, text between fns 159 and 172 and Viney and Jourdain (n 17 above) paras 355, 368, 371 and 373; Dorsner-Dolivet, note under Cass civ 1st, 17 November 1982 (n 176 above) 307. Eg, Cass civ 1st, 20 February 1979, JCP 1979.G.IV.145, Bull civ 1979.I.n68, D 1979.IR.250.

isolated in medical malpractice. This approach should be more generally preferred to the artificial loss of chance analysis, however. As the problem of uncertain causation is one of proof, it is inadequate to attempt to find its solution through concepts, such as loss of chance, that are derived from the modification of substantive legal rules. By relying on loss of chance, the French courts are in fact *confusing an evidential question with a substantive one.* The use of probabilities belongs more appropriately in the domain of assessment of the degree of knowledge of the judge about the events, such knowledge being itself based on the evidence available. Probabilities that have assisted the court in assessing the facts should not have any impact on the application of the substantive rule:

> *Il y a en effet là confusion certaine entre le stade de la détermination des faits, stade où l'évaluation probabiliste doit intervenir, et celui de l'application à ces faits déterminés de la règle de droit. Par un tel procédé, les juges confondent 'avoir 70% de chances d'être coupable' et 'être coupable à 70%': ils appliquent le degré de probabilité à la règle de fond, la condamnation, au lieu de l'appliquer à la preuve.*[280]

Our plea against loss of chance does not necessarily lead to an endorsement of judicial rigidity towards causation, but simply to the argument that French courts have sought the solution in the wrong place. An acceptable alternative to the flexibility offered by the loss of chance theory must and can be found, but it resides in the law of evidence, more precisely in a broader, more flexible, and better articulated use of inferential reasoning.

Conclusion to Chapter 4

The first two approaches experimented with by the judiciaries of Canada, Québec, England, Australia, and France have sought to adapt rules of evidence or civil liability to the aim of insuring compensation for plaintiffs in particular situations. The first, reversal of the burden of proof of causation, remains isolated and more relevant to cases of factual than scientific uncertainty. Nevertheless, it develops interesting justifications for the courts' generosity which could serve in our own

[280] Bénabent (n 210 above) 177. See also: Porat and Stein (n 200 above) 116 and 121. One could however argue that, from a substantive point of view, doctors are held to a legal duty to increase the chances of their patients improving or surviving and that loss of chance seeks to give recognition to a breach of that duty, rather than simply attempting to confront an evidential difficulty, eg, *Rufo v Hosking* (n 23 above) para 24 (Santow J). This argument, which sits more easily in common law than in civil law, is criticised in some Australian decisions as well as by some authors who insist that such duty does not exist: *Chappel v Hart* (n 96 above) 252 (para 50) (McHugh J). See also: A Grubb and J Laing, *Principles of Medical* Law, 2nd edn, (Oxford, OUP, 2004) para 7.30.

enterprise. As for loss of chance, despite its prominence in French medical malpractice, the other jurisdictions have not been won over by its benefits, although English and Australian law has never taken definitive positions against it. The assistance it offers plaintiffs and its capacity for circumventing the injustice of the traditional rules of evidence nevertheless make it an important option to examine further.

Despite rejecting the validity of medical loss of chance in *Laferrière v Lawson* (1991), Gonthier J expressly recognised that the assessment of causation, especially in cases where its existence is uncertain, could be done in a flexible way, with the assistance of factual presumptions as well as the factual and statistical evidence of each case. This underlying principle is at the basis of the last solution studied, namely the courts' willingness to infer or presume causation when they deem appropriate to do so. Such a solution does not, at first sight, hurt the traditional rules of causation; it does not necessitate a modification of existing rules, since the possibility of providing indirect proof of causation already exists within the law of evidence of the four jurisdictions. The particular problems involved in cases of scientific uncertainty have, however, necessitated a reassessment of the fashion in which indirect evidence is assessed by the courts.

This defence of an evidential solution is premised on the belief that dealing with scientific uncertainty in medical malpractice requires neither the devising of new substantive legal rules nor the modification of existing ones. A strong rationale is needed to justify creating alternative legal rules that address causative difficulties that only occur in a limited number of cases and would find no application where there is no uncertainty. One could go even further and argue that there is no rationale for devising *substantive* legal rules in order to address problems of *proof* unless there is a compelling reason to do so.[281] Since the problem of uncertain causation is of an evidentiary nature, the solution should be evidentiary.

The conceptual imbroglio created by the French case law treatment of the indeterminate defendant problem also show the dangers of distorting the existing substantive rules to respond to difficulties of proof. It is interesting to note that French writers have pleaded in favour of solving the problem of the indeterminate defendant through reliance on factual presumptions for that very reason.[282] Dejean de la Bâtie is one of them: '*Mieux vaut reconnaître que, si la règle classique sur la charge de la preuve conduit à une solution inique, cela révèle simplement qu'il faut renverser cette règle au moyen d'une présomption.*'[283]

[281] See also: Savatier (1976) (n 231 above) 501.

[282] Ch 3, text to fn 54.

[283] Dejean de la Bâtie, note under Cass civ 2nd, 19 May 1976, JCP 1978.G.II.18773. He adds, in support of his presumptive solution: '*chacun doit supporter, sur le plan même de la charge de la preuve, les suites de son fait illicite.*'

We believe this affirmation must be nuanced,[284] but we take the view that a simpler and more logical way of tackling problems of proof is to look first within the law of evidence for sufficient rules to address the problem. We submit that one may find there means to address most cases involving evidential uncertainty: inferential reasoning.

[284] To the extent that it advocates the judicial introduction of legal presumptions: ch 5, text between fns 324 and 349.

5

Inferences of Causation

The common law and Québec courts have favoured this evidential means to introduce flexibility in dealing with causative uncertainties. This solution has also been relied on by the French courts, but less extensively. Given that the available evidence in cases of uncertainty often offers little information on which to infer causation, courts have had to devise justifications on which these inferences could validly rest. Following a general introduction to the subject of inferences and factual presumptions of causation (section 1), this chapter examines the different justifications relied on by the courts in the absence of sufficient indirect evidence (section 2), namely those linked to the concepts of risk and danger and the negligent undermining of the plaintiff's means of proof. Finally, it looks at the French courts' willingness to draw *presumptions by elimination* in some cases thought particularly deserving of generosity. This chapter concludes by a critical analysis of the findings (section 3).

Section 1

Inferences and Factual Presumptions

Inferences and factual presumptions play an important role where the causal link between the defendant's fault and the plaintiff's damage is uncertain and cannot be demonstrated under the traditional rules of evidence. The English, Australian and Canadian common law is clear on the legitimacy of inferring causation in cases of evidential uncertainty.[1] In Canada, positive proof of causation in medical malpractice cases is not always necessary and, as of principle, causation can be

[1] England: *Bolitho v City and Hackney Health Authority* [1993] 4 Med LR 381 (CA) (Simon Brown LJ) applying *Wilsher v Essex Area Health Authority* [1987] 1 QB 730; Australia: *Naxakis v Western General Hospital* (1998) 197 CLR 269 (AustHC) 280–81; *Seltsam Pty Ltd v McGuiness* (2000) 49 NSWLR 262 (NSWSC) paras 93 and 143 (Spigelman CJ) (non-medical); Canada: *Snell v Farrell* (1990) 72 DLR (4th) 222; [1990] 2 SCR 311, 330; *Briffett v Gander and District Hospital Board* (1996) 137 Nfld & PEIR 271 (CA) 288.

inferred on the basis of common sense even in the absence of positive or scientific proof of causation.[2]

The civil law jurisdictions have also long recognised that causation can be proven by any means of evidence, including indirect proof[3] adduced by the discretionary drawing of factual presumptions.[4] Québec courts generally approach indirect proof of causation, by relying on a careful assessment of the evidence in order to determine whether the factual, statistical and expert evidence demonstrates on the balance of probabilities the existence of serious, precise, and concordant presumptions of causation.[5] They have not traditionally shown any tendency to draw presumptions of causation too readily.[6] For this reason, many medical malpractice cases involving uncertainty fail.[7]

In France, even though the difficulties in proving causation in medical malpractice cases are solved principally through the loss of chance doctrine, the judiciary also assists victims of damage consequent on a medical act with the help of

[2] *Snell v Farrell* (n 1 above) 330 and ch 2, text to fn 57. Several Canadian cases recognise the possibility of finding causation proven through common sense inferences: *McGowan v King* (OntCtJ, 25 April 1991); *Jourdain (Litigation Guardian of) v Hogg* (OntCtJ, 3 November 1993) paras 34–35; *Robinson v Sydenham District Hospital Corp* (2000) 130 OAC 109 (OntCA) 119; *Lurtz v Duchesne* (2003) OJ no 1540 (OntSCtJ, 16 April 2003) paras 168 and 346; *Aristorenas v Comcare Health Services* (2004) WL 1938380; Carswell Ont 3599 (OntSCtJ, 7 September 2004) paras 68–73; *Fournier v Wiens* (2004) 33 Alta LR (4th) 114 (AltaQB) para 97; *Bear (Litigation Guardians of) v Lambos* (2005) CarswellSask 232 (SaskQB, 28 March 2005) para 45; *O'Grady v Stokes* (2005) ABQB 247, Carswell Alta 578 (AltaQB, 26 April 2005) para 202; *Miller v Budzinski* (2005) BCD Civ J 516; (2004) BCD Civ J Lexis 1530 (BCSC, 24 December 2004) para 469; *Dybongco-Rimando Estate v Jackiewicz* (2001) CarswellOnt 3219 (OntSCtJ, 28 August 2001) para 35;

[3] G Duflo, *La responsabilité des médecins à la lumière de la jurisprudence récente* (Paris, Domat-Montchrestien, 1937) 97; H Lalou, *Traité pratique de la responsabilité civile*, 6th edn, (Paris, Dallo, 1962) para 268; J Ghestin and G Goubeaux, *Traité de droit civil: Introduction générale*, 3rd edn, (Paris, LGDJ, 1990) para 645; J Flour and JL Aubert, *Droit civil: Les obligations 2, Le fait juridique* (Paris, Armand Colin, 1997) para 163; JC Royer, *La preuve civile*, 3rd edn, (Cowansville, Yvon Blais, 2003) para 840.

[4] CcQ, Arts 2846 and 2849 and CN, Art 1353; JL Baudouin and P Deslauriers, *La responsabilité civile*, 6th edn, (Cowansville, Yvon Blais, 2003) para 600; P Lesage-Jarjoura and S Philips-Nootens, *Éléments de responsabilité médicale: Le droit dans le quotidien de la médecine* (Cowansville, Yvon Blais, 2000) 58; D Jutras, 'Réflexions sur la réforme de la responsabilité médicale au Québec' (1990) 31 *Cahiers de droit* 821, 834; A Bernardot and RP Kouri, *La responsabilité civile médicale* (Sherbrooke, RDUS, 1980) para 115; *Boucher v Rousseau* [1984] CA 85, 95; *Laferrière v Lawson* (1991) 78 DLR (4th) 609; [1991] 1 SCR 541, 607; *Lafontaine v Hôtel-Dieu St Jérôme* [1995] RRA 81 (CS) 86; *Therrien v Launay* (2005) WL 434762, Carswell Que 486 (SC, 4 March 2005) paras 77, 87 and 548.

[5] *Montreal Tramways Co v Léveillé* [1933] SCR 456; (1933) 4 DLR 337, 466 and 472 (Lamont J) and 478–79 (Cannon J); *Cloutier v Hôpital Saint Joseph de Beauceville* [1978] CS 943; *Lapointe v Hôpital Le Gardeur* [1989] RJQ 2619 (CA) 2638–39 (Lebel J) (not discussed on appeal: [1992] 1 SCR 351; (1992) 90 DLR (4th) 7); *Camden-Bourgault v Brochu* [2001] RRA 295 (CA) citing *Morin v Blais* [1977] 1 SCR 570 (not reported in DLR); *Therrien v Launay* (n 4 above) para 548.

[6] *Montreal Tramways v Léveillé* (n 5 above) constitutes an exception, however. Some judges have warned against the temptation of too rapidly reaching a conclusion with regards to causation: ironically, Beauregard J in *Gburek v Cohen* [1988] RJQ 2424 (CA) 2442.

[7] Eg, *Bédard v Lavoie* [1987] RRA 83 (CA) 84; *Bureau v Dupuis* [1997] RRA 459 (CS); *Kirschenbaum Green v Syrchin* [1997] RRA 39 (CA) and [1993] RRA 821 (CS); *Kulczycky v Rafferty* [1994] RJQ 1792 (CA); *Zanchettin v DeMontigny* [2000] RRA 298 (CA); *St-Jean v Mercier* [2002] 1 SCR 491; (2002) 209 DLR (4th) 513 and [1999] RJQ 1658 (CA).

factual presumptions of causation. French law features the interesting particularity, despite theoretically requiring causation to be proven with *certainty*, of being ready to presume this certainty in the presence of sufficient probabilities.[8] Some cases mention this possibility explicitly, specifying that it can apply only in the presence of 'high probabilities'.[9] Others are rather vague and state that causation is sometimes deduced from the fact that 'normally' the treatment in question, if carried out without negligence, is followed by a cure;[10] that the damage would 'normally' have been avoided by appropriate therapeutic care;[11] that the type of damage suffered by the plaintiff is 'usually' caused by the presumed fault;[12] that 'in a great number of cases', the damage occurs from the type of fault committed by the defendant;[13] that 'constant biological laws' or 'biological determinism' allow for an identification based on a specific result of the cause of the damage;[14] and, finally, that the defendant's fault is the 'classic cause' of the type of damage suffered by the plaintiff.[15] Thus it appears that a higher than 50 per cent probability is required before certainty is presumed.[16] The tendency of some French cases to rely on high probabilities to presume the certainty of causation nevertheless testifies to the willingness of the French courts to relax the rigidity of their certainty

[8] Trib civ Nîmes, 20 October 1953, JCP 1954.G.II.8222 (note Clavel); Cass civ 1st, 28 June 1960, JCP 1960.G.II.11787: 'Sufficiently probable' hypothesis transformed into certainty; Cass civ 1st, 29 May 1979, JCP 1979.G.IV.257, Bull civ 1979.n156, Gaz Pal 1979.2.somm.417; Bordeaux 5th, 17 February 2004, Juris-Data No 237740: Referring to probabilities, *vraisemblance,* and very high risk; Paris 1st B, 15 January 2004, Juris-Data No 241509: Most probable cause. See also: G Mémeteau, 'Perte de chance en droit médical français' (1986) 32 *McGill Law Journal* 125, 135; and Azard, note under Grenoble 16 May 1962, D 1963.jur.137. Outside medical malpractice: Cass civ 1st, 19 July 1960, Bull civ 1960.G.II.346; Cass civ 2nd, 8 February 1967, Bull civ 1967.2.40; Cass civ 2nd, 6 March 1968, Bull civ 1968.2.53; Cass civ 3rd, 3 October 1974, JCP 1975.G.II.18156 (note Rabut). Against: Cass civ 1st, 4 March 1973, D 1973.somm.79.

[9] Cass civ 1st, 12 November 1968, D 1969.somm.47, D 1969.96; Cass civ 1st, 29 May 1979 (n 8 above); Trib gr inst Paris, 1st July 1991, JCP 1991.G.II.21762 (note Harichaux). See also: F Chabas, 'La perte d'une chance en droit français' in O Guillod, (ed), *Développements récents du droit de la responsabilité civile* (Genève, Centre d'études juridiques européennes, 1991) 131, 154; Dorsner-Dolivet, note under Cass civ 1st, 17 November 1982, D 1984.jur.305, 308 (Case also reported at Bull civ 1982.I.n333, D 1983.380, JCP 1983.G.IV.41, JCP 1983.G.II.20056 (note Saluden)); J Boré, 'L'indemnisation pour les chances perdues: une forme d'appréciation quantitative de la causalité d'un fait dommageable' (1974) I *La semaine juridique* 2620, para 24: 'Reasonable certainty'; G Viney and P Jourdain, J Ghestin, (dir), *Traité de droit civil: Les conditions de la responsabilité*, 2nd edn, (Paris, LGDJ, 1998) paras 368–69: 'Objective foreseeability'.

[10] Aix, 1 December 1949, D 1950.jur.82 (note anon).

[11] Cass civ 1st, 1 June 1976, JCP 1976.II.18483 (note Savatier).

[12] Cass civ 1st, 12 November 1968 (n 9 above).

[13] Cass civ 1st, 29 May 1979, Bull civ 1979.I.n156.

[14] Savatier, note under Cass civ 1st, 27 May 1970, JCP 1971.G.II.16833.

[15] Cass civ 1st, 27 May 1970 (n 14 above): the court presumed both the causal link and the fault on this ground.

[16] The question is rarely evaluated in percentage terms, however. But see: L Dubouis, 'Perte de chances de survie' (1976) *Revue trimestrielle de droit sanitaire et social* 43, 44: If experts have evaluated the chance of survival at 90%, judges may hold the negligence to be the cause of the death; and Paris, 10 March 1966, D 1966.jur.662: Four-in-five chance of survival sufficient to presume causation.

requirement in some cases. Yet when compared to the case law on loss of chance, this alternative attitude remains marginal in French medical liability.

As already discussed in chapter 1, the issue of inferences of causation arises only where there is *uncertainty* in the evidence before the court; it must be impossible to assess causation directly on the basis of the evidence available.[17] This situation is frequently encountered in medical malpractice where the plaintiff's case often depends wholly on whether or not a court is ready to draw an inference of causation.[18] Inferences are not an alternative solution to the non-existence of causation, however. Thus if the direct evidence adduced at trial leads the judge to find that there is no causation between the fault and the damage, the court cannot ignore this result and draw an inference of causation.[19]

Section 2

The Development of Justifications

The application of inferential common law and civil law mechanisms to assess causation proves to be a particularly difficult task in medical negligence cases. As a result of scientific uncertainty, the available lay evidence may provide little information on which to rest even an indirect proof of causation. Moreover, the expert evidence is frequently inconclusive or at best contradictory, and is consequently of little support in drawing a presumption.[20] If common law and civil law rules regarding inferences and presumptions are applied in an orthodox inductive way, this should result in a systematic refusal to draw inferences in such cases.

The study of common law on the subject of inferences of causation in medical negligence is particularly interesting for its courts' willingness to go beyond this difficulty by devising conceptual justifications on the basis of which they have

[17] See also: ch 1, text to fn 166.

[18] MA Jones, *Medical Negligence*, 3rd edn, (London, Sweet & Maxwell, 2003) para 5–18.

[19] Eg, England and Scotland: *Byrnes v Fife Health Board* [1980] SLT 43 (2nd div) 45; *Kay's Tutor v Ayrshire and Arran Health Board* [1987] 2 All ER 417 (HL); *Roughton v Weston Area HA* (2003) EWHC 2731 (QB, 17 November 2003) (no causation); Canada: *Lawrence v Smith* (1991) 84 Alta LR 26 (QB) 39; *Jourdain v Hogg* (n 2 above) para 59; *Grealy v Kuntz* (BCSC, 16 March 1994), treated as evidence rebutting an inference by the Court of Appeal: (1996) BCJ No 1470 (BCCA, 4 July 1996) para 49; *Bigcharles v Dawson Creek and District Health Care Society* (BCCA, 16 May 2001) para 71 (*Bigcharles* can also be interpreted as accepting to draw an inference while finding it rebutted by the evidence presented by the defendant's experts: Paras 69–71); *Roberts v Petersiel* (2005) WL 95201, Carswell Ont 145 (OntSCtJ, 14 January 2005) para 18; Québec: *St-Jean v Mercier* (CA) and (SCC) (n 7 above).

[20] D Jutras, 'Expertise médicale et causalité' in *Congrès du Barreau du Québec* (Montréal, Service de la formation permanente du barreau du Québec, 1992) 897, 906.

considered it permissible to draw causative inferences even in the presence of scarce evidence. This tendency is even more striking, and is applied more liberally, in the current Canadian common law than in England and Australia. It is less obvious in civil law, but interesting developments in France and Québec allow us to affirm that it also exists in these jurisdictions. While our main focus is the medical liability sphere, English man-made industrial disease cases also merit a special attention, since the inferential reasoning in the face of uncertain scientific causation in medical liability has been inspired by these cases.

The main justification experimented with in England, Australia, and Canada is the concept of material increase of the risk of damage. Moreover, Canadian courts have relied on the fact that the information about causation lies within the particular knowledge of the defendant and the defendant has negligently undermined the plaintiff's means of proving causation. Interestingly, Québec courts have been influenced by these Canadian developments, albeit in isolated decisions of the Court of Appeal. In addition, French and Québec courts surmount the hurdle created by the insufficiency of the evidence by relying on justifications based on the notions of creation/increase of a risk and creation of a danger. Finally, French courts have proven ready to provide substantial assistance to special categories of plaintiff by allowing them to demonstrate causation through the presumption-by-elimination technique.

A. Risk

Risk can be relied on in three different types of causative arguments. One may contend that to infer causation, it is sufficient to show that the defendant's fault: i) created a risk of damage for the plaintiff;[21] ii) increased a risk to which the plaintiff was already exposed before his intervention;[22] or, finally, iii) subjected the plaintiff to a danger by creating a substantial risk of damage or by substantially increasing an existing risk. These three types of arguments have played a role in the English, Canadian, Australian, French, and Québec case law.

1. *Common Law: Increase of the Risk of Damage*

The material increase of risk justification was born of the necessity to adapt the test of material contribution to damage to the needs of cases including uncertain causation. It may be recalled that this alternative test for demonstrating causation has proven useful when addressing cases where the cause of the damage comes from two or more contributive sources, including the defendant's wrongdoing, and cannot be wholly attributed to one or the other. The more liberal material

[21] The creation of a risk normally being the consequence of an independent fault.

[22] *Ibid*, except that this situation necessitates the existence of a pre-existing risk.

contribution test considers it sufficient to show that the defendant's negligence *materially contributed*, in a more than *de minimis* way, to producing the damage, even though his act alone was not sufficient to create it.

In common law, the application of the material contribution test soon became problematic in cases in which it was impossible to assess whether or not a contribution to the damage had been made at all by the defendant. Two types of situation brought about this difficulty: alternative cause cases, where the uncertainty of the evidence prevents one from choosing amongst several causes, and cases where the nature of the causative process itself was unknown. In both circumstances, the application of the material contribution test led to a rejection of the claim since it is impossible to know whether the defendant's negligence contributed at all to the occurrence of the injury, although by adding one triggering agent, it did increase the risk of such injury. To address this problem, common law courts resorted to the concept of material increase of risk.

(a) *McGhee v National Coal Board* (1973)

The landmark case of *McGhee v National Coal Board* (1973) introduced the notion of *material increase of the risk of damage* in cases in which the material contribution test could not justify granting recovery to the plaintiff. This notion allows for the argument that by negligently increasing the risk of the final damage arising, the defendant contributes materially to the plaintiff's damage. *McGhee* has been interpreted as both allowing the drawing of an inference of causation (Canada and Australia)[23] and modifying the standard of proof of causation altogether (England, particularly since *Fairchild v Glenhaven*).[24]

McGhee assumes full significance in cases of alternative and unknown causal mechanisms. In these cases, while it is impossible to say that each of the hypothetical causes contributes to the occurrence of the damage, they all nevertheless enhance the general risk of damage to which the plaintiff is already exposed by adding a possible cause of the damage. Consequently, the only way the material contribution test can allow recovery is by equating increase of risk with material contribution. Thereby increase of risk becomes the unifying concept of cumulative, alternative, and unknown causal processes.

It will be recalled that in *McGhee* the plaintiff had contracted dermatitis from exposure to brick dust at work. The evidence was that his employer's failure to provide showers had negligently increased his risk of suffering from dermatitis.

[23] Canada: below, text to n 39. Australia: *Anasson v Koziol* (1996) Aust ACTSC Lexis 68 (ACTSC, 20 December 1996) 48. This interpretation was also adopted in some English cases until recently, eg, *Hotson v East Berkshire Area Health Authority* [1987] 2 WLR 287 (CA) 300; *Wilsher v Essex Area HA* (n 1 above); *Bryce v Swan Hunter Group Plc* [1988] 1 All ER 659 (QB); *Brown v Lewisham and North Southwark Health Authority* [1999] Lloyd's Law Rep Med 110 (CA) 116.

[24] *Fairchild v Glenhaven Funeral Services* [2002] 3 All ER 305 (HL). For a contrary view: A Grubb and J Laing, *Principles of Medical Law*, 2nd edn, (Oxford, OUP, 2004) 447.

The experts were not able to say whether washing after work would have made it more probable than not that the plaintiff would have escaped dermatitis, because the precise nature of its development process was unknown; either dermatitis could be contracted as a result of a single event, one abrasion on the skin, or as a result of an accumulation of abrasions. Only in the latter case could the absence of showers materially contribute to the damage. In the former, it could only increase the risk of disease by multiplying the occasions of contracting it. Under the material contribution test, the plaintiff's claim would therefore fail since the fact of the contribution itself was affected by uncertainty.

To avoid this result, the majority of the House of Lords went beyond the material contribution test. It accepted that in some circumstances, the fact that the defendant's conduct materially increased the risk of damage could be treated as equivalent to materially contributing to the damage when the injury suffered by the plaintiff fell within the ambit of the risk increased by the defendant. The uncertainty was thus resolved by an inference to the effect that the process was cumulative, thereby allowing an analogy with *Bonnington Castings*.[25] Lord Reid and Lord Salmon in particular were of the opinion that where it is impossible for the plaintiff to scientifically prove causation, no useful distinction exists between a source materially contributing to the risk of an outcome and the source materially contributing to the outcome itself. In a case like *McGhee,* in which the way the cause operates is uncertain, Lord Reid was of the opinion that a 'broader view of causation' must be taken. He stated further:

> There may be some logical ground for such a distinction [between materially increasing the risk that the disease will occur and making a material contribution to its occurrence] where our knowledge of all the material factors is complete. But it has often been said that the legal concept of causation is not based on logic or philosophy. It is based on the practical way in which the ordinary man's mind works in the everyday affairs of life. From a broad and practical viewpoint I can see no substantial difference between saying that what the defender did materially increased the risk of injury to the pursuer and saying that what the defender did made a material contribution to his injury.[26]

For Lord Simon, the failure to take steps which would bring about a material reduction of the risk involved a substantial contribution to the injury sufficient to prove causation.[27] As for Lord Salmon, he was of the opinion that it was unrealistic and contrary to ordinary common sense to hold that the negligence which materially increased the risk of injury did not materially contribute to causing the injury.[28] The

[25] JG Fleming, 'Probabilistic Causation in Tort Law' (1989) 68 *Canadian Bar Review* 661, 669. See also: *Brooks v J & P Coates (UK) Ltd* [1984] 1 All ER 702 (QBD) 718.

[26] *McGhee v National Coal Board* [1973] 1 WLR 1 (HL) 4–5.

[27] *Ibid*, p 8. Also relying on *Nicholson v Atlas Steel Foundry and Engineering Co Ltd* [1957] 1 WLR 613 (HL); and *Gardiner v Motherwell Machinery and Scrap Co Ltd* [1961] 1 WLR 1424 (HL).

[28] (N 26 above) 12.

distinction between the two notions, while being 'a fruitful source of interesting academic discussions between students of philosophy', was 'far too unreal to be recognised by the common law'.[29] Finally, Lord Kilbrandon added that where it was shown that the defendants knew that to take a precaution reduced the chance, risk, possibility or probability of contracting a disease and did not take it and the disease had occurred, it was difficult to see how proof of the probability that their failure caused or contributed to the damage could be required.[30] Lord Wilberforce went even further in his minority judgment, as already discussed. He found the case could be decided by shifting to the defendant's shoulders the burden of showing that his breach of duty had not caused the loss.[31]

Some English decisions subsequently relied on the majority's reasoning in dealing with scientific uncertainty.[32] For instance, in *Bryce v Swan* (1988), it was applied to another situation in which the causal mechanism was unknown. The deceased worker was exposed to asbestos dust during successive employment periods for three different owners of shipyards. As a result, he contracted malignant mesothelioma of the pleura, from which he eventually died. His widow argued that the defendants were negligent in failing to take precautions which would have materially reduced the risk. It was known that an increase in exposure to asbestos dust increases the risk of contracting mesothelioma, but unknown how it did so. The risk could possibly rise with exposure because each fibre has a chance of initiating the fatal mutation and the more fibres are inhaled the greater the chance that one will succeed in so doing (alternative mechanism). It could also increase with exposure because the fibres in the lung have a cumulative effect in damaging or overwhelming the body's defence mechanism and thereby facilitate the occurrence of malignancy (cumulative process).[33] Each defendant therefore argued there was no evidence that his own individual breach of duty had caused the sickness.

The Court believed, however, the exposure to dust attributable to each defendant was significant in degree.[34] Consequently, the plaintiff could successfully invoke the *McGhee principle*, namely that where a disease has been caused by a mechanism that is unclear, one can properly *infer* that a breach of duty which increased the risk of the disease thereby contributed to its cause.[35] This would apply, whether the defendant's breaches of duty merely added to the number of possible initiators of the disease or whether they also produced a cumulative

[29] *Ibid*, pp 12–13.
[30] *Ibid*, p 10.
[31] See ch 3, text between fns 22 and 26.
[32] *Kay v Ayrshire* (n 19 above) 421 (Lord Keith) and 422 (Lord Griffiths): Principle accepted but found inapplicable to the facts of the case.
[33] (N 23 above) 665. Compare: *Fairchild v Glenhaven* (n 24 above).
[34] (N 23 above) 666.
[35] *Ibid*, p 667.

impact on the reduction of the body's defence mechanism, since in both cases the risk of disease was increased.[36]

In Canada, *McGhee* was perceived as a reaction against an overly logical conception of factual causation in favour of a more practical, common sense approach, where there is an inherent evidentiary gap which would otherwise have been fatal to the plaintiff's case.[37] While Canadian decisions were divided[38] between the majority approach and Lord Wilberforce's opinion, a group of cases expressed a preference in favour of the majority view, interpreted as relying on material increase of the risk of damage to *infer* causation.[39] For example, in *Haag v Marshall* (1990), Lambert JA stressed that *McGhee* contained an 'inference principle' which applied where it is impossible, in a practical sense, for either party to present evidence which would establish causation. Lambert JA admitted that the inference was not necessarily logical, but believed it permissible on policy grounds:

> The legal inference permitted by the principle may be prodded along by the concept that as between an innocent plaintiff and a defendant who has committed a breach of duty to the plaintiff and by so doing materially increased the risk of loss to the plaintiff, in a situation where it is impossible, as a practical matter, to prove whether the breach of duty caused the loss, it is more in keeping with a common sense approach to causation as a tool of justice, to let the liability fall on the defendant. ...
>
> Whether the inference of causation should in fact be made in any particular case depends on whether it is in accordance with common sense and justice in that case to

[36] *Ibid*, p 671. See also: *Nicholson* where material contribution was applied even though all that was seemingly shown in evidence was an increase of the risk of damage: (n 27 above) 781 (Viscount Simonds), 782 and 784 (Lord Cohen). The repeated references to the increase of the risk of damage lead one to suspect that increase of risk was assimilated to material contribution: 782 (Lord Cohen) and 781 (Viscount Simonds); *Brooks v J&P Coates (UK) Ltd* (n 25 above) 718 where it is unclear whether the Court relied on increase of risk to find causation or whether it took for granted that the causal process involved in this case was cumulative. Compare: *Wintle v Conaust (Vic) Pty Ltd* [1989] VR 951 (VSC).

[37] *Letnik v Metropolitan Toronto (Municipality)* (1988) 49 DLR (4th) 707 (FCA) 721 (MacGuigan J).

[38] See generally: *Snell v Farrell* (n 1 above) 325–26.

[39] GHL Fridman, *The Law of Torts in Canada*, vol 1 (Toronto, Carswell, 1989) 343; M McInnes, 'A Decade in the Supreme Court of Canada' (2000) 62 *Saskatchewan Law Review* 445, 447; EI Picard, *Legal Liability of Doctors and Hospitals in Canada*, 2nd edn, (Toronto, Carswell, 1984) 186. (See also the 1996 edition: EI Picard and GB Robertson, *Legal Liability of Doctors and Hospitals in Canada*, 3rd edn, (Toronto, Carswell, 1996) 222–23); and R Roth, 'Causation and the Burden of Proof: An Age Old Dilemma and a New Age Approach' (1992) 14 *Advocates' Quarterly* 70, 70 and 75. Eg, *Robinson v Sydenham District Hospital Corp* (n 2 above) 116. Outside medical malpractice, England: *Fitzgerald v Lane* [1987] 1 QB 781, 810–11 (appealed on another question: [1989] 1 AC 328 (HL)); *Kirkham v Chief Constable of the Greater Manchester Police* [1990] 2 QB 283, 289; Canada: *Powell v Guttman* (1978) 89 DLR (3rd) 180 (ManCA) 188 and 192; *Dalpe v Edmundston (City of)* (1979) 25 NBR (2nd) 102 (CA); *Edmison v Boyd* (1987) 77 AR 321 (AltaCA) 324; *Letnik v Metropolitan Toronto* (n 37 above) 721 and ff; *Gallant v Fialkov* (1989) 69 OR (2nd) 297 (HCJ) 316 implicitly.

> say that the breach of duty which materially increased the risk ought reasonably to be considered as having materially contributed to the loss.[40]

The course of the law was modified, however, both in Canada and England, by the 1988 decision of the House of Lords in *Wilsher*.

(b) *Wilsher v Essex Health Authority* (1988)

In 1988, in *Wilsher v Essex HA*, the House of Lords reassessed *McGhee* in a medical liability case involving a clear alternative causal mechanism. While it categorically rejected Lord Wilberforce's approach, *Wilsher*'s position on inference of causation is less clear. It may legitimately be asked whether it rejected the *McGhee* majority view or rather limited its application to special cases.

The plaintiff, born three months prematurely, suffered from retrolental fibroplasias (RLF). It was established that the defendant, a young and inexperienced doctor, negligently inserted a catheter into a vein rather than an artery. This negligence increased the risk of RLF by provoking an excess in the administration of oxygen to the baby. There was a higher risk of RLF in premature babies generally, however. Moreover, there was evidence of a link between RLF and several other conditions from which premature babies can suffer (apnoea, hypercarbia, intraventricular haemorrhage, and patent *ductus arteriosus*). Which of these causes was operative was not agreed on. Thus what the defendants did was 'not to enhance the risk that the known factors would lead to injury but to add to the list of factors which might do so.'[41] On this ground, the Court of Appeal, applying *McGhee*, held that the plaintiff could recover even though the existence and extent of the contribution made by the breach could not be ascertained.[42] Browne-Wilkinson V-C dissented; while there was common sense in inferring that a failure to take a precaution against the one possible cause of the injury was a material cause of this injury, when the failure was to take precautions against one of five possible alternative causes, no inference of causation could apply.

A unanimous House of Lords overruled the Court of Appeal's decision and ordered a retrial. Lord Bridge explained the only way the plaintiff's claim could succeed was by establishing, according to the traditional rules of evidence, that the administration of excessive oxygen was more likely the cause than all the other possibilities combined or any single possibility. In accordance with *Bonnington Castings*, the plaintiff could demonstrate this by showing that the breach of the

[40] *Haag v Marshall* (1989) 61 DLR (4th) 371 (BCCA) 379: Rejects the reversal option. See also: O'Sullivan JA in *Powell v Guttman* (n 39 above) 192 which appears to treat *McGhee* as going further than just allowing an inference of causation to be drawn. For other commentaries on *McGhee*: Lord Hope of Craighead, 'James McGhee—A Second Mrs Donoghue?' (2003) 62 *CLJ* 587.

[41] [1986] 3 All ER 801 (CA) 828 (Mustill LJ).

[42] (N 41 above) 829.

duty was at least a material contributor to the damage. In addition, Lord Bridge expressed the following opinion on *McGhee*:

> The conclusion I draw from these passages is that *McGhee v National Coal Board* ... laid down no new principle of law whatever. On the contrary, it affirmed the principle that the onus of proving causation lies on the pursuer or plaintiff. Adopting *a robust and pragmatic approach* to the undisputed primary facts of the case, the majority concluded that it was *a legitimate inference* of fact that the defender's negligence had materially contributed to the pursuer's injury. The decision, in my opinion, is of no greater significance than that and to attempt to extract from it some esoteric principle which in some way modifies, as a matter of law, the nature of the burden of proof of causation which a plaintiff or pursuer must discharge once he has established a relevant breach of duty is a fruitless one (emphasis added).[43]

This common sense inference of material contribution could legitimately be drawn in *McGhee* even though Lord Bridge recognised the causal mechanisms which led to the damage in this case was unclear:

> But where the layman is told by the doctors that the longer the brick dust remains on the body, the greater the risk of dermatitis, although the doctors cannot identify the process of causation scientifically, there seems to be nothing irrational in drawing the inference, as a matter of common sense, that the consecutive periods when the brick dust remained on the body probably contributed cumulatively to the causation of the dermatitis. I believe that a process of inferential reasoning on these general lines underlies the decision of the majority in *McGhee*'s case.[44]

The particular facts of *McGhee* thus warranted the inference drawn. *Wilsher* was very different, since it involved more than one possible distinct and solely sufficient cause. In a case such as this, it was not enough to show a material increase in risk; to succeed, the plaintiff had to demonstrate that the defendant's negligence materially contributed to his loss.

Since *Wilsher* was decided, some have expressed the opinion that it is no longer open to the plaintiff to argue that the defendant has materially increased his risk of damage in order to demonstrate causation.[45] Conversely, others contend that *McGhee* may still be good law, subject to the requirement that the burden of proof remains with the plaintiff and that *Wilsher* left open the possibility for the courts

[43] (N 1 above) 1090. In *Fairchild v Glenhaven* (n 24 above) para 21, Lord Bingham found this passage should no longer be treated as authoritative as it does not reflect the effect of the majority ruling in *McGhee*: Discussed at text to n 81 below.

[44] (N 1 above) 1088. Compare with *Fitzgerald v Lane* (QB) (n 39 above).

[45] RM Jackson and JL Powell, *Jackson and Powell on Professional Negligencem*, 5th edn, (London, Sweet & Maxwell, 2002) 12–249; D Carey, *Medical Negligence Litigation* (Coldfield, CLT Professional Publishing Sutton, 1998) 79. Against: J Stapleton, 'Law, Causation and Common Sense' (1988) 8 *OJLS* 111.

to draw inferences of causation even though the requirement is not met under the traditional rules.[46] There is room for an argument that *Wilsher* did not reject *McGhee* but restricted the application of its *inferential principle* to cases worthy of a *robust and pragmatic approach.*[47] There are in fact many areas of distinction between the two cases. One was thought to lie in the fact that *McGhee* was considered in *Wilsher* to be a case of cumulative causes, while *Wilsher* was a clear case of alternative process.[48] This distinction does not survive closer analysis, however, since the causal mechanism involved in *McGhee* was in fact unknown, and, according to the experts' opinions, could be either cumulative or alternative.[49]

One must therefore look beyond the nature of the causal process and ask whether the primary facts of some cases may legitimate an inference of contribution to the development of the disease even where the causal process is unknown.[50] There are in fact particularities in *McGhee* which may have justified this stand on policy grounds. First, in *McGhee,* there was only one possible agent of the damage, ie, the brick dust.[51] Moreover, this agent, in its tortious and non-tortious form, originated from the same source, the defendant's activities. Both risks were therefore in the defendant's control.[52] In addition, in *McGhee,* a precise pre-existing risk had been enhanced, whereas in *Wilsher,* the risk enhanced was the general risk of suffering injury. These two facts, coupled with the unknown nature of the causal process, could have provided sufficiently strong primary facts in *McGhee* to warrant a 'robust and pragmatic' approach inferring that the two causes operated cumulatively by materially increasing the risk of damage.[53] Conversely, in the typical cases involving alternative causal mechanisms, such as *Wilsher*, the different risks emanate from different sources; often, in addition to the defendant's fault, these include inherent risks in the creation of which the defendant played no role.[54]

Thus *McGhee* and *Wilsher* were two very different cases, and it could be argued that *Wilsher* has simply affirmed that *McGhee* cannot apply to clear alternative cause cases involving non-tortious causes because there does not exist sufficient

[46] WVH Rogers, *Winfield and Jolowicz on Torts*, 15th edn, (London, Sweet & Maxwell, 1998) 207 (no equivalent in 2002 edition); S Deakin, A Johnston and BS Markesinis, *Tort Law*, 4th edn, (Oxford, Clarendon Press, 2003) 190; AM Dugdale and KM Stanton, *Professional Negligence*, 3rd edn, (London, Butterworths, 1998) para 18.04; MA Jones, *Medical Negligence*, 2nd edn, (London, Sweet & Maxwell, 1996) 5–38 (no equivalent in 2003 edition).

[47] *Fairchild v Glenhaven* (n 24 above) para 144 (Lord Rodger); P Cane, *Atiyah's Accidents, Compensation and the Law*, 6th edn, (London, Butterworths, 1999) 93.

[48] Dugdale and Stanton (n 46 above) para 18.05; *Smith v Moscovich* (1989) 40 BCLR (2nd) 49 (BCSC) 54; *The CJD Litigation: Group A and C Plaintiffs* (1998) 54 BMLR 100 (QBD) 101.

[49] As raised by Stapleton (n 46 above) 127; and J Stapleton, 'The Gist of Negligence. Part II: The Relationship Between "Damage" and "Causation"' (1988) 104 *LQR* 389, 402.

[50] Rogers (n 46 above) 207 (no equivalent in 2002 edition).

[51] This distinction is criticised by Lord Hoffmann in *Fairchild v Glenhaven* (n 24 above) para 72.

[52] Fleming (n 25 above) 670.

[53] *Wilsher v Essex Area HA* (n 1 above) 1086–90.

[54] Compare with *Snell v Farrell* (n 1 above).

justification to extend it to such cases. This interpretation tends to be confirmed by the House of Lords' recent decision in *Fairchild v Glenhaven Funeral Services* (2002), in which *McGhee* was revived under strict conditions. The type of limits imposed on the application of *McGhee*, as well as *Fairchild*'s confirmation of the validity of *Wilsher*, appear to confirm that it is the special nature of the case, not some logical ground, which justifies the adoption of this solution.[55]

One must conclude that *Wilsher* has not completely rejected the possibility of inferring causation, of finding it proven, on the basis of increase of risk. For this reason, an examination of the post-*Wilsher* case law is of great interest. Because it has developed completely differently in England and Canada, these two jurisdictions will be treated separately. The impact of the concept of increase of risk in the post-*Wilsher* Australian case law is also briefly analysed.

(c) Subsequent English Case Law

In most of the English medical malpractice cases in which causation has been debated since *Wilsher*, the controversies or uncertainties have been resolved by applying the balance of probabilities requirement to a detailed analysis of the facts and the expert evidence, without necessarily relying on inferential reasoning, with rare references to *Wilsher*, and without addressing the plaintiff's hurdles in demonstrating causation.[56] Even though flexibility in the evaluation of the causal link is insisted on in some recent cases,[57] causation problems are often solved by balancing the value of experts' opinions and by ultimately preferring one over that of others. Many cases rest their choice on the experts' respective experience,[58] their authority and independence,[59] and the clarity and the objectivity of their opinion.[60] The risk of error the courts take by preferring one body of evidence

[55] *Fairchild v Glenhaven* (n 24 above): discussed below at text to nn 67 ff.

[56] England and Scotland: *Byrnes v Fife Health Board* [1980] SLT 43 (2nd div) 45; *Kay's Tutor v Ayrshire and Arran Health Board* [1987] 2 All ER 417 (HL); *Newbury v Bath District Health Authority* (1999) 47 BMLR 138 (HCJ QBD) 5 and 12 (WL); *Smith v National Health Service Litigation Authority* [2001] Lloyd's Rep Med 90 (HCJ QBD) 20 (confusingly assessing causation partly on this basis and partly on the basis of loss of chance); *Roughton v Weston Area HA* (n 19 above) (no causation). See also: *Elvicta Wood Engineering Ltd v Huxley* (CA, 19 April 2000) 13 (industrial disease). Some cases nonetheless rest their analyses on inferential reasoning, eg, *Mirza v Birmingham Health Authority* (QB, 31 July 2001) 8–9; *Webb v Barclays Bank plc* referred to in CA's judgment: [2001] Lloyd's Rep Med 500 (CA).

[57] *Mirza v Birmingham HA* (n 56 above).

[58] *Bull v Devon Area Health Authority* (1989) 22 BMLR 79 (CA); *Taylor v West Kent* [1997] 8 Med LR 251 (QBD); *Elvicta Wood v Huxley* (n 56 above).

[59] *Bull v Devon Area HA* (n 58 above); *Scott v Northern Devon Healthcare Trust* (QB, 31 July 2000) 8.

[60] *Newbury v Bath District HA* (n 56 above); *Scott v Northern Devon Healthcare Trust* (n 59 above) 8; *Elvicta Wood v Huxley* (n 56 above); *Mirza v Birmingham HA* (n 56 above), eg, *Ball v Wirral Health Authority* (2003) All ER (D) 229 (QB, 27 January 2003) paras 69–70: Based on qualifications, fairness of opinions and conformity with the lay evidence; *Gates v McKenna* (1998) 48 BMLR 9 (QB) 25–26 (non-medical); *Markose v Epsom & St Helier NHS Trust* (2004) WL 3154139; EWHC 3130 (QB, 9 December 2004) para 43. See generally: *Gray v Southampton and South West Hampshire Health Authority* (2000) 57 BMLR 148 (QB).

over another is said to be justified because causation does not have to be proven with medical certainty.[61]

In one case, insistence on the application of the balance of probability criterion resulted in the formal rejection of increase of risk reasoning. *Tahir v Haringey Health Authority* (1998) involved the claim of a 15-year-old boy who was admitted to the hospital with mild pyrexia, abdominal pain, and tenderness. After an appendectomy was carried out, his pain persisted and he did not make the usual post-operative recovery. Four days after his admission, he complained of back pain during the night. X-rays of his lower spine showed no abnormality and he was discharged two days later. His pain progressively worsened and he began to suffer urinary retention. He was consequently readmitted, but the final diagnosis of extradural abscess was made only after he was transferred to another hospital, where he subsequently underwent spinal surgery. By the time he had reached the operating theatre, he was suffering from a severe paraparesis. He claimed against the health authority and the doctor who treated him at the first hospital, arguing negligence in failing to act upon his complaints and to diagnose or treat the condition of his spine. At trial, the judge found the defendants negligent but believed that, without negligence, the plaintiff would have been operated on only two to three hours earlier than he had been. Partial compensation was consequently granted. On appeal, both parties agreed that delay increases the neurological deficit and impairs the prospects of recovery. The plaintiff acknowledged, however, that there was insufficient statistical evidence to enable the Court to assess the effect of this additional delay. Rejecting the application of loss of chance, Otton LJ stressed that causation had to be proven on the balance of probabilities by showing at least that the negligence was the sole cause, or a substantial cause, or that it materially contributed to the damage.[62] In his opinion, it was not sufficient to show the delay had materially increased the risk of damage.[63]

The CJD Litigation: Group A and C Plaintiffs (1998) is another interesting example of the current English approach to medical causation.[64] In this case, the application of the balance of probabilities standard was insisted on when dealing with the question of causation between the plaintiffs' Creutzfeldt-Jakob Disease (CJD) and their receipt of cadaverous Human Growth Hormone (HGH) at the end of the seventies. The Court had established that the injection of the infected HGH was tortious only if it had been carried out after 1 July 1977. CJD can be caused by a single injection or dose containing the CJD agent (alternative causal mechanism). It was impossible, however, for the plaintiffs to determine which of the numerous HGH injections they each received had transmitted the disease and consequently whether it had been injected after 1 July 1977. Since the case

[61] Eg, *Elvicta Wood v Huxley* (n 56 above) 13.

[62] *Tahir v Haringey Health Authority* [1998] Lloyd's Rep Med 104 (CA) 107.

[63] *Ibid*, p 108.

[64] *The CJD Litigation: Group A and C Plaintiffs* (n 48 above) (non-medical).

involved alternative causes, the Court believed it could not be assisted by *Bonnington Castings* and *McGhee,* considering the last to be a cumulative cause case. Consequently, it applied the balance of probabilities rule and concluded that if a plaintiff could show he received the majority of doses or injections after 1 July 1977, he would succeed in establishing causation. Thus causation was assessed on the basis of the traditional standard of proof, albeit by relying on a purely statistical assessment of probabilities and thus exemplifying thereby the difficulties of establishing personal causation.[65]

In 2002, a case in the area of industrial diseases has revived *McGhee* in English law, however.[66] In *Fairchild v Glenhaven Funeral Services Ltd*,[67] the House of Lords granted recovery on the basis of an interpretation of *McGhee* going beyond that of *Wilsher* and the Canadian courts, by treating it as a legal test of causation rather than as just permitting a discretionary inference to be drawn when a risk of damage has been materially increased. The three plaintiffs contracted mesothelioma after several years of employment with different employers during which they had inhaled asbestos fibres.[68] Though mesothelioma is clearly caused by asbestos, this case has been complicated by the fact that the causative process of mesothelioma is unknown and medical evidence cannot say on the balance of probabilities whether any particular exposure to asbestos dust at any particular time materially contributed to the plaintiffs' disease: it is equally possible that only one period of employment did so (unknown causal mechanism). In the light, *inter alia,* of *Bonnington, McGhee,* and *Wilsher,* the Court of Appeal had insisted that it be proven on the balance of probabilities that the employers' negligence caused or materially contributed to the whole damage. The Court refused to distort the law in order 'to accommodate the exigencies of a very hard case'.[69] *McGhee* was distinguished by involving only one causative agent, brick dust, originating from a single tortfeasor. It was argued that, in accordance with *Wilsher,* this case cannot be invoked where there is more than one causative agent, and that, for the same reasons, it cannot be used where there is more than one tortfeasor, unless the evidence shows the existence of a cumulative process.[70]

[65] In September 2001, the UK government announced the details of a no-fault compensation scheme for vCJD victims who prove that their illness was contracted as a result of exposure to bovine products in the UK. Trustees however accept as sufficient evidence that the victim was present in the UK for at least five years between 1982 and 1996: JM Williams, 'Variant Creutzfeldt Jakob Disease: Setting Up the vCJD Trust—Operations and Lessons for the Future' (2004) 1 *Journal of Personal Injury Law* 39, 44.

[66] That had arguably been done before however: *Griffiths v British Coal Corporation* [1998] EWJ No 4656 (QB, 23 January 1998) paras 113, 116–17, 119 (industrial disease).

[67] (N 24 above). The House of Lords was dealing with three test cases.

[68] It seems that there was also environmental exposure in this case, but was ignored by the court: J Stapleton, 'Lords a'Leaping Evidentiary Gaps' (2002) 10 *Torts Law Journal* 276, 281.

[69] (N 28 above) para 103 (CA).

[70] *Ibid*, p 104 (CA).

The Court of Appeal's decision in *Fairchild* was reversed by the House of Lords. This Court found all of the defendants liable, on the basis of *McGhee*, for the whole of the plaintiffs' damage, on the grounds that each of them increased the plaintiffs' risk of damage. While it confirmed the general validity of *Wilsher*,[71] the case reinterpreted the *McGhee* material-increase-of-risk test not as allowing an inference to be drawn, but as being an adaptation of the orthodox test of causation made because justice demanded a remedy for the pursuer in such a case.[72] The majority of the Law Lords expressed the opinion that *McGhee* remains a sound authority, and that Lord Bridge's opinion on the 'robust and pragmatic approach' adopted in *McGhee* should no longer be treated as authoritative.[73] They reasonned that *McGhee* does not permit an inference to be drawn, but rather creates a different standard of proof of causation to the effect that, in cases such as *McGhee* and *Fairchild*, causation is demonstrated by showing the defendant negligently materially increased the risk of damage for the plaintiff[74] (or, in the words of Lord Hoffmann, *contributed substantially* to the risk the claimant would contract the disease.)[75] *McGhee* was thus described by the Law Lords as a variation of the ordinary approach to causation;[76] as a different and less stringent test of causation;[77] and as treating material increase of risk as sufficient to satisfy the causal requirement.[78] The justifications adduced for these positions are that in *McGhee*

[71] (N 24 above) paras 21 (Lord Bingham) and 118 (Lord Hutton).

[72] *Ibid*, para 21 (Lord Bingham). *Fairchild* goes arguably further than *McGhee* since it involved a case where one of the defendants undoubtedly caused the plaintiff's injuries, whereas in *McGhee*, it was not known whether the sole defendant's wrongdoing participated at all to the production of the disease: E Peel, '"Loss of a Chance" Revisited: *Gregg v Scott*' (2003) 66 *MLR* 623, 628. The parallel between *McGhee* and *Fairchild* appears indeed erroneous. These two cases involved extremely different fact situations. The first involved scientific uncertainty, while the second was preoccupied with a situation of factual uncertainty. Moreover, in *Fairchild*, the uncertainty related to choosing which of two tortious events had caused the plaintiff's damage (indeterminate defendant problem). In contrast, in *McGhee*, the choice was between one tortious and one non-tortious cause which both emanated from the same defendant. Yet one may legitimately ask why such a distinction should matter, especially if these decisions are predominantly based on policy.

[73] *Fairchild v Glenhaven* (n 24 above) paras 22 (Lord Bingham), 144 and 150 (Lord Rodger).

[74] Compare: *Bryce v Swan* (n 23 above) which, in an exactly similar fact-situation, relied on *McGhee* to *infer* causation.

[75] *Ibid*, para 46 (Lord Hoffmann). The majority decision in *McGhee* does not expressly mention it is inferring causation, although Lord Wilberforce considered the majority decision as relying on inferential reasoning: (n 26 above) 7. Moreover, Lord Simon had made an indirect reference to inferences by citing *Gardiner v Motherwell Machinery and Scrap Co Ltd* (n 27 above); (n 26 above) 9. It has also been interpreted as such by some English cases: Eg, *Bryce v Swan* (n 23 above). Some doctrinal writers treat Fairchild as allowing to draw an inference: C Feeny, P Laleng and D Cooper, 'Mesothelioma, Asbestos and Causation' (2003) *Journal of Personal Injury Law* 1.

[76] (N 24 above) para 35 (Lord Bingham). Lord Bingham admits that his approach or that of drawing legal or factual inferences do not result in much practical difference in this instance. This may explain why the precise nature of the mechanism relied on in *McGhee* was not a consideration: all three possibilities led to the same result as both plaintiff and defendant could not offer any evidence with regard to causation.

[77] *Ibid*, para 45 (Lord Nicholls).

[78] *Ibid*, para 65 (Lord Hoffmann). See also: paras 142 and 144 (Lord Rodger).

the Lords believed they were deciding a question of law[79] and that a factual inference could not be drawn where the medical experts' opinions did not support it.[80]

Lord Hutton disagreed on this point, however, stressing it is permissible to draw common sense inferences which doctors, as scientific witnesses, were not prepared to draw.[81] In his opinion, *McGhee* should be seen as having introduced a *legal inference* of causation binding on trial judges in cases where the employer's breach of duty materially increased the risk of the claimant's contracting a particular disease and the disease has occurred, but where, in the state of existing medical knowledge, the claimant cannot prove by medical evidence that the breach caused the disease.[82]

Although reinstating *McGhee* in English tort law, Lord Hoffmann and Lord Rodger limited its application. Lord Hoffmann imposed five conditions: i) a duty exists specifically intended to protect employees against unnecessary exposure to the risk of a particular disease; ii) this duty is intended to create a civil right to compensation for injury relevantly connected with its breach; iii) the greater the exposure to the agent of the damage, the greater the risk of contracting the disease; iv) except in cases where there has been only one significant exposure to asbestos, medical science cannot prove whose asbestos is more likely than not to have caused the disease; and v) the employee has contracted the disease against which he should have been protected.[83]

Finally, it is noteworthy that the liability was not apportioned on the basis of the extent of the defendant's contribution to the injury. Although this has been criticised,[84] this omission is understandable. Aside from the fact that such apportionment was not requested by the defendants, allowing it in this case would indirectly be accepting a form of proportional assessment of damages which has yet to be admitted in English law. Indeed, since the defendants' contribution in

[79] *Ibid*, paras 150 (Lord Rodger) and 21 (Lord Bingham) citing Lord Reid in *McGhee v National Coal Board* (n 26 above) 3.

[80] Paras 35 (Lord Bingham) and 150 (Lord Rodger). See also: Para 70 (Lord Hoffmann): 'However robust or pragmatic the tribunal may be, it cannot draw inferences of fact in the teeth of the *undisputed* medical evidence' (emphasis added). We disagree: ch 2, text between fns 44 and 64.

[81] *Ibid*, paras 100 and 102. This also corresponds to the Canadian approach.

[82] *Ibid*, para 108.

[83] *Ibid*, para 61. Lord Rodger also notes the need not to extend *McGhee* too far and imposes six conditions: i) inherent causal uncertainty; ii) defendant's wrongdoing materially increased risk claimant will suffer injury; iii) defendant's conduct capable of causing claimant's injury; iv) injury caused by eventuation of kind of risk created by defendant's wrongdoing; v) injury caused by agency operating in essentially same way as agency involved in defendant's wrongdoing; and vi) other possible source of damage is a similar wrongful act or omission of another person or is a similar but lawful act or omission of the same defendant: paras 169–70.

[84] J Stapleton, 'Cause-in-Fact and the Scope of Liability for Consequences' (2003) 119 *LQR* 388, 399; Feeny, *et al* (n 76 above) 9; S Arnell, 'Causation Reassessed' (2002) *Scots Law Times* 265, 267; J Stapleton (2002) (n 68 above) 284 ff and 298 ff; S Green, 'Winner Takes All' (2004) 120 *LQR* 566, 567 ff. Stapleton suggests that apportionment in cases such as *Fairchild* be done on the basis of factors such as the relative length/intensity of exposure or the respective defendants' market-shares.

Fairchild was in the form of a contribution to the increase of the risk of injury, limiting their liability to the extent of that contribution would present close affinities with treating the injury as the loss of a chance.[85] As long as this technique is rejected, apportionment appears conceptually sound only if the causal process is cumulative, the contribution then being to the injury itself.[86]

The Law Lords' decision was clearly and admittedly based on policy rather than principle,[87] motivated by the Court's 'basic sense of justice,'[88] which dictated compensating the victims.[89] The employer–employee relationship between the parties was a prominent consideration, as was the fact that the potential for injustice to the employer was heavily outweighed by the injustice of denying redress to the victim.[90] Another influential factor was that it had been established that the plaintiffs' diseases were caused by exposure to asbestos, partial causation being thereby demonstrated.[91] Finally, the Court was influenced by the fact that, faced with the problem of indeterminacy of the defendant, most jurisdictions have responded by affording remedy to the plaintiff, albeit through recourse to different intellectual mechanisms.[92] It is worth noting that, even though the facts of *Fairchild* could have opened the door to a *Cook v Lewis–Summers v Tice* argument allowing the reversal of the onus of proof of causation, the House of Lords mentioned but did not rely on these North American authorities.[93] Nonetheless, the existence of pro-plaintiff solutions in other common law, and civil law, jurisdictions did influence Lord Bingham:

[85] Although under the material contribution test, causation must a priori be established between the fault and the final injury, which is not the case under loss of chance. Eg, *Lyne v McClarty* (2003) MJ No 29, MBCA 18 (ManCA, 31 January 2003) paras 27 and ff makes a distinction between apportionment and loss of chance, which is overlooked in *Lindahl Estate v Olsen* (2004) 360 AR 310 (AltaQB) paras 136–45, although the point is raised at para 142.

[86] M Fordham, 'Causation in the Tort of Negligence—A Dispensable Element?' (2003) *Singapore Journal of Legal Studies* 285, 299. Stapleton also admits that such apportionment will necessarily be artificial in cases where the defendant's contribution to the total risk is uncertain, however: J Stapleton (2002) (n 68 above) 284 ff and 298 ff.

[87] (N 24 above) para 33 (Lord Bingham).

[88] *Ibid*, para 32 (Lord Bingham). At para 36, Lord Nicholls nonetheless notes that to be acceptable, the law must nevertheless be principled. Compare: *Fitzgerald v Lane* (n 39 above). Also described as an intuitive decision: A Layard, 'Toxic Torts—A Landmark Decision' (2002) 4.4 *Environmental Law Review* 241, 242.

[89] Paras 36 (Lord Nicholls), 33 (Lord Bingham), and 56 (Lord Hoffman).

[90] *Ibid*, para 33 (Lord Bingham). See also: paras 42 (Lord Nicholls) and 63 (Lord Hoffmann).

[91] *Ibid*, para 62 (Lord Hoffmann). Compare: Viney and Jourdain (n 9 above) para 380. Commenting on the indeterminate defendant situations, they argue that a more generous approach is warranted by the fact that causation is partly proven.

[92] *Ibid*, para 156 (Lord Rodger). See also: Lord Bingham, para 32, who adds '[T]here must be some virtue in uniformity of outcome whatever the diversity of approach in reaching that outcome'.

[93] *Ibid*, paras 27, 29–30 (Lord Bingham); 39 (Lord Nicholls); 110 (Lord Hutton); and 164 (Lord Rodger). These cases can be distinguished, however. In *Cook*, each defendant had increased the risk of injury by 50%, while the increases attributed to each defendant in *Fairchild* were much lower. Moreover, all the defendants were not in front of the court in *Fairchild* and, consequently, those who were, were not solely responsible for all the (tortious) sources of the risk: J Stapleton (2002) (n 68 above) 41; Layard (n 88 above) 243.

> If ... a decision is given in this country which offends one's basic sense of justice, and if consideration of international sources suggests that a different and more acceptable decision would be given in most other jurisdictions, whatever their legal tradition, this must prompt anxious review of the decision in question.[94]

One question left partly unresolved in *Fairchild* concerns its applicability to future cases,[95] although the Law Lords were prudent not to encourage unwarranted extensions.[96] Nevertheless, *Fairchild* indirectly confirms the inapplicability of *McGhee* to English medical malpractice cases involving alternative causes, and the continuing dominance of *Wilsher* over these instances. The policy motivations which led the House of Lords to adopt a generous attitude to causation in *Fairchild* are not likely to be present in typical medical malpractice cases involving causal uncertainty. *Fairchild* was found applicable only to two types of situations: where damage is proven to originate from one single type of agent arising from an unidentified defendant, which creates a risk within which the damage falls (*Fairchild*);[97] and where the different possible causes of the damage involve identical risks emanating from only one defendant (*McGhee*). In both these situations, a central, even if not explicit, consideration is the fact that the plaintiff's injury clearly fell within the scope of a risk negligently created by the defendant, thereby partially showing the existence of causation.[98] Very rarely do medical instances of scientific causal uncertainty have this aspect, however; rather, the background risk often originates from a cause foreign to the defendant, not attributed to anyone's fault.[99] In addition, the alternative cause situations in medical litigation rarely involve two faults committed by different defendants, save when the difficulty lies in identifying the defendant in the context of team medical practice; in typical medical malpractice cases, the causal uncertainty concerns the identification of the agent of the damage, not that of the author of the damage. Finally, even though the Law Lords reject *Wilsher*'s interpretation of *McGhee* as allowing the drawing of an inference of causation, they confirm the stand it has taken with regard to the assessment of causation in medical cases involving alternative causal mechanisms. *Fairchild* makes it therefore even more unlikely that English courts will

[94] Para 32.

[95] Fordham (n 86 above) 287.

[96] Paras 73 (Lord Hoffmann); 34 (Lord Bingham); 43 (Lord Nicholls); 118 (Lord Hutton); 169–70 (Lord Rogers) and above text to n 83. See also: Fordham (n 87 above) 297.

[97] Thereby partially proving causation (as in most indeterminate defendant cases).

[98] One must also note the important fact that the link between asbestos and mesothelioma is well-established: Layard (n 88 above) 241.

[99] On the inapplicability of *Fairchild* and *McGhee* to such cases: J Stapleton (2003) (n 84 above) 398, relying on *Fairchild*'s approval of *Wilsher*; M Hogg, 'The Raising of Lazarus: The Resurrection of *McGhee v National Coal Board*' (2003) *Edinburgh Law Review* 80, 81 and 85. Against: Fordham (n 86 above) 298.

be tempted to rely on *McGhee* or increase of risk in medical malpractice law in the future.[100]

This inapplicability was confirmed in *Gregg v Scott* (2004) by the English Court of Appeal and the House of Lords on the basis, *inter alia*, that adopting such a rule in medical liability cases would involve abandoning a good deal of authority, such as *Hotson* and *Wilsher*, which was expressly approved in *Fairchild*.[101] However, the Fairchild 'philosophy' was recently applied in a case involving the breach of a medical duty to inform in *Chester v Afshar* (2005), where the House of Lords accepted the varying of rules of causation based on policy grounds, even in the absence of a negligently caused risk increase.[102]

(d) Subsequent Australian Case Law

Australian cases also seem to reserve their flexible approach to cases of pure causal uncertainty, excluding those involving expert controversy.[103] The idea of material increase of risk has nevertheless also influenced Australian courts to find causation proven, usually through inferential process, in a few important medical cases.[104] In *Chappel v Hart* (1998), McHugh J, stated in the context of the medical duty to inform that if the defendant's wrongful act or omission increased the risk of injury to the plaintiff and that risk eventuates, the defendant's conduct has materially contributed to the injury occurring.[105] Gaudron J was of a smilar opinion:

[100] J Stapleton (2002) (n 68 above) 293; Grubb and Laing (n 24 above) para 7.20. The lack of analogy with the medical malpractice setting also flows from the fact that *Fairchild* (as well as *McGhee)* arose in an occupational context and that all defendants were acting in the pursuit of a commercial profit. Against: Jones (n 18 above) para 5–32 and 5–35.

[101] *Gregg v Scott* [2005] 2 AC 176, para 78 (Lord Hoffmann). See also: para 174: Treated as an 'exception' by Lord Phillips (dissenting on other grounds). See also: *Morris v Blackpool Victoria Hospital NHS Trust* (2004) EWCA CIV 1294 (CA, 13 October 2004) (obiter). It was also confirmed in Australia: *Rufo v Hosking* (2004) NSWCA 391 (1 November 2004) paras 440–41 (Campbell J).

[102] [2005] 1 AC 134; [2005] 3 WLR 927; [2005] 4 All ER 587 (HL). This decision is not thoroughly reviewed here since it involved purely factual uncertainty. For a detailed commentary: L Khoury, '*Chester v Afshar:* Stepping Further Away from Causation?' (2005) *Singapore Journal of Legal Studies* 246. For other commentaries on *Fairchild:* The excellent review and critique of Jones (n 18 above) para 5–27, 5–38; TS Woods, 'Establishing Causation in Negligence: The House of Lords Speaks Again' (2003) 26 *Advocates' Quarterly* 471; W Coley, 'Asbestos Claims' (2003) *Journal of Personal Injury Law* 15; J Stapleton (2002) (n 68 above); Layard (n 88 above); M Hogg (n 99 above); Arnell (n 84 above).

[103] *Epp v Balaton* (2003) 24 Alta LR (4th) 66; [2003] 4 WWR 99 (QB) para 168; *Rufo v Hosking* (n 102 above) para 10 (Hodgson JA).

[104] RP Balkin and JLR Davis, *Law of Torts*, 3rd edn, (Chatswood, NSW, LexisNexis Butterworths, 2004) 319; R Mulheron and J Gordon, 'Juries, Medical Negligence and Causation in the High Court of Australia' (2000) *Tort Law Review* 19.

[105] *Chappel v Hart* (1998) 195 CLR 232 (AustHC) 244 (para 27) and 247 (para 34), specifying at fn 28 that 'increase' includes 'creates'. He did not apply this principle, however, given he found no increase of risk in this specific case. Followed in *Finch v Rogers* (2004) NSWSC 39 (NSWSC, 13 February 2004) para 133 (Kirby J); *Boehm v Deleuil* (2005) WL 1444518, WADC 55 (WADC, 30 March 2005) 115; and *Chapman v Caska* (2005) NSWCA 113 (12 April 2005) para 12 (treated as permitting an inference).

> If ... evidence is to the effect that the injured person would have acted to avoid or minimize the risk of injury, it is to apply sophistry rather than common sense to say that, although the risk of physical injury which came about called the duty of care into existence, breach of that duty did not cause or contribute to that injury, but simply resulted in the loss of an opportunty to pursue a different course of action.[106]

Whether or not this opinion was meant to extend beyond the realm of duty to inform cases, the High Court reiterated this stand outside of this area in *Naxakis v Western General Hospital* (1999), a case dealing with delay in the diagnosis of a burst aneurysm, citing with approval McHugh J's position in *Chappel v Hart.*[107] As for lower courts, they have also adopted this position. For instance, in *Crockett v Roberts* (2002), the Supreme Court of Tasmania accepted (but did not apply) as a correct statement of the law that:

> If a wrongful omission results in an increased risk of injury to the plaintiff and that risk eventuates, a trier of fact is entitled to conclude that the omission caused the injury unless the defendant establishes that the conduct had no effect at all or that the risk would have eventuated and caused the damage in any event.[108]

In 2002, in response to its identification of 'evidentiary gaps' as a major problem in the law relating to causation,[109] the Ipp Report on the review of the Australian law of negligence recommended that legislation recognises that, in appropriate

[106] 239 (para 9).

[107] *Naxakis v Western General Hospital* (n 1 above) 312 (Callinan J) and 279 (para 31) (Gaudron J). It might have been argued, however, that the reference to increase of risk by Gaudron and McHugh JJ in *Chappel v Hart* was limited to assisting the court in distinguishing cases where the realization of the risk is a mere coincidental consequence of the defendant's tort from those in which the doctor's omission to inform had an impact on the realisation of the risk in duty to inform cases: Stapleton (2003) (n 64 above) 410–19.

[108] *Crockett v Roberts* (2002) TASSC 73 (26 September 2002). See also: *Anasson v Koziol* (n 23 above) 48 (*McGhee* treated as permitting a causal *inference*); *Hughes v Minister for Health* (1999) WL 33121042; [1999] WASCA 131 (20 August 1999) para 64; *Chapman v Caska* (n 105 above) para 12 (*ibid*). Outside of medical liability: *Commonwealth v McLean* (1996) 41 NSWLR 389 (CA), 408 (Sperling J). Against: *Bendix Mintex PTY Ltd and ORS v Barnes* (1997) 42 NSWLR 307 (NSWSC), although the notion of increase of risk transpires heavily from Mason P's analysis, as he himself admits: 319. See also: 342 (Beazley JA) and 348–49 (Stein J, dissenting). See also, on the role of increase of risk in the assessment of causation, outside of medical liability: *Birkholz v RJ Gilbertson Pty Ltd* (1985) 38 SASR 121; *Wallaby Grip (BAE) PTY Ltd (In Liq) v Macleay Area Health Service* (1998) NSW Lexis 2423 (NSWSC, 18 December 1998) 12–13 (mesothelioma case), treating material increase of risk as permitting an inference of material contribution, but refusing to apply it in this case despite the finding that the higher the exposure to asbestos, the more likely a person will contract mesothelioma: 15–17; *ICI Australia Operations Pty Ltd v Walsh* (1997) Aust Torts Rep 81–452; *EM Baldwin & Sons Pty Ltd v Plane* (1999) Aust Torts Rep 81–499; *Seltsam Pty Ltd v McGuiness* (n 1 above) paras 102–9: this case insists that the plaintiff must prove that the increase of risk did cause or materially contributed to the injury, however, which is contradictory to the rule that infers contribution or finds it proven based on evidence of increased risk, para 118. See also: J Gunson, 'Turbulent Causal Waters: The High Court, Causation and Medical Negligence' (2001) *Tort Law Review* 53, 70–75.

[109] Commonwealth of Australia, *Review of the Law of Negligence, Final Report* (Canberra, September 2002), Part 7, para 7.27.

cases, proof that the negligence materially contributed to the harm or risk of harm may be treated as sufficient to establish factual causation, nothwithstanting an inability to satisfy the but-for test[110] The report advised that this be done on normative grounds, by considering whether or not and why responsibility for the harm should be imposed on the negligent party,[111] adding that the detailed criteria for determining this issue should be left to common law development.[112] The recommendations were incorporated in the most part by State and Territory legislatures and given legislative effect—by adopting broader language without reference to the notion of risk, however.[113] Thus, Australian law has proved willing within its common-sense, flexible approach to factual causation to refer to, and sometimes apply, the concept of material increase of risk, but only in a small number of medical negligence cases.

(e) Subsequent Canadian Case Law

Even though Canadian law accepted *Wilsher* as authoritative, it took a completely different turn. In *Snell v Farrell* (1990),[114] the Supreme Court of Canada directly addressed the question of the impact of *McGhee* in light of *Wilsher*. It also clarified the Canadian position with regard to inferences of causation in medical malpractice cases. The defendant doctor performed surgery on a 70-year-old woman to remove a cataract from her right eye. After injecting a local anaesthetic into the retrobulbar muscles behind the eyeball, the defendant noticed a discoloration which he interpreted as a small retrobulbar bleed. On palpating the eye, he found it was not hard and that there were no signs of retrobulbar haemorrhage. He waited 30 minutes and proceeded with the surgery. Following the operation, there was blood in the eye's vitreous chamber. Nine months later, when the chamber cleared, the defendant doctor realised that the optic nerve had atrophied and that the plaintiff had lost her eyesight. The interesting feature of this case was the existence of three mutually exclusive possible causes of the loss of the plaintiff's optic nerve's blood supply which had led to its atrophy. One possible cause was pressure due to retrobulbar haemorrhage. This inherent risk may occur in 1 per cent to 3 per cent of cases but could also have been caused by the defendant negligently continuing the surgery despite the presence of blood in the eye. The loss of blood supply could also have been the result of a stroke in the eye, likely to occur in a

[110] *Ibid*, para 7.32.

[111] *Ibid*, para 7.33.

[112] *Ibid*.

[113] Civil Liability Act 2002 (NSW) §5D(2); Civil Liability Act 2003 (Qld) §11(2); Civil Liability Act 1936 (SA) §34(2); Civil Liability Act 2002 (Tas) §13(2); Civil Liability Act 2002 (WA) §5C(2); Civil Law (Wrongs) Act 2002 (ACT) §45(2); Wrongs Act 1958 (Vic), §51(2). On the Ipp Report: SS Clark and R McInnes, 'Unprecedented Reform: The New Tort Law' (2004) 15 *Insurance Law Journal* 1; D Ipp, 'Negligence: Where Lies the Future?' (2003) 23 *Australian Bar Review* 158; H Luntz, 'Turning Points in the Law of Torts in the Last 30 Years' (2003) 15 *Insurance Law Journal* 1.

[114] (N 1 above).

patient suffering, as the plaintiff did, from high blood pressure or diabetes. Finally, the plaintiff also had severe glaucoma, which can, over a long period, cause optic nerve atrophy. No expert was able to state with certainty what caused the atrophy in this particular case or when it occurred. They did, however, testify that where there is bleeding other than the obvious pinprick of the needle, the operation should not be continued. The defendant was therefore at fault in this respect. Relying on *McGhee v National Coal Board* (1973), the New Brunswick Court of Queen's Bench, confirmed by the Court of Appeal, granted the claim; the plaintiff had *prima facie* proven that the defendant's actions caused her injury and the defendant did not satisfy the requirement of the onus shifted to him.

The Supreme Court of Canada also granted the claim, although on completely different grounds. Sopinka J, writing for a unanimous Court, recalled that in most cases, the traditional principles of causation are sufficient for the task of evaluating causation. He expressed himself in favour of flexibility in the assessment of the burden and standard of proof of causation in medical malpractice cases, however. While he believed that the legal or ultimate burden should remain with the plaintiff, he clearly agreed with the possibility of drawing an inference of causation in medical malpractice cases, even in the absence of direct scientific proof of its existence.[115]

Despite Sopinka J's emphasis that in most cases the traditional principles of causation remain applicable, the subsequent cases and doctrine treated the flexible approach and the possibility of inferring causation he advocated as a general rule in medical malpractice cases.[116] Yet in Sopinka J's judgment, one cannot easily identify the exact circumstances in which such an inference of causation is warranted. Campion and Dimmer agree, however, observing that 'it is expected that the principles in *Snell v Farrell* will be applied in medical negligence cases where appropriate.'[117] That their prediction has been fulfilled is unfortunately doubtful.

Sopinka J makes it clear that an inference of causation is justified in cases in which the facts regarding causation are within the defendant's particular knowledge and the defendant's negligence undermines the plaintiff's means of proving causation; the case was in fact decided on this basis.[118] It is less clear whether he considered valid an inference based on the material increase of the risk of damage by the defendant, although he acknowledges the authority of *Wilsher v Essex Area HA*

[115] *Ibid*, p 330.

[116] AM Linden, *Canadian Tort Law*, 7th edn, (Markham, Butterworths, 2001) 112 (he compares this mechanism with *res ipsa loquitur*); L Klar, *Tort Law*, 3rd edn, (Scarborough, Carswell, 2003) 402 and fn 75; MA Ross, 'Rules of the Road to Judgment in Medical Malpractice Cases: Standard of Care and Causation' (1998) 20 *Advocates' Quarterly* 274, 283. But some cases still refuse to draw inferences of causation because of absence of evidence, eg, *Rothwell v Raes* (1988) 54 DLR (4th) 193 (OntHCJ); (1990) 76 DLR (4th) 280 (OntCA); *Grealy v Kuntz* (BCSC), *aff'd* (BCCA) (n 19 above).

[117] JA Campion and DW Dimmer, *Professional Liability in Canada* (looseleaf) (Toronto, Carswell, 1998) 3–31.

[118] See below, text to n 179.

(1988) in Canadian law.[119] Klar is more assertive and believes that *Snell*'s allowance of an inference of cause even where there is no scientific evidence of a probable connection between negligence and injury amounts to accepting the essential principle of *McGhee*.[120] To jump from the willingness of inferring causation in the absence of scientific evidence to the acceptance of the rationale of *McGhee* is surely too precipitate. Sopinka J does not expressly accept that an inference of causation can be based on the material increase of the plaintiff's risk of damage. There are however two hints in support of this position. First, Sopinka J implies that *Wilsher* accepted, as of principle, the House of Lords majority decision in *McGhee*:

> Decisions in Canada after *Wilsher* accept its interpretation of *McGhee*. In the circumstances in which *McGhee* had been previously interpreted to support a reversal of the burden of proof, an inference was now permissible to find causation, notwithstanding that causation was not proven by positive evidence.[121]

A second hint is found in Sopinka J's comment that, instead of reversing the burden of proof on the basis of material increase of risk (as per Lord Wilberforce in *McGhee*), the trial judge in *Snell v Farrell* could have equally granted the plaintiff's claim by drawing an inference of causation. Indeed he stated that had the trial judge applied the principles of causation described in inter alia, *McGhee* and *Wilsher*, he would have drawn an inference of causation and such inference would have been fully warranted on the evidence.[122] However, Sopinka J makes no mention of increase of risk as the ground for this inference.

These two excerpts from Sopinka J's decision could imply that he accepted causation could be inferred on the basis of a material increase of risk by the defendant. This interpretation is debatable, however. Sopinka J also rejects what he refers to as *McGhee's* two 'alternatives', simply proving that the defendant created a risk of injury or imposing on the defendant the risk of disproving causation, except where defendants having a 'substantial connection to the injury are escaping liability because plaintiffs cannot prove causation'.

Whether or not Sopinka J really meant to expressly recognise this possibility, the subsequent Canadian common law cases,[123] as well as some

[119] *Snell v Farrell* (n 1 above) 326.

[120] Klar (n 116 above) 403.

[121] (N 1 above) 326. This is obviously not what Lord Bridge meant in *Wilsher v Essex Area HA* (n 1 above) 326. Sopinka J cites the following cases in support of his assertion: *Rendall v Ewert* (1989) 60 DLR (4th) 513 (BCCA); *Kitchen v McMullen* (1989) 62 DLR (4th) 481 (NBCA); *Westco Storage Ltd v Inter-City Gas Utilities Ltd* (1989) 59 Man R (2d) 37 (CA); *Haag v Marshall* (n 40 above).

[122] *Snell v Farrell* (n 1 above) 335. Sopinka J distinguishes *Snell v Farrell* from *Wilsher v Essex Area HA* on the ground that the experts' evidence in *Wilsher* was seriously in conflict, while in *Snell* the experts were simply unable to reach any conclusion. It is hard to understand how this distinction can be the basis of the choice of causative approach.

[123] Eg, *Lankenau Estate v Dutton* (1991) 79 DLR (4th) 705 (BCCA); *Levitt v Carr* [1992] 4 WWR 160 (BCCA); *Taylor v Hogan* (1994) 119 Nfld & PEIR 37 (NfldCA).

commentators,[124] interpreted it as supporting such a rule. Sopinka J's opinion has in fact been applied in such a way as to give vitality to the majority opinion in *McGhee* in medical liability instances.[125] Canadian case law is also fascinating for the lenient way in which it has applied this material increase of risk reasoning.

In *Webster v Chapman* (1997), the fact that the doctor's conduct was fraught with obvious risks was sufficient to infer causation. A woman was prescribed a drug called Coumadin by a specialist to treat a pelvic thrombosis. Thereafter, her family doctor told her of the danger of becoming pregnant in her medical condition, without, however, warning her of the potential harm that the medication could cause to foetus. Despite this advice, the woman became pregnant. She consulted the defendant doctor when she was 8 weeks pregnant, but he erroneously assessed her pregnancy at 11 weeks. He expressed concern about her having become pregnant but nonetheless negligently told her to continue taking her medication. He arranged for her to have an ultrasound examination and see an obstetrician, who immediately advised her to stop taking the medication. The infant was born with serious morphological and neurological congenital anomalies. The trial judge and the Court of Appeal found the defendant negligent for omitting to consult with a specialist and advise the mother of the risks involved in continuing to take the drug while pregnant. It was not disputed that the damage was caused by the ingestion of Coumadin during the pregnancy and that the morphological anomalies had been suffered before the plaintiff consulted the defendant. In the medical knowledge of the time, however, it was unknown whether or in what manner Coumadin could affect the development of the central nervous system (unknown causal mechanism). The experts were able only to say that its ingestion during the first trimester of pregnancy *could* result in the kind of damage afflicting the plaintiff. Consequently, the defendant contended that the plaintiff's damage had already occurred when he committed his fault.

The trial judge agreed with this submission, which was, however, rejected by the Court of Appeal. The latter found the defendant liable on the ground that the failure to terminate the woman's medication when she became pregnant materially increased the risk of damage to the foetus.[126] Material increase of the risk of

[124] JB Archibald, 'Proof of Causation Revisited: *Snell v Farrell*' (1991) 1 *Journal of Environmental Law and Practice* 227, 231. Against: D Cheifetz, 'Materially Increasing the Risk of Injury as Factual Cause of Injury: *Fairchild v Glenhaven Funeral Services Ltd in Canada*' (2004) 29 *Advocates' Quarterly* 253, 255 and 262, interpreting Sopinka J's rejection of Lord Wilberforce reversal of the burden of proof approach as a rejection of the possibility to draw inferences based on increase of risk. The same error appears in *Allen (Next Friend of) v University Hospitals Board* (2002) AJ no 1041; ABCA 195 (AltaCA, 27 August 2002) para 19.

[125] PH Osborne, *The Law of Torts*, 2nd edn, (Toronto, Irwin Law, 2003) 56: The 'gradual easing of the burden of proof sparked by McGhee continues'; Klar (n 116 above) 402: '[W]hile rejecting the bold principle of McGhee, Sopinka J adopted its spirit ...' The only 'bold principle' clearly rejected in *Snell v Farrell* is Lord Wilberforce's reversal of the onus approach, however.

[126] *Webster v Chapman* (1997) 155 DLR (4th) 82 (ManCA) 93. See also: *Suchorab v Urbanski* (1997) 156 Sask R 46 (QB) 55 *a contrario*.

damage was, on the basis of Lord Salmon and Lord Reid's judgments in *McGhee*, equated to material contribution to the injury and was thus sufficient to infer causation. This conclusion was reached despite the fact that the medical experts were unable to quantify the increase of risk and even though the risk to which the mother was subjected before the defendant's intervention was objectively greater than the risk flowing from the defendant's negligence.

Taylor v Hogan (1994) affords another interesting example. The patient complained to the defendant doctor of low abdominal pain radiating to her right side, headaches, nausea and painful sexual intercourse. Wrongly suspecting a recurrence of endometriosis when she was actually suffering from constipation, the defendant performed a laparoscopy in the course of which the patient's colon was punctured. A second surgery was immediately required to repair it. Within 24 hours of the second intervention, the patient suffered from a thrombosis of the right cerebral artery (a stroke). The trial judge and the Court of Appeal found the defendant negligent for not taking the means to discover the patient had been suffering from chronic constipation for some years. In addition, the procedure had been performed negligently. Causation was more difficult to assess, since the experts were unable to agree on the stroke's exact aetiology and to determine definitively whether it had been the result of the second surgery. One expert believed, however, that a reasonable inference of causation could be drawn on the basis of different observations, such as the patient's raised platelet count before the second surgery, which, combined with the increased coagulation of the blood during the stress of the surgery, *could* have contributed to the stroke. In addition, this expert relied on the temporal relationship between the surgery and the onset of the stroke.

While admitting that there was no scientific evidence or knowledge available to demonstrate what caused the stroke, the trial judge reiterated the principle that his decision did not have to be based on medical certainty but on the balance of probabilities. He found, however, that causation had not been proven, given that the patient had had four previous operations under general anaesthetic without suffering from a stroke. The Court of Appeal reversed that decision. Insisting that *Snell* imposes a less onerous burden on plaintiffs in cases of medical malpractice, the Court was of the opinion that an inference of causation could be drawn, since the evidence showed that the defendant's negligence created a risk and the injury occurred within the area of the risk. Moreover, there was no positive medical opinion to rebut such an inference.[127]

Finally, in *Robinson v Sydenham District Hospital Corp* (2000), the Ontario Court of Appeal dealt with the claim of a man who had fractured his finger when he accidentally tripped over his dog. The defendant doctor realigned the fracture and immobilised it. When the cast was removed less than a month later, all four

[127] (N 124 above) 50–51.

of the plaintiff's fingers were stiffened in the position in which they had been immobilised. They stiffened further until they closed up completely into a fist. After two operations, the patient's hand was reopened but remained without function. The Court of Appeal agreed with the trial judge that the defendant had negligently immobilised the plaintiff's hand. On appeal, the defendant contested the trial judge's statement that the language of *Snell* allowed the plaintiff to prove only that the defendant had created a risk of harm and that the injury occurred within the area of the risk. The Court of Appeal agreed that this proposition was rejected in *Snell* but only to the extent that it justified reversing the burden of proof. Creation of a risk could, however, support drawing an inference of causation adverse to the defendant.[128] The Court believed that the trial judge had made a correct application of this principle when he found causation proven on the basis of the defendant doctor's failure to minimise the risks of the treatment to which the plaintiff was subjected.[129] The trial judge's conclusion was not only supported by the medical evidence but was 'also a reasonable common sense inference from the totality of the evidence.'[130]

In *Levitt v Carr* (1992), the Court of Appeal also relied on material increase of risk, although in applying slightly different reasoning. The plaintiff was referred to the defendant because of a persistent bowel complaint. Crohn's disease was diagnosed and the claimant treated with steroid therapy. Because the patient's symptoms did not improve, the defendant performed surgery during which he discovered that the plaintiff was in fact suffering from ulcerative colitis, a condition similar to Crohn's disease. The misdiagnosis was, however, not negligent, since both conditions require high dosage steroid therapy. A rare, randomly occurring but known side effect of such therapy is avascular necrosis.[131] The patient's femoral head eventually suffered from this condition, which entailed hip replacement surgery. The trial judge found the defendant at fault for pursuing the steroid treatment for a period of 18 weeks, even after the patient's condition deteriorated, while the recognised duration of this treatment was then limited to a maximum of 6 weeks. It was unknown, however, whether the avascular necrosis was caused by the steroid treatment that took place within the accepted period of 4 to 6 weeks or by the treatment administered afterwards (alternative causal process). Consequently, the plaintiff could prove only that the defendant had increased his chances of developing this condition.

On the basis of *Bonnington, McGhee,* and *Wilsher*, Wood J found causation proven, as he believed that both periods of treatment probably contributed

[128] (2000) 130 OAC 109 (OntCA) 116. This case takes for granted that the test could apply to the *creation* of a new risk.

[129] *Ibid*, 119.

[130] *Ibid*. See also: *Briffett v Gander & District Hospital Board* (n 1 above). The drawing of an inference was unnecessary in this case, however, given how high the increase of risk was (70%–75% or 90% depending on the expert).

[131] Death of bone tissue as a result of being deprived of blood supply.

cumulatively to the development of the damage. Since the time length of the negligent treatment was almost twice as long as the maximum length universally recognised and accepted as reasonable, the increase of risk was material within the meaning of the term used by Lord Reid in *Bonnington Castings v Wardlaw*.[132] Applying *Snell* and *Wilsher*, the Court of Appeal confirmed this decision; it was open to the trial judge to infer from the evidence that the duration of the treatment beyond 6 weeks materially increased the risk of damage and that this material increase in risk was a contributing cause of the damage.[133] The case is interesting for its emphasis on the extent of the increase of risk needed to meet the *material* condition of the test. This contrasts with many Canadian cases which in practice consider a mere increase or creation of a risk on the part of the defendant sufficient to meet the requirement.

The study of the Canadian cases shows that the courts have tended to a liberal interpretation of *Wilsher* and *Snell,* with the result that material increase of risk is still relied on by the Canadian medical malpractice case law,[134] Moreover, with the exception of *Levitt,* the above case law shows a tendency in Canada to consider the mere increase of a risk sufficient to meet the requirement of material increase of risk-material contribution to the damage. It is striking that most of the cases applying material increase of risk do not pay attention to the quantification of the extent of the risk created or increased by the defendant. The above cases also show that once material increase of the risk is relied on, it makes no difference whether the causal process involved is alternative, cumulative, or unknown. Finally, these cases demonstrate that it is unlikely that *Fairchild v Glenhaven Funeral Services* (2002) will have an impact on Canadian medical malpractice. The concept of material increase of risk has long been interpreted in Canadian medical malpractice instances as permitting an inference of causation to be drawn. As the authority for such an interpretation comes from the highest court, in *Snell v Farrell* (1990),

[132] (N 123 above) 180. It was not necessary to rely on increase of risk, however, if the causal process was indeed cumulative which may be doubted given the experts' opinions.

[133] *Ibid*, pp 185–86. See also: *Dixon Estate v Holland* [1997] 1 WWR 130 (BCSC) 136 interpreting *Levitt v Carr* as involving a two-set approach: i) it is open to the trial judge to infer material increase of risk from the evidence; ii) he can thereafter also conclude that this material increase of risk was a contributing cause in the plaintiff's damage.

[134] See also: *Fawaz v Abdel-Shahid* (2002) CarswellOnt 2509 (OntSCtJ, 18 July 2002) para 3; *Ibrahim v Hum* (2004) 33 Alta LR (4th) 323; (2005) 6 WWR 564 (AltaQB) paras 141 and 145: Based on a decrease of chances of recovery of less than 50%. Against: *Allen v University Hospitals Board* (n 124 above) para 19; *Van Dyke v Grey Bruce Regional Health Centre* (2005) OJ no 2219, ONC Lexis 2415 (OntCA, 3 June 2005) para 40; and *O'Grady v Stokes* (n 2 above) para 123 (both on the basis of the civil law case of *St-Jean v Mercier* which was grounded on considerations very specific to this jurisdiction). For other more general references to *Snell* in Canadian caselaw: *Allen v University Hospitals Board* (n 124 above) paras 18–19; *Dobie v Dlin* (2002) BCJ No 507, BCSC 356 (8 March 2002) para 192 (*obiter*); *Lurtz v Duchesne* (n 2 above) para 345; *Williamson v Kozak* (2003) AJ no 1467, ABQB 953 (AltaQB, 21 November 2003) para 59; *Grass (Litigation Guardian of) v Women's College Hospital* (2003) OJ no 5313 (OntSCtJ, 31 December 2003) para 94; *Smith (Guardian ad litem of) v Grace* (2004) BCJ No 583, BCSC 395 (BCSC, 23 March 2004) para 8.

and is already 15 years old, it appears likely that the Canadian courts will remain faithful to this interpretation.[135]

Two tendencies emerge in the post-*Snell* period in Canada. A first, exemplified by the cases commented above, shows a willingness to rely on inferential reasoning to resolve causation difficulties, sometimes resting heavily on the concept of increase of risk. Another movement tends rather to reserve *Snell*'s generous pro-plaintiff attitude towards cases of 'true' uncertainty which excludes cases where the evidence is controversial[136] or where the parties have adduced 'direct', 'credible', 'clear', 'specific' or 'ample' expert evidence on the issue of causation[137]; these are rather resolved on the weighing of the value of the experts' opinions.[138]

The common law increase of risk reasoning, even if it has not been constant, appears to have had an influence, even if unacknowledged, on Québec law.

[135] Unless the Supreme Court of Canada itself has the occasion to state whether Sopinka J's adoption of the inference interpretation in *Snell v Farrell* has been misapprehended. It should be noted that Canadian courts have not, in the past, hesitated to depart from English developments, however. Eg, the *Anns*' test of duty of care (*Anns v Merton London Borough Council* [1978] AC 728 (HL)) continued to apply in Canada even after it was rejected by the House of Lords in *Murphy v Brentwood District Council* [1991] 1 AC 398 (HL); *Kamloops v Nielsen* (1984) 10 DLR (4th) 641; [1984] 2 SCR 2; *Canadian National Railway Co v Norsk Pacific Steamship Co* (1992) 91 DLR (4th) 289; [1992] 1 SCR 1021; *Cooper v Hobart* [2001] 3 SCR 537; 206 DLR (4th) 193.

[136] Eg, in Canada: *Smith v Grace* (n 135 above). See also: *McLeod v Ridyard* (2001) CarswellBC 18; BCSC 158 (26 January 2001) para 73 and, doubtfully, in *Cottrelle v Gerrard* (2003) OJ No 4194; (2004) CarswellOnt 1623 (CA, 22 April 2004) 32–33. In Québec: *Chouinard v Robbins* (QuéCA, 10 December 2001) para 83 (Rochette J, dissenting). The distinctions are not always made, however, and there are cases where causation is said to be inferred when it is actually based on accepted positive scientific evidence, eg, *Lurtz v Duchesne* (n 2 above) para 372.

[137] *Lawrence v Smith* (n 19 above) 39; *Bigcharles v Dawson Creek* (n 19 above) para 71 (*Bigcharles* can also be interpreted as accepting to draw an inference while finding it rebutted by the evidence presented by the defendant's experts: paras 69–71); *Jourdain v Hogg* (n 2 above) para 59; *Grealy v Kuntz* (trial judge) (n 19 above), treated as evidence rebutting an inference by the Court of Appeal: (N 19 above) para 49; *Dobie v Dlin* (n 134 above) para 208 (*obiter*); *M(CP) (Guardian ad litem of) v Quinn* (2004) BCD Civ J Lexis 1506; (2005) BCD Civ J 256 (BCSC, 29 November 2004) para 141; *Roberts v Petersiel* (n 19 above) para 18; *Bystedt (Guardian ad litem) v Hay* (2004) BCJ No 401; BCCA 124 (BCCA, 4 March 2004) para 122 (trial judgment, cited at para 57 of the majority CA's judgment). See also: *Moore v Castlegar & District Hospital* (1998) ACWSJ Lexis 81040; 1998 ACWSJ 518529; 77 ACWS (3rd) 677 (BCCA) paras 11–12, referring to (1996) 25 BCLR (3rd) 188 (BCSC) para 22; *Cottrelle v Gerrard* (n 137 above) 32–33; *Smith v Grace* (n 135 above); *O'Grady v Stokes* (n 2 above) para 203; *Miller v Budzinski* (n 2 above) para 474 and 476.

[138] *Bigcharles v Dawson Creek & Dist Health Care* (n 19 above) 71; *Bystedt v Hay* (n 137 above) para 122 (trial judgment, cited at para 57 of the majority CA's judgment); *Allen v University Hospitals Board* (n 124 above) paras 29–31 (commenting on the first instance judgment); *Grass v Women's College Hospital* (n 134 above) para 149; *Meyers (Next Friend of) v Stanley* (2003) AJ No 685, ABQB 468 (AltaQB, 27 May 2003) paras 82–84 (nevertheless referring unnecessarily to material increase of risk); *Trajdos (Litigation Guardian of) v Bala* (2003) OJ no 4953 (OntSCtJ, 11 December 2003) paras 216–17; *Wilson v Byrne* (2004) WL 1201437; Carswell Ont 2314, OJ No 2360 (OntSCtJ, 4 June 2004) paras 90–91. On the applicability of *Snell: Dobie v Dlin* (*obiter*) (n 134 above); *Michener v Doris* (2003) BCJ No 2301; BCSC 1541 (BCSC, 8 October 2003) para 185, relying on *Moore v Castlegar & District Hospital*. In some cases, however, inferences have been drawn without any justifications, and although the court had evidence in front of it to address the issue, eg, in *Lurtz v Duchesne* (n 2 above) paras 360–61 and 372. See also: *Epp v Balaton* (n 103 above); *Zaiffdeen v Chau* (2004) AJ No 513; ABQB 331 (AltaQB, 30 April 2004) para 48 (erroneously assimilates but-for and material contribution tests).

2. *Québec*

(a) Increase of Risk

Perhaps as a result of the common law influence, the concept of risk has also been relied on by the Québec courts to justify a generous evaluation of causation. Thus the creation by the defendant of a risk, or the increase of a risk to which the plaintiff has already been exposed, has had an impact on the way Québec courts approach causation. Reference to risk in relation to causation remains relatively rare in Québec cases, however. It nevertheless has played a central role in some decisions involving scientific causal uncertainties. The most important is *Gburek v Cohen* (1988), the facts of which have already been stated.[139] In the Court of Appeal, the majority judges, Chouinard and Mailhot JJ, found the defendant at fault because of the insufficiency of the kidney and audiogram tests carried out during the treatment of the defendant's meningitis with a toxic antibiotic. The causal link between these omissions and the plaintiff's deafness was uncertain, since the tests could only allow for detection of a situation which the defendant could then only attempt to remedy. It was in fact disputed whether the tests, if carried out, would have shown anything abnormal.

The majority of the Court of Appeal nevertheless found serious, precise, and concordant presumptions of causation between the defendant's fault and the plaintiff's deafness. The factual elements on which they were based show that the concepts of danger and risk were not far from their thoughts. These were the fact that the hearing loss was consequent on the treatment; that the prolonged use of gentamycine was, to the knowledge of the defendant and the medical community, dangerous; that this danger, as well as the risk of deafness, increased with the duration of the treatment; that the negligently omitted renal tests *and* audiograms *could* have revealed the warning signs of the plaintiff's hearing problem; and that they would have allowed for a reassessment of the treatment and a decrease in the dose, suspension of medication, or replacement of gentamycine with another medicine.[140] Thus the majority judges' factual presumption was based in great part on the plaintiff's subjection to a danger the defendant knew of, or the fact that he knowingly increased the risk of hearing loss to which the plaintiff was already subjected.[141]

[139] See: ch 1 above, text to fn 246.

[140] (N 6 above) 2436 and 2440. This conclusion was reached without discussing the defendant's argument that normal blood concentrations of the antibiotic could have caused the deafness. The majority believed that if the defendant had taken the recommended precautions, he would have been able, in different ways, to avoid the plaintiff's damage, a fact not demonstrated in evidence, however. Compare: *Bolitho v City and Hackney HA* (n 1 above).

[141] Beauregard J, in his minority decision, relies more openly on the concept of risk. He does so in order to reverse the burden of proof, however: ch 3, text between fns 58 and 64. Compare with *Kay v Ayrshire* (n 19 above) 420 (Lord Keith); 421 (Lord Griffiths); 425 (Lord Mackay).

In *Dodds v Schierz* (1986), the Québec Court of Appeal also relied on increase of the risk, albeit implicitly. The patient was the victim of a cerebral haemorrhage (stroke) which left her partially paralysed. The year before, the defendant had prescribed birth control pills for her in the knowledge of her medical history of phlebitis. The plaintiff contended that, in the circumstances, the defendant's prescription had been negligent, since phlebitis constitutes a contraindication to the use of birth control pills. She also claimed that the contraceptives had been the most probable cause of her damage, to which the defendant replied that it could be explained by other causes. While stressing that there was a *relationship* between birth control pills and stroke, the experts could not say that there was a *causal relationship* between the two. Nevertheless, the trial judge and the Court of Appeal found the defendant at fault and that his fault had, on the balance of probabilities, caused the plaintiff's damage.[142] This conclusion was based on the fact that phlebitis constitutes a clear contraindication for prescribing birth control pills as it *could* lead to strokes. The Court also relied on the fact that in a great number of cases birth control pills had in fact caused cerebral injury to women suffering from phlebitis.

This case is interesting for deeming causation proven, even though the experts had not given a favourable opinion on causation. Moreover, the decision was based on an abstract scientific possibility of causation, without an analysis of the probability of causation in the specific case at hand. While the trial judge discussed and discarded any other possible causes of the stroke, such as vasculitis and arteriosclerosis, the Court of Appeal does not mention the possible alternative causes of the stroke and insists solely on the statistical probability of causation.

Finally, in *Chouinard v Robbins* (2001), the Court of Appeal of Québec found causation in an alternative causes case on the basis that defendant's fault had increased the seriousness of hyponatremia, from which the patient already suffered and which could, in itself, cause permanent damage to the brain.[143] More specifically, the delay in treating the patient's condition, by increasing the seriousness of the hyponatremia increased *the risk of brain damage*. This was sufficient to demonstrate causation, although the expert evidence had suggested that brain injury could have been caused by hyponatremia even in the absence of delay.[144]

Some Québec judges have rejected, expressly or implicitly, risk as a sufficient basis for presuming causation, however. The Court of Appeal of Québec arguably did so in *St-Jean v Mercier* (1999). The plaintiff was claiming compensation for the paraparesis affecting his legs. He had argued it had been caused by the defendant orthopaedist's delayed treatment of a fracture of his dorsal spine following an accident in which he was hit by a car while hitchhiking on

[142] *Dodds v Schierz* [1986] RJQ 2623 (CA) 2628 and 2636. See also: *Villemaire-Grenier v Lachapelle* [1989] RRA 38 (CQ) 43–44; *Kulczycky v Rafferty* (CA) (n 7 above) *a contrario.*

[143] (N 136 above) paras 12, 17 (Robert J).

[144] As admitted by Robert J, *ibid*, para 18. Against: Rochette J, dissenting, paras 77 and 83.

the side of a highway. In response to one of the plaintiff's arguments, the Court interpreted *Snell* and *Laferrière* as having limited the importation of *McGhee* into Canadian law. It stressed that it is not sufficient, in proving causation, to show that the defendant created a risk and the damage occurred within the scope of that risk.[145] A close reading of this opinion reveals that the Court of Appeal meant to restrict its rejection to the reliance on risk as a justification for reversing the burden of proof of causation, not for presuming it.[146] The Supreme Court of Canada (2002), when confirming the Court of Appeal's position on this issue, expressed a more general objection to reliance on this concept, however. It added that to the extent that increase of risk is a separate means of proof with a less stringent standard to satisfy, *Snell v Farrell* and *Laferrière v Lawson* should have put an end to 'such attempts at circumventing the traditional rules of proof on the balance of probabilities.'[147]

(b) Creation of a Danger

The creation by the defendant of a situation that is objectively dangerous has been the main concept on which the Québec courts dealing with medical malpractice claims have relied to presume causation despite the scarcity of the evidence.[148] This remains infrequent, however. Moreover this justification is usually referred to in *obiter dicta* or deduced *a contrario*. Finally, its application as a strict rule was recently rejected by the Supreme Court of Canada. Examination of this concept is nonetheless worthwhile, as it opens the door to interesting parallels between the Québec, common law and French approaches.

The principle is that, when the defendant's fault presents a clear danger to the plaintiff's health and security and this danger subsequently materialises, causation can be presumed. Cases identify its origin in the following obiter dictum of Gonthier J in *Laferrière v Lawson* (1991):

> The plaintiff is aided in establishing his or her case by presumptions (as provided by art 1205 *CCLC*) and by such factual and statistical evidence as will aid the judge in appreciating what Moisan J described properly as ... 'reasonable and prudent behaviour', 'the natural order of things', 'the sequence of cause and effect' and, generally, 'the normal and ordinary course of events'. The judge will want to pay especially close attention to the various causal properties of the doctor's fault as well as the particular character of the damage which has manifested itself. In some cases, where a fault presents clear danger for the health and security of the patient and where such danger materializes, it *may* be reasonable for a judge to presume the causal link between the fault and such damage, 'unless there is a demonstration or a strong indication to the contrary' (*Morin v Blais* . . .). If, after all has been considered, the judge is not satisfied that the fault has, on his or her

[145] (N 7 above) 1666. Approved by the Supreme Court of Canada: (n 7 above) para 116.
[146] Because of its implicit referral to *Cook v Lewis* [1951] 1 DLR 1; [1951] SCR 830.
[147] (N 7 above) para 116.
[148] Baudouin and Deslauriers (n 4 above) para 591 and cases cited at fns 52–55.

assessment of the balance of probabilities, caused any actual damage to the patient, recovery should be denied. To do otherwise would be to subject doctors to an exceptional regime of civil responsibility (emphasis added).[149]

The concept was relied on, in obiter, in *Stéfanik v Hôpital Hôtel-Dieu de Lévis* (1997). The plaintiffs, expecting twins, were under the regular care of the first defendant doctor. When the mother noticed that the babies were moving less than usual, she went to the first defendant's clinic where she was seen by the second defendant. This doctor reassured her by saying that on examination, he had heard two heartbeats. The next day, after discharging green mucus, the mother went to the hospital in a state of emergency. There, the death of one baby was acknowledged. Delivery was induced and the second baby was born with a significant neurological deficit. He died 7 years later. Both doctors were found at fault for not carrying out the tests which could have allowed for detection of the problem. In addition, the second defendant was found negligent for not transferring the mother to a hospital for further tests after being informed of the diminution of foetal movement. With regard to causation, the plaintiffs contended that since fault was shown, the burden of disproving causation should be shifted to the defendants' shoulders. They nevertheless also pleaded that the most probable cause of the babies' problems was growth retardation associated with the 'transfuser syndrome', which would have been detected had proper tests been carried out. The defendants contested the reversal of the burden of proof contention and argued that the most probable cause of the accident was either a detached placenta, which could not have been detected by any test or some other, unknown cause.

The Court, after noting that the Supreme Court of Canada does not require causation to be proven with certainty, found it was demonstrated on the balance of probabilities, since tests would have probably revealed the problem and prompted an earlier delivery. Morin J added that the Court did not have to adopt the plaintiffs' hypothesis to reach this conclusion, since the rule expressed by Gonthier J in *Laferrière v Lawson* could apply. Indeed, the defendants' faults involved the 'obvious risk' of not diagnosing the problem in the twins' development, which could lead to the adverse consequence that happened in this case. In such circumstances, Morin J thought it reasonable to presume causation even without being convinced that the plaintiffs' hypothesis was the most probable.[150]

In *Prat v Poulin* (1997), the creation of a danger justification was also applied, this time in the ratio decidendi of the judgment. The defendant doctor had not

[149] (N 4 above) 608 (*obiter*) (reference omitted). *Morin v Blais* does not support the rule expressed in this paragraph but only the words 'unless there is a demonstration or strong indication to the contrary'. Against: RP Kouri, 'From Presumptions of Fact to Presumptions of Causation: Reflections on the Perils of Judge-made Rules in Quebec Medical Malpractice Law' (2001) 32 *Revue de droit de l'Université de Sherbrooke* 213, 233.

[150] *Stéfanik v Hôpital Hôtel-Dieu de Lévis* [1997] RJQ 1332 (CS) 1354.

advised his patient to stop taking birth control pills before undergoing two surgical interventions. The day after the second one, she suffered a thrombosis of the cerebral artery, a risk suspected at the time of the operation. In the years preceding, the health ministry had recommended that women stop taking oral contraceptives before undergoing major surgery. These recommendations were based on the risk of thrombosis of the veins, but they also advised assuming a relationship between oral contraceptives and arterial thrombosis. The Superior Court and the Court of Appeal found the defendant negligent for not complying with the recommendation. The fact that the thrombosis *could* have been caused by the combined effect of oral contraceptives and surgery, as well as the fact that the defendant was at fault, were sufficient for Beauregard J to apply the rule. He was of the opinion that the doctor's fault had created a danger for his patient and that consequently he bore the burden of 'disproving' causation on the basis of *Laferrière v Lawson*.[151] It is noteworthy that the risk of thrombosis of the cerebral artery, while clearly acknowledged, was not quantified by either court. Moreover, the defendant's argument that a thrombosis of the cerebral artery can happen spontaneously, without any surgical intervention and even to a woman who has never taken oral contraceptives was not considered sufficient to rebut the presumption.[152]

The Supreme Court of Canada has recently put a halt to the expansion of the creation of a danger rule ... by contesting that it is a *rule*. In *St-Jean v Mercier* (2002), Gonthier J stressed that his reference to this notion in *Laferrière v Lawson* had been misapprehended. He insisted that it was merely a reiteration of the traditional approach to factual presumptions, and did not create another means of proof in Québec civil law in the establishment of the causal link.[153] After *St-Jean,* concepts of risks and danger are rarely to be found in the Québec case law as justifications for a more lenient approach to causation.[154] Interestingly, *St-Jean* had a similar impact on Canadian common law. In *Allen (Next Friend of) v University Hospitals Board* (2002),[155] the Alberta Court of Appeal relied on this case, as well as on *Snell v Farrell,* to state that it is insufficient for the plaintiff to show that the defendant created a risk of harm and that the harm subsequently occurred within the ambit of the risk created. Such stand appears surprising not only because

[151] *Prat v Poulin* [1997] RJQ 2669 (CA) 2693.

[152] See also: *Bureau v Dupuis* [1997] RRA 459 (CS) (*a contrario*); *Mainville v Cité de la Santé* [1998] RJQ 2083 (CS) 2099 (*obiter*); *St-Jean v Mercier* (n 7 above) 1666 (CA) (contradicted on this point by the Supreme Court of Canada: (n 7 above) para 116). See also: *Gburek v Cohen* (n 6 above) 2440 (Chouinard J), predating *Laferrière v Lawson* but referring inter alia to the creation of a danger to presume causation.

[153] (N 7 above) para 116.

[154] Eg, of cases referring to risk or danger in the assessment of causation: *Lauzon v Ranger* (QuéSC, 25 November 2002) para 82 (risk); *Lacombe v Hôpital Maisonneuve-Rosemont* (2004): paras 32 and 40 (danger).

[155] (N 124 above) para 19. See also: *O'Grady v Stokes* (n 2 above) para 123.

St-Jean is a civil law case based on considerations very specific to this jurisdiciton,[156] but also because *Snell* was interpreted as advocating the reverse proposition as far as *inferences* based on increase of risk are concerned.[157]

The notions of danger and risk have also come into play to address uncertain causation in France, through the concept of *création fautive d'un risque* (faulty creation of a risk) and *création d'un état dangereux* (creation of a dangerous state of affairs). Moreover, the concept of increase of risk has also played a role in French medical law cases.

3. *France*

(a) *Création Fautive d'un Risque*

The notion of risk has played a role in cases where the doctor is the creator of a risk which has been fulfilled. In these cases the sole fact that the doctor has negligently exposed his patient to an abnormal risk which has materialised, and thereby made his patient lose a chance of avoiding the damage, is sufficient to justify *full* compensation of that damage even if causation between the doctor's fault and the damage is not proven with certainty.[158] The Cour de cassation's decision on 27 May 1998,[159] relied on this idea. The plaintiff became pregnant with her fifth child after the defendant physician provoked ovulation at her request. The defendant subsequently agreed to artificially induce the birth so that the child would be born on his patient's wedding anniversary. A haemorrhage ensued and led to the patient's death. The highest Court agreed with the Court of Appeal that the defendant breached his obligation not to subject his patient to an unjustified risk and to refuse demands which exposed her, without therapeutic justification, to the major risk associated with an induced birth despite her background and non-favourable delivery conditions. Moreover, it found the defendant negligent in his post-operative care of the haemorrhage and this negligence in direct and certain relation to the damage. It is uncertain whether the Court relied on the first or last fault to find liability and whether the Court's reliance on the creation by the defendant of an unjustified risk was intended to qualify the fault rather than establish causation. Even so, the identification of the fault as the creation or increase of a serious and unjustified risk facilitated the proof of causation by allowing the Court to focus on the fact that the damage is the fulfilment of the risk

[156] The power of civil law courts to 'create' presumptions that are more akin to legal, rather then factual, presumptions.

[157] See above, text between nn 116 and 127.

[158] Viney and Jourdain (n 9 above) paras 369 and 373. They emphasise that this reasoning is mostly relied on in cases of breach of the obligation to inform to justify either full compensation or compensation for the lost chance of taking a decision which could have averted the damage. See also: C Müller, *La perte d'une chance* (Berne, Staempfli, 2002) paras 123–25.

[159] See also: Cass civ 1st, 20 February 1979, JCP 1979.G.IV.145, Bull civ 1979.I.n68, D 1979.IR.250.

created. Thus it avoided the difficult question of determining whether an appropriate reaction to the haemorrhage would have prevented the death.

Another interesting example in the area of products liability flows from the Court of Appeal of Versailles' assessment, on 2 May 2001, of the relationship of cause and effect between an anti-hepatitis B vaccine and the appearance of multiple sclerosis.[160] Multiple sclerosis was diagnosed 3 months after the plaintiff received two injections of the vaccine and the victim consequently claimed against the vaccine's manufacturer. Despite the fact that the relationship between anti-hepatitis B vaccine and the development of multiple sclerosis was still scientifically hypothetical, the Court found it had been legally proven. The Court relied on the fact that the expert report did not exclude the possibility of a link between the two; that a press release of the *Agence de sécurité sanitaire* had concluded there was a risk of developing this disease, especially in the presence of a special susceptibility to it; and that this risk was mentioned in the vaccine package and in a medical dictionary. Moreover, around a hundred persons vaccinated at approximately the same time had presented with the symptoms of the disease. Finally, the decision of the *Direction générale de la santé* to compensate some of the victims demonstrated, in the opinion of the Court, that the causal link was at least *possible*. In this specific case, it found causation proven because of the time concomitance between the vaccine and the appearance of the symptoms and the absence of other possible causes. Even though causation could not be objectively demonstrated from a scientific point of view, it was considered proven in the specific case at hand on the basis of serious, precise, and concordant presumptions.[161] This decision was however quashed by the Cour de cassation on September 2003 on the basis of the scientific uncertainty surrounding general (abstract) causation between multiple sclerosis and the hepatitis B vaccine.[162]

(b) *Création d'un État Dangereux*

In some French cases involving causal uncertainty, a tendency has arisen to presume causation when the defendant has created an objectively dangerous state of affairs followed by a damage which is the normal and foreseeable fulfilment of the risk created by the fault.[163] French courts tend, in these cases, to deal with the uncertainties affecting causation by relying on the probability or the objective foreseeability of the damage. It is not clear whether these cases consider the creation of the danger in itself to be negligent but it appears reasonable to believe

[160] D 2001.IR.1592.

[161] See also: Cass civ 1st, 18 December 1979, JCP 1980.G.IV.93 (*a contrario*).

[162] Cass civ 1st, 23 September 2003: JCP 2003.G.II.10179 (note Jonquet, Maillols, Mainguy and Terrier) (Also reported at: D 2004.898, 899 ((note Serinet and Mislawski), Pet Aff 2004.n12.p14 (note Gossement), Pet Aff 2004.n81.p9 (note Mémeteau), JCP 2003.Entreprise et Affaires.II.1749 (note Faict et Mistretta), D 2004.1344 (note Mazeaud)).

[163] Viney and Jourdain (n 9 above) para 369.

that an independent fault must be proven. A review of the French case law shows that creation of a danger justification does not occupy a significant place in the French field of medical negligence, however.[164]

(c) Increase of Risk

Finally, French courts sometimes rely on the idea of increase of risk to presume causation in cases involving alternative causation. For example, on 23 May 1973, the Cour de cassation found causation proven on the ground, *inter alia*, that the defendant had increased the risk of damage to which his patient was already exposed.[165] The defendant radiologist had injected a contrast agent called methiodal into his patient. Following the injection, the patient's pelvis became paralysed and she suffered from paresis of her lower limbs. The patient's doctor was not found at fault for prescribing the injection, since the use of this specific product was necessary, other tests being untrustworthy. Moreover, the probability of accidents caused by the product was low and not foreseeable in the plaintiff's case. Yet the radiologist had injected a dose of 17cc rather than the recommended 10cc. The defendant argued that causation between the injection and the damage had not been demonstrated, since the expert attributed the damage to the patient's unforeseeable intolerance for the contrast agent. The Cour de cassation dismissed the argument on the ground that the expert's report also stated the overdose was unusual and '*pas heureuse*' and had increased the chances of neurological damage.[166] This was sufficient to show causation.

In addition, the language of fault appears sometimes to be used to cover up the fact that causation is presumed. On 5 March 1974, the Cour de cassation agreed with the Toulouse Court of Appeal that the defendant was at fault for increasing the risks normally involved in the delivery of his patient's baby without good cause. He had done so by using 'acrobatic forceps' which caused a crack in the plaintiff's bladder. The evidence had shown that this technique was abandoned by

[164] Save perhaps in Cass civ 1st, 5 March 1974, D 1974.IR.127. Cases which rely on the concept involve mainly road accidents pre-dating the adoption of the Loi du 5 juillet 1985; accidents provoked by a person to whom a thing was entrusted or left in dangerous conditions; damage caused by a person the care of whom was entrusted to another; and cars stolen because of the lack of care of their owners. Viney and Jourdain (n 9 above) para 369 and cases cited at fns 151–61, in particular: Cass civ 2nd, 9 February 1972, D 1972.Somm.158; Cass civ 1st, 3 October 1974 (n 8 above); Cass civ 2nd, 12 June 1975, JCP 1976.G.II.18444; Cass civ 2nd, 11 March 1976, JCP 1976.G.IV.157; Cass civ 3rd, 2 December 1980, JCP 1981.G.IV.69; Cass civ 3rd, 4 March 1980, JCP 1980.G.IV.196; Cass civ 1st, 4 February 1992, Resp civ et ass 1992.comm.194. See also: P Jourdain *Droit à la réparation: Lien de causalité,* Jurisclasseurs, Fasc 160 (Paris, Éditions techniques, 1993) 17–18 and cases cited. Against: Cass civ 1st, 23 May 1973, Gaz Pal 1973.2.885 (note Doll), JCP 1975.G.II.17955 (note Savatier), Bull civ 1973.1.n181, JCP 1974.G.II.17643 (note Savatier).

[165] Cass civ 1st, 23 May 1973 (2nd case) (n 164 above). See also: Cass civ 1st, 5 February 1991, D 1991. somm.358 (note anon).

[166] Risk was also part of the assessment of fault in this case. See also: Cass civ 1st, 20 February 1979 (n 159 above), similarly involving the injection of *méthiodal.*

science because of its danger and lack of conformity with the known scientific knowledge. Despite the wording of the decision, reliance on increase of risk was not necessary to qualify the fault, which was otherwise demonstrated. By relying on this notion, however, the Court could easily reach a positive conclusion with regard to causation without any discussion as to whether or not the damage had not rather flowed from the normal risk undertaken by the plaintiff.[167] Thus, despite the fact that increase of risk is mentioned in relation to fault, it appears here to have been relied on to presume causation.

Cases addressing the claims of the HCV and HIV victims of the contaminated blood scandal in France are also instructive on this subject, as one observes great reliance on the idea of comparative risks and increase of risk. The need to refer to these concepts flows from the fact that courts are always confronted with a pre-existing risk of contamination, which they must compare to the risk negligently introduced by the blood transfusion or the injection of blood products.[168] The decision of the Dijon Court of Appeal on 16 May 1991,[169] is particularly instructive, even though it is not concerned with medical liability. The plaintiff, a haemophiliac, was seriously injured in a car accident in 1984, following which he received several transfusions. He claimed compensation from the driver of the car in which he was a passenger after discovering that he was infected with HIV. The problem was to determine whether his infection was the consequence of the accident or had been contracted previously through no fault of the defendant (alternative causal process). During his hospitalisation, the plaintiff received a minimum of 168,000 units of Factor VIII as well as 20 units of blood. In comparison, in treatment for his haemophilia, he had received 8190 units of Factor VIII since the discovery of the HIV epidemic in France. Moreover, the experts determined that before the accident he ran less than a 20 per cent risk of being contaminated because he was using products prepared locally. The probability of contamination associated with the accident varied between 93 per cent and 95.35 per cent, since the blood and blood products came from the Paris region. The Court decided the plaintiff's contamination was the normal and foreseeable fulfilment of the risk associated with the massive transfusions he received after the accident because of the higher probability that they caused the damage.

This case is remarkable for its use of pure objective probabilities in choosing between alternative causes. On the basis of the respective risks they carried, the Court found the accident, not the pre-existing condition, was the cause of the infection, since the increase of risk provoked by the defendant's fault was substantial and the ultimate risk considerably higher than the pre-existing risk. This

[167] This case is probably more appropriately classified in the category of faulty creation of a risk, since the increased pre-existing risk was the general risk involved in every delivery of a baby.

[168] The contaminated blood cases are discussed below, at text between nn 202 and 274.

[169] D 1993.242 (note Kerckhove), aff'd by Cass civ 1st, 17 February 1993, Bull civ 1993.I.80, RTDC 1993.589 (note Jourdain).

reasoning is applied notwithstanding the fact that the contamination could equally have come from the blood products given to plaintiff after the accident or from those previously received, since only one injection of blood products is sufficient for the virus to be transmitted (alternative causes).[170] Other decisions have similarly decided causation on the basis of a comparation between the background risk and the risk of contamination introduced by the transfusion.[171]

The limited number of cases clearly referring to the concept of increase of risk makes it difficult to conclude to a general tendency to find causation based on the creation or increase of a risk in France. Nevertheless, the idea of risk as a ground for *full* compensation is noticeably present in France, a fact that is interesting to examine in conjunction with the prominence of loss of chance in French law.

A last justification on which the courts, especially in Canada, have relied on to justify inferring causation is the defendant's particular knowledge of the causal facts and his negligent undermining of the plaintiff's means of proving causation.

B. Negligent Undermining of the Plaintiff's Means of Proof

Some argue that as a policy matter, ease of proof is a consideration which may be relied on when deciding who should bear the legal burden of proof in civil proceedings[172] and may justify placing the burden of proof on the shoulders of the party who is best placed to discharge it.[173] This option has not, however, been generally adopted in English and Canadian medical malpractice.[174] It was in fact rejected in England in the 1978 Pearson Report[175] and by the Supreme Court of Canada the year before in *Joseph Brant Memorial Hospital v Koziol.*[176] One may ask, however, whether it could be a consideration sufficient to infer causation. As

170 See also: Cass civ 1st, 20 February 1979 (n 159 above); Paris, 17 September 1993, aff'd by Cass civ 1st, 9 July 1996, Bull civ 1996.I.n306, Resp civ et ass 1996.comm.385; Paris 1st B, 15 January 2004 (n 8 above): The high risk related to injection of plasma made from a large number of donors was a factor in the decision to presume causation, Bordeaux 5th, 17 February 2004 (n 8 above). Outside medical liability: Cass civ 1st, 9 February 1972 (n 165 above); Cass civ 1st, 4 January 1974, D 1974.IR.87.

171 CAA Paris 3rd A, 14 November 2002, Juris-Data No 206451; Paris 1st B, 10 June 2004, Juris-Data No 243118; Paris 1st B, 10 June 2004, Juris-Data No 249876.

172 R Emson, *Evidence*, 2nd edn, (London, MacMillan, 2004) 448.

173 Implicit in *Hurst v Evans* (1917) 1 KB 352 (Lush J) 356–57.

174 But it was relied on to reverse the burden of proof of causation in a manufacturer's liability case: *Hollis v Dow Corning Corp* (1995) 129 DLR (4th) 609; [1995] 4 SCR 634, 683–84, by analogy with *Cook v Lewis* (n 146 above). Sopinka J's decision in *Snell v Farrell* seems to open the door to such argument in medical liability: ch 3, text to fn 39.

175 Great Britain, *Report: Royal Commission on Civil Liability and Compensation for Personal Injury (The Pearson Report)* (London, Cmd 7054, Her Majesty's Stationery Office, 1978) para 1336 (with regard to burden of proving *negligence*).

176 *Joseph Brant Memorial Hospital v Koziol* (1977) 77 DLR (3rd) 161; [1978] 1 SCR 491, 500–1: the Supreme Court of Canada rejected an argument based on *Cook v Lewis* (n 146 above) (Rand J). See also: *Look v Himel* (OntHCJ, 25 June 1991); *Pike v Peace Arch District Hospital Society* (BCSC, 23 August 1985): The Court refused to find causation proven but denied costs to the hospital because of its nursing staff's failure to maintain proper records.

stated in the Canadian case of *Allen (Next Friend of) v University Hospitals Board* (2002), how much evidence of causation is needed before drawing an inference depends on 'who holds the knowledge or how much knowledge exists'.[177] The Canadian Supreme Court has responded positively to the above question in *Snell v Farrell* (1990).

This decision has been prominently referred to by Canadian cases in relation to the possibility of drawing inferences based on increase of risk.[178] Yet the Supreme Court of Canada's decision to infer causation in this case was itself based on another factor, namely the defendant's particular knowledge of the facts related to causation and the undermining, by his negligence, of the plaintiff's possibilities to prove causation:

> In many malpractice cases, the facts lie particularly within the knowledge of the defendant. In these circumstances, very little affirmative evidence on the part of the plaintiff will justify the drawing of an inference of causation. . . .
>
> The legal or ultimate burden remains with the plaintiff, but in the absence of evidence to the contrary adduced by the defendant, an inference of causation *may* be drawn although positive or scientific proof of causation has not been adduced. If some evidence to the contrary is adduced by the defendant, the trial judge is entitled to take account of Lord Mansfield's famous precept. This is, I believe, what Lord Bridge had in mind in *Wilsher* when he referred to a 'robust and pragmatic approach to the . . . facts' . . . (emphasis added)[179]

In *Blatch v Archer* (1774), Lord Mansfield indeed stated: 'It is certainly a maxim that all evidence is to be weighed according to the proof which it was in the power of one side to have produced, and in the power of the other to have contradicted.'[180]

On the basis of the above, the Supreme Court of Canada inferred causation in this case on the ground that the defendant was in a better position to observe what occurred during the medical intervention and interpret it from a medical point of view. Moreover, by negligently continuing the operation despite the presence of blood in the plaintiff's eye, he made it impossible for her or anyone else to detect the presence of haemorrhaging. Two considerations were thus central to the decision: the fact that the defendant had a privileged understanding of the situation; and the fact that the causal uncertainty had been created by the defendant's negligence.

[177] *Allen v University Hospitals Board* (n 124 above) para 19. See also: *Bear v Lambos* (n 2 above) para 46.

[178] Facts summarised ch 1, text to fn 244.

[179] (N 1 above) 328–30. The courts have discretion to draw or not the presumption.

[180] (1774) 1 Cowp 64, 983 ER 969, 970.

Very few Canadian common law cases have relied on this notion subsequently and their treatment of it is not always clear.[181] However, the undermining of the plaintiff's means of proving causation through the defendant's negligence was explicitly the basis of the inference of causation drawn in *Heidebrecht v Fraser-Burrard Hospital Society* (1996). The plaintiff suffered significant brain damage consequent on a bacterial meningitis. He had developed meningitis after a frontal craniotomy was performed by the defendant neurosurgeon for the removal of a large tumour which had caused the plaintiff's loss of vision. The British Columbia Supreme Court had found the defendant neurosurgeon negligent for not carrying out a lumbar puncture when the plaintiff manifested signs of meningitis, a rare but known consequence of frontal craniotomy. The assessment of causation involved difficulties because of controversy amongst the experts as to whether the puncture would have produced normal results had it been carried out when it should have. The uncertainty affecting causation was thus precisely caused by the negligent omission to carry out the test.[182] Consequently, Henderson J, on the basis of *Snell v Farrell*, adopted a 'robust and pragmatic approach' and inferred causation. This finding rested on the fact that causation does not need to be determined with scientific precision and that it is not essential that a medical expert support the plaintiff's theory of causation with a firm opinion to find the defendant liable.[183]

Even though it originated in a common law case, this approach not surprisingly made its way to the Québec courts as another justification for adopting a more lenient attitude towards causation. Reliance on this concept is mainly found, however, in minority opinions by Beauregard J of the Québec Court of Appeal. For instance, in *Houde v Côté* (1987), Beauregard J presumed causation between general anaesthesia and the plaintiff's partial paralysis, despite the experts' controversial opinions on this question. This presumption was based on the doctor's omission to adequately complete his patient's file, thereby preventing the claimant

[181] *Meringolo (Committee of) v Oshawa General Hospital* (1991) 46 OAC 260 (CA) 272 (*obiter*); *Scott (Crick) v Mohan* (1993) 142 AR 281 (AltaQB); *Pierre (Next Friend of) v Marshall* [1994] 8 WWR 478 (AltaQB) 506; *Stewart v Pettie* (1995) 121 DLR (4th) 222; [1995] 1 SCR 131, 154 (non-medical); *Dixon Estate v Holland* (n 133 above) 135–36; *Ostby v Bondar* (1998) 218 AR 132 (QB) 146; *Bigcharles v Dawson Creek* (n 19 above) paras 27–29 (Southin J, diss); *Rogers v Grypma* (AltaQB, 7 November 2001) para 311; *Wilson v Byrne* (n 138 above) para 83. See also: *Bigcharles v Dawson Creek* (n 19 above) paras 69–71: the Court implicitly accepts that an inference could be drawn on this basis, but rejected the claim on the ground that the defendants had adduced substantial expert evidence in support of their causation theory. Some cases emphasise that the lack of information about causation is due to the defendant's omission, but do not draw inferences on this basis: *Dobie v Dlin* (n 134 above) para 21; *Meyers v Stanley* (n 138 above) para 76; *Trajdos v Bala* (n 138 above) para 82; *Bystedt v Hay* (n 137 above) para 95 of the trial judge's judgment, cited at para 56 of the CA's majority judgment.

[182] *Heidebrecht v The Fraser-Burrard Hospital Society* (BCSC, 10 October 1996) para 105.

[183] *Ibid*, paras 108–9. Eg, the reverse situation encountered in *Bigcharles v Dawson Creek* (n 19 above) para 23 (Southin J, diss). In this case, the plaintiff had participated in the destruction of his own means of proof. His long period of unconsciousness after a car accident, caused by consumption of alcohol, had deprived the attending physicians of an important diagnosis tool.

from proving causation.[184] In his view, when the patient cannot prove causation because of the doctor's omission to make a complete report of his intervention, there is a presumption against the doctor that the damage is the result of his fault.[185] Beauregard J reiterated this opinion in *Gburek v Cohen* (1988),[186] where the defendant had negligently omitted to carry out tests. He accepted that the notion could ground a presumption of material increase of risk which itself could lead to the reversal of the onus of proof of causation.[187] Once again, he noted that if the evidence shows the defendant has prevented the plaintiff from proving the probable cause of his injury, the court can presume causation.[188]

The particular knowledge by the defendant of the causative facts or the negligent undermining of the plaintiff's means of proving causation have not been relied on in English law to justify drawing inferences of causation in medical malpractice.[189] The insufficiency of medical notes and records is sometimes emphasised but does not play a critical part in the assessment of causation. It is mentioned to stress the difficulties the parties and court have had to confront[190] or as an indication of unexplained carelessness.[191] There are, however, some isolated indications that the courts might be more willing to draw inferences when the defendant's actions prevent the plaintiff from proving causation;[192] or to assess causation more leniently. In *Webb v Barclays Bank* (2001),[193] weight was given to this concept to grant compensation, albeit for the plaintiff's lost chances.[194] The defendant doctor was found negligent for omitting to carry out necessary investigations before advising his patient to submit to an amputation after she had badly hurt her polio-affected knee. The amputation was subsequently carried out. It was impossible to determine, however, what advice the doctor would have given her if he had carried out the appropriate inquiries.[195] This uncertainty was caused by the fact that because of the defendant's omission,

[184] *Houde v Côté* [1987] RJQ 723 (CA) 729–30.

[185] *Ibid*, p 730 (*obiter*) (Chouinard J also stresses the incomplete records in the patient's medical file: 736–37). See also: Deschamps J in *Zanchettin v Demontigny* (n 7 above) 312.

[186] Facts exposed at ch 1, text to fn 246.

[187] *Gburek v Cohen* (n 6 above) 2447 also in a minority opinion.

[188] See also: *Dame Cimon v Carbotte* [1971] CS 622 626; *Massinon v Gys* [1996] RJQ 2258 (QuéCS) 2277 and 2280 (*obiter*). Against: Owen J in *Gouin-Perreault v Villeneuve* [1986] RRA 4 (QuéCA) 9–10.

[189] It is relied on in other areas, however: LD Smith, *The Law of Tracing* (Oxford, Clarendon Press, 1997) 77–78.

[190] *Paddison v Walsall Health Authority* [February 2000] Med Lit 3 (QB) 4.

[191] *Skelton v Lewisham and North Southwark HA* [1998] Lloyd's Rep Med 324 (QB). But see: *Rhodes v Spokes and Farbridge* [1996] 7 Med LR 135.

[192] *Ratcliffe v Plymouth and Torbay Heath Authority* (1998) 42 BMLR 64 (CA) 83 (*obiter*).

[193] (N 56 above).

[194] Against the recommendations of both counsel. The question was not reviewed on appeal, since both parties agreed that the judge was wrong in law not to have applied the balance of probabilities requirement.

[195] It was also difficult to determine what the plaintiff herself would have done had she been properly advised, a difficulty compounded by the fact that she had not testified at trial.

which led to the amputation, it was no longer possible to examine the litigious knee. The trial judge placed the blame for the evidential gaps partly on the doctor's shoulders:

> We have therefore, a situation where the very omissions which have been proved against the defendant are those which preclude the claimant from advancing the evidence necessary to establish causation. I cannot believe that the law could possibly countenance such a manifestly unjust situation by insisting on a balance of probabilities approach in circumstances such as these.[196]

In Australia, an approach favourable to the plaintiff was adopted by some courts in cases where the 'facts are particularly within the knowledge' of the defendant, but not in medical negligence cases and usually in relation to evidence of fault.[197] In the context of medical liability, the fact that the defendant's negligence has caused the unavailability of important causal evidence has been considered a justification for granting damages for loss of a chance, however.[198]

The idea of negligent undermining of the plaintiff's means of proving causation also is found in some French judgments. For example, the Paris Tribunal de grande instance referred to it on 1 July 1991,[199] when deciding whether or not to draw a factual presumption in favour of a patient who had contracted HIV following a blood transfusion. Her difficulties in proving causation between the transfusion and her condition were exacerbated by the fact that the medical staff had omitted to note down the identification numbers of the units used for the transfusion. After examination of the circumstances of the case and elimination of all other possible causes of contamination, the Court found it was 'highly probable' the transfusion had been the cause of the damage. It was willing to ignore the remaining causative uncertainty, since it was due to the defendant's omission. On appeal, the Court of Appeal of Paris reached the same conclusion,[200] also noting the clinic's negligence in omitting to identify the provenance of the blood units, thereby preventing the experts from reaching certainty as to the causal link.[201]

[196] Cited in CA's judgment: (N 56 above) 5.

[197] *Hampton Court Ltd v Crooks* (1957) 97 CLR 367 (AustHC) 371–72 (Dixon J); *Wallaby Grip (BAE) PTY Ltd (In Liq) v Macleay Area Health Service* (n 108 above) 14, referring to *Parker v Paton* (1941) 41 SR 237 (HC) 243; *Bendix Mintex v Barnes* (n 108 above) 317–78 (Mason P) and 339 (Beazley JA). In the Autralian law of evidence, this takes the name of the 'scintilla principle': P Bayne, *Uniform Evidence Law: Text and Essential Cases* (Leichhardt, NSW, Federation Press, 2003) para 4.370.

[198] *Gavalas v Singh* (2001) 3 VR 404 (VicCA) 417.

[199] JCP 1991.G.II.21762 (note Harichaux).

[200] Paris, 28 November 1991, D 1992.jur.85 (note Dorsner-Dolivet), JCP 1992.G.II.21797 (note Harichaux), Gaz Pal 1992.I.120 (note Paire) (quashed: Cass civ 1st, 12 April 1995, JCP 1995.G.II.22467 (note Jourdain)).

[201] Question not discussed on appeal: Cass civ 1st, 12 April 1995 (n 200 above). A similar reasoning justified the granting of damages for loss of the chance to prove causation or to be granted compensation: Aix-en-Provence 10th, 13 January 2005, Juris-Data No 270996.

There is only one area in which French courts have relied extensively on factual presumptions to find causation proven. Where the plaintiff is claiming compensation for HIV or HCV contamination allegedly caused by blood transfusions received in the early 1980s, presumptive reasoning is resorted to by the French judiciary in a very liberal fashion through the technique of proof by elimination.

C. Presumptions by Elimination (France)[202]

1. *Generalities*

French courts have extensively relied on what may for the purpose of this study be called *presumptions by elimination* (or negative presumptions).[203] Instead of inducing the proof of causation on the basis of the conjunction of all the elements of the case, causation is presumed from the absence of some specific elements of fact. This *negative* assessment may lead the court to decide that there is no other explanation for the damage beyond the defendant's fault.[204] This process of proof by elimination thus seeks to select as a cause the one that remains when all other probable causative factors have been ruled out.[205]

This reasoning by elimination has been of special assistance to the French courts in dealing with claims by the victims of the contaminated blood scandal. In many countries, the early 1990s witnessed scandals linked to the transfusion of contaminated blood during the preceding decade and France was no exception. The risk of transmission of HIV by blood had been known internationally since June 1981, and as early as October 1984, the efficiency of heating techniques for treating blood was recognised in the United States. Nevertheless, it was only on 1 August 1985, that the systematic screening of blood donors became compulsory in France. As a result of this delay, several individuals transfused between 1978 (when the HIV epidemic started in Europe) and 1985 became infected. The same delay allowed the spread of the hepatitis C virus (HCV). Transfusion of contaminated blood is undeniably a very efficient way to transmit the HIV virus, with

[202] Presumptions by eliminations have been argued in other jurisdictions, but not always with success, eg, *Platter v Sonatrach* (2004) CILL 2073 (QB) para 98, a case involving an HIV infection contracted after receiving an intravenous injection of vitamin C at the defendant's clinic. Rejecting the plaintiff's negative presumption arguments, the court concludes: '(T)his is not a case where the Sherlock Holmes dicta of eliminating the impossible and treating whatever remains as the truth, applies.'

[203] Originally, this technique has been used in cases involving damage allegedly caused by supersonic bangs: P Jourdain, 'Responsabilité civile et contamination par le virus du SIDA à la suite de transfusions' (1992) *Revue trimestrielle de droit civil* 117, 118, G Viney, 'Chronique Responsabilité civile' (1992) I *La semaine juridique* 501, 502.

[204] R Savatier, *et al*, *Traité de droit médical* (Paris, Librairies Techniques, 1956) 319.

[205] Also resorted to in common law, eg, *British Columbia Electric Railway Co v Clarke* [1950] 3 DLR 161 (SCC) 163–64 (Taschereau J) and 169 (Locke J).

nearly 100 per cent of tainted blood recipients being infected.[206] HIV can also be transmitted through the reception of whole blood, blood cellular components, plasma, and clotting factors used in the treatment of haemophilia.[207] Haemophiliacs who received concentrated clotting factors composed of blood components from potentially thousands of donors prior to 1984–85 run a substantial risk of HIV infection.[208]

This situation gave birth to a large body of criminal, administrative, and civil cases in the French courts.[209] Since 1991, the French legislature has taken the matter in hand, however, by creating a compensation fund for HIV victims.[210] Victims are nevertheless not precluded from making their civil claims instead.[211] Many victims indeed claimed compensation for the damage caused by the alleged negligence of the French State, the Centre National de Transfusion Sanguine, and

[206] Z Matsuda, JA Hellinger and M Essex, 'Human Immune Deficiency Virus and Other Retroviruses' in SL Gorbach, JG Bartlett and NR Blacklow, (eds), *Infectious Diseases*, 2nd edn, (Philadelphia, WB Saunders, 1998) 2096.

[207] C Del Rio and JW Cuuran 'Epidemiology and Prevention of Acquired Immunodeficiency Syndrome and Human Immunodeficiency Virus Infection' in GL Mandell, JE Bennett and R Dolin, (eds), *Principles and Practice of Infectious Diseases*, 6th edn, (New York, Churchill Livingstone, 2005) 1490.

[208] *Ibid.*

[209] Compare: *Walker Estate v York Finch General Hospital* (2001) 198 DLR (4th) 193; [2001] 1 SCR 647, in which the Supreme Court of Canada refused to presume causation on the basis of the failure to take adequate precautions to deter persons known to pose a risk from donating blood (Plaintiff W's claim) because the identified donor testified that he would have given blood even if the defendant's screening techniques had not been negligent. See also: LJ Neoh, 'A Comment on *Walker Estate v York-Finch General Hospital*' (2000) 23 *Advocates' Quarterly* 370 generally, and 382–85. The scarcity of the case law on this issue in Canada and Québec is explained by the fact that the federal government has set up a compensation fund for victims of post-transfusion HIV (upon proof of the causal link between the infection and a transfusion received between 1978–89). Moreover, in response to a class action suit, it has offered payments to hepatitis C victims infected between 1986 and 1990 who waive rights to sue the government or the Canadian Red Cross Society. Provincial assistance plans also exist in Ontario, Québec, and Manitoba for HCV victims infected before 1986 or after 1990. See generally: JJM Shore and M Vardy, 'Obligation de l'État d'aider financièrement les personnes atteintes du VIH par suite d'une transfusion de sang ou de dérivé sanguin' (1990) 31 *Cahiers de droit* 871; BM Dickens, 'Justice, Compensation and Hepatitis C' (2000) 18 *Windsor Yearbook of Access of Justice* 226. See also: the Krever report, which recommends replacing the tort liability system with a no-fault system, a recommendation that was not followed: Commission of Inquiry on the Blood System in Canada, *Final Report*, vol 3 (Ottawa, Canadian Government, 1997) 1029–45, particularly 1044–45. On 30 May 2005, the Canadian Red Cross publicly recognised its responsibility for distributing harmful blood products to Canadians and, as compensation, offered scholarships and a grant for academic research on medical accidents: http://www.redcross.ca/main.asp?id=013578&tid=001 (23 August 2005).

[210] Loi no 91–1406 du 31 décembre 1991 portant diverses dispositions d'ordre social, JO 4 January 1992, 178. It introduces a legal presumption of causation which operates once the applicant demonstrates that he is infected with HIV and has received a transfusion or injections of blood products in the litigious period: §47IV. See generally: H Margeat, 'Sang et droit: L'indemnisation des victimes' [1993] *Gazette du Palais* 977, 979–82; ML Morançais-Demeester, 'Contamination par transfusion du virus du sida: responsabilités et indemnisation' [1992] *Dalloz* 189, 192–94; M Lebeau, 'Responsabilité et contamination post-transfusionnelles' [1999] *Gazette du Palais* 880, 835, 836–37.

[211] Trib gr inst Nice, 27 July 1992, D 1993.jur.38 (note Vidal); CE 5th and 7th sub-s, 27 Febuary 2002, Juris-Data No 063658.

regional transfusion centres.[212] In addition, the private medical clinics or public hospitals where the transfusions were received, as well as the doctors and medical staff in charge of them, were also sued.[213] Before the French civil courts, however, HIV and HCV victims claiming compensation must face a greater hurdle: to prove with certainty that the transfusion is responsible for their infection. When the blood donor can be traced, this does not present great difficulties.[214] Nonetheless, even then, causation may be hard to establish, since it must also be determined whether the identified donor was already contaminated at the time of the donation. Such verifications are vain if the donor is identified many years after the transfusion, as often happens in the HCV cases. In any event, in most instances, the donor's identity is impossible to establish. This is especially so when plasma or clotting factors are transfused, since their preparation necessitates a large number of donors.[215] In other cases, even though the donor should theoretically be identifiable, this is made impossible because the patient's file is incomplete and does not specify the origin of the blood received, for example through a lot number. Consequently, direct proof of causation is often impossible to attain.

Faced with the extent of the human drama prompted by the spread of HIV and HCV through the use of contaminated blood in the first half of the 1980s, French courts recognised the victims' need for assistance in their attempts to obtain compensation. They have done so both by facilitating the proof of the transfusion centres' and private clinics' faults, and by allowing the victims to present indirect proof of causation between their damage and the transfusions received. Rejecting the claim of an alleged victim of the contaminated blood scandal for lack of evidence obviously appeared unjust to the French courts. Instead, they accepted the proof of causation through the finding of serious, precise, and concordant factual presumptions.[216] Through the conjunction of high probabilities when certain factual conditions are met and the insistence on the absence of other alternative causes, the courts find sufficient

[212] Such centres are in charge of collecting blood, treating plasma, producing blood products, and providing medical care: H Margeat, 'Séropositivité, sida et jurisprudence' [1991] *Gazette du Palais* 580, 583. The *Centres de transfusion sanguine* (CST) have a monopoly on the storage and distribution or blood. They are under the State's tutelage: Morançais-Demeester (n 210 above) 189.

[213] Claims have also been made against those whose negligence necessitated the transfusion, eg, the faulty driver who caused the accident, which in turn led to the need for a transfusion: Trib gr inst Bobigny, 19 December 1990, Gaz Pal 1991.I.233 (note anon); Dijon 1st, 16 May 1991, D 1993.242 (note Kerckhove) (aff'd Cass Civ 1st, 17 February 1993 (n 169 above)); Paris 1st, 26 November 1991, D 1992.IR.70, Gaz Pal 1992.G.II.580, Paris, 7 July 1989, Gaz Pal 1989.2.752; or the surgeon whose medical fault necessitated the transfusion: Versailles 1st ch, 1st sect, 30 March 1989, JCP 1990.G.II.21505 (note Dorsner-Dolivet). These claims create specific causative difficulties which are not discussed here, however.

[214] Paris, 7 July 1989 (n 213 above); Trib gr inst Bobigny, 19 December 1990 (n 213 above); Trib gr inst Nice, 27 July 1992 (n 211 above).

[215] Trib gr inst Bordeaux, 17 February 1992, Gaz Pal 1992.II.somm.404.

[216] HIV victims claims, eg, Cass civ 1st, 17 February 1993 (n 169 above) 590–91; Cass civ 2nd, 20 July 1993, Bull civ 1993.II.n273, Resp civ et ass 1993.comm.378; Cass civ 1st, 14 November 1995, Bull civ 1995.I.n414, JCP 1996.I.3985, par13 (note Viney); Jourdain (1992) (n 203 above) 118–19. HCV victims claims, eg, Cass civ 1st, 9 July 1996 (n 170 above); Cass civ 1st, 23 November 1999, Bull civ 1999.I.n324, Resp civ et ass 2000.comm.48 (claim rejected, however).

justification to presume causation. More specifically, an elimination process is usually relied on and causation presumed when no other element can explain the infection.

This type of reasoning is easier to apply to the HIV cases than to claims by hepatitis C victims. In HIV cases, findings that result from the process of proof by elimination are certainly validated by the fact that the molecular biology of the human immunovirus is now better understood than is the case for many other viruses.[217] Moreover, its means of transmission are also well known.[218] Applying elimination reasoning is much more complex in HCV cases, however. Although blood is a clear vector of the virus,[219] many modes of transmission are currently not well determined[220] and uncertainty about the virus's aetiology makes it difficult to prove causation by elimination. A second difficulty concerns the slow manifestation of the sicknesses flowing from HCV infection. At first, hepatitis C is asymptomatic or minimally symptomatic.[221] The virus's presence is often detected only when a complication emerges decades after the transfusion, usually over 20 years later.[222] Moreover, even if an identified donor is shown not to have HCV in his blood, this is not conclusive, since it is possible, with time, for a person to be cured of hepatitis C with complete disappearance of the antibodies.[223]

[217] FR Cleghorn, *et al*, 'Human Immunodeficiency Viruses' in Mandell, *et al* (n 206 above) 2119.

[218] The main ones being transmission through blood or blood products, sharing of needles by intravenous drug users, sexual contact, and passage from mother to child: J Ambroziak and JA Levy, 'Epidemiology, Natural History and Pathogenesis of HIV Injection' in K Holmes King, *et al*, (eds), *Sexually Transmitted Diseases*, 3rd edn, (New York, McGraw-Hill, 1999) 251; Matsuda, *et al* (n 206 above) 2095–96; JJ Champoux and WL Drew, 'Retrovirus, Human Immunodeficiency Virus and Acquired Immunodeficiency Syndrome' in KJ Ryan, (ed), *Sherris Medical Microbiology: An Introduction to Infectious Diseases*, 4th edn, (Norwalk, Appleton & Lange, 2004) 609; MH Merson and P Piot, 'Global Perspectives on Human Immunodeficiency Virus Infection and Acquired Immunodeficiency Syndrome' in Mandell, *et al* (n 206 above) 1469; Del Rio, *et al* (n 207 above) 1488. The probability of transmission by other means is very low: PL Épée, 'Problèmes médico-légaux soulevés par le SIDA' [1991] 2 *Gazette du Palais* 575.

[219] WL Drew, 'Hepatitis Viruses' in KJ Ryan, (ed), *Sherris Medical Microbiology: An Introduction to Infectious Diseases*, 3rd edn, (Norwalk, Appleton & Lange, 1994) 551.

[220] In the 1995 edition of Mandell *et al*, Lemon and Brown report that in half of the cases, the modes of transmission and the aetiology are unknown: SM Lemon and EA Brown 'Hepatitis Virus' in GL Mandell, JE Bennett and R Dolin, (eds), *Principles and Practice of Infectious Diseases*, 4th edn, (New York, Churchill Livingstone, 1995) 1482. In the 2005 edition, Thomas, *et al* rather state that outside of blood, saliva, tears, seminal fluids, ascetic fluid and cerebrospinal fluid, very little information is available as to the potential infectivity of other body fluids: DL Thomas, SC Ray and SM Lemon, 'Hepatitis C' in Mandell, *et al* (n 206 above) 1964. One of the main, unambiguous sources is the sharing of syringes for preparing and injecting drugs: SM Lemon and MJ Alter, 'Viral Hepatitis' in Holmes, *et al* (n 208 above) 374, 377; RS Koff, 'Hepatitis C' in Gorbach, *et al* (n 206 above) 865. Opinions have long been divided about sexual transmission, but the balance of evidence now favours occasional sexual transmission: Holmes (n 208 above) 374 and 377; Koff (n 220 above) 865.

[221] Lemon and Alter (n 220 above) 375.

[222] *Ibid*, p 376; Thomas, *et al* (n 220 above) 1959; Koff (n 220 above) 866. If the delay of detection of the virus in the blood is short, this excludes causation as it takes between eight to twelve weeks to detect HCV in blood: Thomas, *et al* (n 220 above) 1957 and 1478–79; Lemon and Alter (n 220 above) 375. The same conclusion follows if there is less than two years between the transfusion and the appearance of cirrhosis: Y Lambert-Faivre, 'L'hépatite C post-transfusionnelle et la responsabilité civile' (1993) *Dalloz* 291, 292.

[223] Lambert-Faivre (n 222 above) 292.

2. *HIV Infected Plaintiffs*

The main defendants in the HIV cases have been the transfusion centres,[224] which are treated more severely by the imposition of a contractual obligation of result[225] in the provision of non-defective blood products.[226] Until April 2005, private clinics were held only to an obligation of means,[227] and were found at fault only if it was shown they had the possibility of controlling the quality of the blood transfused,[228] which was rarely the case. Finally, doctors are also bound to an obligation of means[229] and have no obligation to verify the quality of the blood transfused.[230] But whoever the defendant, and whether or not the defendant's obligation is one of means or result, the victims are not exempted from proving causation between their damage and the transfusion.[231] While the sources of HIV infection are well known, the existence of several possible discrete origins complicates the task of HIV victims attempting to prove causation. In order to assist the HIV victims faced with this difficulty, the French courts have in many cases been prepared to find causation proven on the basis of factual presumptions where a sufficiently *probable* causal link is shown.[232] In the absence of any other predisposition, the probability of contamination is often considered so high that compensation is granted almost automatically.[233] The high probability of infection is not always expressly relied on, however. Often, rather the courts stress the absence of other explanations

[224] Contractual claims against transfusion centres are based on the mechanism of *stipulation pour autrui*: Cass civ 1st, 12 April 1995 (n 200 above); Margeat (n 210 above) 983; Lebeau (n 210 above) 35; Jourdain (1992) (n 203 above) 120.

[225] B Gimbert, 'Responsabilité médicale et transfusion sanguine' (1998) 27 *Petites affiches* 10, 12.

[226] Trib gr inst Paris, 1 July 1991 (n 9 above). Confirmed in, eg, Paris, 28 November 1991 (n 200 above); Cass civ 1st, 12 April 1995 (n 200 above); Cass civ 1st, 14 November 1995 (n 216 above). See also: Morançais-Demeester (n 210 above) 191; JS Bergé, 'Risque et faute dans la contamination transfusionnelle' [1996] *Gazette du Palais* 737; Lebeau (n 210 above) 35; Margeat (n 212 above) 584; Viney (1992) (n 203 above) 502; Gimbert (n 225 above) 10.

[227] Margeat (n 212 above) 584. In the past, this question was controversial, as some courts held the private clinics to an obligation of result: Jourdain (1992) (n 203 above) 120 and Viney (1992) (n 203 above) 502, both relying on *L'affaire Fourgeron*: Paris, 28 November 1991 (n 200 above). The Cour de cassation recently reversed this stand and imposed an obligation of result on a private clinic: Cass Civ 2nd, 21 April 2005, Juris-Data N° 28163.

[228] Bergé (n 226 above) 737.

[229] Jourdain (1992) (n 203 above) 120; Gimbert (n 225 above) 10. Against: Trib gr inst Paris, 1 July 1991 (n 9 above).

[230] Paris, 28 November 1991 (n 200 above), Gaz Pal 16 February 1992 (note Paire), D 1992.85 (note Dorsner-Dolivet), JCP 1992.G.II.21797 (note Harichaux); Jourdain (1992) (n 203 above) 120. Doctors are in fact prohibited from doing so, as transfusion centres have a monopoly on the quality control of blood: Gimbert (n 225 above) 10.

[231] Some argue that obligations of result encompass a presumption of causation, however: Viney and Jourdain (n 9 above) para 367; P Jourdain, *Droit à la réparation: Lien de causalité*, Fasc 160 (Paris, Juris-classeurs éditions techniques, 1993) 15 and P le Tourneau and L Cadiet, *Droit de la responsabilité civile* (Paris, Dalloz, 1998) para 819.

[232] Dorsner-Dolivet, note under Paris, 28 November 1991 (n 200 above).

[233] Without any need of relying on loss of chance: Dorsner-Dolivet, note under Versailles ch 1 sec 1, 30 March 1989 (n 213 above).

for the plaintiff's damage,[234] which is considered sufficient to presume causation. Overall, judges assess causation in a very liberal way and their decisions are usually in the plaintiff's favour, even though it is not possible to exclude all other possibilities in every case.[235]

In general, when the transfusion was performed between 1978 and August 1985,[236] the presumption of causation is first based on the following basic positive clues:[237] the existence of several transfusions; the discovery of the HIV infection within the normal period for the appearance of the antibodies; the proof that at least one donor belonged to a risk group, or was HIV positive, at the moment of the blood donation.[238] Even when the donor cannot be identified, a negative inquiry is undertaken to eliminate other possible causes flowing mainly from risk factors in the life style of the person transfused. The courts verify whether the plaintiff is a member of a risk group;[239] whether he has travelled in countries where the concentration of HIV infections is particularly high;[240] and whether his sexual behaviour puts him at risk.[241] The serology of the members of the plaintiff's family is also scrutinised.[242] Finally, it is inquired whether there are other risk factors in the plaintiff's medical history, as for example other blood transfusions, haemophilia, or previous infections usually related to HIV.[243] The absence of these elements increases the probability of a link between the transfusion or injection of blood products and the plaintiff's infection; this probability may be transformed into certainty.[244] It is not necessary that every positive and negative factor stated above be present to apply the presumption and the courts are often satisfied with only a few of them.[245]

The judgment of 1 July 1991 by the Paris Tribunal de grande instance[246] probably provides the most interesting illustration of this reasoning. A woman was infected with HIV after receiving three units of blood following the birth of her last child in May 1984. The medical staff omitted to note down the identification

[234] Paris, 26 November 1991 (n 213 above); Trib gr inst Paris, 5 February 1992, JCP 1992.G.IV.1762 (the Court insists on the exceptional gravity of the damage); Montpellier, 13 February 1992, JCP 1992.G.IV.2094; L'Épée (n 213 above) 577.

[235] Dorner-Dolivet, note under Versailles 1st ch, 1st sect, 30 March 1989 (n 213 above).

[236] Trib gr inst Bordeaux, 17 February 1992 (n 215 above). See also: Margeat (n 212 above) 583.

[237] Trib gr inst Paris, 1 July 1991 (n 9 above); Paris, 28 November 1991 (n 200 above); Morançais-Demeester (n 210 above) 192; Lebeau (n 210 above) 37.

[238] Trib gr inst Bobigny, 19 December 1990 (n 213 above); Trib gr inst Nice, 27 July 1992 (n 211 above).

[239] Eg: Trib gr inst Paris, 1 July 1991 (n 9 above); Trib gr inst Nice, 27 July 1992 (n 211 above).

[240] Trib gr inst Paris, 1 July 1991 (n 9 above); Trib gr inst Nice, 27 July 1992 (n 211 above); L'Épée (n 219 above) 577.

[241] Trib gr inst Paris, 1 July 1991 (n 9 above); Trib gr inst Bordeaux, 17 February 1992 (n 215 above).

[242] *Ibid*; L'Épée (n 218 above) 577.

[243] Trib gr inst Nice, 27 July 1992 (n 211 above).

[244] Morançais-Demeester (n 210 above) 192.

[245] Trib gr inst Bordeaux, 17 February 1992 (n 215 above).

[246] (N 199 above) confirmed by Paris, 28 November 1991 (n 200 above) (not discussed on appeal: Cass civ 1st, 12 April 1995 (n 200 above)). See also: Toulouse, 5 November 1991, Gaz Pal 1992. 2.somm.405.

numbers of the blood used. Despite the absence of formal identification of the donors, the Court concluded one of them was infected with HIV and consequently that the transfusion caused the plaintiff's condition. This finding was based on the delivery to the clinic of four units of blood of the plaintiff's blood type two days before the transfusion. In the opinion of the medical expert, it was very probable that the three units used for the transfusion were amongst the four delivered, since the plaintiff had a rare blood type and the chance was slim that another patient with the same blood type had a transfusion at the same time. Moreover, the blood units are always used within two days of their reception and the time lapse between the exit of the units from the transfusion centre and the transfusion was compatible with the assertion that they were meant for her. Finally, the blood of one of the four donors had been also used for a transfusion to a newborn baby who thereafter died of post-transfusion AIDS.[247] In addition to all these elements, the Court looked at the plaintiff's personal situation to eliminate other possible causes: she was married at 21 years old, had two children, and was divorced by her husband (who was HIV negative) when he learned that she was infected; she was not a drug user and had never travelled in regions where there is a high concentration of HIV; finally, she had never suffered from infections frequently associated with HIV. These circumstances led the Court to the conclusion that it was highly probable the plaintiff had received blood from the donor responsible for the newborn's infection. The remaining uncertainty was ignored because it was due to the clinic's fault in not recording the blood's lot numbers.[248]

Because of the courts' insistence on the absence of other alternative causes, a great hurdle arises when elements in the plaintiff's history lead the experts to believe that the infection may have been contracted through other means. This hypothesis principally affects haemophiliacs who receive Factor VIII, a clotting factor prepared with blood originating from several non-identifiable donors, as treatment.[249] Only one infected donor is sufficient for HIV to be transmitted (alternative causes). Therefore, if a haemophiliac previously received a blood transfusion or clotting factor or other blood products non-negligently, as well as during the litigious period, and was thereafter diagnosed with HIV infection, it may be an impossible task to link his infection to the negligent injection of blood or blood products. This was the problem faced by the Dijon Court of Appeal on 16 May 1991 (the haemophiliac in a car accident case).[250] It will be remembered

[247] *Acquired immunodeficiency syndrome*, the active manifestation of HIV.

[248] The Cour de cassation rejected an argument that reasoning based on the absence of other causes has the effect of reversing onto the defendant the burden of showing that the plaintiff could have contracted HIV from other sources: Cass civ 2nd, 20 July 1993 (n 216 above) on appeal from Toulouse, 5 November 1991 (n 246 above).

[249] Margeat (n 212 above) 579.

[250] D 1993.242 (note Kerckhove), *aff'd*, Cass civ 1st, 17 February 1993 (n 169 above).

that in this case, the uncertainty was resolved by the drawing of a presumption based on a pure calculation of scientific probabilities based on risk assessment.[251]

3. *Post-transfusion Hepatitis C*

Despite the difficulties related to the proof of causation in post-transfusion HCV cases, French courts have also presumed it on a basis similar to the one relied on in the HIV cases,[252] sometimes coupled with reasoning based on risk. An instructive example is the Cour de cassation decision of 9 July 1996[253] confirming the Paris Court of Appeal decision of 17 September 1993. The two Courts had examined the claim of an HCV victim who had received a large quantity of concentrated red blood cells and fresh plasma during operations consequent on a road accident. Causation was found despite the absence of demonstration that the blood products used were infected and the fact that the expertise attributed 43 per cent of HCV cases to unknown causes.[254] Besides the Courts' emphasis on the increased risk of HCV contamination owing to the amount of units transfused, other relevant elements were the absence of previous transfusions, pre-existing hepatitis condition or any risk factor. Statistical causation was therefore rejected in favour of a more personal causative analysis based on increase of the risk of damage and elimination of other causes

On 14 November 1995, the Cour de cassation also granted compensation to a man infected with HCV. A haemophiliac, in 1985 he had received Factor VIII following a surgical intervention. Two years later, his HCV infection was discovered. Besides noting the absence of other possible causes, the Court drew attention to the experts' assessment at over 80 per cent of the risk of HCV infection after administration of the clotting products. Moreover, the absence of proper testing at the time and of precautions showed, in the opinion of the Court, the products could not have been otherwise than infected. Thus the very high probability of a relationship between the injection of blood products and the contamination, in addition to the absence of other causes, prompted the Court to infer causation.

In HCV cases, courts also generally tend to be generous overall, rejecting compensation where the probability of an alternative explanation is high. In one

[251] Above, text to n 169.

[252] Paris, 20 December 1996, Gaz Pal 1998.I.somm.98 (note Vray); Metz 1st, 21 January 2004, Juris-Data No 234287, despite the contrary conclusions of the medical expert. It does not always succeed, eg, Cass civ 1st, 16 July 1998, Bull civ 1998.I.n261; Cass civ 1st, 23 November 1999 (n 216 above). See also: Lambert-Faivre (n 222 above) 293; Gimbert (n 225 above) 10; and Lyon 1st, 9 September 2004, Juris-Data No 253284: Causation presumed although direct evidence showed that one of the donors tested positive to HCV.

[253] Cass civ 1st, 9 July 1996 (n 170 above).

[254] Other decisions mention that unknown causes of hepatitis C contamination are evaluated at 30%: Paris 1st B, 10 June 2004 (243118) (n 171 above).

example, the plaintiff was a nurse, professionally exposed to the risk of contamination, who, in the months preceding her transfusion, had both had a wisdom tooth extracted under general anaesthesia and been exposed to an epidemic of hepatitis C at her work place.[255]

4. *From Factual to Quasi-legal Presumptions*

Recent developments have arguably gone further than the above discretionary drawing of factual presumptions. Jourdain indeed argues that the factual presumptions of causation usually drawn by the courts in HIV/HCV cases have now been transformed by the Cour de cassation into a substantive legal rule.[256] He rests his argument on three cases of the first civil chamber, dated 9 May and 17 July 2001[257] and dealing with the claims of HCV victims. In the three cases, the Cour de cassation justified the transfusion centres' liability in the same manner: where a person demonstrates that his contamination has occurred after he received blood transfusions and that he has not been subjected to any other individual modes of transmission, it is for the transfusion centre to show that its blood products were not defective. In the three cases, the plaintiffs met this test by showing that they had received blood transfusions, they had previously been in perfect health, and the origin of their infection could not be found in their lifestyle and personal history. In Jourdain's opinion, the above decisions create a rule of law, since the trial judge's discretion is limited to the evaluation of fulfilment of two conditions, namely the existence of a blood transfusion and the absence of other modes of transmission.[258] The rule stated by the Cour de cassation, however, may be nothing more than a reformulation of the presumption-by-elimination technique used by French courts in this line of cases, with an attempt to grant it a weightier probative value.

In 2003, the Cour de cassation refused to extend this reasoning to cases of multiple sclerosis allegedly caused by injections of the anti-hepatitis B vaccine,[259] quashing a decision by the Court of Appeal of Versailles, which had partially relied

[255] Cass civ 1st, 23 November 1999 (n 216 above).

[256] P Jourdain, 'Imputabilité d'une contamination virale à une transfusion sanguine: la preuve par exclusion du lien de causalité érigée en présomption de droit' (2001) *Revue trimestrielle de droit civil* 889, 889. See also: F Chabas, note under Cass civ 1st, 18 June 2002, Gaz Pal 2003.572, somm.n207; YM Serinet and P Mislawski, note under Cass civ 1st, 23 September 2003 (n 162 above).

[257] Cass civ 1st, 17 July 2001, Bull civ 2001.I.n234 and Cass civ 1st, 9 May 2002, Bull civ 2002.I.n130. Confirmed in Cass civ 1st, 18 June 2002 (n 256 above) (presumption however reversed) and Cass civ 1st, 2 July 2002, Juris-Data No 015089.

[258] (N 256 above) 890. Eg, Cass civ 1st, 16 July 1998 (n 252 above); Cass civ 1st, 28 March 2000, RTDC 2000.577, 579 (note Jourdain) (also reported at Bull civ 2000.I.n108, 72, Gaz Pal 2000.somm.1705; Cass civ 1st, 18 June 2002 (n 256 above). In the 18 June 2002 case, the Cour de cassation cites as other modes of transmission: travel in endemic countries and contacts with infected individuals.

[259] Cass civ 1st, 23 September 2003 (n 162 above). Followed in Angers 1st B, 30 March 2005, Juris-Data No 273651. See also: L Neyret, 'Vaccination contre l'hépatite B: fin de débat judiciaire?' [2003] *Dalloz*

on a reasonning by elimination to presume the causal link.[260] The rejection was based on the absence of scientific evidence of the transmission of multiple sclerosis by the anti-hepatits B vaccine, multiple sclerosis having an unknown aetiology. This distinguishes such cases from the transfusions instances described above since it is well-established that HIV and HCV can be transmitted through blood vectors, thus providing evidence of 'partial causation'.[261]

5. *Administrative Courts and Statutory Intervention*

The Conseil d'État has also proved willing to presume causation in HIV and HCV transfusion cases, in the absence of risk factors personal to the patient.[262] In the 1995 *Sanchez* case, the highest administrative court based its decision on the fact that, despite the uncertainty of the expert's conclusion on causation, the latter had qualified as 'manifest' the causal link given the absence of testing of one donor and the lack of any risk factors associated with the patient. It also took into account the fact that the infection could not be linked to an operation the patient had undergone 4 years before the transfusion; and, finally, that the clinical evolution of her ailment suggesting a primo HIV invasion had followed the transfusions she received.[263] Other cases have considered causation proven where the donors or some of them could not be identified or tested, or on the basis of the absence of risk factors other than the transfusion, insisting that it is for the defendant hospital to prove the harmlessness (*innocuité*) of the blood transfused, thereby presuming causation.[264]

2579; V Rebeyrol, 'Les effets secondaires des médicaments et la responsabilité des laboratoires producteurs' (2005) 137 *Petites affiches* 16; YM Serinet and P Mislawski, note under Cass civ 1st, 23 September 2003 (n 162 above) 899, L Pitet, 'Responsabilité du fait des produits : sagesse et force du lien de causalité' [2004] *Gazette du Palais* 869, 871. For a critique: Jonquet, *et al* (n 162 above) para 10; D Mazeaud, note under Cass civ 1st, 23 September 2003 (n 162 above) 1345.

[260] Versailles, 2 May 2001: D.2001.somm.p1592, RTDC 2001.891 (note Jourdain). See also: Versailles 3rd, 12 September 2003, Resp civ et ass 2004.n11.comm.344 (note Radé): Causation presumed between the anti-hepatitis B vaccine and a Guillain-Barré syndrome.

[261] See also: Angers 1st B, 30 March 2005 (n 259 above); D Mazeaud, note under Cass civ 1st, 23 September 2003 (n 162 above) 1345; YM Serinet and P Mislawski, note under Cass civ 1st, 23 September 2003 (n 162 above) 900, Rebeyrol (n 259 above).

[262] CAA Marseille 1st, 6 December 2001, Juris-Data No 197099; CAA Paris 3rd A, 20 March 2001, Juris-Data No 155641; CAA Paris 3rd A, 14 November 2002 (n 171 above).

[263] CE 3rd and 5th sub-s 24 February 1995, Gaz Pal 1995.22 (*Sanchez*), quashing CAA Lyon plénière, 9 July 1992, JCP 1992.G.IV.n3073, p 336: on the ground, *inter alia,* that one donor had not been identified. The plaintiff was a nurse, however, but no risk factor in her behaviour had been demonstrated in her particular case.

[264] Trib adm Strasbourg 2nd, 10 February 1994, Gaz Pal 1994.pan adm.152; CAA Paris 3rd, 5 May 1998, Juris-Data No 048489 (occupational infection); CAA Paris plénière, 12 February 1998, Juris-Data No 050464; CAA Paris 3rd A, 20 March 2001 (n 262 above); CAA Paris 3rd ch, 8 November 2004, No 01PA03602. See also: CAA Bordeaux 2nd, 26 May 1999, Juris-Data No 106626: The court emphasises the absence of risk factor, but adds that one donor was shown to have been infected.

Since the adoption of the *Loi du 4 mars 2002*, all HCV victims, whether treated in a public hospital or a private clinic, benefit from a legislative presumption of imputability,[265] upon the proof that the contamination followed a transfusion.[266] The plaintiff must first provide the court with evidence demonstrating the causal link between the transfusion or injection of blood products and the contamination. If he succeeds, it is for the defendant to show that the transfusion has not caused the contamination.[267] The plaintiff's *prima facie* causal demonstration can be made with the help of factual presumptions,[268] and some judges rely on the presumptions by elimination reasoning in this respect. Decision have relied on, *inter alia* but not cumulatively, the time concomitance between the transfusion and the onset of the symptoms of contamination; the impossibility to identify donors; the existence of other modes of contamination, such as a nosocomial transmission;[269] other invasive procedures before the onset of the symptoms; drug use, acupuncture, or possible sexual transmission; the plaintiff's state of health before the receipt of the blood or blood products; other risks factors, for instance those linked to the plaintiff's profession.[270] The presence of some these factors does not lead to the automatic rejection of the claim, however.[271] Once the plaintiff has made his demonstration, the transfusion centre cannot defend itself by simply arguing that the blood products were also provided by another source; he must

[265] Also described as a presumption of causality, eg, Paris 1st B, 10 June 2004 (249876) (n 171 above). This seems erroneous since some causal evidence must be provided by the plaintiff.

[266] §102 and critique of B Legros, 'État des lieux sur les différents régimes d'indemnisation des conséquences des accidents médicaux' (2004) *Médecine et droit* 1, 9.

[267] Applied in Aix-en-Provence 10th, 9 November 2004, Juris-Data No 257370; Paris 1st B, 10 June 2004 (243118) (n 171 above); Paris 1st B, 10 June 2004 (249876) (n 171 above); Bordeaux 5th, 17 February 2004 (n 8 above); Paris 1st B, 15 January 2004 (n 8 above); Cass civ 1st, 18 January 2005, Gaz Pal, 6–7 avril 2005.juris. 23 (note Guigue). Also applied by the administrative courts: CAA Nantes 2nd, 3 February 2004, Juris-Data No 244840; CAA Nancy 3rd, 29 January 2004, No 99NC01114; CAA Marseille, 3rd ch, 28 April 2005, No 02MA01822; CAA Nancy 3rd, 27 January 2005, No 00NC00918; CAA Marseille 3rd, 10 June 2004, No 00MA00844.

[268] Paris 1st B, 10 June 2004 (249876) (n 171 above).

[269] Transmission through other medical acts, eg: CAA Paris 3rd A, 14 November 2002 (n 171 above); CAA Nancy 3rd, 27 January 2005 (n 267 above). It is not sufficient simply to hypothetically raise the possibility of nosocomial transmission in a case where the plaintiff has undergone other medical procedures; this other mode of transmission must be proven: Paris 1st B, 10 June 2004 (249876) (n 171 above). See also in administrative law: CAA Nantes 2nd, 3 February 2004 (n 267 above); CAA Marseille 3rd, 28 April 2005 (n 267 above).

[270] These factors are not cumulative and courts are often contented with a few of them, eg, Aix-en-Provence 10th, 9 November 2004 (n 267 above); Paris 1st B, 10 June 2004 (243118) (n 171 above); Paris 1st B, 10 June 2004 (249876) (n 171 above); Paris 1st B, 15 January 2004 (n 8 above): The high risk related to injection of plasma made from a large number of donors was also a consideration in this case; Cass civ 1st, 18 January 2005 (n 267 above). See also in administrative law: CAA Marseille 3rd, 10 June 2004 (n 267 above); CAA Nancy 3rd, 27 May 2004, No 99NC01942; CAA Nancy 3rd, 29 January 2004 (n 267 above); CAA Nancy 3rd, 27 January 2005 (n 267 above).

[271] Paris 1st B, 10 June 2004 (249876) (n 171 above) (acupuncture); Paris 1st B, 15 January 2004 (n 8 above) (risky sexual behaviour). Both alternative contamination sources were ignored on the basis that the contamination risk associated with them was much lower than that associated with blood transfusions.

show that this other source played a role in the contamination. It is not necessary to prove that one of the donors was infected, but the defendant can exonerate himself by showing that none of the donors were.[272] Doubt benefits the plaintiff.[273] If the claim is granted, compensation is paid by the State.[274]

The HIV/HCV case law provides an outstanding example of a generous approach to causation clearly based on legitimate equity concerns and offering full compensation in cases of alternative causal mechanisms affected by uncertainty.

D. Others

Finally, the judiciary of the five jurisdictions also shows a tendency to draw presumptions of causation when the fault is serious, when there is time concomitance between the fault and the damage, and when a regulation has been breached. These instances are not particular to medical negligence but may play a general role in dealing with scientific uncertainties.

Commentators in France and Québec observe that when the defendant's fault is serious, courts are tempted to presume causation or more easily conclude for its existence.[275] The line of French cases regarding HIV/HCV victims tends to confirm the willingness of the courts to assist plaintiffs in light of particularly serious faults or of faults leading to particularly serious consequences.[276] In addition, even though simple concomitance in time is generally not considered sufficient to establish causation through the mechanism of presumptions,[277] some cases draw inferences on this basis.[278] Finally, since the Supreme Court of Canada civil law

[272] Aix-en-Provence 10th, 9 November 2004 (n 268 above).

[273] It is unclear whether this section of the provision is meant to reverse the legal burden of proof. We are of the opinion that it simply indicates that the plaintiff will be successful should the defendant not succeed in rebutting the presumption, thereby resulting in a shifting of the evidential burden. CAA Nancy 3rd, 27 January 2005 (n 268 above): the administrative tribunal when applying s 102 did not reverse the burden of proof, nor impose a presumption of responsibility.

[274] Through the *Établissement français du sang*.

[275] France: B Starck, H Roland and L Boyer, *Obligations 1) La responsabilité délictuelle*, 5th edn, (Paris, Litec, 1996) para 1074 and cases cited (involving breach of the duty to inform), inter alia, Cass civ 1st, 11 February 1986, JCP 1987.G.II.20775 (note Dorsner-Dolivet); Viney and Jourdain (n 9 above) 192 and 200 (when the fault creates a danger); J Carbonnier, *Droit civil 4) Les obligations*, 22nd edn, (Paris, PUF, 2000) 391; Québec: *Dubé v Québec (PG du)* [1997] RRA 555 (CS) (summary) (non-medical); Bernardot and Kouri (n 4 above) para 115; Baudouin and Deslauriers (n 4 above) para 581 and cases cited at fn 26. These can be paralleled with presumptions based on the notion of creation of a danger: above, text between nn 149 and 153. See also: WS Malone, 'Ruminations on Cause-in-Fact' (1956) 9 *Stanford Law Review* 60 84, commenting on *Summers v Tice*.

[276] Compare: *Walker Estate v York Finch* (n 210 above).

[277] Jourdain (n 232 above) 8.

[278] Eg, in medical liability: *Ostby v Bondar* (n 182 above) 145–46; Jourdain (2001) (n 257 above) 891 and cases cited, involving supersonic bangs followed by the collapse of a wall, Cass civ 1st, 12 November 1968 (n 9 above). See also: *BC Electric R Co v Clarke* (n 206 above) 164; Versailles, 2 May 2001, D 2001.IR.1592; Paris 1st B, 16 October 2003, Juris-Data No 230703; *Brouillet v Brouillet* (QuéSC, 1 October 2002) paras 40–41.

decision in *Morin v Blais* (1977), it has been accepted in Québec that, unless there is a strong indication or proof to the contrary, causation may be presumed if a binding regulation laying down elementary standards of care had been breached; that breach was immediately followed by an accident; and the standard of care was expressly designed to prevent the accident.[279] *Morin v Blais* involved a road accident allegedly caused by an inadequate signalling device on the rear of a tractor and has been applied restrictively thereafter and never to medical cases.[280] Nevertheless, the case is interesting as it demonstrates a willingness to find causation when the damage falls within the ambit of a risk created by the defendant. Similarly, some Australian cases appear to accept that causation or material contribution may be presumed on the sole basis of the proof of breach of a duty followed by injury.[281] In *Chappel v Hart* (1998), Gaudron J stated that once a physical injury has occurred, breach of a duty is treated as materially causing or contributing to that injury unless there is sufficient reason to the contrary: 'breach of a duty coupled with an incident of the kind that might thereby be caused is enough to justify an inference'.[282]

Conclusion to Section 2

The results of the empirical review above show that English courts are generally not easily convinced to draw inferences and factual presumptions of causation in medical liability cases involving scientific uncertainty.[283] The cases demonstrate a

[279] (N 5 above) 580. Applied in *Boucher v Rousseau* (n 4 above) 96 (non-medical) (Against: Monet J, diss at 94). See also: *Dame Charest v Ouellet* [1971] CA 616, 619 and ff involving very similar facts.

[280] Against: P Deslauriers and SE Chebin, 'Perspectives québécoises sur la responsabilité médicale' (1999) 101 *Revue du notariat* 299, 308: It could apply to the breach of a *norme de prudence* provided for in the Code of Ethics of Physicians RRQ M–9, r4 if the rule's purpose is to prevent the occurrence of the accident in question. In *Zanchettin v Demontigny* (n 7 above) 310–12 the court rejected the application of *Morin v Blais* to the breach of a general recommendation to resuscitate patients, since it was not dictated by an elementary standard of care designed to prevent damage.

[281] *Chappel v Hart* (n 105 above) 273 (para 93) (Kirby J), citing *Betts v Whittingslowe* (1945) 71 CLR 637 (AustHC) 649 (Dixon J), itself referring to *Vyner v Waldenberg Bros Ltd* [1946] 1 KB 50 and not finding it necessary to inquire whether the latter case meant more than drawing an inference on this basis. Although it was not clear whether Kirby J meant to reverse the burden of proof or infer causation, his decision was interpreted as effecting the latter, eg, *Zaltron v Raptis* (2001) WL 808376, SASC 209 (4 July 2001) para 90 (medical duty to inform), treated as a shift of the evidentiary burden; *Lock v Lock* (2001) WL 122672, WASCA 20 (7 February 2001) (non-medical) para 60. See also: D Hamer, 'Chance Would Be a Fine Thing: Proof of Causation and Quantum in an Unpredictable World' (1999) 23 *Melbourne University Law Review* 557, 616 and ff.

[282] Para 8, also citing *Betts v Whittingslowe* (n 281 above) 649 (Dixon J). See also: para 68 (Gummow J); *Naxakis v Western General Hospital* (n 1 above) paras 36 (Gaudron J), 76 (Kirby J), also citing *Betts*. See the comments of I Freckelton and K Petersen, *Controversies in Health Law* (Sydney, Federation Press, 1999) 125–26.

[283] M Davies, *Textbook on Medical Law*, 2nd edn, (London, Blackstone, 1998) 125.

return to the traditional values and rules in England, while in Canada part of the case law adopts an expansive view of the English developments and a willingness to apply *McGhee* to medical malpractice instances. In Australia, reliance on the concept of increase of risk has been timid, albeit in important High Court medical negligence cases. Québec medical liability cases adopt a stand as restrictive as recent English developments, refusing to presume causation in the presence of scarce or controversial evidence; more expansive approaches are used by a minority of judges. France stands aside from the other jurisdictions. While exercising restraint (save in the HIV/HCV cases) in its reliance on the possibility of presuming causation in the area of medical malpractice, it has moved towards a radical solution, namely the allowance of proportional recovery.

Based on the results of this empirical study, section 3 embarks into a critical discussion of the developments described above.

Section 3

Critical Analysis

In many cases, recourse to indirect evidence of causation becomes necessary when the direct evidence remains too uncertain to allow for any conclusion, positive or negative, to be reached about causation. Assessing causation on the basis of indirect evidence is particularly difficult in cases fraught with scientific uncertainty, however, because of the scarcity or contradictory nature of the evidence and because the possibility of an alternative cause of the damage—inherent medical risks or the plaintiff's pre-existing negative state of health—always lurks in the background.

The usual inferential process proceeds to a study of the individual facts of the case which are known and in evidence in order to assess the existence of an unknown fact. Inferences and factual presumptions are normally seen as empirical and pragmatic matters. In common law, they are theoretically based on probabilities, on the 'usual course of events', which ensure a rational connection between the known and the unknown facts.[284] Similarly, French law views them as an essentially evidential process.[285] The civil law judge's presumptive intellectual process is normally based on experience and observation and follows from the

[284] P Murphy, *Murphy on Evidence*, 8th edn, (London, Blackstone, 2003) 685.

[285] R Barraine, *Théorie générale des présomptions en droit privé* (Paris, LGDJ, 1942) 107; R Decottignies, *Les présomptions en droit privé* (Paris, LGDJ, 1950) para 106.

expression of a probability or likelihood[286] and the normal course of events.[287] Consequently, in both legal traditions, inferences and factual presumptions are generally drawn on the basis of a careful assessment of the individual facts of the case and experts' opinions in order to assess the probability of existence of the unknown facts.

Factual presumptions and inferential reasoning do not therefore necessarily assist the plaintiff faced with one of the situations presented above, as his claim may be rejected because of the lack of *known* facts on which to ground his proposed inference or because of their uncertainty. In such a situation, however, the plaintiff can count on the readiness of some courts to rest their inference on justifications previously devised in similar cases, thereby avoiding the uncertainty that study of the individual facts of the case and assessment of the probability of existence of causation could have led to. The instances of inferences examined in section two are indeed not always grounded on a purely fact-based analysis of the whole of the evidence, but are sometimes deduced from a single pre-determined factual element, whether the creation or increase of a risk, the creation of a danger, or knowledge of the causative information-negligent undermining of the plaintiff's means of proof.[288] All the evidence may still be carefully assessed, but at the stage of the defendant's effort to rebut the presumption.

In addition, a trend common to many cases in the area of causal uncertainty is their insistence on justifying inferences drawn on the basis of the judges' common sense.[289] The importance given to this notion prompts a fundamental question. Given the extent of dissatisfaction with the approaches adopted for addressing uncertain causation, can common sense indeed be grounding the judicial assessment of the advisability of inferring causation?

Admitting that there can be a principled basis to the drawing of judicial inferences, and that these can find their root in the judge's common sense rather than in fact-based evaluation of probabilities, may appear *prima facie* objectionable, as it erodes the normal factual inductive process at the basis of the judge's discretionary power. It must therefore be asked whether such reasoning is an admissible part of inferential reasoning in either common law or civil law, especially given that strict adherence to the requirement for careful study of the facts of the case

[286] Ghestin and Goubeaux (n 3 above) para 649; J Carbonnier, *Droit civil: Introduction*, 27th edn, (Paris, PUF, 2002) para 175 (about legal presumptions); Decottignies (n 285 above) paras 2–3; P Brun, *Les présomptions dans le droit de la responsabilité civile* (Grenoble, Thèse de doctorat, Université de Grenoble II, 1993) 21.

[287] Decottignies (n 285 above) para 106; Dejean de la Bâtie, note under Cass civ 2nd, 19 May 1976, JCP 1978.G.II.18773 (note Dejean de la Bâtie); Brun (n 286 above) 386.

[288] In that sense, they are more akin to legal presumptions.

[289] Ch 2, text to fn 54.

as the basis of presumption is invidious to the plaintiff in cases of scientific uncertainty. This section therefore addresses the legitimacy of the courts' intellectual process in inferring causation. It first discusses the validity of grounding inferences on the judge's common sense (A). It then asks whether presumptions of fact and inferences may be legitimately grounded on systematised justifications or basic facts that serve as precedents for similar cases (B). It finally critiques the justifications themselves (C).

A. Common Sense Inferences

Judicially and outside the court, Lord Hoffmann has attempted to explode the myth that causation is simply a matter of common sense. Part of his critique is that when judges say a test is based on common sense, they are concealing an absence of legal reasoning.[290] It is indeed reasonable to suspect the concept is used in both traditions to conceal policy considerations and their influence on judicial decision making.[291] It may even be suspected to act as a multi-purpose, only seemingly objective and logical, concept providing a convenient motive for the judge's *subjective* or *intuitive* decision.[292] Common sense should, however, mean more than that.

A common sense approach, while having the advantage of being fundamentally flexible,[293] may nevertheless result in uncertainty and arbitrariness. Lord Hope recently objected that: 'On its own common sense, and without more guidance, is no more reliable as a guide to the right answer in this case than an appeal to the views of the traveller on the London Underground.'[294] Common sense

[290] G Vos, 'Linking Chains of Causation: An Examination of New Approaches to Causation in Equity and the Common Law' (2001) 60 *CLJ* 337, 337; *Fairchild v Glenhaven* (n 24 above) para 53. See also: PBH Birks, *An Introduction to the Law of Restitution* (Oxford, Clarendon Press, 1989) 21–22 on 'constructive reasoning', ie, the fact that language can be used intentionally or unintentionally to obfuscate the true basis upon which legal disputes are resolved.

[291] *Wilsher v Essex Area Health Authority* [1988] 1 AC 1074 (HL) 1088 (Lord Bridge); *March v E & MH Stramare Pty Ltd* (1991) 171 CLR 506 (AustHC) 531 (McHugh J, diss); NJ Mullany, 'Common Sense Causation—An Australian View' (1992) 12 *OJLS* 431, 436 and 439; P Cane, *Atiyah's Accidents, Compensation and the Law*, 5th edn, (London, Butterworths, 1993) 104–5 (no equivalent in the 1999 edition) (n 49 above); McInnes (n 45 above) 445; Deakin, *et al* (n 46 above) 186; MA Jones, *Medical Negligence* (London, Sweet & Maxwell, 1996) (n 18 above) para 5–24 (no equivalent in the 2003 edition): inferences are no less fictional simply because they are described as 'common sense' or 'pragmatic'. Generally: Stapleton (n 45 above). See also: ch 2 (policy considerations), text between fn 75 and 91.

[292] *Fairchild v Glenhaven* (n 24 above) para 53 (Lord Hoffmann). See also: R Travers, 'Medical Causation' (2002) 76 *Australian Law Journal* 258, 267.

[293] BS Markesinis, 'La politique jurisprudentielle et la réparation du préjudice économique en Angleterre: une approche comparative' (1983) *Revue internationale de droit comparé* 31, 45–46.

[294] *Chester v Afshar* (n 102 above) paras 83–84. He agrees with Lord Hoffmann's comments in *Environment Agency (formerly National Rivers Authority) v Empress Car Co (Abertillery) Ltd* [1999] 2 AC 22, 29 and ff that common sense answers to questions of causation will differ according to the purpose for which the question is asked, para 84.

justifications have also been criticised as allowing tribunals of fact to determine legal responsibility by applying their own idiosyncratic values.[295] Finally, they have been considered meaningless in cases where expert evidence is needed to assess causal connections.[296]

It has been argued that common sense is of little value as an explanation and cannot justify decisions by itself.[297] Indeed, a central problem resides in the fact that common sense is not a uniform or normative concept. Empirical research by psychologists into this notion and that of the *ordinary man* has in fact shown that their application does not produce uniform results,[298] since common sense does not mean the same thing for everyone.[299] Lloyd-Bostock points out that differing perceptions of cause may be seen in terms of differences in context, motive, personality, experience, information sought, interpretation, and level of certainty required.[300] She argues:

> Though empirical observations of attributions actually made may help identify the rules governing them, the ordinary man seen in this way is not the average, consensus, majority voter, or whatever, of actual people, but a kind of *personification of prescriptive rules* supposedly actually in use (emphasis added).[301]

Insistence on the application of common sense notions of causation may thus sanction inconsistency in the case law[302] and, leaving this concept without precise meaning, may have the effect of allowing decisions based solely on '*sentiment*' (feelings)[303] and rules which depend on the area of the law concerned and the judge's sympathy for the victim. Nowhere in the medical malpractice cases that invoke the notion of common sense is it defined, however.

A first step towards identifying a meaning for common sense consists of recognising that in the context of medical liability, common sense is not to be advanced as a justification for decisions, even though in practice it has sometimes been used

[295] *March v Stramare* (n 291 above) 533 (McHugh J, dissenting). McHugh J's point seems to have been centred on distinguishing the factual causation stage from the legal causation stage, refusing to allow that the first be assessed on the basis of anything other than the but-for test. McHugh J also relies on the research of Lloyd-Bostock to criticise this notion.

[296] *March v Stramare* (n 291 above) 533. See also: A Porat, A Stein and SM Cohen, 'Indeterminate Causation of Damages: An Essay on Holtby, Allen, and Fairchild' (2003) 23 *OJLS* 667, 688–89.

[297] S Lloyd-Bostock, 'The Ordinary Man, and the Psychology of Attributing Causes and Responsibility' (1979) 42 *MLR* 143, 164.

[298] Lloyd-Bostock (n 297 above).

[299] Travers (n 292 above) 267; Rogers (n 46 above) 212–13; HLA Hart and T Honoré, *Causation in the Law*, 2nd edn, (Oxford, Clarendon Press, 1985) 1.

[300] (N 297 above) 165 and 167.

[301] *Ibid*, pp 147–48.

[302] Mullany (n 291 above) 439. See also: England: Travers (n 292 above) 259; Stapleton (n 45 above) 123–24; Cane (1993) (n 47 above) 104–6; Hart and Honoré (n 299 above) 1–2, 9 and 26 and ff. Against: MJ Powers and NH Harris, *Clinical Negligence*, 3rd edn, (London, Butterworths, 2000) 899.

[303] P Esmein, 'Le nez de Cléopâtre ou les affres de la causalité' (1964) 33 *Dalloz* 205.

as such. Rather, it indicates the attitude the judge should have towards the evidence.[304] It has to do with the way the decision-making process should be carried out rather than what the right view of the nature of causation should be. Decisions that reflect the tendency of judges to infer causation despite scientific uncertainties should consequently not be termed *common sense decisions* or *decisions grounded on common sense*. Common sense cannot serve as *the* justification, as it may permit judges to abdicate the difficult task of adjudicating causation by clothing value judgments in the guise of rules and to seek to justify a desired conclusion with the illusion of intellectual argument.

This said, one must try to give meaning to common sense.[305] Legal commentators have made remarkable efforts in attempting to define this notion as used in the general context of assessment of causation and fault.[306] Our aim is not to critique these interesting developments but rather to concentrate on the sense the phrase can legitimately have in relation to the specific question of evidence of causation in medical malpractice.

In instances involving scientific uncertainty, common sense is regularly contrasted with scientific, mathematical, and philosophical assessments of causation.[307] It must therefore at the very least refer to the distance judges must maintain from the different theories of causation developed by legal theorists, as well as the scientists' or statisticians' knowledge and understanding of causal relationships.[308] It has also been referred to in relation to the idea that courts should not be paralysed by scientific causal uncertainty, since legal and scientific causation are different concepts.[309] Common sense may also signify that the treatment of uncertain evidence by the judge may be motivated by moral, sociological, and political considerations that would not be taken into account in a purely scientific causal analysis.[310] Finally, it may serve as a reminder that the judge should also ground his assessment of causation on his view of what constitutes the *normal course of events*, which should be based on the *whole of* the lay, medical, and statistical evidence, and should not be dictated by the expert witnesses.

Consequently, in medical malpractice litigation, common sense, if one insists on using the phrase, *need* not refer to more than the different propositions of the

[304] Travers (n 292 above) 259: It is an injunction to judges and jurors to do their best in a difficult situation.

[305] On the need to define legal notions in order to efficiently use them: Viney and Jourdain (n 9 above) para 334.

[306] Hart and Honoré (n 299 above) 26 and ff; Stapleton (n 45 above) 122 and ff; Lloyd-Bostock (n 297 above).

[307] Eg, *Alphacell Ltd v Woodward* [1972] AC 824 (HL) 834 (Lord Wilberforce) and 847 (Lord Salmon); *Wilsher v Essex Area HA* (n 1 above) 1088.

[308] Against: Mullany (n 291 above) 437: Resort to expert evidence makes appeal to notions of common sense meaningless.

[309] *Letnik v Metropolitan Toronto (Municipality)* (n 37 above) 707 (non medical).

[310] For a review of some of these, see: ch 2, text between fn 80 and 86.

case law with regards to the independence of the judge's mind when addressing causal uncertainty.[311] The real danger of arbitrariness arises when these propositions are hidden behind the general rubric of *common sense* and one is no longer able to identify precisely what is being invoked. Removing the rubric and discussing and defining the various considerations and factors which play a role in a given decision-making process removes the danger of arbitrariness and the need for an all-embracing concept such as that of common sense.

On the basis of the review conducted in the preceeding chapters of the positions taken by courts and commentators concerning the way the tribunal of fact should assess direct and indirect evidence of causation in medical malpractice, we submit that courts could incorporate greater flexibility into their decisions to infer causation if they formally adopted the following propositions as the basis of their common sense *approach*:

i) causation is not to be assessed in a scientific, mathematical, or statistical way;

ii) evidence of a *possible* link should be sufficient at the stage of assessing abstract causation. At the personal level, statistical and epidemiological data should have limited impact, since the concern is to establish personal causation rather than an objective possibility of causal link. They are acceptable as a guide but should not dictate any fixed solution to the judge;

iii) expert evidence should be placed on the same level as factual evidence. It should carry weight, especially when it is uncontroversial; but there should be acknowledgement, as in Canadian common and civil law, that the tribunal may find causation proven even if the medical opinion is inconclusive in this respect;

iv) in the presence of scientific controversy on the issue of causation, the judge is allowed to make a choice influenced by the lay evidence and other considerations. Choice can also flow from a judgment on the value of the expert witnesses' opinions. Such judgment should be resorted to as a means of evaluating the weight of the evidence, however, not of settling expert controversies with regard to causation;

v) rather than using the expression 'common sense' to refer to undisclosed policy considerations, the latter should be expressed clearly and openly, and be accompanied by proper justification; and finally

vi) recourse to the burden of proof as the basis of decisions should be strictly a last resort, used in cases in which examination of the evidence, lay and expert, and evaluation of policy considerations do not lead to a firm conclusion, whether based on direct or indirect evidence, about causation.

[311] The question of the general role the notion may have in addressing causation is beyond the scope of this text.

In practice, however, judicial flexibility and independence in assessing causation is difficult to exercise in cases in which this evaluation depends heavily on expert evidence. This difficulty may explain the need the courts have had to look for guidance in previously drawn inferences.

B. Inferential Reasoning Process

1. Common Law

Inferring facts on the basis of previously drawn inferences in similar circumstances is not uncommon in common law.[312] This process, often referred to as *factual presumptions*, occurs where one item of circumstantial evidence almost always suggests an inference, whether with greater or lesser persuasiveness.[313] Thus, judicial precedent or familiarity, recurring circumstantial evidence may be labelled factual presumption, maxim, or doctrine.[314] Some have objected, however, that the label *factual presumptions* tends to falsely imply that some types of evidence are inherently more probative than others and obscures the reasoning process undertaken by the tribunal of facts.[315] Judges are in fact not compelled as a matter of law to draw these inferences.[316] In addition to these, judicially created legal inferences or presumptions do not present particular difficulties in common law, as they flow from the judge's prerogative as creator of law.

A recent Canadian case nevertheless drew attention to the importance, before drawing inferences of causation, of balancing the individual facts of each case. In *Anderson v Wilson* (1999), it had to be decided whether there was a common issue of causation amongst the different parties to a class action. In 1996, a public health inspector identified a possible link between the defendant's clinics, which provided electroencephalogram tests (EEGs), and an outbreak of hepatitis B. A group of plaintiffs claimed negligence and breach of contract, alleging they contracted the sickness during the taking of EEGs at these clinics. Proof of causation was problematic, since assessment of whether there was a temporal connection between the contraction of hepatitis B and the treatment depended on each patient's serologic data. Further difficulty flowed from the existence of other risk factors for hepatitis B such as lifestyle, age, blood transfusions, recent travel to

[312] MN Howard, R Bagshaw and SL Phipson, *Phipson on Evidence*, 15th edn, (London, Sweet & Maxwell, 2000) 70.

[313] DW Elliott, *Elliott and Phipson on the Law of Evidence* (London, Sweet & Maxwell, 1987) 90. It can be based on one item of evidence: Emson (n 172 above) 458.

[314] J Sopinka, SN Lederman and AW Bryant, *The Law of Evidence in Canada*, 2nd edn, (Toronto, Butterworths, 1999) 98 and ch 1, text between fns 175 and 181.

[315] Emson (n 172 above) 458.

[316] Sopinka, *et al* (n 314 above) 597. In contrast, rebuttable legal presumptions compel the court to a set determination *in the absence of evidence to the contrary*.

high-risk areas, sexual partners, and IV drug use.[317] Even though the defendant had increased the risk of contracting hepatitis B for all these patients (who were allegedly 500 times more likely to have it than the general population), the court refused to find a common issue concerning causation. It stressed the need to look at the facts of each case and the whole of the evidence and to evaluate all the other possible causes, each of which could vary according to plaintiff. Only once this exercise had been conducted would the court be able to assess whether causation could be inferred.[318] Thus the court was conscious that the assessment of *all* the facts of a case, not solely the increase of risk, even if substantial, must be part of a judge's decision to presume causation or not.[319]

This case may, therefore support the idea that inferences of causation should not be drawn solely on the basis of a pre-approved formula applicable in every case, without close scrutiny of the particular facts of a case and other possible alternative causes.[320] A similar opinion was recently voiced by the Court of Appeal of British Columbia in *Bigcharles v Dawson Creek and District Health Care Society* (2001):

> I do not view the principle in Snell as being one to permit a trial judge to leap to a conclusion by way of an inference without a full consideration of the evidence during the weighing process. If that process leads to a conclusion that neither party has made out its case on a balance of probabilities where, as here, there is a substantial body of evidence led by the defendants on the issue of causation, it is in my opinion open to the trial judge to decline to draw an inference on this issue.[321]

This view is consistent with the position that inferences can be relied on only where the study of the facts and expert opinions reveals uncertainty with regard to causation.[322] Should uncertainty persists after examination of the whole of the evidence, there does not appear to be any conceptual objection in common law to grounding an inference on justifications previously relied on by the case law in similar cases.

[317] (1999) 175 DLR (4th) 409 (OntCA).

[318] On the basis of *Snell v Farrell: Anderson v Wilson* (1999) 175 DLR (4th) 409 (OntCA) 682.

[319] See also: *Fitzgerald v Lane* [1987] 1 QB 781, 810–11 (appealed on another question: [1989] 1 AC 328 (HL)) 809: *McGhee* does not absolve the judge from the duty of making a decision on a pure question of historical facts, if it is possible.

[320] It is also compatible with the idea that such examination may take place in rebuttal and consequently fall to the defendant to conduct.

[321] Hollinrake JA refused to draw an inference based on the defendants' negligent undermining of the plaintiff's means of proving causation: (BCCA, 16 May 2001) paras 69–71. See also: *National Trust Co v Wong Aviation Ltd* (1969) 3 DLR (3rd) 55; [1969] SCR 481 on the importance of grounding inferences on the whole of the evidence.

[322] Ch 1, text to fn 166.

2. Civil Law

In Québec civil law, Kouri has objected to civil law judges' empowerment to create legal presumptions,[323] which is how he views Québec cases of presumption of causation. Judicial presumptions of causation must, he insists, be based on the circumstances of each particular case.[324] Kouri's comments raise the excellent point that, before advocating a principled approach to inferential reasoning, one must assess whether the judicial creation of presumptive rules serving as precedents violates the conceptual coherence of civil law:

> It should be noted that as in the case of other forms of proof with the exception of presumptions of law, presumptions of fact cannot serve to create presumptions of fault or of causation. Only a text of law can create a legal presumption. Unlike legal presumptions, which exempt a party from having to provide complete proof, presumptions of fact serve as a means of proving certain factual elements. Moreover, presumptions of fact are a form of inductive reasoning signifying that one proceeds from individual facts to arrive at general conclusions, or in other words, that one infers an outcome from the observation of particular circumstances. If one were to proceed on the basis of a general postulate set out in advance in order to infer a certain result in a given fact-situation, this would constitute a form of deductive reasoning and thus antithetical to civilian presumptions of fact.
>
> Obviously, when the courts set out a rule of general application under which an inference of causation may be drawn, (as in the cases of *Morin* and *Lawson*), one is no longer in the realm of inductive reasoning but rather in the presence of a general legal presumption of praetorian origin which would appear, at first blush, to usurp the role of the legislator and to run counter to article 2811 CCQ.[325]

Kouri's position is legitimate given the wording of the French and Québec civil codes, as well as the French doctrine's traditional understanding of the intellectual process leading to a judicial presumption and the role played by the judiciary in the drawing of presumptions. On the other hand, his argument ignores French developments on these subjects. French cases and doctrine have in fact acknowledged for at least the past 50 years the existence of judicially created legal presumptions.

The need for a legislative text for the creation of a legal presumption is clearly expressed in the French Code.[326] Yet a significant proportion of the French doctrine and case law supports the view that a legal presumption can exist without

[323] The creation of legal presumptions is indeed within the powers of the legislator, not the judge: CN, Art 1350 CN and CcQ, Art 2847.

[324] Kouri (n 149 above) 240.

[325] *Ibid*, p 237. Kouri was referring to the tendency in Québec cases to presume causation when the defendant has submitted the plaintiff to a danger.

[326] As well as in the travaux préparatoires of the CN: G Aron, *Théorie générale des présomptions en droit privé* (Paris, Pedone, 1895) 36.

a text if a *jurisprudence constante* (unbroken line of authority) establishes it.[327] French cases have in fact not hesitated to extend existing legal presumptions beyond their original scope or to create new ones.[328] Many commentators have noted the existence of these praetorian presumptions, amongst them Pothier, Gény, Decottignies, and Barraine.[329] In 1946, Mimin argued that French courts do establish systematised presumptions:

> *Or, au voisinage de ces présomptions légales, le droit judiciaire montre un ordre d'autres présomptions. Bien plus fortes que les présomptions de fait ou présomptions de l'homme ou indices et qui en cas d'admissibilité se pèsent librement, elles ressemblent aux présomptions légales. Elles ont la même énergie. Convenues vraies a priori, elles admettent généralement la preuve contraire mais jusque là ne peuvent être méconnues. Elles s'imposent au juge, du moins tant que celui-ci ne trouve rien pour les renverser. La doctrine les cite ou devrait les citer comme des marques de droit coutumier. La jurisprudence les énonce comme des principes et souvent la Cour de cassation a brisé des arrêts qui les traitaient comme simples présomptions de fait et croyaient pouvoir les écarter sans preuve contraire. Nous les appellerons quasi-légales parce que, non écrites dans la loi, elles ont cependant force de loi.*[330]

In a given category of litigation, the problems of evidence may always take the same form, and, since the same presumptive reasoning may be used each time a case involving such problem is heard by a court, precedents may form on which courts may thereafter rely. Thus, on the basis of typical fact situations and the clues that usually accompany them, a factual presumption may be transformed into an obligatory *judicial* presumption,[331] if the Cour de cassation gives its assent to such decisions.[332] While such presumptions are not assimilated to legal presumptions, they have the same characteristics.[333]

[327] Or a *coutume.* Barraine (n 285 above) para 223; Goubeaux (n 286 above) para 1006; Dejean de la Bâtie, note under Cass civ 2nd, 19 May 1976 (n 287 above). See also: the criticism of Aron (n 326 above) 36–41.

[328] A Bénabent, *La chance et le droit* (Paris, LGDJ, 1973) 156; J Dupichot and D Guével, *Contrats et obligations: Présomptions,* Jurisclasseur civil 1349–53, Fasc 155 (Paris, Éditions techniques, 1997) para 18.

[329] RJ Pothier, *Traité des obligations* (Paris, Libr de l'oeuvre de Saint-Paul, 1883) paras 839 and ff; F Gény, *Science et technique en droit privé positif,* t III (Paris, Sirey, 1921) 327–30; Decottignies (n 285 above) para 114; Barraine (n 285 above) paras 156 and ff and 223 and ff. See also: H Motulsky, *Principes d'une réalisation méthodique du droit privé* (Paris, Sirey, 1948) 133 and ff; Brun (n 286 above) 19; Dupichot and Guével (n 328 above) para 116 and ff; J Devèze, *Contribution à l'étude de la charge de la preuve en matière civile* (Grenoble, Service de reproduction des thèses de l'Université des sciences sociales de Grenoble, 1980) para 356; J Normand, *Le juge et le litige* (Paris, LGDJ, 1965) para 333; YM Serinet and P Mislawski, note under Cass civ 1st, 23 September 2003 (n 162 above) 899.

[330] P Mimin, 'Les présomptions quasi-légales' (1946) I *La semaine juridique* 578.

[331] *Ibid,* a judge can usually refuse to draw it in the presence of contrary proof, however. See also: JM Auby, note under CE, 3rd and 5th sub-s, 22 December 1976, JCP.1978.G.II.18792: The difference between such presumptions and factual ones lies in the fact that the judge has meant to bind himself in the former case.

[332] Decottignies (n 285 above) para 115; Brun (n 286 above) 20.

[333] Mimin (n 330 above); Decottignies (n 285 above) para 115.

The French doctrine has acknowledged that considerations of equity contribute to the courts' decisions in drawing praetorian presumptions in the area of civil liability.[334] Barraine observes that these presumptions have usually been created for serious reasons, under the influence of moral, economical, and social considerations and to protect certain groups of individuals for serious reasons of public interest.[335] He adds that the creative role of the judiciary has always tended towards the same goal: facilitating the obtaining by victims of compensation they can legitimately expect.[336]

Of course, none of the authors above had in mind the instances of presumption of causation discussed in this chapter;[337] but in their recent theses, Brun (1993) and Potier (1996) assimilate presumptions of causation based on *création d'un état dangereux* and *création injustifiée d'un risque*, as well as the loss of chance cases, to this category.[338] Moreover, le Tourneau and Cadiet acknowledge the existence of 'presumptions of causation' alongside factual presumptions.[339] They also include loss of chance cases in this category.[340] Finally, Jourdain has recently argued that the Cour de cassation has implemented a new judicial presumption of causation in the area of contaminated blood transfusion litigation.[341]

This question is absent from the Québec literature and case law. The reason appears to be that the question has been ignored, rather than that discussion has led to consensus in the doctrine and case law on the subject. With the exception of Kouri, no one has explicitly discussed the question; only Gonthier J, in *St-Jean v Mercier* (2002), comes close to expressing an opinion in this regard in the area of medical liability. As may be recalled, he rejected the notion that a distinct means of proof exists that is based on the idea of creation of a danger or increase of risk.

[334] Brun (n 286 above) 364.

[335] Barraine (n 285 above) paras 334, 348 and 362.

[336] *Ibid*, para 237.

[337] But Barraine refers to presumptions of causation created by the Cour de cassation in the context of industrial accidents: *ibid* paras 290 and 336. Other oft-cited examples include the presumption of responsibility for the deeds of things, judicially created on the basis of art 1384.1 CN; the presumption of ownership of the possessor; the generalisation of the obligation of good faith; the presumption of solidarity in commercial affairs; and the presumption to the effect that the vendor knows the defects of the thing he sells.

[338] Brun (n 286 above) 98 and 104. Brun describes loss of chance as a partial presumption of causation. He also includes, p 20, all factual presumptions drawn by the trial judge in circumstances in which the defendant is unable in practice to rebut them; C Potier, *Les présomptions de causalité* (Paris, Mémoire de DEA, Paris I Panthéon Sorbonne, 1996) 12–16. Auby is also of the opinion that loss of chance is in fact a presumption of causation: Auby (n 331 above).

[339] le Tourneau and Cadiet (n 231 above) para 819.

[340] As well as instances of *obligations de résultat* which, they believe, to implicitly include a presumption of causation. For other examples: para 819.

[341] Cass civ 1st, 9 May 2001; Bull civ 2001.I.n130, D 2001.2149 (rap Sargos) and Cass civ 1st, 17 July 2001 (n 257 above).

He reminded that these concepts can be invoked only when assessing the existence of clues present in the individual facts of the case within a traditional presumptive process.[342]

An orthodox vision of the role of the judge in drawing presumptions, based on a literal and restrictive interpretation of the Civil Code's provisions and an insistence on the court's exclusive role as interpreter of legislation, may in large part explain the restrictive Québec attitude towards presumptions of causation in medical malpractice.[343] Yet in practice, Québec judges addressing civil cases, like their French counterparts, do not generally hesitate to use their interpretative powers to devise rules of law.[344] This is especially striking in civil liability, in which the generality of Article 1382 CN and Articles 1457–58 CcQ[345] has prompted the need to define the limits of civil liability judicially.[346] Moreover, Québec law's distinct position towards judicially created presumptions cannot find justification in the different wording of the provisions of the Civil Code of Québec concerning proof by presumptions; these are in fact almost identical to the corresponding French articles, with only a few differences in style rather than substance.[347] As both Codes clearly state that legal presumptions are those established by the legislator, Québec sources have undoubtedly shown greater respect for codal provisions than their French colleagues. It may nevertheless be asked whether such a literal interpretation of the Code is warranted.

This text does not plead in favour of creation of a *quasi-legal presumption* of causation that could apply generally to medical liability cases, however. The probative impact granted to such presumptions conflicts with the judicial discretion we consider necessary in this field, as well as the crucial importance of studying the individual facts and expert opinions in order to achieve the most personal assessment of causation possible. One should remain wary of adopting a wholly systematic inferential reasoning process, given that presumptions drawn in this area will rarely be rebuttable in practice, as the causal uncertainty often affects defendant and plaintiff alike. Some exception to this general principle may be warranted in some cases, however, as we will argue.

[342] *St-Jean v Mercier* (n 7 above) 298 and above, text between nn 146 and 148.

[343] The more generous Québec standard of proof may also play a role in this strict position. Morever, this stand is certainly influenced by the general desire to protect the integrity of civil law in a jurisdiction surrounded by the common law tradition.

[344] JL Baudouin, 'The Impact of the Common Law on the Civilian Systems of Louisiana and Quebec' in J Dainow, (ed), *The Role of Judicial Decisions and Doctrine in Civil Law and in Mixed Jurisdictions* (Baton Rouge, Louisiana State University Press, 1974) 6, 10 and 12.

[345] And their predecessors, Arts 1053 and 1065 CcL-C.

[346] PA Crépeau, *La responsabilité civile du médecin et de l'établissement hospitalier* (Montréal, Wilson & Lafleur, 1956) 39–40.

[347] Compare: Arts 2846 CcQ and 1349 CN; 2847 Arts CcQ and 1350 CN; and Arts 2849 CcQ and 1353 CN.

The French position nevertheless has important implications and provides useful teachings. It shows that presumptive reasoning in civil law allows for systematised reasoning in cases presenting similar difficulties. It also demonstrates that the judicial power for presumptive reasoning in civil law is less limited than is thought in Québec. It also argues for the courts' showing greater openness to considerations other than a strict examination of the specific facts of the case when assessing the advisability of presuming causation.

These considerations are consonant with the discretion civil law judges should enjoy when assessing indirect evidence. As already seen, the French doctrine considers the tribunal's power to draw factual presumptions is not limited by the requirement that only serious, precise, and concordant presumptions be entertained. On the contrary, Québec writers tend to treat this requirement as a strict condition.[348] Strictly applied, the requirement leads to the rejection of most medical claims involving scientific uncertainty, however. The scarcity of evidence, the contradictions in the experts' opinions, and the fact that there is almost always a possibility that damage may have flowed from a risk intrinsic to the treatment or from the plaintiff's pre-existing condition may in themselves prevent the requirement from being met.[349]

There is room for the argument that the criterion of seriousness, precision, and concordance should not be applied so rigidly that it leads to injustice in cases involving scientific uncertainty. In appropriate circumstances, there should be no objection to relaxing the way satisfaction of this criterion is assessed in order to deal adequately with cases in which the evidence affords limited factual clues on which to base a presumption. Moreover, judicial discretion of this nature should go as far as legitimising reliance on previously drawn presumptions.

3. *The Justifications*

This section has addressed two crucial components of the inferential process relied on by the courts in the area of medical malpractice, namely the insistence on rooting the judges' inferences in common sense, and the possibility of relying on previously drawn presumptions in similar instances and transposing the justifications developed therein to subsequent cases. It has argued that the notion of common sense in the context of uncertain scientific causation cannot constitute a justification for the courts' inferences. Rather, it should serve as a guide in the adoption by the judge of the proper attitude towards uncertain causal evidence, one that is not dictated to by the philosophical or scientific approaches to causation;

[348] Royer (n 3 above) para 842; A Nadeau and R Nadeau, *Traité pratique de la responsabilité délictuelle* (Montréal, Wilson & Lafleur, 1971) para 645. See also: *Therrien v Launay* (n 4 above) para 548.

[349] Jutras (n 20 above) 906, fn 24. These elements can also allow the defendant to rebut a presumption the court is willing to draw. In this case, the burden is on the defendant to prove the probability of an alternative cause, however.

that acknowledges the gap between legal and scientific causation; and the need to remain independent from the expert evidence and base decisions on the whole of a case's evidence. Further, this section has sought to show that systematised factual presumptive reasoning is a possible option for the judiciary, even in civil law, where the French courts have relied on it several times to date. There thus does not appear to be any categorical conceptual objection to adopting justifications that could apply uniformly to inferential reasoning in cases of the same nature. Nevertheless, we have emphasised the importance of careful assessment of the individual facts of each case in order to preserve fairness to the defendant.

Recognising that judicial presumptions may be grounded on a systematic approach and that common sense is not a justification for decisions intensifies the need to carefully analyse and rethink the justifications on which common and civil law courts have grounded inferences of causation. The following section therefore asks whether the justifications relied on by courts of civil and common law jurisdictions and studied in this chapter are admissible bases for presumptive reasoning.

Where information is incomplete, it is difficult to insist the judge's decision rest mainly on logic and probabilities; on the other hand, much inferential reasoning is empirical and thus cannot be decided in advance. The drafting of guidance for applying inferential reasoning must seek to balance these two realities. This last section discusses which considerations beyond the individual facts of the case are valid and weighty enough to create precedents.

C. Critique of the Justifications

In the course of the examination of the case law in section 2 of this chapter, several types of justification were encountered. These included the origin of the background risk, the extent of the risk created or increased by the defendant, whether the risk increased or created by the defendant is so great that it creates a danger for the plaintiff, and the particular knowledge of the relevant facts by one of the parties or the disappearance of the means of proving causation through the fault of one party.[350] These developments show a real struggle on the part of the judiciary to find objective and straightforward justifications for the courts to rely on when drawing inferences. Pre-established justifications for presuming causation provide a very convenient way to deal with the problem and take a decision without the complications of close examination of the facts of the case and expert controversies. Even though this approach may have legitimate aims, however, recourse to 'pre-established truths'[351] should be eschewed when it leads to injustice to the defendant.

[350] See also: F Chabas 'Vers un changement de la nature de l'obligation médicale' (1973) I La semaine juridique 2541.

[351] The expression is of Brun (n 286 above) 368.

In *Seyfert v Burnaby Hospital Society* (1986), McEachern CJSC said that it would be contrary to principle to hold a defendant responsible for damage he may not have caused 'unless there is a compelling legal reason why the court should reach such a conclusion.'[352] One must also be wary of the awkward possibility, if inferences are drawn too readily, that plaintiffs contending with uncertainty may obtain compensation more easily than those who have resolved it. For these reasons, a central question is whether the justifications cited by the courts of the four jurisdictions in assisting plaintiffs constitute compelling legal reasons for doing so. The present section is thus dedicated to a critique of the justifications relied on by the courts of England, Australia, Canada, Québec, and France for presuming causation in cases involving alternative mechanisms, namely the concepts of risk and increase of risk, danger, and negligent undermining of the plaintiff's means of proof.

In what follows, we argue that most of the justifications so far developed by the courts as bases for inferring causation are unacceptable conceptually or in their practical application in the context of medical malpractice. Moreover, most are inadequate to the task of ensuring better compensation to the plaintiff while maintaining fairness for the defendant. Finally, taken in isolation, most do not provide compelling enough grounds for presuming causation. The present section undertakes to address the concepts of risk, danger, and negligent undermining of the means of proof in order to determine: i) whether they have the inherent value necessary for basing inferences of causation solely on their presence; and, if not: ii) whether they are still relevant factors to put in the presumptive balance.

1. *The Idea of Risk*

(a) Material Increase of Risk in Common Law

Despite the authority of *Fairchild v Glenhaven Funeral Services* (2002), in which McGhee was interpreted not as introducing an inference of causation, but as an alternative test for proving causation,[353] the analysis of the concept of increase of risk is here maintained under the inference category for two reasons. First, the position adopted in *Fairchild* is unlikely to become a binding authority for cases of medical liability as already argued.[354] Second, in Canada, the only jurisdiction which has been willing, except at the Supreme Court level, to address causal uncertainty in medical malpractice on the basis of *McGhee*, it is interpreted as involving an inferential principle.[355] In Australia, material increase of risk has also been

[352] (1986) 27 DLR (4th) 96 (BCSC) 102.

[353] Above, text to n 72.

[354] Above, text between nn 96 and 100.

[355] Above, text to n 39. In fact, the exact mechanism employed in *McGhee* had no practical relevance, since the defendant had no more evidence to offer than the plaintiff because the causal uncertainty was due to the uncertain aetiology of the plaintiff's disease.

invoked predominantly with regard to the application of inferential reasoning.[356] Finally, it is preferable to limit the impact of this concept in medical malpractice to the justification of a discretionary inference. Material increase of risk does in fact fit squarely within inferential reasoning, which typically infers from a known fact (eg, the increase of a risk) the existence of an unknown fact (eg, material contribution or causation).[357] Moreover, while the approach taken in *McGhee* and *Fairchild* may be justified in the field of industrial diseases, considerations apply in the field of medical malpractice that make it inadvisable to draw hasty parallels between the two.

The identity of the creator and beneficiary of the risk, and the social imbalance between him and the plaintiff, are interesting considerations in the context of cases of pharmaceutical products liability, industrial pollution, and industrial diseases, where risks have often been created at the victim's expense in the pursuit of an economic activity, with a view to commercial profit.[358] In such fields, the policy incentive for having the rules of causation operate less favourably to the defendant are stronger and favour making the defendant bear the risk of uncertainty.[359] They cannot assume the same significance in the medical sphere, however. Even though there exists an imbalance of power between patient and doctors, and though the latter do take risks from which their patients may suffer, these risks are usually not primarily the result of their misdeeds. The pre-existing situation of the plaintiff is usually negative, one not of life and health but of sickness and death. Moreover, the origin of the pre-existing risk is often found outside the medical act, whether in the human condition or in a previous event or fault unrelated to the medical act. In contrast, cases of work-related diseases involve situations where the defendant is often the creator of the pre-existing risk.[360] Moreover, the doctors' lack of foresight of these risks may flow from the inherently unpredictable nature of the human condition[361] or from the limited ability of medical science to predict and control risk. Special consideration is due to the fact that uncertainty is an inherent part of medical practice, and the doctor is a fallible person engaged in what is often closer to art than exact science.[362] Further, while medical risks are inherent in the activity

[356] (N 108 above).

[357] Lord Hutton in *Fairchild v Glenhaven* (n 24 above) para 108. It is also difficult to understand how, considering the case law's agreement on rejecting Lord Wilberforce's reversal of the onus of proof, the House of Lord could adopt a solution even more burdensome for the defendant.

[358] Compare with *Hollis v Dow Corning Corp* (n 174 above) 675 (LaForest J): It is 'highly desirable from a policy perspective to hold the manufacturer to a strict standard'; and in England: *Ratcliffe v Plymouth and Torbay Heath Authority* (1998) 42 BMLR 64 (CA) 85.

[359] On the utilitarianism of benefits and burdens and the modern concept of 'the polluter pays': M Davies, *Textbook on Medical Law*, 2nd edn, (London, Blackstone, 1998) 113.

[360] C Larroumet, 'L'indemnisation de l'aléa thérapeutique' [1999] *Dalloz* 33, 37.

[361] G Boyer-Chammard and P Monzein, *La responsabilité médicale* (Paris, PUF, 1974) 116.

[362] France: R Savatier, 'Une faute peut-elle engendrer la responsabilité d'un dommage dans l'avoir causé?' [1970] *Dalloz* 123, 125; Québec: *Dupont v St Martin* (SCC, 19 December 1922) (Mignault J).

in question, they are undertaken for a purpose totally different from that pursued in the industrial context. The prime beneficiary of the risk is usually the patient and the society as a whole. The social utility of medicine is arguably more deserving of protection than the pursuit of an economic activity. These considerations militate against drawing too readily parallels between medical malpractice and industrial disease cases and in favour of treating the notion of risk, if this concept is retained, as part of the inferential reasoning process.[363] True, in cases of uncertainty, it may in practice make no difference whether one infers causation, reverses the burden of proving causation, or finds causation automatically proven on the basis of increase of a risk, however. Unless the defendant possesses special knowledge of the causal facts, the result of all of these techniques is the same.

The Practical Application of the Concept—The idea of material increase of the risk of damage is attractive to plaintiffs in cases of uncertain alternative causation or unknown causal process, as it adapts the material-contribution-to-the-damage requirement to their conceptual needs. It also serves for both cumulative and alternative cause cases without introducing the hurdle of a distinction difficult to apply in practice. In fact, when there is an evidentiary gap, the distinction between material contribution and material increase of risk might be difficult to draw.[364] It could even be argued that the distinction loses most of its value if it is agreed that the material contribution to the injury test can be met by proof of very little contribution, as well, indeed, as in cases in which the fact of contribution cannot be assessed. This thus provides a further incentive to equate the two, since it may be impossible in many cases to assess the extent of the contribution otherwise than in terms of increase of risk.[365] The only tangible benefit derived from the distinction would then be exclusion of clear cases of alternative causation. The potential impact of the idea of material increase of risk appears thus to be great. Consequently, its proper assessment is crucial. It may be objected that such an undertaking is irrelevant considering that *Wilsher* has prompted the return, in alternative cause cases involving non-tortious factors, to a more traditional approach to causation in which increase of risk has no impact.[366] Yet the concept has current relevance given its impact in a series of Canadian Court of Appeal and Australian medical liability cases of the past decade.

[363] True, this argument is not unassailable. The marketing of pharmaceutical products is also undertaken for the public's benefit, and to claim that doctors have no financial and scientific interest in their patients' treatment can be doubted.

[364] MA Jones, *Textbook on Torts*, 8th edn, (London, Blackstone, 2002) 233; *McGhee v National Coal Board* (n 26 above) 12–13 (Lord Salmon).

[365] Eg, arguably: *Nicholson v Atlas Steel Foundry and Engineering Co Ltd* (n 27 above). See also: Jones (1996) (n 18 above) 5–23 (no equivalent in the 2003 edition).

[366] Confirmed in *Fairchild v Glenhaven* (n 24 above) paras 22 (Lord Bingham); 118 (Lord Hutton) and 149 (Lord Rodger).

If we invoke the meaning ascribed to the *material* requirement in *Bonnington Castings v Wardlaw*, mere increase of risk, as long as it is not trivial, would appear sufficient to meet the test.[367] Yet in *Nowsco v Canadian Propane* (1981), Bayda JA noted the need to show the magnitude of the risk in order to ensure that the causation requirement is not bypassed:

> Rather the breach of duty contemplated must be such that the risk it creates is of a magnitude that would prompt one to say about that risk 'it is so unreasonable that injury is more likely to occur than not'. In the parlance of the ordinary man one must be able to say that the creator of the risk was 'certainly asking for trouble'.[368]

Yet the Canadian case law has not understood material as a requirement entailing, as Bayda JA implies, an increase of risk that would meet the balance of probabilities test, and we submit the test was not introduced to address cases that could be solved under traditional principles. Examination of the Canadian cases that have applied this concept after 1990 shows that the extent of the risk created or of the increase of the risk is never quantified or commented on, and it appears that a mere increase of the risk is sufficient to infer causation.[369]

Beyond the problems caused by the courts' generous application of the concept, it has inherent difficulties that militate against giving this notion a determinative role in medical malpractice litigation. The main criticisms are these: it forces exaggerated recourse to statistical evidence; it may give credibility to an argument identifying the increase of risk as the damage suffered by the plaintiff; there are inconsistencies in rejecting loss of chance while admitting inferential reasoning based on increase of risk; and, finally, reliance on increase of risk within the assessment of causation leads to confusion of the fault and causation requirements.

Recourse to Statistical Evidence—One of the problems resulting from reliance on increase of risk as a justification for inferring causation is the indirect encouragement to resort solely to statistics in order to make a *prima facie* case for causation. This line of reasoning will allow a plaintiff to fully recover upon demonstration, for instance, that the doctor's failure to treat him has increased his risk of not recovering by 10 per cent, since it has been shown statistically that prompt treatment decreases the risk of suffering from this ailment by 10 per cent. Statistical evidence of this kind automatically grants the plaintiff full success on

[367] Thus the defendant can be held liable even if, statistically, the increase of risk is less than 51%: R Meeran, 'Problems of Causation in Environmental Personal Injury' (1992) *Solicitors' Journal* 804, 804.

[368] *Nowsco Well Service Ltd v Canadian Propane Gas & Oil Ltd* (1981) 122 DLR (3rd) 228 (CA) 246 (non-medical case).

[369] Above, text between nn 125 and 135, with the exception in *Levitt v Carr* (n 123 above).

the causation issue, even though he may be unable to prove that he would have been a member of this lucky group of patients.[370] In other words, by grounding the argument about recovery on a purely objective statistical link, the concept removes the obligation to conduct a personal analysis of causation. The potential for injustice to the defendant is clear, since he must pay full damages to a person whose disability may flow, in reality, from some other source.[371]

Increase of Risk as Damage—The same example shows that there is a very fine line between this reasoning and one that uses the concept of increase of risk to enable a plaintiff to claim damage that has not yet materialised. It is in fact theoretically possible to assimilate increase of risk to a head of damage admissible for compensation. The plaintiff could claim compensation for the increased risk of damage the defendant's fault has provoked, rather than for the final damage, death, or injury.[372] Thereafter, he can fulfil the lighter task of proving, on the balance of probabilities, causation between the increased risk or the risk created and the defendant's negligence. Gibbs JA, who found causation proven on the basis of a material increase of the risk in *Smith v Moskovitch* (1989), acknowledged this possible confusion: 'Risk is not injury. There is no cause of action for risk whether material or not. It is only when the risk leads to injury that there is a claim, the claim being founded upon the negligence implicit in creating the risk, and even then the claim can only be maintained if the causal link is proven.'[373]

Causative arguments based on mere increase of risk may thus provoke great over-deterrence by opening the door to endless claims, given that each medical fault increases the risk of damage to the patient. Of course, this adverse impact may be limited by restricting the admissibility of the argument to cases in which the damage has actually been manifested. With or without this restriction, inferences based on increase of risk remain controversial because of their resemblance to the loss of chance argument.

Parallel with Loss of Chance—In cases allowing the loss of chance argument, it is sufficient to prove that the fault increased the risk of damage and to claim compensation in proportion to this increase of risk.[374] By increasing the risk of the plaintiff's suffering the illness, the defendant has in effect reduced the latter's

[370] J Stapleton, *Disease and the Compensation Debate* (Oxford, Clarendon Press, 1986) 47: This test has the potential of over-internalising losses to the defendant to a greater degree than the all-or-nothing balance of probabilities test. Stapleton adds that over-internalisation may be reduced by the subsequent causal apportionment of damages which takes into account other possible sources of risk, however.

[371] Cane (n 47 above) 93; Jones (n 364 above) 231–32; Stapleton (n 49 above) 403–4.

[372] The argument then becomes the mirror image of loss of chance.

[373] *Smith v Moscovich* (1989) 40 BCLR (2nd) 49 (BCSC) 53. We disagree that negligence is always implicit in the creation of a risk. See also: *Powell v Guttman* (n 39 above) 188; *Merlin v British Nuclear Fuels* Plc [1990] 2 QB 557 (non-medical).

[374] Jutras (n 20 above) 905.

chances of avoiding fulfilment of the risk.[375] Consequently, rejecting compensation of a lost chance constitutes refusal to grant compensation for the fact that the defendant's fault has merely increased a risk of damage to the plaintiff. Acceptance of inferential reasoning based on increase of risk is thus hard to reconcile with rejection of the loss of chance argument.[376] If partial recovery afforded by loss of chance is inadmissible, it is *a fortiori* illogical to grant full compensation on the mere finding of an increased risk. The change of wording from chance to risk does not conceal the fact that the reasoning is the same and that one is giving with one hand what one is refusing with the other; compensation of lost chances is refused while inferences of causation based on the increase of risk flowing from the loss of the very same chance are admitted.

The potential impact of presumptions based on increase of risk is actually more worrisome than that of loss of chance. While loss of chance allows recovery only for a portion of the final damage, reliance on material increase of risk permits *full* compensation. In the example above, while the plaintiff will be refused recovery for 10 per cent of his final injury on the basis that loss of chance is inadmissible in medical malpractice, he will nevertheless still be able to rely on material increase of risk to entitle him to full compensation, a 10 per cent risk not being in the *de minimis* range.[377] The absence of discussion of how far the defendant's fault aggravated the risk, or of quantification of the background non-negligent risk the plaintiff was already exposed to, intensifies the clash between the two stands: loss of chance at least forces some quantification of the increase of risk-loss of chance in order to measure the amount of compensation. This yields another awkward contrast between the material increase of risk approach advocated in *McGhee* and the loss of chance doctrine: the less that is known about the risk, the greater the potential award of damage.[378]

A way to address this criticism is to argue that medical loss of chance cases such as *Hotson* and *Laferrière* are cases of alternative causation involving a non-faulty agent, to which the notion of material increase of risk does not apply in any event. But the critique remains relevant to Canadian and Australian case law, since the concept has not been applied so restrictively there. Another counter-argument may be found in the fact that, in the example mentioned, there is no uncertainty, since it is known that the risk was increased by 10 per cent. Consequently, the primary condition for *McGhee* to apply is absent. Again, it is hard to justify why cases

[375] This has led some to argue that *McGhee* was in fact concerned with loss of chance: G Robertson, 'Overcoming the Causation Hurdle in Informed Consent Cases: The Principle in *McGhee v NCB*' (1984) 22 *University of Western Ontario Law Review* 75, 90; M Hogg, 'Lost Chances in Contract and Delict' (1997) *Scots Law Times* 71, 73.

[376] This was noticed by Lord Mackay in *Hotson v East Berkshire AHS* (n 23 above) 786.

[377] Meeran (n 367 above) 805.

[378] Jones (1996) (n 46 above) para 5–38 (no equivalent in the 2003 edition).

in which the increase of risk is non-quantified but known to be less than 50 per cent should be treated more generously at the causation level than cases in which one is able to assess the exact extent of the increase of risk.

Confusing Fault and Causation—Increase of risk reasoning is also fraught with conceptual problems. Equating a mere increase of risk with material contribution to the damage leads to the danger of confusing the fault and causation requirements and of ultimately dispensing the plaintiff from proving causation by deducing it from the sole existence of the fault. It is in fact more appropriate to situate creation and increase of risk of damage in the context of fault and foreseeability of damage, rather than factual causation.[379] These concepts are usually relied on when determining whether the standard of the reasonable person is met, by helping identify the kinds of precaution the defendant should have taken when carrying on his activities. Creating or increasing a risk is not necessarily faulty, but it can become negligent if it constitutes a departure from how the reasonable person would have acted. Granting that material increase of risk necessitates proof of simple increase of risk, it becomes clear that allowing causation to be shown on this basis confuses the fault and causation requirements and may lead to the effective disappearance of the causation condition.[380] Since it is always possible to argue that the defendant's negligent actions or omissions have created or increased a risk of damage to the plaintiff,[381] this position has a perverse effect: liability comes to be based solely on fault and damage.[382] The problem is solved if one adds to the material increase of risk test the requirement of demonstrating the link between the negligent increase of risk and realisation of the risk, thereby treating increase of risk solely as an element of negligence. This reintroduces the traditional evidential requirement, however, and, with it, the causative problem which inferences based on increase of risk was intended to overcome.[383]

(b) Increase of Risk and Creation of a Danger in Civil Law

All of the above comments also apply to reliance on increase of risk and creation of a danger in civil law. In particular, the conceptual objection to the effect that increase of risk is an element of fault, not causation, applies equally to both Québec and

[379] *Bolton v Stone* [1951] AC 850 (HL); *Fairchild v Glenhaven* (n 24 above) para 132 (Lord Rodger); EJ Weinrib, 'A Step Forward in Factual Causation' (1975) 38 *MLR* 518, 523. Eg, England: *Yates v Rockwell Graphic Systems Ltd* [1988] 1 ICR 8 (QB) 15; *Cobbing v Chase Farm Hospitals NHS Trust* (Barnet County Ct, 11 September 1998) summarised at [1999] JPIL 167; Canada: L Klar, *Tort Law* (n 116 above) 315–16; Linden (n 116 above) 119 and ff; EI Picard and GB Robertson, *Legal Liability of Doctors and Hospitals in Canada*, 3rd edn, (Toronto, Carswell, 1996) 193 and ff and cases cited at fn 125.

[380] *Nowsco v Canadian Propane* (n 368 above) 245 (non-medical). Bayda J solves the problem by adding a requirement of magnitude of the risk. See also: Klar (n 116 above) 398.

[381] *Nowsco v Canadian Propane* (n 368 above) 246.

[382] Robertson (n 375 above) 84 and 88; Weinrib (n 379 above) 523.

[383] Eg, *Seltsam Pty Ltd v McGuiness* (n 1 above) paras 102–9.

French law. In these jurisdictions, the notions of danger and risk are usually part of the assessment of the fault requirement and have been of use to the courts mainly in the assessment of the objective potential for damage arising from an activity.[384] The creation of a risk or danger is considered negligent if it occurs without the taking of all the reasonable precautions necessary to avoid causing damage.[385] The mere fact of creating a risk of damage is not considered in itself a fault, however.[386]

In theory, the concept of creation of a danger, invoked in Québec especially, is more acceptable, as it guarantees limitation of liability through the idea of *danger* when properly applied. In the usual sense of the word, the extent of the risk created or increased by the defendant should be central to the notion of creation of a danger, as danger implies that a *significant risk has been created* or that an already existing risk *has been significantly increased,* and that damage has occurred within the area of the risk.[387] Interpreted in this fashion, there appears to be little objection to such a justification, since the significance of the risk ensures that the balance shifts in favour of probable causation, in harmony with the balance of probabilities requirement, although the latter is thereby assessed on a purely statistical basis.[388]

This interpretation is not reflected in the case law, however. In their practical application of this concept, Québec courts show no real concern with the quantification of the risk created or aggravated, and the concept of danger itself is not discussed. Moreover, some cases have seen fit to apply this justification even when the defendant's fault has merely increased the risk of occurrence of the damage[389] by finding danger upon the proof that the type of fault committed by the defendant *could* cause the damage that arose in the specific case. Danger is thereby emptied of its meaning and used in a fashion similar to the common law judicial reliance on material increase of risk, thereby becoming subject to the objections expressed above.

The recent decision of Gonthier J in *St-Jean v Mercier* (2002) negates the view that judicial presumptions may be drawn automatically by Québec courts on the basis of single concepts such as creation of a danger and treats it as one of the factors to take into account in the court's presumptive reasoning, not as creating another means of proof.[390] To the extent that creation of a danger is equated with a mere increase of risk, one must agree with Gonthier J's stand.

[384] G Schamps, *La mise en danger: Un concept fondateur d'un principe général de responsabilité. Analyse de droit comparé* (Paris, LGDJ, 1998) 816 and 821.

[385] *Ibid*, p 822 and fn 1016.

[386] *Ibid*, p 822 and cases cited at fn 1015. The unnecessary creation of a danger potentially leading to damage has sometimes been considered to be in itself careless: 823 and texts cited at fn 1017.

[387] *Danger* can also refer to a low risk of damage of a great magnitude.

[388] It may be argued that presumptive reasoning is therefore not required in either Québec or common law when invoking this concept.

[389] Above, text between nn 149–152 and Jutras (n 20 above) 907, fn 29.

[390] (N 342 above) para 114. Compare: *Roughton v Weston Area Health Authority* (n 19 above).

2. Negligently Created Causal Uncertainty

The most interesting factor is that relating to the defendant's special knowledge of information about causation and his negligently undermining the plaintiff's means of proving it.[391] This is the only consideration that touches on the bases of the rules about burden and standard of proof in the two systems, namely allocation of the risk of uncertainty and judicial error and the principle of equality of the parties before the evidence. When one party possesses information, or had the means of possessing information, to which the other party does not have access, it can be argued that the traditional principle of allocation of the risk of evidence loses its meaning. In such situations, the law's traditional choice of who should bear the risk of absence or insufficiency of the evidence constitutes a clear injustice. If the rules of evidence are really about deciding who bears the risk of uncertainty in the evidence, there is a strong rationale for departing from the orthodoxy when the uncertainty has been negligently created by one of the parties. To relax the stringency of the burden resting on the plaintiff is no more than a pragmatic means to redress the balance between plaintiff and defendant.

Wigmore notes that the 'principle' of placing the burden of proving a fact on the party who presumably has peculiar means of knowledge enabling him to prove it has been advanced as a special test for solving some cases. He believes, however, that this consideration furnishes no universal working rule and that it 'merely takes its place among other considerations of fairness and experience as a most important one to be kept in mind in apportioning the burden of proof in a specific case.'[392] Others have drawn attention to the fact that common law courts are inclined to require proof from the party to whom the least difficulty or embarrassment will be caused by the burden,[393] and that this may even justify putting the onus on the defendant in certain cases.[394] In France, the doctrine has argued that the law should take into account the inequalities of the parties *vis-à-vis* the evidence[395] and the fact that one party has the best ability to adduce evidence.[396] But the French writings also make no claim that this factor should be an autonomous and sufficient criterion.

[391] It is relied on expressly in *Snell v Farrell* (n 1 above) to infer causation in a medical malpractice case.

[392] JH Wigmore, *Evidence in Trials at Common Law*, vol IX (Boston, Little Brown, 1940) §2486. See also: R Demogue, *Notions fondamentales de droit privé* (Paris, A Rousseau, 1911) 550 and ff.

[393] Murphy (n 285 above) 81.

[394] Eg, *Levison v Patent Steam Carpet Cleaning Ltd* (1978) QB 69 (non-medical).

[395] R Legeais, *Les règles de preuve en droit civil* (Paris, LGDJ, 1955) 170; Devèze (n 329 above) 544.

[396] H Mazeaud, L Mazeaud and J Mazeaud, *Traité théorique et pratique de la responsabilité civile délictuelle et contractuelle*, t II, 6th edn, (Paris, Montchrestien, 1965) para 694; P Esmein, 'Le fondement de la responsabilité contractuelle' (1933) *Revue trimestrielle de droit civil* 627, 642 and ff.

Can the idea of particular knowledge of the facts justify by itself presuming causation or dispensing the plaintiff from proving it in medical liability?[397] This is a crucial question, especially considering that accepting this justification as the sole ground for a reversal of the burden of proof or a presumption of causation means the judge may relax evidentiary standards according to which party is best equipped to discharge the proof regarding the unknown element, thereby subjecting legal rules to imperatives of proof.[398] Moreover, Motulsky raises an interesting point by finding it shocking that a party may lose a case solely on the basis that proof would have been easier for him, when in reality no proof was possible. He argues further that the notion of 'ease of proof' involves the danger of purely subjective assessment.[399] It is indeed difficult to identify exactly when a party will have sufficient knowledge of the causative information to allow an exception to the usual allocation of risk between the pleaders.

In the specific field of medical negligence, there are formidable obstacles to contending that *better knowledge of the causative facts* should determine who bears the risk of uncertainty.[400] The strongest objection is that grounding a causative finding solely on the fact that the doctor is 'in a better position to observe what occurred' and interpret it from a medical point of view[401] is over-reaching. After all, in most medical cases, imbalance of knowledge is a factor; this fact evacuates the notion of meaning in this area. Doctors always have some degree of control over the causative information during a medical intervention, being best placed to observe what is happening and understand it. The imbalance of knowledge between the parties is exacerbated by the fact that most patients do not have any scientific background.

In addition, any argument based on the appropriateness of obliging defendants to better control risks before acting may be less valuable in medical cases than in cases such as those of pharmaceutical product liability and industrial diseases. The idea of particular knowledge of the causal information runs into fewer objections in cases concerned with risks created or increased for the purpose of deriving profits out of their exploitation, as for example, in cases of environmental pollution caused by an industry or of the marketing of pharmaceutical products or other products which are known or suspected to have adverse consequences on human health, such as cigarettes. In these situations, the necessity of encouraging responsible and thorough inquiries into all the possible negative consequences of

[397] Brun (n 286 above) 380.

[398] X Lagarde, *Réflexion critique sur le droit de la preuve,* t 239 (Paris, LGDJ, 1994) 227 and 232. Lagarde insists that stating that proof must be undertaken by the party who is best placed to do so is equivalent to stating that legal rules may depend on imperatives of proof; R Delisle, D Stuart and D Tanovich, *Evidence: Principles and Problems*, 7th edn, (Toronto, Carswell, 2004) 34–35, in the criminal law context.

[399] Motulsky (n 329 above) 139.

[400] See generally: Devèze (n 329 above) 519.

[401] *Snell v Farrell* (n 1 above) 335–36.

the commercial activity in question is much more compelling then in medical malpractice cases.

By contrast, in medicine, risks are often created and increased, even if negligently, with a view to benefiting patients and more generally society as a whole.[402] Moreover, requiring of medical practitioners perfect control of information about the risks associated with the treatments and procedures they undertake could result in paralysis in the exercise of medicine and the avoidance of treatments which could be beneficial to the patient but involve uncertainty that in normal circumstances is of an acceptable degree.

The idea of justifying a presumption of causation on the basis of the *negligent undermining by the defendant of the plaintiff's means of proof* is more appealing. Such justification should be relied on only if the lack of information created by the defendant is instrumental in preventing the plaintiff from proving causation, however.[403] Under these conditions, we defend it as a valid consideration in *inferring* causation. To reflect the suggested restriction, we address this justification under the title of *negligently created causal uncertainty.*

Grounding inferred causation solely on the negligent creation of uncertainty in the causative evidence is problematic from a purely conceptual point of view, however. It matches hardly any of the requirements of a negligence action. In the current state of medical liability in civil and common law, it is not a fault in itself:

> [I]t is no wrong to another to make it difficult for him to prove a case and, if such a category of wrongdoing were to be introduced, it would constitute an arbitrary form of strict liability, since defendant could often not know in advance whether his conduct was likely in the outcome to present difficulties of proof to a potential victim.[404]

This objection can be responded to by arguing that the concept takes on meaning and weight only where an independent act of negligence on the defendant's part has prevented assessment of causation. If a distinct fault is proven which has the effect of undermining the possibility for the plaintiff of proving causation, the objection dies out. There are several situations in common and civil law in which the defendant doctor may wrongfully impair the plaintiff's means of proving causation as a consequence of an independent act of negligence, for instance the failure to diligently update the patient's records with the relevant information about treatment and its consequences or the omission to carry out relevant and necessary tests which could have clarified what unfolded.[405]

402 This prompts the interesting question of whether the compensation of these risks should be undertaken by the society as a whole through, for example, state compensation funds. This question is, unfortunately, beyond the scope of this work.

403 This condition is suggested by Kouri (n 149 above) 217.

404 Hart and Honoré (n 329 above) 425 criticising *Cook v Lewis* (n 146 above).

405 Eg, *Crits c Sylvester* [1956] OR 132; *aff'd* [1956] SCR 991; *Ostby v Bondar* (1998) 218 AR 132 (QB) 144.

Even though one may link the plaintiff's inability to prove causation to a specific recognised type of medical fault, this leaves a causative problem. These faults often only increase the plaintiff's risk of damage, as where the defendant has not carried out necessary tests. In other cases, for example where a fault was committed in the maintenance of medical records, proving causation between such fault and the plaintiff's damage becomes simply impossible. It is indeed difficult logically to view responsibility for the negligent creation of causal uncertainty as a contributing factor in the occurrence of the final injury.[406] The incorporation of this concept into the causative analysis is thus dubious, unless the head of damage is redefined as the loss of the chance of arguing a successful case in court. Such redefinition, easier to defend in France, would however prompt the objections already expanded on.[407]

Consequently, if negligent responsibility for the causal uncertainty is to be taken into account when assessing causation, then it must be acknowledged that it is not for conceptual reasons but because it provides a policy argument in favour of assisting the plaintiff. As a policy ground, the idea is in fact very interesting.[408] The negligent undermining of the plaintiff's means of proving causation is a pragmatic and rational reason for more readily presuming causation, since, in these cases, the fundamental basis of the traditional rules of proof has been distorted through one party's negligence. Despite the willingness underlying the rules regarding the standard and burden of proof to keep the risk of error to the minimum, the traditional rules of evidence are clearly bound to favour the defendant in every case fraught with factual or scientific uncertainty with regard to the proof of causation. Since allocating the burden of proof mainly involves a choice of who should bear the consequences of uncertain evidence, there is as a matter of policy no objection to forcing the party who has negligently created the absence of causal evidence to bear its consequences.[409] Such argument applies a fortiori to the less radical presumptive stand. There is room to argue that the uncertainty and the risk of judicial error should then be placed on the defendant's shoulders, either by reversing the burden of proof or, preferably, by introducing a presumption of causation.

[406] Eg, Paris 1st B, 7 October 2004, Gaz Pal 6–7 avril 2005.24 (note Guigue); Aix-en-Provence 10th, 13 January 2005 (n 201 above); *Therrien v Launay* (n 4 above) para 477; and above, text to n 201. The impossibility to prove causation is not, as of yet, a recognised head of damage for which a plaintiff can obtain compensation from the defendant. A Porat and A Stein, *Tort Liability under Uncertainty* (Oxford, OUP, 2001) 160 and ff suggest that it should.

[407] And it has been applied in some French cases, eg, Aix-en-Provence 10th, 13 January 2005 (n 201 above). See the distinction between cases where the running of the chance has been halted (classic) and those in which the chance could be taken, as would be the case here: ch 4.

[408] McInnes (n 39 above) 449 supports this approach.

[409] This has the additional advantage of encouraging the party in control of the information to behave more responsibly. Some argue for a reversal of the burden of proof in such circumstances: D Giesen, *International Medical Malpractice Law: A Comparative Law Study of Civil Liability Arising from Medical Care* (Boston, Martinus Nijhoff, 1988) paras 1073–74 and cases cited at fn 53, inspired by the German Federal Supreme Court case law.

This idea is in fact not new. The courts are already prompted by this occurrence to introduce more generous rules of evidence in several jurisdictions[410] and attach legal consequences to the fact that the plaintiff is prevented from proving causation because of the defendant's fault. This element plays a role in the decision to reverse the burden of proof in cases involving indeterminate defendants in Canada and, indirectly through *in solidum* liability, in France and Québec. It is also relied on in diverse sectors of common law, as a rule of law and equity to the effect that if one wrongfully creates an evidentiary difficulty, it is resolved against one.[411] In particular, common law's willingness to resolve evidential uncertainties against the party who has created them can be traced back to 18th century case law, in *Armory v Delamirie* (1722), where the court resolved on this basis uncertainty as to the value of a jewel against the defendant, a goldsmith, who had refused to produce it in evidence.[412] The Supreme Court of Canada has also expressly recognised, in a medical liability context, that the incidence of the ultimate burden of proof can be altered when the underlying rationale for its allocation is absent in a particular case.[413] The negligent creation by the defendant of a causal uncertainty fatal to the plaintiff's case does affect the underlying justification for the existing standard and burdens of proof. It should therefore not only be a weighty consideration in the courts' willingness to adopt a generous attitude towards indirect evidence, but in itself justify drawing a presumption of causation, absent contrary evidence from the defendant.[414] Because of the particularities of the medical liability context already expanded on and the clear rejection in this area of reversal of the burden of proof in cases of uncertainty, a rebuttable presumption grounded on this fact is advocated.

[410] Rogers (n 46 above) 186–87: An inference adverse to the defendants can be drawn where two defendants are sued and the plaintiff's difficulties in proving causation are due to the defendant's failure to call available evidence (no equivalent in the 2002 edition). Eg, the position of the German law: Giesen (n 409 above) 419 and cases cited at fns 32 and 36; 521 and cases cited at fn 51; W Van Gerven, J Lever and P Larouche, *Cases, Materials and Text on National, Supranational and International Tort Law* (Oxford, Hart Publishing, 2000) 460; Fleming (n 25 above) 671.

[411] LD Smith, *The Law of Tracing* (Oxford, Clarendon Press, 1997) 77–78 and cases cited at fns 48–52. This rule allows no finding of contrary evidence in the law of tracing.

[412] (1722) 5 Stra 505, 93 ER 664: The court assessed at its highest value the piece of jewellery in question.

[413] *Snell v Farrell* (n 1 above) 321 citing *National Trust Co v Wong Aviation Ltd* (1969) 3 DLR (3rd) 55; [1969] SCR 481. See especially: 487–89 where the Supreme Court of Canada discusses the possibility of reversing the burden of proof in bailment cases when the bailee is the best placed to explain what happened to the chattel that has disappeared.

[414] To the same effect: Kouri (n 149 above) 240. See also: Porat and Stein (n 406 above) 161 and, generally: 160–206. These authors suggest the introduction in common law of the 'evidential damage doctrine'. This doctrine creates a new form of negligence which holds the defendant liable if his wrongful actions have impaired the plaintiff's ability to establish the facts necessary for him to succeed in his claim or reduced his chances of doing so. It is based on the demonstration that evidential damage constitutes a distinct type of loss: damage to a person's autonomy. The extent of the liability would be equal to the value of the missing information derived statistically from its potential to

D. Suggested Approach

The courts' search for rational legal grounds for presuming causation in cases of uncertainty has failed in many respects. It is hardly acceptable, however, to resign ourselves to living with this conclusion, since it leads back to strict adherence to the traditional rules of evidence, which, in the vast majority of cases fraught with causal uncertainty, frustrate the law's compensatory objectives.

Although the above conclusion puts in jeopardy our contention that inferences and presumptions afford the most acceptable tool for dealing with uncertain causation in medical malpractice, we still maintain it. With the exception of cases which can be amply justified by equity concerns, such as the French HCV/HIV cases, the evaluation of causation should remain a discretionary fact-based exercise allowing the court to take into account the whole of the factual and expert evidence, which may reveal information making the balance shift towards the defendant. For this reason, inferential reasoning is to be generally preferred in medical liability. Moreover, causation depends too heavily on the facts of each case to allow for reliance on strictly framed concepts applied in an automatic manner; generally, this militates against the adoption of all-purpose justifications that prompt automatic presumptions. Underlying this position is the belief that the difficult task of assessing causation in cases of scientific uncertainty must not be avoided by devising doubtful concepts conceived solely to obviate this difficulty. The courts should not shirk their responsibilities, but grapple with these evidential difficulties on their own terms.

The possible impact that factual presumptions can have on the defendant in cases of evidential uncertainty strengthens the argument presented against treating the factors discussed above as determinative of liability (except to the extent conceded). In cases fraught with scientific uncertainty, rebutting a factual presumption of causation becomes a difficult task for the defendant unless he benefits from some special knowledge unavailable to the plaintiff. When the defendant must cope with the same evidential difficulties as the plaintiff, calling upon the former to demonstrate alternative cause ultimately imposes the consequences of evidential uncertainty on him.[415] The drawing of an automatic presumption from scarce evidence may lead in effect to the same consequences as pure reversal of the burden of proof.[416] If this occurs, it should prompt strong objections, since this

establish causation (compare with a similar reasoning adopted by some French courts, above n 407). Though the authors attempt to respond to objections, their idea carries great difficulties, inter alia of causation, foreseeability and evaluation of damages. Moreover, agreeing with this solution would be inconsistent with our argument that one should not adopt a detour through substantive law to address evidential difficulties: Section D below. See also: Porat, *et al* (n 296 above) 697–700.

[415] Jones (1996) (n 18 above) para 5–24 (no equivalent in the 1996 edition).

[416] Implicitly admitted by Sopinka J in *Snell v Farrell* (n 1 above) 335. See also: JG Fleming, *The Law of Torts*, 9th edn, (London, Sweet & Maxwell, 1998) 227.

option has been rejected as a general tool in medical malpractice in the five jurisdictions studied, and we have concluded that no policy consideration is weighty enough to support this solution in this specific area.

Thus, factual inferences need to be primarily based on the judge's weighing of the bulk of the expert and lay evidence in the flexible fashion suggested above. Even though the factual evidence of increase of the pre-existing risk of damage, and creation of a new risk or of a danger have been judged insufficient as isolated justifications for the drawing of a presumption, they can form legitimate considerations, *amongst others,* to take into account in the judge's discretionary assessment of the probative weight of the indirect evidence. For instance, the comparison of the background risk with the risk attributable to the defendant is clearly a relevant consideration and may provide a reliable and weighty clue to put in the presumptive balance. The judge should have the discretion to decide what weight he will give to these factual elements in the light of the whole of the evidence and whether to disregard them altogether, however.

Where the defendant's negligence has prevented the plaintiff from proving causation, one may legitimately go further, however, and argue that, under certain conditions, the negligent creation by the defendant of the causal uncertainty should have determinative weight and justify the implementation of a rebuttable legal inference or, in civil law terms, a judicial presumption. While such a stand will find limited conceptual objections in common law, it is more difficult to justify in civil law as a judicial creation unless a *jurisprudence constante* establishes it.

Besides this last case, we reiterate our insistence on resorting solely to factual inferential reasoning in this area of litigation. True, insisting on one specific intellectual mechanism rather than another may be criticised as artificial in cases of scientific uncertainty. Whether one presumes causation, reverses the burden of proving it, creates a new test of causation, or creates a fiction, the result is exactly the same when the defendant suffers from the same evidential uncertainties as the plaintiff: causation is taken for granted although it cannot be proven by the plaintiff or disproven by the defendant. Where evidence is available to the defendant which the plaintiff has no access to, however, the choice of mechanism will determine how stringent the rule will be for the defendant, and for that reason, the exact nature of the mechanism adopted deserves attention.[417]

[417] The debate as to the nature of the court's intellectual process is of great significance to the topic of the power of review of the appellate courts, a question beyond the scope of this study, however.

Conclusion to Chapter 5

In *Snell v Farrell* (1990), Sopinka J summarises the root of the problems arising in this area of litigation by observing that the dissatisfaction with the traditional approach to causation 'stems to a large extent from its too rigid application by the courts in many cases.'[418] Increased flexibility in the assessment of direct and indirect evidence of causation constitutes in fact a key step towards a solution to causal uncertainty that will not detract from the traditional rules of proof of causation.[419]

The plea for flexibility finds its justification in the fact that, in their practical application in medical malpractice cases fraught with uncertainty, the traditional standards of proof are more burdensome to the plaintiff than the law requires them to be in theory and lead in most cases to the rejection of his claim. As a consequence, in a series of similar cases, the existing rules of evidence have been fatal to the substantive rules of civil liability. In such circumstances, through a more flexible evidential approach, the judicial assessment of causation should account for the additional burden plaintiffs are forced to bear in practice.[420]

In 1950, Decottignies wrote in his famous text on presumptions in private law that '*toute facilité que le législateur accorde dans le domaine de la preuve renforce l'efficacité du droit.*'[421] He was referring to legislative creation of presumptions, but his observation can be transposed to our study. Relaxation of the attitude to direct and indirect evidence of causation and greater and more open reliance on inferential reasoning in order to redress evidential inequalities between the parties is required in this specific area of the law, to ensure rules of extra-contractual and contractual civil liability and of negligence law apply efficiently. It addresses the fact that the rights of plaintiffs are systematically ignored in cases of scientific uncertainty. As Decottignies states, '*Un droit sans preuve est sans intérêt pour son titulaire.*'[422]

418 (N 1 above) 328. See also: Weinrib (n 379 above) 522: problems may stem from a vision that sees them as normative.

419 S Philips-Nootens, 'La perte de chance: détournement du lien de causalité ou dommage distinct?' (1990) 50 *Canadian Bar Review* 611, 615.

420 See also: *Fairchild v Glenhaven* (n 24 above) paras 9 (Lord Bingham) and 62 (Lord Hoffmann).

421 (N 285 above) para 6.

422 *Ibid*, para 6.

Final Analysis and Conclusion

Section 1

General Review

Several decades of theoretical effort have failed to prevent the emergence of practical problems in the demonstration and assessment of causation between medical fault and injury. Courts in England, Australia, Canada, France, and Québec have had to deal with these difficulties with little guidance. Decisions in individual cases have shaped a case law which, although it has established interesting principles, has often lacked coherence and sometimes overlooked the long-term practical consequences of its conceptual creations. The present text has attempted to provide a comprehensive picture of these developments, to situate them in relation to one another, and to test their validity against existing legal principles. The end in view has not been to propose modifications to the existing law of evidence and civil liability in common and civil law, but rather to engage with the problem of causal uncertainty in medical malpractice without violating the existing legal framework of each system. Our premise has been the inadequacy of framing conceptual shortcuts to a desired outcome without directly addressing causative uncertainty. We have thus aimed to provide realistic and immediate assistance in the understanding and treatment of causal uncertainty. It is our hope that we have enhanced the understanding of the problem of uncertain causation and articulated some approaches that will make the exercise of dealing with it less burdensome for courts and parties.

This book has pinpointed strengths and weaknesses in each of the five jurisdictions' judicial responses to causal uncertainty in medical liability. The efforts by each system to balance the desire to compensate plaintiffs with fairness to defendants can serve as a conceptual inspiration or warning to those of the others. The tendency of Québec courts is to remain strictly faithful to the traditional principles of civil liability and evidence law and avoid the liberalism characterising the French judiciary. French courts are expansive in their assessment of causation, show less concern for protecting the medical profession, and more actively pursue compensatory and punitive aims. In its preference for flexibility, Canadian and

Australian jurisprudence diverge from the conservatism of English medical liability, which is closer to the Québec courts' attitude.[1]

In the first chapter, we examined the context in which scientific uncertainties with regard to causation occur, as well as the general rules concerning the assessment of causation in civil law and common law. This brief outline demonstrated that the causal requirement involves difficulties both theoretical and practical. Further, a brief examination of the rules of evidence showed that, applied in an orthodox way, they may lead systematically to refusal of compensation for plaintiffs dealing with causal uncertainties in medical liability cases. The unfairness of this situation has led the judiciaries of England, Australia, common law Canada, Québec, and France to seek solutions within existing legal principles and by devising new tools. An examination of these tools in chapters 3, 4 and 5 showed that, after a few decades of expansive reasoning leading the courts to rely on notions of risk and contribution in order to infer causation, the English courts have returned to a more traditional approach in evaluating causation in medical malpractice cases involving scientific uncertainty, displaying strict attachment to the balance of probabilities rule and seldom resorting to inferential reasoning. Reversal of the burden of proof and loss of chance have not been retained as options in the current English case law on medical liability. Comparatively, Canadian lower courts have shown an expansive tendency in their willingness to rely on the concept of material increase of risk to infer causation even in cases in which the background risk and the increase of risk were difficult to assess. Moreover, the highest Court has proven ready to infer causation on the basis of the defendant's superior knowledge of the causative information and his negligent undermining of the plaintiff's means of proof of causation, an option rarely followed thereafter, however. Reversal of the burden of proof is limited to very specific situations rarely found in typical medical uncertainty cases; and loss of chance has clearly been rejected, the Canadian common law courts considering the civil law judgment in *Laferrière v Lawson* (1991) to be authoritative. Our brief overview of Australian law has also revealed a similar willingness to relax traditional principles, by allowing the loss of chance argument in some lower courts decisions, and not rejecting it straightforwardly in the High Court, despite refusing to apply it in particular cases. Moreover, the technique of inference based on increase of risk has also been noted in this jurisdiction and recognised by the High Court, although rarely applied in medical negligence cases.

Québec is an interesting jurisdiction, both for its historical reluctance to extend causation too far in medical litigation and for the confused state of its Court of Appeal case law. There are very few instances of presumed causation in medical

[1] Aside from the policy-driven decision in *Chester v Afshar* (2004) [2005] 1 AC 134; 3 WLR 927; 4 All ER 587.

liability cases, factual presumptions not being readily drawn and resting on a strict examination of the facts of the case and the expert evidence. Beyond this traditional vision of proof of causation, a few cases are set apart by their willingness, in order to presume causation, to rely on the creation by the defendant of a danger for the plaintiff, the negligent impairment by the defendant of the plaintiff's means of proving causation, or the idea of risk. Québec also presents the distinguishing feature of having taken a clear position on loss of chance, rejecting its application in medical liability. As for France, it stands to one side because of the prominent place it gives to the loss of chance doctrine, an approach that makes it the most generous jurisdiction of the five. French reliance on loss of chance overshadows recourse to reversal of the burden of proof and especially reliance on inferential reasoning in medical malpractice. Nevertheless, through the idea of probability and risk as well as recourse to presumptions by elimination, factual presumptions are also resorted to in France as a way of finding causation proven in cases involving uncertainty. The distinctiveness of the French courts' position in this field is of great interest when paralleled with the Québec developments. Even though these two jurisdictions possess similar rules of *responsabilité civile* and despite the fact that the Québec case law usually considers the French developments in this field of law as authoritative, their development has been completely different with regard to proof of causation in medical liability.[2]

The empirical study conducted in chapters 3, 4, and 5 underlined the varied techniques relied on by the judiciaries of the four jurisdictions in their efforts to provide a rationale for their decisions to assist plaintiffs facing causal uncertainty in medical malpractice. But have their efforts succeeded? This text has addressed this question taking a critical look at the solutions. Having taken a position in favour of inferential reasoning, it has analysed, in chapter 5, the intellectual technique currently relied on by the courts to infer causation and the justifications on which the courts rest the inferences of causation they prove willing to draw.

Section 2

Review of the Critique of the Solutions

The disparities in attempts by the judiciaries of the five jurisdictions under study to devise ways of addressing evidential uncertainty are symptomatic of the need

[2] Although this may be explained by the higher standard of proof applicable in French law, as well as the role of causation as a restrictive tool: See ch 1, text to fn 94 and between fns 147 and 158.

for clarification and critical analysis of the judicial approaches to causal uncertainties. So is the confusion in the definition and application of some of the concepts involved. This text has sought to defend two arguments. First, the solutions developed by the four jurisdictions in dealing with uncertain causation in medical cases are for the most part inadequate for the task. Reversal of the burden of proof and reliance on loss of chance should be rejected. More precisely, reversal of the burden of proof is an unrealistic option for the judiciary in the current state of the law. The courts of all five jurisdictions are currently reluctant to adopt it. In addition, the justifications on which it is based do not find application in medical liability, although the negligent undermining of the plaintiff's means of proving causation is a relevant consideration here. As for loss of chance, it opens the door to overwhelming difficulties which can be avoided by existing adequate alternatives, even in France. Its overreaching impact on the foundations of the law of civil liability and evidence, as well as other conceptual and policy problems it gives rise to, led to its being firmly rejected above.

In light of these critiques, we have defended the view that the solution to this evidential problem is . . . evidential. It lies in the two remaining solutions tackled by the judiciary: reliance on inferences and factual presumptions which takes into account the need for flexibility in cases involving uncertainty. While objecting to a rigid and orthodox approach to causal uncertainty, this text has rejected the French expansive tendencies evinced in the concept of proportional recovery, because of the conceptual difficulties they give rise to and their ultimate overreaching impact on the rules of civil liability. It has also opposed the rigidity of part of the current case law, which leads to almost systematic refusal to compensate the plaintiff in presence of uncertain causation, arguing in favour of a flexible approach. The preferred solution lies between these two extreme positions, and the Supreme Court of Canada case law provides inspiration in this respect. Its advocacy of a more flexible approach to the assessment of evidence of causation is in harmony with the argument defended in chapter 5 that the solution to this evidential problem does not lie in modifying the substantive rules of civil liability or evidence law, or creating new ones to address evidential difficulties, but rather in re-evaluating the way indirect evidence of causation is judicially assessed. Problems introduced by loss of chance and the four jurisdictions' general opposition to the reversal of the burden of proof confirm the validity of this stand. Many of the courts' efforts have thus been misplaced; the real question is how traditional principles of evidence of causation should be applied, *not how they may be departed from.*[3]

[3] To the same effect, but defending a different approach: D Klimchuk and V Black, 'A Comment on *Athey* v *Leonati:* Causation, Damages and Thin Skulls' (1997) 31 *University of British Columbia Law Review* 163, 177.

Section 3

The Alternative–Cumulative Causes Distinction

Before recalling the solution ultimately defended, one must first note that the critical review of the different solutions developed judicially was conducted without regard to the cumulative/alternative causal mechanism distinction.[4] True, the case law reviewed has demonstrated that these categories often play a central role in English common law, in the determination of the rules applicable to cases of uncertain causation, especially in the industrial diseases cases.[5] They have also played a role in some medical liability cases, such as *Snell v Farrell* (1990)[6] and *Wilsher v Essex Area HA* (1988).[7] The distinction between cumulative and alternative processes in fact determines in English law whether the approach adopted is a generous one or one of strict application of the orthodox rules of proof of causation: i) cumulative causation cases merit a plaintiff-friendly approach through application of the material contribution test (*Bonnington*); ii) alternative causation cases must be addressed in the traditional way, even in cases involving uncertainty (*Wilsher*); iii) unknown causal mechanism cases must be addressed in the same way as alternative causation cases. A more lenient approach is warranted where the different possible causes of the damage involve identical risks emanating from only one defendant (*McGhee*) or, in some specific cases, from different possible causes which are all tortious (*Fairchild*).

There are indeed grounds for treating alternative causal processes with prudence. In instances involving cumulative causes, the defendant's act or omission always participates to some degree in the occurrence of the damage. Conversely, in alternative causal mechanisms cases, especially those involving non-tortious alternative causes, the possibility that the plaintiff's actions have not contributed at all to causing the damage clearly and not surprisingly prompts the courts to be more careful before linking them to the whole damage on the basis of a discretionary inference. The much greater risk of condemning an innocent person at least partly justifies treating them more strictly.[8] There are consequently more compelling reasons to show prudence when dealing with alternative cause cases in which non-tortious alternative causes exist: *into this category fall most medical cases involving uncertainty*.[9] Consequently medical liability instances must not be treated lightly.

[4] Ch 1, text between fns 253 and 260.

[5] Eg, *McGhee v National Coal Board* [1973] 1 WLR 1 (HL); *Fairchild v Glenhaven Funeral Services* [2002] 3 All ER 305 (HL) par14 (Lord Bingham).

[6] *Snell v Farrell* (1990) 72 DLR (4th) 222; [1990] 2 SCR 311.

[7] *Wilsher v Essex Area Health Authority* [1988] 1 AC 1074 (HL).

[8] Against: R Meeran, 'Problems of Causation in Environmental Personal Injury' (1992) *Solicitors' Journal* 804, 805.

[9] MA Jones, *Medical Negligence*, 3rd edn, (London, Sweet & Maxwell, 2003) paras 5–38.

The argument above is also seriously flawed, however. In alternative causes cases, while the existence of contribution is itself unknown, the alternative explanations are either 0 per cent contribution or 100 per cent contribution, and thus the defendant's possible contribution is potentially of much greater extent than in cumulative cases. Moreover, the fact that very little (indeed, even non-quantified) contribution is sufficient to meet the material contribution test reduces the factual difference existing between the two mechanisms. If the goal is as far as possible to avoid committing errors, the question is not easily resolved, since the possibility of error is serious in both cases. These same observations apply to unknown mechanisms cases. The possibility of the process being cumulative nevertheless makes these cases better candidates for the court's generosity.

There are other dangers in relying too heavily on this dichotomy, especially given the fact that the distinction may be difficult to draw in practice when causation if fraught with uncertainty.[10] This has been strongly pleaded by Jones:

> It is not entirely clear why the courts should want to make such fine distinctions when dealing with different types of factual uncertainty. It may be pure chance whether a defendant's negligence enhances an existing risk or adds a new risk factor, even if it is possible to distinguish between such risks. In some cases, it may simply be unknown whether an illness is the result of a cumulative effect or of a single event the risk of which has been enhanced by the defendant. In the face of such uncertainty it would seem strange to attach much significance to the distinction between cumulative and discrete causes, although it may be conceded that in practice, if not in logic, it may be easier to infer that 'there must have been some contribution' in cases of cumulative causes and/or the enhancement of a single risk factor.[11]

This position is reinforced by the fact that the distinction has no determinative impact on medical malpractice in the other jurisdictions. Canadian law has avoided the necessity for definitively qualifying the causal process by inferring causation in medical liability on the basis of material increase of risk, which applies equally to both cumulative and alternative causal mechanisms. Moreover, reliance on the defendant's negligent undermining of the plaintiff's means of proof does not necessitate differentiating between these mechanisms.[12] In civil law, the dichotomy also has minimal impact. In the exceptional Québec decisions where the concepts of increase of risk and creation of a danger are relied on to presume causation, the nature of the process involved is not a consideration.[13] The same observation

[10] *McGhee v National Coal Board* (n 5 above); *Bryce v Swan Hunter Group Plc* [1988] 1 All ER 659 (QB); *Fairchild v Glenhaven Funeral Services* (n 5 above).

[11] Jones (n 9 above) para 5-027.

[12] *Cook v Lewis* [1951] 1 DLR 1; [1951] SCR 830 applies solely to alternative tortious causes cases, however.

[13] It is relevant where the alternative causes are all tortious, however: CcQ, Art 1480.

applies to French law where, in addition, loss of chance allows partial recovery without needing to draw distinctions between cumulative and alternative mechanisms. Finally, the case law on HIV and HCV contamination in France gives a good example of the willingness of the French Courts to presume causation in clear cases of alternative causal process. The more willing the courts are to adopt solutions that can apply indistinctively to both processes—such as loss of chance and inferences based on risk, danger, or the negligent undermining of the plaintiff's means of proof—the more the distinction between cumulative and alternative mechanisms loses its relevance. Consequently, because of its uneven impact on the determination of the applicable rules and the fact that the dichotomy may also be affected by uncertainty, the alternative–cumulative causal mechanism distinction has not been granted a central role in the resolution of causal uncertainty in medical malpractice. It is crucial, however, to understand that, when relaxing causation principles, *caution* is especially advisable in cases clearly involving alternative causal processes.

Section 4

Flexibility and the Evidential Solution

The analysis carried out in chapters 2 to 5, especially as regards the Supreme Court of Canada medical malpractice case law of the last 10 years, undergirds our argument that the answer to this question lies in injecting flexibility into the process of assessing the evidence while ensuring respect for the integrity of the current systems; or, in the words of Bénabent, '*[E]ssayer, sans nuire à la sécurité qui doit naître du droit, de dépouiller celui ci d'une rigidité excessive*'[14] Such flexibility can be justified in the area of medical malpractice, especially in cases fraught with scientific uncertainty, by the fact that in this field the standard of proof of causation, although no different in theory, is much more burdensome to the plaintiff in practice. Courts are consequently right to take steps to redress the balance. It may be argued that the difficulty in question is offset by plaintiffs' recourse to expert testimony. In reality, however, the frequency of expert controversy and the difficulties plaintiffs face in finding experts willing to support their theory of causation render this an inadequate means of redressing the balance.

There exists a broad spectrum of options between untrammelled generosity and rigidity, however. The key to dealing with scientific causal uncertainties is found in situating judicial discretion appropriately within this spectrum. One must take

[14] A Bébabent, *La chance et le droit* (Paris, LGDJ, 1973) 203, expressed in a different context.

particular care in carrying out this task because of the special considerations that come into play in the medical context and the potential for infringing patients' interests with excessively severe rules of liability. In chapter 5, we have sought to give flexibility concrete meaning by supplying content to the notion of common sense frequently relied on in medical malpractice. This has led us to argue that flexibility can be deployed in a manner informed by a better understanding of the role of expert evidence in medical litigation and the differences between explanations of causal interactions in science and the law. Moreover, there does not appear to be any theoretical obstacle, however, to resting common law inferences or even civil law factual presumptions on elements other than factual and expert evidence and a strict assessment of the probability of the existence of causation. Both common law and French civil law accept the possibility of systematised presumptive reasoning by resorting to inferences previously drawn in similar situations, when the individual facts of the case support such a conclusion.

Our premise is thus that the problem of uncertain causation can be tackled without fundamental changes to the rules of civil liability and evidence law, favouring instead the flexible use of existing evidential means, inferences, and factual presumptions. The problems specific to the application of these techniques in cases of uncertain causation has however made their careful examination essential.

The courts of the jurisdictions studied have recognised this evidential option, as we saw in chapter 5, and applied it. They have also dealt with the difficulty of engaging in inferential reasoning when the evidence is limited, by devising justifications for presuming causation. Thus our stand in favour of relying on inferential reasoning to address scientific uncertainty has lead inevitably to a critical assessment, not only of the courts' intellectual process when resorting to this means of evidence, but also of the different justifications relied on by the courts to give an appearance of objectivity to their decisions.

In chapter 5, we contended that factual inferences of causation cannot rest solely on concepts such as the unquantified creation of danger or risk or the mere increase of risk. These notions can only have acceptable meaning in medical liability if they form part of the court's discretionary assessment of the whole of the indirect evidence. The assessment of the individual facts of the case should remain the basis of causal inferences, given the importance of personal over abstract causation. The extent of the judge's discretion when inferring elements of fact make it legitimate to give clear weight to these elements, however.

Greater weight must be given to any negligent creation by the defendant of causal uncertainty preventing the plaintiff from proving causation. When this circumstance exists, asking who should bear the consequences of the evidential uncertainty leads inevitably to the answer, *the party who negligently created it*, ie, the defendant. Such technique seeks to pragmatically redress a balance one of the parties has negligently altered. Though it does not fit within any of the conditions of liability, it appears acceptable as a means of preserving the fundamental justification of the rules on the burden and standard of proof. Although we have opted, on this basis, for the drawing of a rebuttable presumption rather than the reversal of the onus of proof, the choice of one or the other approach will not have consequences unless both parties provide equally probable explanations for the cause of the damage.

In adopting the positions summarised above, we seek to protect both parties' interests: the approaches proposed will give plaintiffs much needed assistance. They will also adequately protect the principle of fairness to defendants. They remain to some extent favourable to the defendant physicians, in that they do not solve once and for all the problems of proof and inequality of information plaintiffs have to deal with. Compensatory objectives remain difficult to meet even under this proposal, and the problems plaintiffs face in this area of litigation remain worthy of attention and redress. Despite our advocacy for more flexibility in the assessment of causation and greater and better reliance on inferential reasoning, in most cases, plaintiffs will continue to remain under-compensated when flexibility is difficult to attain, either because the facts of the case are too uncertain to prompt inferences; or because the judge is incapable of affirming his independence from the medical expertises because of the technicality of the matter; or where the uncertainty is not the result of negligence but rather of the limitations of medical science.

Our approach does not solve all problems and it does not claim to do so. Rather, it hopes to prompt reflection and discussion about the relative merits of the different justifications used to ground presumptions of causation and the place that inferential reasoning should take in determining causation in cases involving scientific uncertainty. Raising the different problems the judicial solution of difficulties of proof of causation have led to will hopefully take a step towards the finding of a solution.

Section 5

Alternative Solutions?

One cannot conclude without wondering, at least briefly, whether a legislative solution could overcome the difficulties that remain in spite of the different judicial solutions studied.[15] It is doubtful whether legislative action, taking the form

[15] Eg, JA Bazley and AJA Fitzgerald in *EM Baldwin & Son Pty Ltd v Plane* (1999) Aust Tort Reports 65,621 (NSWCA) 65,623 and 65,650 (mesothelioma case).

of a compulsory first-party insurance, a state compensation fund or a statutory relaxation of the burden or standard of proof of causation, would solve all causation problems.[16] Indeed, the flexibility required by the assessment of causation can hardly be replicated in a statute. Moreover, its inherently fact-based nature may preclude the adoption of an all-purpose rule aimed at solving all instances of causal uncertainty. It is also striking that several statutes seeking to improve victims' compensation possibilities, normally through no-fault compensation schemes, often maintain the causal requirement.[17] Others merely restate solutions or tools that already exist in the law,[18] sometimes reproducing in legislative form rules (and their associated uncertainties) developed by the case law.[19] Introducing general exceptions to traditional causal priniciples in medical liability cases via statute (eg, through a presumption of causation)[20] would bring to the fore a conflict of interests between those who prioritise assisting patients and those who prioritise protecting the medical profession and (public) health care systems. It is thus a complex issue that cannot be readily resolved.

[16] Beyond the difficulties raised above, one may also note that under no-fault compensation schemes, proof of causation is often facilitated by the setting up of a predetermined list connecting certain ailments with their causes, thus limiting the associations possible under the scheme. Moreover, when causal requirements are maintained, administrative bodies may still not be better equipped than courts to make such causal connections: JS Forstrom, 'Victim Without a Cause: The Missing Link Between Compensation and Deterrence in Toxic Tort Litigation' (1987) 18 *Environmental Law* 151, 177 about the Japanese Pollution-related Health Damage Compensation Law of 1973.

[17] Eg, Danish Patient Insurance Act, §1–2: the connection between the injury and the examination, treatment or the like must be shown on a preponderance of evidence; New Zealand Injury Prevention, Rehabilitation, and Compensation Act 2001, §20 [available at www.legislation.co.nz (23 August 2005)]: the claimant must show that injury was caused by an accident within the meaning of §25, which excludes injury caused by a gradual process, disease, or infection that is not work-related (§26). See also: §32 for causal requirements concerning 'treatment injury'; one must prove that the injury was caused by treatment ((1)(b)), which excludes injury caused, *inter alia*, by underlying health conditions ((2)(a)); Sweden's 1996 Patient Tort Act, §6–7 [available at www.lof-forsakring.com/pdf/patient_injury.pdf (23 August 2005)] under which the patient must show with preponderant probability the causal link between the injury and the doctor's conduct; CSP, §L3111-9 (compulsory vaccination): injury must be imputable directly to the vaccination.

[18] Eg, §102 of the Loi du 4 mars 2002 which simply restates the possibility for the plaintiff to prove the link between an HCV infection and a transfusion through factual presumptions; §L1142-1 CSP: although hospitals and clinics may be held liable without fault for nosocomial infections and medical accident, the infections and accidents must be imputable to acts of prevention, diagnostic or health care.

[19] As the recent reforms in Australian law demonstrate: Civil Liability Act 2002 (NSW) §5D and E; Civil Liability Act 2003 (Qld) §11–12; Civil Liability Act 1936 (SA) §34–35; Civil Liability Act 2002 (Tas) §13–14; Civil Liability Act 2002 (WA) §5C and D; Civil Law (Wrongs) Act 2002 (ACT) §45–46; Wrongs Act 1958 (Vic) §51–52 and comments of Kirby J in *Finch v Rogers* (2004) NSWSC 39 (13 February 2004) para 146.

[20] For an interesting example of causal relaxation through statutory action, see the presumption of causation established by the Tobacco Damages and Health Care Costs Recovery Act 2000 of British Columbia, SBC c 30, §3(1).

Final Conclusion

Until a definitive solution to these problems is found, a change of attitude towards the evidence is one step towards a better balancing of the interests of the plaintiff and the defendants in medical malpractice litigation. This can be achieved, as argued, by greater flexibility in the assessment of the lay and expert evidence and in the reliance on inferential reasoning; more articulate justifications, fact based and encompassing careful study of the *whole of the evidence*, which may include giving consideration to negligently caused increase of risk of injury; greater independence *vis-à-vis* scientific evidence; and weightier impact to negligently created causal uncertainty.

The judicial flexibility advocated by this book is informed by a broader perspective, that of a recognition that the human body is not a mechanical whole whose functioning can be accounted for the way a machine can be explained by an engineer. It is still to a great extent a mysterious and unexplained entity over which no one, not even the physician, has perfect control: 'The human body is not a man-made engine. . . . The Greek tragedian Aeschylus addressed the unforeseen predicaments of human frailty in terms of the sport of the gods.'[21]

A precise mechanical explanation for human biological phenomena is impossible and each person's biological identity is unique. To practice flexibility in the assessment of causation is thus also to reflect the fact that mathematical precision does not exist—and perhaps should not be sought—in the present state of knowledge about the human body. The law of medical negligence can and should incorporate into its approach to causation the reality of the holistic and puzzling nature of the human body, the limitations of the scientific explanatory processes, and the inherently uncertain nature of both human health and medical science.

[21] Cited in *Ratcliffe v Plymouth and Torbay Heath Authority* (1998) 42 BMLR 64 (CA) 72.

BIBLIOGRAPHY

Textbooks

General, Comparative and Others

J Ambroziak J and JA Levy, 'Epidemiology, Natural History and Pathogenesis of HIV Infection' in KK Holmes et al eds, *Sexually Transmitted Diseases* (3rd edn, New York, McGraw-Hill, 1999)

JJ Champoux and WL Drew, 'Retrovirus, Human Immunodeficiency Virus and Acquired Immunodeficiency Syndrome' in KJ Ryan ed, *Sherris Medical Microbiology. An Introduction to Infectious Diseases* (3rd edn, Norwalk. Appleton & Lange, 1994)

FR Cleghorn, MS Reitz, M Popovic and RC Gallo, 'Human Immunodeficiency Viruses' in GL Mandell, JE Bennett and R Dolin eds, *Principles and Practice of Infectious Diseases* (6th edn, New York, Churchill Livingstone, 2005)

R David and C Jauffret-Spinosi, *Les grands systèmes de droit contemporains* (10th edn, Paris, Dalloz, 1992)

C Del Rio and JW Curran 'Epidemiology and Prevention of Acquired Immunodeficiency Syndrome and Human Immunodeficiency Virus Infection' in GL Mandell, JE Bennett and R Dolin eds, *Principles and Practice of Infectious Diseases* (6th edn, New York, Churchill Livingstone, 2005)

WL Drew, 'Hepatitis Viruses' in KJ Ryan ed, *Sherris Medical Microbiology. An Introduction to Infectious Diseases* (4th edn, Norwalk, Appleton & Lange, 2004)

D Giesen, *International Medical Malpractice Law: A Comparative Law Study of Civil Liability Arising from Medical Care* (Boston, Martinus Nijhoff, 1988)

S Jasanoff, *Science at the Bar* (Cambridge, Harvard University Press, 1995)

RS Koff, 'Hepatitis C' in SL Gorbach, JG Bartlett and Blacklow NR eds, *Infectious Diseases* (2nd edn, Philadelphia, WB Saunders Company, 1998)

SM Lemon and MJ Alter, 'Viral Hepatitis' in KK Holmes et al, *Sexually Transmitted Diseases* (3rd edn, New York, McGraw-Hill, 1999)

SM Lemon and EA Brown, 'Hepatitis Virus' in GL Mandell, JE Bennett and R Dolin eds, *Principles and Practice of Infectious Diseases* (4th edn, New York, Churchill Livingstone, 1995)

Z Matsuda, JA Hellinger and M Essex, 'Human Immune Deficiency Virus and other Retroviruses' in SL Gorbach, JG Bartlett and NR Blacklow eds, *Infectious Diseases* (3rd edn, Philadelphia, WB Saunders Company, 2004)

MH Merson and P Piot, 'Global Perspectives on Human Immunodeficiency Virus Infection and Acquired Immunodeficiency Syndrome' in GL Mandell, JE Bennett and R Dolin eds, *Principles and Practice of Infectious Diseases* (6th edn, New York, Churchill Livingstone, 2005)

C Müller, *La perte d'une chance* (Berne, Staempfli, 2002)

A Porat and A Stein, *Tort Liability under Uncertainty* (Oxford, OUP, 2001)

WP Keeton ed, *Prosser and Keeton on the Law of Torts* (5th edn, St Paul, West Publishing Co, 1984)

DL Thomas, SC Ray and SM Lemon, 'Hepatitis C' in GL Mandell, JE Bennett and R Dolin eds, *Principles and Practice of Infectious Diseases* (6th edn, New York, Churchill Livingstone, 2005)

WT Tsushima and KK Nakano, *Effective Medical Testifying. A Handbook for Physicians* (Oxford, Butterworths-Heinemann, 1998)

W Van Gerven, J Lever and P Larouche, *Cases, Materials and Text on National, Supranational and International Tort Law* (Oxford, Hart Publishing, 2000)

C Von Bar, *The Common European Law of Torts* vol 1 (Oxford, Clarendon Press, 1998)

JH Wigmore, *Evidence in Trials at Common Law* vol IX (Boston, Little Brown & Co, 1940)

—— *The Science of Judicial Proof* (3rd edn, Boston, Little, Brown & Co, 1937)

K Zweigert and H Kötz (T Weir trans), *Introduction to Comparative Law* (3rd edn, Oxford, Clarendon Press, 1998)

England

T Anderson and W Twining, *Analysis of Evidence. How to do Things with Facts* (London, Weidenfeld and Nicolson, 1991)

R Bagshaw, *Cross and Wilkins: Outline on the Law of Evidence* (7th edn, London, Butterworths, 1996)

PBH Birks, *An Introduction to the Law of Restitution* (Oxford, Clarendon Press, 1989)

M Brazier, *Medicine, Patients and the Law* (3rd edn, Harmondsworth, Penguin, 2003)

P Cane, *Atiyah's Accidents, Compensation and the Law* (5th edn, London, Butterworths, 1993)

—— *Atiyah's Accidents, Compensation and the Law* (6th edn, London, Butterworths, 1999)

D Carey, *Medical Negligence Litigation* (Sutton Coldfield, CLT Professional Publishing, 1998)

JF Clerk, *Clerk & Lindsell on Torts* (16th edn, London, Sweet & Maxwell, 1989–94)

Sir R Cross, *Cross and Tapper on Evidence* (9th edn, London, Butterworths, 1999)

M Davies, *Textbook on Medical Law* (2nd edn, London, Blackstone, 1998)

IH Dennis, *The Law of Evidence* (2nd edn, London, Sweet & Maxwell, 2002)

AM Dugdale and KM Stanton, *Professional Negligence* (3rd edn, London, Butterworths, 1998)

DW Elliott, *Elliott and Phipson on the Law of Evidence* (London, Sweet & Maxwell, 1987)

R Emson, *Evidence* (2nd edn, London, MacMillan, 2004)

D Fairgrieve, *An Anglo-French Comparative Law Study of the Loss of Chance Doctrine in Medical Negligence Cases* (MJur Thesis, University of Oxford, 1997)

JG Fleming, *The Law of Torts* (9th edn, London, Sweet & Maxwell, 1998)

M Freeman and H Reece eds, *Science in Court* (Dartmouth, Ashgate, 1998)
R Goldberg, *Causation and Risk in the Law of Torts* (Oxford, Hart Publishing, 1999)
—— 'The Role of Scientific Evidence in the Assessment of Causation in Medicinal Product Liability Litigation' in H Reece ed, *Law and Science* (Oxford, OUP, 1998) 55
A Grubb and J Laing, *Principles of Medical Law* (2nd edn, Oxford, OUP, 2004)
HLA Hart and T Honoré, *Causation in the Law* (2nd edn, Oxford, Clarendon Press, 1985)
RF Heuston and RA Buckley, *Salmond & Heuston on the Law of Torts* (21st edn London, Sweet & Maxwell, 1996)
AM Honoré, 'Causation and Remoteness of Damage' in A Tunc ed, *International Encyclopedia of Comparative Law* ch 7 vol XI (The Hague, Tübingen, 1971)
MN Howard, R Bagshaw and SL Phipson, *Phipson on Evidence* (15th edn, London, Sweet & Maxwell, 2000)
RM Jackson and JL Powell, *Jackson & Powell on Professional Negligence* 1st suppl (4th edn, London, Sweet & Maxwell, 1998)
RM Jackson and JL Powell, *Jackson & Powell on Professional Negligence* (5th edn, London, Sweet & Maxwell, 2002)
MA Jones, *Textbook on Torts* (7th edn, London, Blackstone, 2000)
—— *Medical Negligence* (3rd edn, London, Sweet & Maxwell, 2003)
A Keane, *The Modern Law of Evidence* (5th edn, London, Butterworths, 2000)
BS Markesinis and SF Deakin, *Tort Law* (4th edn, Oxford, Clarendon Press, 1999)
P Murphy, *Murphy on Evidence* (8th edn, London, Blackstone, 2003)
—— *Evidence & Advocacy* (5th edn, London, Blackstone, 1998)
D Nelken, 'A Just Measure of Science' in M Freeman & H Reece eds, *Science in Court* (Dartmouth, Ashgate, 1998) 11
MJ Powers and NH Harris, *Clinical Negligence* (3rd edn, London, Butterworths, 2000)
H Reece, *Law and Science* (Oxford, OUP, 1998)
WVH Rogers, *Winfield & Jolowicz on Tort* (16th edn, London, Sweet & Maxwell, 2002)
LD Smith, *The Law of Tracing* (Oxford, Clarendon Press, 1997)
J Stapleton, *Disease and the Compensation Debate* (Oxford, Clarendon Press, 1986)
M Stockdale and C McAlhone, *The Elements of Evidence* (3rd edn, Newcastle upon Tyne, Northumbria Law Press, 1997)
C Tapper, *Cross and Taper on Evidence* (10th edn, London, Butterworths, 2004)
S Uglow, *Evidence: Text and Materials* (London, Sweet & Maxwell, 1997)
T Ward, 'Law's Truth, Lay Truth and Medical Science' in H Reece ed, *Law and Science* (Oxford, OUP, 1998) 243
T Weir, 'Loss of a Chance—Compensable in Tort? The Common Law' in O Guillod ed, *Développements récents du droit de la responsabilité civile* (Genève, Centre d'études juridiques européennes, 1991)

Australia

RP Balkin and JLR Davis, *Law of Torts* (3rd edn, Chatswood, NSW, LexisNexis Butterworths, 2004)
P Bayne, *Uniform Evidence Law. Text and Essential Cases* (Leichhardt, NSW, The Federation Press, 2003)
B Bennett, *Law and Medicine* (North Ryde, NSW, LBC Information Services, 1997)

I Callinan, 'Legal Rules Governing the Requirement of Causation in Tort Law' in I Freckelton and D Mendelson eds, *Causation in Law and Medicine* (Hampshire, Ashgate Dartmouth, 2002)

JW Carter and DJ Harland, *Contract Law in Australia* (4th edn, Chatswood, NSW, Butterworths, 2002)

G Edmond and D Mercer, 'Rebels without a Cause? Judges, Medical and Scientific Evidence and the Uses of Causation' in I Freckelton and D Mendelson eds, *Causation in Law and Medicine* (Hampshire, Ashgate Dartmouth, 2002)

I Freckelton and H Selby, *Expert Evidence: Law, Practice, Procedure and Advocacy* (2nd edn, Pyrmont, NSW, Law Book Co, 2002)

I Freckelton and K Petersen, *Controversies in Health Law* (Sydney, The Federation Press, 1999)

J Gans and A Palmer, *Australian Principles of Evidence* (2nd edn, Sydney, Cavendish Publishing Limited, 2004)

JD Heydon, *Cross on Evidence (Australia)* (7th edn, Sydney, Butterworths, 2004)

A Ligertwood, *Australian Evidence* (2nd edn, Sydney, Butterworths, 1993)

H Luntz, 'Loss of Chance' in I Freckelton and D Mendelson eds, *Causation in Law and Medicine* (Hampshire, Ashgate Dartmouth, 2002)

PJM MacFarlane, *Health Law in Australia & New Zealand* (Sydney, The Federation Press, 2000)

J Stapleton, 'Scientific and Legal Approaches to Causation' in I Freckelton and D Mendelson eds, *Causation in Law and Medicine* (Hampshire, Ashgate Dartmouth, 2002)

F Trindade and P Cane, *The Law of Torts in Australia* (3rd edn, Victoria, OUP, 1999)

M Wallace, *Health Care and the Law* (3rd edn, Pyrmont NSW, Lawbook Co, 2001)

Canada

JA Campion and DW Dimmer, *Professional Liability in Canada* (looseleaf, Toronto, Carswell, 1998)

R Delisle, D Stuart and D Tanovich, *Evidence: Principles and Problems* (7th edn, Toronto, Carswell, 2004)

GHL Fridman, *The Law of Torts in Canada,* vol 1 (Toronto, Carswell, 1989)

—— *The Law of Contract in Canada* (4th edn, Scarborough, Carswell, 1999)

L Klar, *Tort Law* (3rd edn, Scarborough, Carswell, 2003)

AM Linden, *Canadian Tort Law* (7th edn, Markham, Butterworths, 2001)

AM Linden and LN Klar, *Canadian Tort Law. Cases, Notes & Materials* (11th edn, Toronto, Butterworths, 1999)

PH Osborne, *The Law of Torts* (Toronto, Irwin Law, 2000)

EI Picard, *Legal Liability of Doctors and Hospitals in Canada* (2rd edn, Toronto, Carswell, 1984)

EI Picard and GD Robertson, *Legal Liability of Doctors and Hospitals in Canada* (3rd edn, Scarborough, Carswell, 1996)

J Sopinka, SN Lederman and AW Bryant, *The Law of Evidence in Canada* (2nd edn, Toronto, Butterworths, 1999)

France

G Aron, *Théorie générale des présomptions légales en droit privé* (Paris, Pedone, 1895)
R Barraine, *Théorie générale des présomptions en droit privé* (Paris, LGDJ, 1942)
J Bell, S Boyron and S Whittaker, *Principles of French Law* (Oxford, OUP, 1998)
A Bénabent, *Droit civil. Les obligations* (4th edn, Paris, Montchrestien, 1999)
—— *La chance et le droit* (Paris, LGDJ, 1973)
W Bobleter, *Le lien de causalité entre un traumatisme et ses conséquences corporelles probables* (Paris, Mémoire DESS, Paris II Assas, 1990)
G Bourgeois, P Julien and M Zavaro, *La pratique de l'expertise judiciaire* (Paris, Litec, 1999)
G Boyer-Chammard and P Monzein, *La responsabilité médicale* (Paris, PUF, 1974)
P Brun, *Les présomptions dans le droit de la responsabilité civile* (Grenoble, Thèse de doctorat, Université de Grenoble II, 1993)
J Carbonnier, *Droit civil. Introduction* (27th edn, Paris, PUF, 2002)
—— *Droit civil. 4) Les obligations* (22nd edn, Paris, PUF, 2000)
D Chabanol, *La pratique du contentieux administratif* (5th edn, Paris, Litec, 2003)
F Chabas, *L'influence de la pluralité des causes sur le droit à la réparation* (Paris, LGDJ, 1967)
—— 'La perte d'une chance en droit français' in O Guillod ed, *Développements récents du droit de la responsabilité civile* (Genève, Centre d'études juridiques européennes, 1991) 131
R Chapus, *Droit du contentieux administratif* (11th edn, Paris, Montchrestien, 2004)
P Conte and P Maistre du Chambon, *La responsabilité civile délictuelle* Coll Le Droit en Plus (Grenoble, Presses universitaires de Grenoble, 1994)
R Decottignies, *Les présomptions en droit privé* (Paris, LGDJ, 1950)
M Deguergue, 'Causalité et imputabilité' in *Jurisclasseur administratif*, Fasc 830 (Paris, Éditions techniques, 2000)
R Demogue, *Notions fondamentales de droit privé* (Paris, A Rousseau, 1911)
J Devèze, *Contribution à l'étude de la charge de la preuve en matière civile* (thesis, Université des sciences sociales de Grenoble, 1980)
G Duflo, *La responsabilité des médecins à la lumière de la jurisprudence récente* (Paris, Domat-Montchrestien, 1937)
J Dupichot and D Guével, *Contrats et obligations. Présomptions* Fasc 155, Jurisclasseur civil 1349–1353 (Paris, Éditions techniques, 1997)
J Favier, *La relation de cause à effet dans la responsabilité quasi délictuelle* (thèse de doctorat, Université de Paris, 1951)
J Flour and JL Aubert, *Droit civil. Les obligations. 2) Le fait juridique* (Paris, Armand Colin, 1997)
M Garnier, V, J and T Delemarre, *Dictionnaire des termes de médecine* (24th edn, Paris, Maloine, 1995)
F Gény, *Science et technique en droit privé positif*, t III (Paris, Sirey, 1921)
J Ghestin and G Goubeaux, *Traité de droit civil. Introduction générale* (3rd edn, Paris, LGDJ, 1990)
P Jourdain, *Droit à réparation. Lien de causalité* Fasc 160, Jurisclasseur civil (Paris, Éditions techniques, 1993)

X Lagarde, *Réflexion critique sur le droit de la preuve,* t 239 (Paris, LGDJ, 1994)
H Lalou, *Traité pratique de la responsabilité civile* (6th edn, Paris, Dalloz, 1962)
L Larombière, *Traité et pratique des obligations,* t 5 (Paris, Durand, 1857)
C Larroumet, *Droit civil. Les obligations, le contrat,* t III (5th edn, Paris, Economica, 2003)
R Legeais, *Les règles de preuve en droit civil* (Paris, LGDJ, 1955)
P le Tourneau and L Cadiet, *Droit de la responsabilité civile* (Paris, Dalloz, 1998)
M Lombard et G Dumont, *Droit administratif* (Paris, Dalloz, 2003)
G Marty and P Raynaud, *Droit civil: Introduction générale à l'étude du droit,* t I (2nd edn, Paris, Sirey, 1972)
H, L and J Mazeaud, *Traité théorique et pratique de la responsabilité civile délictuelle et contractuelle,* t II (6th edn, Paris, Montchrestien, 1965)
G Mémeteau, *Le droit médical* (Paris, Litec, 1985)
—— *La responsabilité civile médicale en droit comparé français et québécois* (Montréal, CRDPCQ, 1990)
J Normand, *Le juge et le litige* (Paris, LGDJ, 1965)
H Motulsky, *Principes d'une réalisation méthodique du droit privé* (Paris, Sirey, 1948)
J Penneau, *La responsabilité médicale* (Paris, Sirey, 1977)
—— *Faute et erreur en matière de responsabilité médicale* (Paris, LGDJ 1973)
M Planiol and G Ripert, *Traité pratique de droit civil français. Les obligations* t6 (Paris, LGDJ, 1925–34)
RJ Pothier, *Traité des obligations* (Paris, Libr. de l'oeuvre de Saint-Paul, 1883)
C Potier, *Les présomptions de causalité* (Mémoire DEA, Paris I Panthéon Sorbonne, 1996)
G Ripert and J Boulanger, *Traité de droit civil* t II (Paris, LGDJ, 1957)
J Rivero et J Waline, *Droit administratif* (19th edn, Paris, Dalloz, 2002)
R Rodière, *La responsabilité délictuelle dans la jurisprudence* (Paris, Librairies Techniques, 1978)
R Savatier, J Savatier, JM Auby and H Pequignot, *Traité de droit médical* (Paris, Librairies Techniques, 1956)
G Schamps, *La mise en danger: un concept fondateur d'un principe général de responsabilité* (Paris, LGDJ, 1998)
B Starck, *Droit civil. Les obligations* (Paris, Librairies techniques, 1972)
B Starck, H Roland and L Boyer, *Introduction au droit* (5th edn, Paris, Litec, 2000)
——, H *Obligations. 1) La responsabilité délictuelle* (5th edn, Paris, Litec, 1996)
D Veaux, *Contrats et obligations (Preuve)* Fasc 133 (Fasc 10), Jurisclasseur civil 1271–1381 (Paris, Éditions techniques, 1997)
J Vincent and S Guinchard, *Procédure civile* (27th edn, Paris, Dalloz, 2003)
G Viney (J Ghestin, dir), *Traité de droit civil. Les obligations. La responsabilité: conditions* (Paris, LGDJ, 1982)
G Viney and P Jourdain (J Ghestin, dir), *Traité de droit civil. Les conditions de la responsabilité* (2nd edn, Paris, LGDJ, 1998)
G Viney and B Markesinis, *La réparation du dommage corporel. Essai de comparaison des droits anglais et français* (Paris, Economica, 1985)

Québec

J-L Baudouin and P Deslauriers, *La responsabilité civile* (6th edn, Cowansville, Yvon Blais, 2003)

J-L Baudouin, 'The Impact of the Common Law on the Civilian Systems of Louisiana and Quebec' in J Dainow ed, *The Role of Judicial Decisions and Doctrine in Civil Law and in Mixed Jurisdictions* (Baton Rouge, Louisiana State Univ Press, 1974)

L Baudouin, *Le droit civil de la province de Québec; Modèle vivant de droit comparé* (Montréal, Wilson & Lafleur, 1953)

A Bernardot and RP Kouri, *La responsabilité civile médicale* (Sherbrooke, RDUS, 1980)

P-A Crépeau, *L'intensité de l'obligation juridique ou des obligations de diligence, de résultat et de garantie* (Montréal, Yvon Blais, 1989)

—— *La responsabilité civile du médecin et de l'établissement hospitalier* (Montréal, Wilson & Lafleur, 1956)

L Ducharme, *Précis de la preuve* (5th edn, Montréal, Wilson & Lafleur, 1996)

S Gaudet, 'L'application de la notion de perte de chance en droit médical' (Paper presented at the ICAJ's Conference: *Responsabilité médicale et hospitalière. Aspects juridiques et éthiques,* Montréal, October 1990)

D Jutras, 'Expertise médicale et causalité' in *Congrès annuel du Barreau du Québec* (Montréal, SFPBQ, 1992) 897

H Kélada, *Notions et techniques de preuve civile* (Montréal, Wilson & Lafleur, 1986)

L Khoury, 'L'incertitude scientifique en matière civile et la preuve d'expert', in P Patenaude, (dir), *L'interaction entre le droit et les sciences experimentales:* Actes du colloque, 15 May 2001 (Sherbrooke, RDUS, 2001).

C Larroumet, *Réflexions sur la responsabilité civile. Évolution et problèmes actuels en droit comparé* (Montréal, Institut de droit comparé, Université McGill, 1983)

P Lesage-Jarjoura and S Philips-Nootens, *Éléments de responsabilité médicale. Le droit dans le quotidien de la médecine* (Cowansville, Yvon Blais, 2000)

Y-M Morissette, 'L'influence du droit français sur le droit de la preuve au Québec' in HP Glenn ed, *Droit québécois et droit français: communauté, autonomie, concordance* (Cowansville, Yvon Blais, 1993) 423

A Nadeau and R Nadeau, *Traité pratique de la responsabilité civile délictuelle* (Montréal, Wilson & Lafleur, 1971)

Office de révision du Code civil, PA Crépeau (Chair) *Rapport sur le Code civil du Québec* vol I (Québec, Éditeur officiel, 1978)

Québec, Ministère de la Justice *Commentaires du ministre de la Justice: Le Code civil du Québec* t I (Québec, Publications du Québec, 1993)

J Pineau and M Ouellette, *Théorie de la responsabilité civile* (2nd edn, Montréal, Thémis, 1980)

J-C Royer, *La preuve civile* (3rd edn, Cowansville, Yvon Blais, 2003)

M Tancelin, *Des obligations. L'acte illégitime et les modes d'exécution* (Montréal, Wilson & Lafleur, 1993)

FP Walton, *Le domaine et l'interprétation du Code civil du Bas-Canada* trad M Tancelin (Toronto, Butterworths, 1980)

Reports

Ipp Report: DA Ipp, Commonwealth of Australia, *Review of the Law of Negligence, Final Report* (Canberra, September 2002)

Great Britain, *Report: Royal Commission on Civil Liability and Compensation for Personal Injury (The Pearson Report)* Cmdn 7054 (London, Her Majesty's Stationery Office, 1978)

South Australian Law Reform Committee, *87th Report Relating to Claims for Injuries from Toxic Substances and Radiation Effects*, No 87 (1985)

Periodicals

United Kingdom

S Arnell, 'Causation Reassessed' (2002) *Scots Law Times* 265

P Atiyah, '*Res Ipsa Loquitur* in England and Australia' (1972) 35 *MLR* 337

A Boon, 'Causation and the Increase of Risk' (1988) 51 *MLR* 508

S Chapman, 'Apportionment of Liability between Tortfeasors' (1948) 64 *LQR* 26

W Coley, 'Asbestos Claims' (2003) *Journal of Personal Injury Law* 15

F Cownie, 'Medical Negligence—A Question of Policy?' (1987) *Professional Negligence* 95

C Feeny, P Laleng and D Cooper, 'Mesothelioma, Asbestos and Causation' (2003) *Journal of Personal Injury Law* 1

JS Forstrom, 'Victim Without a Cause: The Missing Link Between Compensation and Deterrence in Toxic Tort Litigation' (1987) 18 *Environmental Law* 151

C Foster, 'Last Chance for Lost Chances' (2005) *New Law Journal* 248

D Gerecke, 'Risk Exposure as Injury: Alleviating the Injustice of Tort Causation Rules' (1990) *McGill Law Journal* 797

R Goldberg, 'The Contraceptive Pill, Negligence and Causation: Views on Vadera v. Shaw' (2000) 8 *Medical Law Review* 316

S Green, 'Winner Takes All' (2004) 120 *LQR* 566

T Hill, 'A Lost Chance for Compensation in the Tort of Negligence by the House of Lords' (1991) 54 *MLR* 511

—— 'Lost Chances in Contract and Delict' (1997) *Scots Law Times* 71

—— 'The Raising of Lazarus: The Resurrection of *McGhee v National Coal Board*' (2003) *Edinburgh Law Review* 80

Lord Hope of Craighead, 'James McGhee—A Second Mrs. Donoghue?' (2003) 62 *CLR* 587

N Jansen, 'The Idea of a Lost Chance' (1999) 19 *OJLS* 271

A Layard, 'Toxic Torts—A Landmark Decision' (2002) 4.4 *Environmental Law Review* 241

S Lloyd-Bostock, 'The Ordinary Man, and the Psychology of Attributing Causes and Responsibility' (1979) 42 *MLR* 143

M Lunney, 'Chances of Recovery in Tort: *Allied Maple Group v Simmons & Simmons*' (1996–7) 7 *King's College Law Journal* 101

BS Markesinis, 'La politique jurisprudentielle et la réparation du préjudice économique en Angleterre: une approche comparative' (1983) *Revue internationale de droit comparé* 31

R Meeran, 'Problems of Causation in Environmental Personal Injury' (1992) 136 *Solicitors' Journal* 804
C Miller, 'Coal Dust, Causation and Common Sense' (2000) 63 *MLR* 763
E Peel, 'Loss of a Chance' Revisited: *Gregg v Scott*' (2003) 66 *MLR* 623
A Porat, A Stein and SM Cohen, 'Indeterminate Causation of Damages: An Essay on Holtby, Allen, and Fairchild' (2003) 23 *OJLS* 667
H Reece, 'Losses of Chances in the Law' (1996) 59 *MLR* 188
W Scott, 'Causation and Material Contribution' (1999) *Health Care Risk Reports* 12
—— 'Causation in Medico-legal Practice: The Lost Opportunity Cases' (1998) *Health Care Risk Reports* 6
—— 'Causation in Medico-Legal Practice: A Doctor's Approach to the "Lost Opportunity Cases" (1992) 55 *MLR* 521
J Stapleton, 'Law, Causation and Common Sense' (1988) 8 *OJLS* 111
J Stapleton, 'The Gist of Negligence. Part II: The Relationship Between "Damage" and "Causation"' (1988) 104 *LQR* 389
J Stapleton, 'Cause-in-Fact and the Scope of Liability for Consequences' (2003) 119 *LQR* 388
M Stauch, 'Causation, Risk and Loss of Chance in Medical Negligence' (1997) 17 *OJLS* 205
G Vos, 'Linking Chains of Causation: An Examination of New Approaches to Causation in Equity and the Common Law' (2001) 60 *CLJ* 337
EJ Weinrib, 'A Step Forward in Factual Causation' (1975) 38 *MLR* 518
G Williams, 'Causation in the Law' (1961) *CLJ* 62
JM Williams, 'Variant Creutzfeldt Jakob Disease: Setting Up the vCJD Trust—Operations and Lessons for the Future' (2004) 1 *Journal of Personal Injury Law* 39

Australia

SS Clark and R McInnes, 'Unprecedented Reform: The New Tort Law' (2004) 15 *Insurance Law Journal* 1
I Freckelton, 'Editorial' (1999) 7 *Journal of Law and Medicine* 5
J Gunson, 'Turbulent Causal Waters: The High Court, Causation and Medical Negligence' (2001) *Tort Law Review* 53
D Hamer, 'Chance Would Be a Fine Thing: Proof of Causation and Quantum in an Unpredictable World' (1999) 23 *Melbourne University Law Review* 557
T Honoré, 'Medical Non-Disclosure, Causation and Risk: *Chappel v Hart*' (1999) 7 *Torts Law Journal* 1
D Ipp, 'Negligence. Where Lies the Future?' (2003) 23 *Australian Bar Review* 158
H Luntz, 'Turning Points in the Law of Torts in the Last 30 Years' (2003) 15 *Insurance Law Journal* 1
G Masel, 'Damages in Tort for Loss of Chance' (1995) *Torts Law Journal* 1
R Mulheron and J Gordon, 'Juries, Medical Negligence and Causation in the High Court of Australia' (2000) *Tort Law Review* 19
NJ Mullany, 'Common Sense Causation—an Australian View' (1992) 12 *OJLS* 431
J Stapleton, 'Lords a'Leaping Evidentiary Gaps' (2002) 10 *Torts Law Journal* 276
—— 'The Golden Thread at the Heart of Tort Law: Protection of the Vulnerable' (2003) 24 *Australian Bar Review* 1

R Travers, 'Medical Causation' (2002) 76 *Australian Law Journal* 258
SM Waddams, 'Damages: Assessment of Uncertainties' (1998) 13 *Journal of Contract Law* 1

Canada

JB Archibald, 'Proof of Causation Revisited: *Snell v Farrell*' (1991) 1 *Journal of Environmental Law and Practice* 227
A Beever, 'Cause-in-Fact: Two Steps out of the Mire' (2001) 51 *University of Toronto Law Review* 327
D Cheifetz, 'Materially Increasing the Risk of Injury as Factual Cause of Injury: *Fairchild v Glenhaven Funeral Services Ltd* in Canada' (2004) 29 *Advocates' Quarterly* 253
G Demeyere, 'The "Material Contribution" Test: An Immaterial Contribution to Tort Law: A Comment on *Briglio v Faulkner*' (2000) 34 *University of British Columbia Law Journal* 317
BM Dickens, 'Justice, Compensation and Hepatitis C' (2000) 18 *Windsor Yearbook of Access of Justice* 226
JG Fleming, 'Probabilistic Causation in Tort Law' (1989) 68 *Canadian Bar Review* 661
D Gerecke, 'Risk Exposure as Injury: Alleviating the Injustice of Tort Causation Rules' (1990) 35 *McGill Law Journal* 797
D Klimchuk and V Black, 'A Comment on *Athey v Leonati:* Causation, Damages and Thin Skulls' (1997) 31 *University of British Columbia Law Review* 163
M McInnes, 'Causation in Tort Law: A Decade at the Supreme Court of Canada' (2000) 63 *Saskatchewan Law Review* 445
—— 'Causation in Tort Law: Back to Basics in the Supreme Court of Canada' (1997) 35 *Alberta Law Review* 1013
L-J Neoh, 'A Comment on *Walker Estate v York-Finch General Hospital*' (2000) 23 *Advocates' Quarterly* 370
B Pardy, 'Risk, Cause and Toxic Torts: A Theory for a Standard of Proof' (1989) 10 *Advocates' Quarterly* 277
G Robertson, 'Overcoming the Causation Hurdle in Informed Consent Cases: the Principle in *McGhee v NCB*' (1984) 22 *University of Western Ontario Law Review* 75
MA Ross, 'Rules of the Road to Judgment in Medical Malpractice Cases: Standard of Care and Causation' (1998) 20 *Advocates' Quarterly* 274
R Roth, 'Causation and the Burden of Proof. An Age Old Dilemma and a New Age Approach' (1992) 14 *Advocates' Quarterly* 70
TS Woods, 'Establishing Causation in Negligence: The House of Lords Speaks Again' (2003) 26 *Advocates' Quarterly* 471

France

H Aberkane, 'Du dommage causé par une personne indéterminée dans un groupe déterminé de personnes' (1958) *Revue trimestrielle de droit civil* 516
J-L Aubert, 'Responsabilité civile. Dommage. Perte d'une chance. Aggravation du préjudice. Réparation complémentaire' (1990) *Répertoire du Notariat Defrénois* 746
JS Bergé, 'Risque et faute dans la contamination transfusionnelle' *Gazette du Palais* 1996.doct.737

J Boré, 'L'indemnisation pour les chances perdues: une forme d'appréciation quantitative de la causalité d'un fait dommageable' *La semaine juridique* 1974.I.2620

F Bouvier, 'La responsabilité médicale' *Gazette du Palais* 1984.doct.284

F Chabas, 'Vers un changement de nature de l'obligation médicale' *La semaine juridique* 1973.I.2541

A Charaf Eldine, 'La théorie de la perte d'une chance sanitaire (devant la Cour de cassation et le Conseil d'État)' (1983) 19 *Revue trimestrielle de droit sanitaire et social* 48

F Descorps Declère, 'La cohérence de la jurisprudence de la Cour de cassation sur la perte de chance consécutive à une faute du médecin' *Dalloz* 2005.742

L Dubouis, 'Perte de chances de survie. Médecin omettant de pratiquer un traitement adéquat. Absence de responsabilité pénale et civile' (1976) *Revue trimestrielle de droit sanitaire et social* 43

—— 'Perte d'une chance de survie. Indemnisation' (1971) *Revue trimestrielle de droit sanitaire et social* 66

G Durry, 'Sur un probable revirement de jurisprudence en matière de réparation de la perte d'une chance de guérison ou de survie' (1983) *Revue trimestrielle de droit civil* 547

—— 'Faute médicale et perte de chances de survie' (1972) *Revue trimestrielle de droit civil* 408

—— 'Jurisprudence française en matière de droit civil' (1971) *Revue trimestrielle de droit civil* 377

—— 'La faute du médecin diminuant les "chances de guérison" du malade' (1969) *Revue trimestrielle de droit civil* 797

—— 'La faute du médecin diminuant les "chances de guérison" du malade' (1967) *Revue trimestrielle de droit civil* 181

P Esmein, 'Le nez de Cléopâtre ou les affres de la causalité' *Dalloz* 1964.chr.33

—— 'Le fondement de la responsabilité contractuelle' (1933) *Revue trimestrielle de droit civil* 627

B Gimbert, 'Responsabilité médicale et transfusion sanguine' (1998) 27 *Petites Affiches* 10

J Huet, 'Perte d'une chance: du plus ou moins classique' (1986) *Revue trimestrielle de droit civil* 117

D Jacotot, 'Vers la généralisation de l'obligation de sécurité dans le domaine de la responsabilité médicale' (1997) *Petites Affiches* 25

P Jourdain, 'Imputabilité d'une contamination virale à une transfusion sanguine: la preuve par exclusion du lien de causalité érigée en présomption de droit' (2001) *Revue trimestrielle de droit civil* 889

—— 'Sur la perte d'une chance' (1992) *Revue trimestrielle de droit civil* 109

—— 'Responsabilité civile et contamination par le virus du SIDA à la suite de transfusions' (1992) *Revue trimestrielle de droit civil* 117

—— 'Responsabilité civile. Conditions de la responsabilité' (1989) *Revue trimestrielle de droit civil* 81

X Lagarde, 'Finalités et principes du droit de la preuve' *La semaine juridique* 2005.G.771

Y Lambert-Faivre, 'L'hépatite C post-transfusionnelle et la responsabilité civile' *Dalloz* 1993.chr.291

C Larroumet, 'L'indemnisation de l'aléa thérapeutique' *Dalloz* 1999.chr.33

M Lebeau, 'Responsabilité et contamination post-transfusionnelles' *Gazette du Palais* 1999.doct.880

B Legros, 'État des lieux sur les différents régimes d'indemnisation des conséquences des accidents médicaux' (2004) *Médecine et droit* 1

P Leroy, 'Le juge judiciaire et le lien de causalité médicale' (1994) 90 *Petites Affiches* 19

N Lesourd, 'La perte d'une chance' *Gazette du Palais* 1963.2.doctr.49

P L'Épée, 'Problèmes médico-légaux soulevés par le SIDA' *Gazette du Palais* 1991.2.doctr.575

X-Y Li-Kotovtchikhine, 'Le certain en droit civil' (1999) 133 *Petites Affiches* 12

H Margeat, 'Sang et droit. L'indemnisation des victimes' *Gazette du Palais* 1993.977

H Margeat, 'Séroposivité, sida et jurisprudence' *Gazette du Palais* 1991.580

G Marty, 'La relation de cause à effet comme condition de la responsabilité' (1939) *Revue trimestrielle de droit civil* 685

F Maury, 'Victimes du VHB (vaccin contre l'hépatite B): Faut-il attendre une certitude scientifique pour les indemniser?' (2004) *Médecine et droit* 125

D Mayer, 'La "garde" en commun' (1975) *Revue trimestrielle de droit civil* 197

G Mémeteau, 'Perte de chance en droit médical français' (1986) 32 *McGill Law Journal* 125

G Mémeteau, 'Perte de chance et responsabilité médicale' *Gazette du Palais* 1997.1367

P Mimin, 'Les présomptions quasi-légales' *La semaine juridique* 1946.I.578

M-L Morançais-Demeester, 'Contamination par transfusion du virus du sida: responsabilités et indemnisation' *Dalloz* 1992.chr.189

C Müller, 'La perte d'une chance médicale en droit comparé et suisse' (2003) 9 *Revue générale de droit médical* 105

L Neyret, 'Vaccination contre l'hépatite B: fin de débat judiciaire?' *Dalloz* 2003.2579

L Pitet, 'Responsabilité du fait des produits: sagesse et force du lien de causalité' *Gazette du Palais* 2004.doctr.869

IE Postacioglu, 'Faits simultanés et le problème de la responsabilité collective' (1954) 52 *Revue trimestrielle de droit civil* 438

V Rebeyrol, 'Les effets secondaires des médicaments et la responsabilité des laboratoires producteurs' (2005) 137 *Petites Affiches* 16

R Savatier, 'La responsabilité médicale en France (Aspects de droit privé)' (1976) *Revue internationale de droit comparé* 493

—— 'Le droit des chances et des risques dans les assurances, la responsabilité civile dans la médecine et sa synthèse dans l'assurance de responsabilité médicale' (1973) 44 *Revue générale des assurances terrestres* 457

—— 'Une faute peut-elle engendrer la responsabilité d'un dommage sans l'avoir causé?' *Dalloz* 1970.chr.123

B Starck, 'La pluralité des causes de dommage et la responsabilité civile. La vie brève d'une fausse équation: causalité partielle = responsabilité partielle' *La semaine juridique* 1970.I.2339

V Tacchini-Laforest, 'Réflexions à propos de la perte de chances' (1999) 142 *Petites Affiches* 7

A Tunc, 'Perte d'une chance de guérison par suite d'une erreur de diagnostic' (1963) *Revue trimestrielle de droit civil* 334

I Vacarie, 'La perte d'une chance' (1987) 3 *Revue de la recherche juridique* 903

P and F Vayre, 'Le médecin expert judiciaire. Mission pour responsabilité professionnelle' *Gazette du Palais* 2001.doctr.425

G Viney, 'Chronique Responsabilité civile' *La semaine juridique* 1992.G.I.501

Québec

D-A Bellemare, 'L'homme de science devant les tribunaux' (1977) 37 *Canadian Bar Review* 465

A Bernardot, 'Le médecin et les présomptions de fait' (1971) 2 *Revue de droit de l'Université de Sherbrooke* 75

P-A Crépeau, 'La responsabilité civile du médecin' (1977) 8 *Revue de droit de l'Université de Sherbrooke* 25

—— 'La responsabilité médicale et hospitalière dans la jurisprudence québécoise récente' (1960) 20 *Revue du Barreau* 433

P Deschamps, 'L'obligation de moyens en matière de responsabilité médicale' (1991) *Assurances* 575

P Deslauriers and S-E Chebin, 'Perspectives québécoises sur la responsabilité médicale' (1999) 101 *Revue du Notariat* 299

CC Emanuelli, 'Le droit comparé selon une perspective canadienne' (1980) 40 *Revue du Barreau* 75

CD Gonthier, 'Chronique. Le témoignage d'experts: à la frontière de la science et du droit' (1993) 53 *Canadian Bar Review* 187

M Guy, 'Le Code Civil du Québec: Un peu d'histoire, beaucoup d'espoir' (1993) 23 *Revue de droit de l'Université de Sherbrooke* 453

D Jutras, 'Réflexions sur la réforme de la responsabilité médicale au Québec' (1990) 31 *Cahiers de droit* 821

RP Kouri, 'From Presumptions of Fact to Presumptions of Causation: Reflections on the Perils of Judge-made Rules in Québec Medical Malpractice Law' (2001) 32 *Revue de droit de l'Université de Sherbrooke* 213

K Lippel, 'L'incertitude des probabilités en droit et en médecine' (1991-2) 22 *Revue de droit de l'Université de Sherbrooke* 445

K Lippel, K Messing, S Stock and N Vézina, 'La preuve de la causalité et l'indemnisation des lésions attribuables au travail répétitif: rencontre des sciences de la santé et du droit' (1999) 17 *Windsor Year Book Access Justice* 35

AT Mécs, 'Medical Liability and the Burden of Proof' (1970) 16 *McGill Law Journal* 163

S Philips-Nootens, 'La perte de chance: détournement du lien de causalité ou dommage distinct?' (1990) 50 *Canadian Bar Review* 611

I Parizeau, 'Le lien de causalité ... au bord du gouffre' (1989) 49 *Canadian Bar Review* 514

JJM Shore et M Vardy, 'Obligation de l'État d'aider financièrement les personnes atteintes du VIH par suite d'une transfusion de sang ou de dérivé sanguin' (1990) 31 *Cahiers de droit* 871

OS Tyndale, 'The Quebec Law of Evidence Compared with that of France' (1934) 12 *Canadian Bar Review* 641

Others

KM Clermont and E Sherwin, 'A Comparative View of Standards of Proof' (2002) 50 *American Journal of Comparative Law* 243

M Fordham, 'Causation in the Tort of Negligence—A Dispensable Element?' (2003) *Singapore Journal of Legal Studies* 285

R Fumerton et K Fress, 'Causation and the Law: Preemption, Lawful Sufficiency, and Causal Sufficiency' (2001) *Law and Contemporary Problems* 83

L Khoury, '*Chester v Afshar:* Stepping Further Away from Causation?' (2005) *Singapore Journal of Legal Studies* 246

WS Malone, 'Ruminations on Cause-in-Fact' (1956) 9 *Stanford Law Review* 60

JA McLaughlin, 'Proximate Cause' (1925–26) 39 *Harvard Law Review* 149

RW Wright, 'Actual Causation vs. Probabilistic Linkage: The Bane of Economic Analysis' (1985) 14 *Journal of Legal Studies* 435

INDEX